Converging Media, Diverging Politics

Converging Media, Diverging Politics

A Political Economy
of News Media in the
United States and Canada

Edited by David Skinner,
James R. Compton,
and Michael Gasher

A Division of
ROWMAN & LITTLEFIELD PUBLISHERS, INC.
Lanham • *Boulder* • *New York* • *Toronto* • *Oxford*

LEXINGTON BOOKS

A division of Rowman & Littlefield Publishers, Inc.
A wholly owned subsidiary of The Rowman & Littlefield Publishing Group, Inc.
4501 Forbes Boulevard, Suite 200
Lanham, MD 20706

PO Box 317
Oxford
OX2 9RU, UK

British Library Cataloguing in Publication Information Available

Library of Congress Cataloging-in-Publication Data

Converging media, diverging politics : a political economy of news media in the
united states and canada / edited by David Skinner, James R. Compton, and
Michael Gasher.
    p. cm.
 Includes bibliographical references and index.
 ISBN 0-7391-0827-1 (cloth : alk. paper) — ISBN 0-7391-1306-2 (pbk. : alk. paper)
 1. Journalism—United States. 2. Journalism—Canada. 3. Mass media—
Ownership—United States. 4. Mass media—Ownership—Canada. 5. Convergence
(Telecommunication) I. Skinner, David, 1956– II. Compton, James Robert, 1963–
III. Gasher, Mike, 1954– IV. Title.

 PN4867.C62 2005
 071—dc22   2005014125

Printed in the United States of America

 ⊚™ The paper used in this publication meets the minimum requirements of
American National Standard for Information Sciences—Permanence of Paper
for Printed Library Materials, ANSI/NISO Z39.48-1992.

Contents

Prologue

Has a Free Press Helped to Kill Democracy?

Robert Jensen

Cable news channels, twenty-four hours a day. The Internet, with more Web sites than one could visit in a lifetime. Broadcast television news. And newspapers. And magazines. A world overflowing with words and images, with talk of politics everywhere in the media, and the media everywhere in our lives.

In a democracy, the free flow of information is crucial if citizens are to be meaningful political actors and make good on the possibilities of popular sovereignty. Therefore, in a democracy, this overflow of information could be taken as evidence of the success of journalism and mass media.

Which leaves us pondering a difficult question: How do we overcome the failure of success?

I borrow the term from a plant scientist, Wes Jackson.[1] In describing industrial agriculture, Jackson uses the term "the failure of success" to explain the paradox of decreasing soil fertility and increasing yields. There is less topsoil, and less fertile topsoil, yet yields increase. The answer to the paradox is in farmers' shift from soil to oil; the decrease in soil fertility is being temporarily offset through the artificial means of chemical fertilizers, pesticides and herbicides. The failure is in the long term; yield increases through such measures cannot continue indefinitely. Such a system, no matter how much is produced, is neither healthy nor sustainable.

In similar fashion, the high yield of information gives the illusion that democracy is vibrant. There is more information available than ever before. Even if one brackets out the huge amount that is about celebrities, entertainment, sports, and other nonpolitical topics, the quantity of political information available is staggering. Quantity, yes, but of what quality? Do the high yields of talk about politics really mean democracy is healthy? If we can turn on a television set and hear politics being talked about, does that mean that meaningful politics is going on?

After twenty-five years spent working, at various times, as a journalist, professor, and/or political activist, it has never seemed clearer to me that democracy is in trouble, and that journalism and mass media are deeply implicated in that trouble. The problem in North America today is not primarily the threat of repression of political activity or expression by governments, though such threats continue to exist (for example, the targeting of Arabs and South Asians for arbitrary detention after September 11, 2001, or the violent response to peaceful protests of the Free Trade Area of the Americas meetings in Miami in November 2003). More destructive to democracy is the atrophying of meaningful political engagement in the lives of the majority of people.

Therein lies the paradox: In the United States and Canada, which by any measure rank high on the list of the most affluent societies in the history of the world, many people have the resources (time, money, education) to engage in politics, with no shortage of information available to them, living in systems that offer expansive guarantees of freedom of participation and expression. Yet in all of my traveling, speaking, writing, and teaching, I hear a consistent message from ordinary people that they believe there is no room for them in politics.

The causes of this political disengagement are complex, but no doubt the failures of journalism and mass media are a part of the equation. These problems are encapsulated in a comment from a first-year student at the University of Texas, who, when asked why not only did he never expect to be politically active himself, but why he thought people who were passionate about politics were a bit odd, said simply:

"Look at what's on TV—politics is such a joke."

In a culture in which television defines reality for a large number of people, his assessment can't be brushed off as simple immaturity. In at least two ways, he is right. First is a recognition that what passes for political debate on TV is a fraud. Pundits on talk shows argue loudly but rarely put forth a coherent argument (if by "argument" we mean the presentation of propositions that lead to a rational conclusion). Politicians typically are paired in inane right vs. left pseudo-debates in which neither person responds to the other and viewers are left with the feeling that the real problems and potential solutions were never on the table, which can easily lead viewers to want to avoid politics altogether. Second is the realization that contemporary journalists routinely do not make good on their obligation to be the critical, independent sources of information and analysis that citizens need. Though people will differ in their critique of journalism, there is a common feeling across political positions that journalism isn't providing the quality of coverage people need.

What should citizens in a democracy expect from journalism? Certainly journalists cannot by themselves fix a failing political system, but a more vigorous journalism would be of great help to citizens struggling to engage politically. It isn't difficult to articulate criteria for such a journalism. Here's a short list of what people need from journalists, and brief thoughts on how journalism fails us, using the coverage of the 2003 Iraq War as an example:

- a truly independent source of factual information. Contemporary news provides lots of information, but because of the inordinate power given to official sources (primarily government and corporate) in the professional practices of journalists, news accounts are often dominated by "facts" that come from those power centers, not from independent inquiry. In the war, journalists became conduits for a variety of fabrications, distortions, and half-truths from the Bush administration about alleged weapons of mass destruction and terrorist ties in Iraq. But because those claims came from "credible" sources (no matter how many times such officials lie, they somehow remain credible), they were repeated over and over in the news.
- the historical, political, and social context to make sense of those facts. We all recognize that no matter how often we say we want "just the facts," that no one can make sense of the world from a hodge-podge of factual assertions; we need a framework within which to understand facts. While journalists can't be expected to provide a historical treatise on every subject they report on, the almost complete absence of such context in daily reporting leaves people crippled in trying to come to judgment. Reporting on the war suffered greatly from this absence; the political history of the region started in the 1990s for most journalists, with the critical history of U.S. policy in the Middle East largely ignored.
- exposure to the widest range of opinion available in the society. On this count, the failure is most apparent and appalling. The vast majority of voices allowed into mainstream media are within the moderately liberal to reactionary right-wing spectrum. Progressive and left-wing ideas are consistently marginalized when they are allowed to appear at all. During the war, the idea of balance seemed to be fulfilled by having current military officers and retired military officers on news programs. Current Bush administration officials were balanced with former Clinton officials, who typically endorsed the same basic philosophy with, at best, minor disagreements over tactics.

To be alarmed by this state of affairs, we need not hearken back to some mythical golden age of journalism and politics, pretending that we once had a great democracy untainted by power. Democracy faces challenges in every era. We can look to the past and see clearly the ways in which democracy was diminished—the use of state and private violence to crush dissent, the disenfranchisement of large segments of the population, and the direct legal repression of speech and press. Such threats are clear, especially in hindsight. But progress on those fronts should not delude us into thinking that problems on other fronts can be ignored. As formal freedoms have expanded and formal barriers to political participation have dropped, the struggle for economic and political control among different classes and groups continues. And in a mass-mediated society, the mass media are one place where that struggle goes on.

Historically, that struggle has been between those who want to keep power in the hands of a fairly narrow elite (a kind of managerial democracy, run by supposed experts, allegedly to the benefit of all but in reality to serve primarily that elite) and those who want power to be as widely disbursed as possible (what is commonly known as participatory democracy, in which the system is judged by whether people have meaningful control over their own lives). In the managerial conception, citizens' role is to ratify the decisions of experts and professional politicians through regular voting. In the participatory conception, citizens' role is to be actively engaged not just in selecting representatives but also in defining the agenda and having a role in determining policy alternatives.

Today, we are moving toward a society in which even impoverished notions of managerial democracy seem idealistic, as the quality of public discourse continues to degrade. We live in an era in which policy proposals are treated not as topics for discussion by the people but products to be sold to them. Forget democracy-as-participation. Even democracy-as-ratification is unrealistic. Today, we have democracy-as-stupefaction. The goal of politicians and their consultants seems to be to stupefy, to dull the faculties of people, just as product advertising leaves people stupefied. To borrow from the dictionary definition, politics seems to be designed to leave people in "a state of suspended or deadened sensibility." And all too often, journalists aid in this process rather than contesting it.

Given that most journalists are led to the craft by a sense of commitment to democracy and a belief that journalism can be a positive force in society, why are journalists increasingly part of the problem and not the solution? Understanding the reasons requires analysis of the political economy of media, the professional practices of journalists, and the ideological climate in which they work—all of which constrain journalists from doing the work they might want to do or, in many cases, from even recognizing what kind of critical, independent work is necessary.

In an age of corporate consolidation and technological convergence, the pressures mount and the constraints intensify. News managers grow ever more conscious of the bottom line, leading inexorably to more pressure to treat news not as the lifeblood of democracy but as one more commodity to sell, and to treat news workers not as skilled craftspeople with some autonomy but employees producing that commodity.

What are the motive forces behind these trends? How do they play out in newsrooms, boardrooms, and society at large? Where have elected officials and regulators failed us? And how can citizens and journalists work to reverse the decline? The chapters in this book offer detailed and sophisticated analyses of these issues.

Can we overcome the failure of success? Just as in the struggle to move beyond industrial food production to sustainable agriculture, one can sketch the main tasks in moving from a corporatized, commodified media production system to a democratic communication network. We must articulate the values crucial for the long-term health of the system, identify the institutions and practices that create obstacles to living those values, work out the bold but hard-headed strategies needed to break down the obstacles, experiment with new ways of living and working, and dig in for the long haul. Progressive change is within our grasp, though not necessarily in this moment.

These matters are not purely academic; citizens need such analyses to defend themselves and democracy. And the outcome matters. In some sense, North America in the twenty-first century can be seen as the ultimate fulfillment of democracy. The question is, will it also be the end of democracy?

NOTE

1. Wes Jackson, *New Roots for Agriculture*, (Lincoln: University of Nebraska Press, 1980).

1

Mapping the Threads

David Skinner, James R. Compton, and Mike Gasher

What is journalism for? What purpose do the news media serve in contemporary American and Canadian society? These simple, yet fundamental questions inform every chapter in this book.

In specific terms, this collection of essays considers, from a range of vantage points, how corporate and technological convergence in the news industry in the United States and Canada impacts journalism's expressed role as a medium of democratic communication. But more generally, and by necessity, it speaks to larger questions about the role that the production and circulation of news and information does, can, and should serve, using as its objects of study the news industries of two North American neighbors. Aside from sharing a 5,000-mile border, the United States and Canada are among the richest and most democratic countries in the world, endowed with strong free-press traditions. They serve as models for the kind of technological resources and expertise that give meaning to the expression "information society."

Yet this book adopts a critical stance. Set against the backdrop of escalating neoliberal economic policies, shifting trade regimes, and the intensive and extensive capitalization of communication industries in general, it draws upon the heritage of critical political economy to consider how the intensified concentration of news media ownership, ongoing processes in the commodification of news and information, and the implementation of new technologies are foreclosing not only upon the range of ideas and diversity of perspectives found in American and Canadian news coverage but upon the possibilities for journalism itself. Consideration of media reform initiatives is also included: from journalism education to the development and maintenance of independent, community, and alternative media.

While the historical domination of Canadian media by American media products has been well documented, the news environments in the two countries have to a large degree escaped this trend and remain largely distinct.[1] Recently, however, a number of interrelated trends have begun to frame and animate the development of these environments in both jurisdictions, presenting possibilities for drawing them closer together. It is these trends that call this collection into being. They include:

- corporate and technological convergence, which allow once-distinct news organizations to work together, to harmonize their efforts in both the journalistic and the business realms, in different media markets, even across distinct media (especially newspapers, TV, and Internet);
- deregulation, by which governments and regulators roll back their powers of intervention, and reregulation, by which states increasingly relegate governance of the news and information industries to market forces that transcend regional and national boundaries;
- rising pressures for flexible labor regimes along with worker resistance to those regimes;
- concerns about the reform of journalism education, and whether journalism school should encompass something more than vocational training;
- intense competition for increasingly mobile investment capital, whereby media ownership belongs increasingly to armies of faceless shareholders with a stronger commitment to capital accumulation than to any particular industry;
- the fragmentation and reaggregation of audiences, which challenge conventional notions of community, including those communities which constitute formal polities;
- reinforced barriers to entry as the product of the size and scope of contemporary media companies;
- the re-purposing of material and human resources, so that the same content serves several media platforms and journalists become content producers whose work can be adapted to print, broadcast, and on-line forms;
- the cross-promotion of media properties, whereby news and advertising content encourages corporate brand loyalty among audiences and advertisers;
- and subsequent changes in patterns of media representation, which result from the integration of promotional and journalistic content and create new conflicts of media interest.

In the face of these similarities and overlaps, the essays in this volume focus on the forces that structure journalism and the news media in both countries, examining the ways in which they are nuanced by local, regional, and national circumstances, and, at the same time, the way these forces exert pressure for both the further integration of these markets as well as the development of new avenues for journalistic expression. In Canada, concerns over transnational corporate integration are being heightened by increasing debate over allowing greater levels of foreign ownership of Canadian broadcast and newspaper outlets.

There is a great deal at stake in the debate over corporate concentration and, more recently, convergence in the news industries. There are, most obviously, the economic stakes of shareholders and advertisers who seek to maximize return on their investments. But there are also the interests of news workers, whose investment of labor suffers very restricted mobility in a concentrated and converged industry environment. There are the political stakes of formally constituted political parties and interest groups who want to get their messages on the public agenda. Then there are social stakes, the everyday concerns of Americans and Canadians who, as both consumers and, more importantly, community members and citizens, depend on the news media to help them understand the forces and events that animate and shape their lives. Again, what is journalism for, and how does the production of news and information serve these stakeholders, whose interests are often at odds with one another?

Over the last several decades, the mediascape has been very rapidly transformed, a product of technological innovation, fundamental policy shifts, and massive corporate mergers.[2] On both sides of the border, a number of writers have illustrated how "convergence"—the buzzword of this era—has taken place at several levels: at the technological level, as voice, video, data, and other services have been integrated into single broadband networks; at the corporate level, as companies that once operated in industries and fields held separate by technological and regulatory divides restructure in an effort to gain competitive advantages in this shifting environment; at the level of markets, as newly converged corporations struggle to expand and redefine markets and product lines; and at the level of labor, as news and information workers struggle to find new forms of collective representation in this shifting environment.[3]

As chapters 2 and 3 illustrate, in technological terms, convergence is not a new phenomenon. What is new, however, is the ongoing dismantling of regulatory barriers that have historically given form to both media markets and patterns of representation, the digitization and networking of information systems that allow for increasing flexibility in the production, distribution, and consumption of news and information products, and the increasingly global reach of media companies as they strive to capitalize on these new political and technical arrangements.

This collection is motivated by the need to fill a gap in the critical analysis of these trends in the political economy of news production. While there have been a number of important recent critical works analyzing the impacts of convergence on media industries in both the United States and Canada, the impact of neoliberal policies and new information networks on continental integration, and the role of media industries in the development of transnational digital capitalism, the impacts of these changes on news production, and the patterns of representation that flow from it, remain underexamined.[4]

Framed by a North American political economic tradition that has, by one count, been developed over four generations of researchers,[5] writers in this volume assume that news media are embedded in larger macro-structures of power—i.e., ownership, the market, the state, and other forms of dominant social relations—which limit and direct their work in the interest of capital and/or dominant social groups. They draw attention to the stratified nature of North American society, placing a particular focus on economic ownership, the governing logic of capital accumulation, and the ways in which this logic plays out in the structure and operation of large, increasingly vertically and horizontally integrated profit-seeking media corporations.[6] And they consider how both the ongoing dismantling of regulatory frameworks and the digitization and networking of information systems that allow for the increasing flexibility in the production, distribution, and consumption of news and information products are shifting patterns of representation and, in the process, giving a shrinking number of owners increasing play in framing editorial policies and positions. From this perspective, media organizations and institutions can be seen to operate according to a logic that serves the interests of owners, shareholders, and advertisers, not the diverse, and often divergent, interests of civil society—interests which can, and often do, come into conflict with the core logic of news media production. To a large part, it is this corporate logic that underlies the events that are reshaping American and Canadian media markets.

TWO JURISDICTIONAL CONTEXTS

Canadians and Canadian scholars spend a great amount of time differentiating Canadian and American experience, particularly in the realms of communication and culture. This collection turns that on its head somewhat, in that we address both what is common and what is particular. While in both countries, media associated with news production and carriage have traditionally come under three different regulatory regimes—one for print, another for broadcast, and a third for telecommunications common carriers—in Canada regulation is generally less formal and codified than in the United States.

In the United States, regulation is framed by the First Amendment, antitrust rules and the powers of the Federal Communications Commission.

While the First Amendment provides the news media with a kind of talisman against government regulation, historically antitrust regulation and the diversity principles enforced by the FCC provided for at least some corporate diversity in media markets—even though the idea of diversity has itself been the subject of heated debate.[7] In Canada, however, regulation has generally been less rigorous in character. In the face of an historically small population, large land mass, a shortage of investment capital, and the often overwhelming presence of American media products, the Canadian state has played an active role in promoting the development of media industries. Sometimes directly, sometimes indirectly through regulatory bodies such as the Canadian Radio-Television and Telecommunications Commission (CRTC), the federal government has encouraged oligopolies and even granted monopolies in media markets.[8] Consequently, regulations governing concentration of ownership have been more fluid and flexible in Canada than those in the United States. In both jurisdictions, however, there has been a long-standing concern over the concentration of ownership and the ways in which corporate imperatives color news production.

In the late nineteenth and early twentieth centuries, the development of mass advertising combined with fast presses and cheap newsprint to create the ground on which contemporary newspaper chains grew. In the United States, Scripps and Hearst were among the first to exploit the economies of scale of chain ownership. Following their lead, the Southam family began to assemble the first Canadian newspaper chain in 1897. Some of the advantages of the new corporate structure were reduced editorial costs captured by sharing editorials, features, and news stories, as well as reduced material costs when buying paper and ink in bulk.[9] Journalistic style changed to meet with this new commercial regime. "Objectivity" replaced partisan news reporting as papers sought to increase both circulation and profits by appealing to a mass market rather than particular political interests, and sensationalized news coverage, with its "blaring headlines and exaggerated drama," became a key marketing tool as newsstands and newspaper hawkers targeted pedestrians on the streets of the burgeoning urban centers.[10]

Mass advertising also brought its own imperatives. In a competitive market, newspapers divide circulation and advertising among themselves, driving up the cost of each paper they produce. But in a monopoly situation, newspapers are able to maximize both circulation and advertising revenue. The savings made through such economies of scale are evidenced in the fact that advertising rates "per thousand" readers are often cheaper in monopoly markets than in their competitive counterparts. Starting in the early twentieth century, this logic slowly began to wind its way through newspaper markets across the United States and Canada, driving amalgamations and creating single newspaper towns.[11] Chains took hold faster in the United States than in Canada, however. In the United States in 1933, chains accounted for about thirty-seven percent of national daily circulation and about forty-six percent of Sunday circulation.[12] In Canada, at about the same time, there were 116 newspapers owned by ninety-nine publishers.[13]

As advertising took hold, writers were quick to point out its influence on content. As Will Irwin argued in a 1911 article detailing the influence of advertising on news production:

> What does the advertiser ask as a bonus in return for his business favor? Sometimes a whole change of editorial policy—as when the Pittsburgh newspapers were forced to support a candidate for the bench chosen by the department stores; more often the insertion of personal matter of no news value in itself; most often the suppression of news harmful to himself, his family, or his business associates.[14]

Through the late 1920s and early 1930s, advertising and its commercial imperative put a stamp on broadcasting, too, as the commercial networks, designed to maximize return on advertising to national and regional audiences, gained control of the system in the United States.[15] Meanwhile in Canada, control of the system by the government-owned Canadian Broadcasting Corporation tended to slow the development of the commercial model at the national level, but commercial development proceeded apace at the local level. In both countries, newspaper and radio cross-ownership assumed growing proportions.

In the years immediately following World War II, the burgeoning consumer society provided the context for dramatic growth in newspaper advertising and circulation, as well as commercial radio.[16] But the increasingly commercial character of the media alarmed cultural and intellectual elites on both sides of the border, and in both the United States and Canada inquiries were struck to consider the form and direction of growth.

In the United States, the inquiry was a private-sector initiative and arose in the wake of a wave of discontent over increasing press concentration "and the perception of irresponsible behavior by media and media owners."[17] Reportedly spawned during a board meeting of the Encyclopaedia Britannica directors, the Commission on Freedom of the Press (Hutchins Commission) was financed through a $200,000 (U.S.) donation from Time Inc. and $15,000 (U.S.) from Encyclopaedia Britannica Inc. Led by Robert Hutchins, president of the University of Chicago, the commission was underpinned by an elitist belief that the "agencies of mass communication . . . can exert an influence over the minds of their audience too powerful to be disregarded."[18] Set against the ideal that a free and responsible press is the cornerstone of democracy, the commissioners found the system ailing. Competition in the news media was declining and the number of sensationalist tabloids on the rise. Proprietors instructed reporters to play down "uninteresting" facts and figures concerning government policies, taxation, and spending. And there was much evidence of owners and managers shaping news coverage to fit their own political views and commercial interest.[19] In addition to a general report, the commission published six special studies on subjects ranging from freedom of the press to the government and mass communication to policy proposals for film and radio. But while the members of the commission held common concerns for growing commercialization and concentration of ownership, they disagreed over what to do about it, particularly concerning the proper role and form of government intervention. The compromise was to call upon the government, the press, and the public to work together to create a more responsible news media. Most of the commission's thirteen recommendations were vague. One called for "an independent agency to appraise and report annually upon the performance of the press," others placed the onus for improving public communication upon government and nonprofit institutions, rather than upon industry itself.

In Canada, where the state has been much less reticent to take an active hand in shaping political and economic development, the postwar inquiry into media was sponsored by the government. The Royal Commission on National Development in the Arts, Letters and Sciences (Massey Commission) was struck in 1949 and led by Vincent Massey, chancellor of the University of Toronto. In keeping with the Canadian federal government's historic concern for promoting nationalist perspectives across the country's far-flung geography, Massey's mandate was much broader than Hutchins's. The commission spent two years investigating Canadian "culture," including the state of the arts, university funding, and the mass media. The commission's report blatantly subscribed to an elite-centered, intellectual vision of culture and drew a stark contrast between high cultural forms and the burgeoning "mass culture"—particularly American mass culture—that underwrote much of the development of the broadcast and film industries. Dependence on American "newspapers, periodicals, books, maps and endless educational equipment" was also decried.[20] As the commission noted, "The American invasion by film, radio, and periodicals is formidable." The commission added, "It cannot be denied . . . that a vast and disproportionate amount of material coming from a single alien source may stifle rather than stimulate our own creative effort; and, passively accepted without any standard of comparison, this may weaken critical faculties."[21]

When dealing with Canadian-owned media, however, the commission was less attuned to their growing commercial character. Despite escalating private ownership and commercial influence in broadcasting, Massey claimed that broadcasting was a "public service," not "an industry."[22] The commission was also generally unconcerned about the common ownership of newspaper and radio stations, noting that despite the fact that considerable cross-ownership existed they found "no evidence of any abuse of power as a result."[23] Moreover, the commission generally abstained from any critical examination of newspapers, claiming that such a line of inquiry "lies far beyond our competence." The commission went on to afford the press the benefit of the doubt in how they discharged their responsibilities, noting that "it is their privilege to give such emphasis to the news as, in their judgment, will make the paper more attractive, popular and successful."[24]

Thus, while in the immediate postwar period the burgeoning commercial climate sprouted inquiries into the media in both the United States and Canada, the broader social context that animated each of them sent them down different paths. While drawing on a libertarian heritage Hutchins set out to consider commercial influence on the media and the role of the press in political discourse, Massey's more explicitly conservative gaze was set more broadly on the role of the media in developing "national" life. Both decried the role of commercial imperatives in undermining the "higher" political and social functions of the media. But while, for Hutchins, the crux of the problem lay between the exercise of blatant self-interest by media owners and an American public that did not understand "how far the performance of the press falls short of the requirements of a free society in the world today,"[25] for Massey the central villain was American mass culture and its impact on the Canadian public. And while for Hutchins, government intervention was pared on the philosophical edge of the First Amendment, Massey's conservatism generally granted Canadian proprietors commercial reign of their organizations.

While no direct action resulted from either study, both left their marks on media development. Hutchins's ruminations provided the cornerstones for the "social responsibility" theory of the press, which became a focal point for journalism education and animated further consideration of the role and responsibility of the press in both countries. In Canada, Massey's concern over the presence of American media in Canadian markets would contribute to fostering protectionist measures in a range of industries. However, under the ideological sway of the hegemony of private capital neither were able to challenge the prerogatives of private capital that drove market consolidation in both countries. And, while in both the United States and Canada, levels of concentration of ownership would continue to rise, in Canada the situation would be complicated by efforts to, on one hand, maintain Canadian control of media operations, while at the same time allowing industry to capture the benefits of economies of scale in a small market.

RISING CONCENTRATION

Consolidation proceeded in both countries through the 1950s and 1960s. Various villains were found to be animating the problem, including inheritance taxes that "forced" aging proprietors to sell out to chains before their heirs were left with huge tax bills. At the heart of the problem, however, remained the private profit motive and the economic benefits of the synergies captured through economies of scale.

Though not in all cases, capturing the benefits of these economies of scale seemed to undermine journalistic values. Chain ownership tended to lessen the number of reporters and editorial voices across the papers owned by the chain while, at the same time, increasing the scope of potential editorial meddling by owners and managers. Cross-ownership, where one company owned newspaper and broadcast media, exacerbated these problems—particularly if the company held different media properties in the same market. Worst of all for some critics, however, was conglomerate ownership, whereby media properties represented just a portion of the companies' corporate holdings. As Nicholas Johnson, an FCC commissioner, testified before the 1970 Special Senate Committee on the Mass Media in Canada, "a very large conglomerate corporation is likely to treat a mass media subsidiary as something in the nature of a public relations or advertising company." [26]

Rising concentration through the 1960s caught the interest of government agencies on both sides of the border. In a bid to capture some of the benefits of amalgamation without the necessity of corporate marriage, rival newspaper companies began to enter into joint-operating agreements, in which they would share office space, printing facilities, and sometimes advertising and other business functions while maintaining separate news rooms. This led to antitrust investigations in both countries and, following on the heels of prosecutions in the United States, the adoption of the 1970 Newspaper Preservation Act.[27] But while some saw the act as an innovative way to preserve diversity in media markets, others saw the legislation as a blatant case of political pandering "that would make life difficult for independent operators."[28] One Canadian case illustrates well the difficulties in enforcing anticombines legislation in the capital-intensive news industry.

In 1957 a series of events shifted the structure of the newspaper market in Vancouver, British Columbia, from one morning and two evening papers, all independently owned, to one evening and one morning paper, both owned by one company that was jointly owned by two of the three former proprietors. The amalgamation served to reduce the operating expenses of the two remaining papers and secure their market positions. In a subsequent investigation of this market restructuring, the Restrictive Trade Practices Commission found that although there was "no question that the competitive situation" of the two papers was "affected substantially" by placing their ownership in one company, "developments in other cities in North America indicate that economic factors press toward a reduction in the number of newspapers or the number of publishers in cities which had previously supported several independent dailies." [29] Consequently, the commission found that the joint operating agreement "does not immediately represent as serious a danger to the public interest . . . as a newspaper monopoly in the hands of a single owner" and that on the grounds of economic necessity, the arrangement be allowed to stand.[30] Thus, even though they appeared to represent the lesser of two necessary evils, these kinds of arrangements were allowed to proceed, despite the fact that they increased the barriers to entry for any new possible competitors.[31]

Ongoing consolidation through the 1960s also prompted the FCC to adopt a range of ownership rules prohibiting the cross-ownership of broadcast networks and cable systems (1970), a cable system and a television station in the same market (1970), and a newspaper and a broadcast station in the same market (1975).[32] In Canada, similar forces precipitated the 1970 Special Senate Committee on the Mass Media (the Davey Committee). However, as Skinner and Gasher illustrate in chapter 3, despite the fact that the committee found that ongoing concentration left the media system open to a range of abuses, little was done to curb these developments in Canada. Indeed, Davey's recommendations were reminiscent of Hutchins's, particularly with respect to calling for an independent press council "that would monitor the press the way the press monitors society," and calling for actors other than the proprietors—in this instance, the public and journalists—to take an active hand in helping improve press quality.[33]

Solutions to what was often perceived as the growing problem of concentration continued to elude authorities on both sides of the border through the 1970s. In 1978, the U.S. Federal Trade Commission held a two-day symposium on concentration of ownership, but in 1980 concluded that "there is relatively little the Commission can do" as economies of scale seemed to be at the heart of the problem. Moreover, because chain newspapers generally operate in distinct geographical locations, the commission argued that it was difficult to challenge them on antitrust grounds.[34] In Canada, apparent collusion on the part of Canada's two largest newspaper chains to monopolize the Vancouver, Ottawa, and Winnipeg markets prompted a Royal Commission on Newspapers. But, as illustrated in chapter 3, while the Commission made sweeping recommendations for restructuring the industry, political pressure from publishers and the intervention of an election forestalled any change.

As part of a constitutional reform package in 1982, Canada adopted a Charter of Rights and Freedoms, which included as one of its "fundamental freedoms" the right to "freedom of the press and other media of communication." However, this right has been little help in the struggle over news media ownership because, as Robert Everett and Frederic Fletcher point out, it "grants media organizations freedom to pursue interests that may not coincide with broader social objectives and needs."[35] Moreover, they go on to suggest, the ability to enforce normative principles in the media sector has been weakened by the influence of powerful publishers, lobbying by private sector interests, traditional libertarian rhetoric, and a "lack of will to implement declared principles."[36]

Media amalgamations leading up to the 1980s were only a prelude to much greater empire-building in both the United States and Canada. In the early 1980s, the Reagan administration set the stage for the reregulation (i.e., regulation by market forces) of media markets, and a whole new set of conglomerates and cross-media giants emerged. In 1985, Capital Cities took over the American Broadcasting Corporation, General Electric acquired NBC, and Loews Corp. took control of CBS. Also in that year, Rupert Murdoch managed to challenge FCC foreign ownership rules and establish the Fox network.[37] By 1986, of all U.S. cities with a daily newspaper, 98 percent had only one newspaper management.[38] Consolidation proceeded, as in both Canada and the United States daily newspaper chains expanded their holdings of weekly papers, capitalizing on increasing economies of scale and rationalizing advertising markets.

As Mosco and Schiller note, these changes were not only the product of a liberalized domestic market, but forces opposed to further consolidation, such as "trade unions, educators, voluntary associations, and public interest organizations" had been weakened during the Reagan era and were unable to waylay this neoliberal agenda.[39] The Time-Warner merger in mid-1989 capped off a decade of unprecedented concentration in the United States that created a handful of entertainment conglomerates with commanding market positions at home and abroad.

In 1989, the Canada-U.S. Free Trade Agreement initiated the further integration of the two countries' trade and investment policies, part of a broader strategy to liberalize trade globally, a strategy which includes the North American Free Trade Agreement, the World Trade Organization, and discussions toward the establishment of a hemispheric trade zone for the Americas. In the negotiations with the United States, Canada won a concession exempting cultural production from *full* compliance with the requirements of free trade, permitting the Canadian government to take policy action to support its cultural industries. While this "cultural exemption" has been taken up in subsequent trade negotiations, its policy value is uncertain because it permits trade partners to take retaliatory action if Canadian policy action in the cultural field has a detrimental economic impact on a trade partner.[40] On another front, in 1997 the United States won a WTO challenge to Canada's protectionist magazine policy, forcing the Canadian government to revise legislation and roll back restrictions on foreign ownership, split-run editions, and the tax deductibility of advertising expenditures.[41]

In Canada, the early 1990s saw the hyperconcentration of the Canadian newspaper market as Conrad Black's Hollinger Corp. acquired properties accounting for almost half of the country's daily circulation. Black was heralded by some as the "savior" of the Canadian newspaper business because he was willing to invest in the industry when others (e.g. Thomson Inc.) were moving their capital into more promising information and advertising vehicles. Black, for example, established a new national daily, the *National Post*, in October 1998, the first substantial investment in the Canadian newspaper industry in almost three decades. But Black's interest in newspapers had its price; he was a hands-on proprietor who exerted considerable influence on editorial content and imposed radical restructuring that resulted in major layoffs, particularly among journalists.[42] Hollinger's domination of the Canadian newspaper industry was short-lived, however, as the Internet and the digitization of information began to open up new possibilities for both creating and consolidating media markets, and as Hollinger's debt load forced Black to divest properties.

In 1996, policy decisions taken by the federal governments in both the United States and Canada opened the door for the corporate convergence of media markets that had long been kept separate by regulatory fiat. In the United States, the 1996 Telecommunications Act, the first successful revision of the 1934 Communications Act, removed longstanding television and radio ownership limits and reframed regulation as a vehicle to encourage competition within and across traditional media boundaries. The act had the effect of increasing ownership concentration, especially in the radio industry. In the United States today, about 80 percent of daily newspapers are group-owned, with three companies—Gannett, Knight Ridder, and Tribune—accounting for more than 25 percent of daily newspaper circulation. Only twenty-nine U.S. cities can boast two or more dailies with separate editorial staffs. All the major U.S. television networks are owned by conglomerates—NBC (General Electric), ABC (Disney), CBS (Viacom), Fox (News Corp.)—and an increasing number of radio stations have become group-owned, with Clear Channel Communications and Infinity Broadcasting (a division of Viacom) the largest. AOL's purchase of Time Warner in 2001 was a clear signal that on-line media were part of the media cross-ownership picture. The last few years have seen continued liberalization of media markets in the United States, as both the courts and the FCC have moved to roll back regulations governing cross-media ownership, diversity, and ownership caps.[43] When the Federal Communications Commission sought in June 2003 to further reduce the restrictions governing media ownership, public pressure from a range of sources compelled Congress and the courts to take a second look.

In Canada, the federal government's Convergence Policy Statement altered the regulations which had previously kept the newspaper, broadcasting, and telecommunications industries separate and distinct, and paved the way for cross-media consolidations. Mergers in 2000 radically transformed the Canadian mediascape. CanWest Global, which already owned the Global television network, bought the Southam Newspaper Group and became overnight the country's principal daily newspaper publisher. The telecommunications company Bell Canada Enterprises (BCE) bought the CTV television network and the country's prestigious national newspaper, *The Globe and Mail*. Finally, the newspaper company Quebecor bought the cable-television provider Videotron and the French-language television network TVA. In Canada, then, these three media companies own major news media operating in the newspaper, television and on-line industries.

These latest rounds of consolidation have prompted concerns in both countries. In the United States, the ways in which consolidations have impacted the media's representation of the "news world" has drawn particular concern, in terms of: foreclosing on local coverage; the growing trend toward "infotainment"; and representation of the "war on terrorism"—on the home front, in Afghanistan, and in Iraq. In the aftermath of the September 11, 2001, attacks on the World Trade Center and the Pentagon, *Harper's* editor Lewis H. Lapham sought news coverage that would provide "[i]nformed argument about why and how America had come to be perceived as a dissolute empire;" question "the supposed omniscience of the global capital markets;" contrast the growing income gap between rich and poor; and draw crucial distinctions between "the ambitions of the American national security state and the collective well-being of the American citizenry."[44] He would be disappointed. In the wake of the U.S.-led invasion of Iraq, major news organizations, and in particular 24-hour cable news operations, engaged in a corporate branding battle—each striving to cloak themselves in the patriotism of the flag. Criticism of the invasion was scarce as both MSNBC and Fox News adopted the U.S. government's logo for the conflict: "Operation Iraqi Freedom." Anchors, enthralled by the spectacle of military power, enthused on air about the effectiveness of the Pentagon's "Shock and Awe" aerial bombardment of Baghdad. Radio stations owned by Clear Channel went so far as to organize public rallies in support of the Bush White House's war policies.[45] A year after the invasion, Disney would try to block its Miramax division from distributing a documentary by filmmaker Michael Moore that criticized the Bush White House's handling of the September 11 tragedy.

In Canada, recent concern has focused on the rather ham-fisted tactics of CanWest Global, whose managers, as Leslie Regan Shade recounts in chapter 5, sought to impose a range of editorial sanctions and a centralized editorial line which compelled its member newspapers to publish the same "national editorials" from coast to coast. Inadvertently, CanWest did more than any critic to revive public debate over corporate concentration and convergence in Canada. While readers and former Southam publishers protested and attended public rallies—and rival daily newspapers took up the subject in their news and opinion columns—governments took notice. Quebec's provincial government was the first to act, by first holding public hearings on press concentration in 2001 and then establishing a consultative committee in 2003 to recommend legislative action. Both houses of the federal parliament subsequently joined the debate. The House of Commons Standing Committee on Canadian Heritage conducted a 2003 review of broadcasting in Canada, with particular attention to media ownership, and the Senate Committee on Transportation and Communications, chaired by former *Montreal Gazette* editor Joan Fraser continues to hold public hearings examining the quality and diversity of news and information.

The essays in this volume reflect the tensions underlying these contemporary events. The first part of the collection sets the stage for subsequent discussions. In chapter 2, Robert Horwitz charts the legal and political context of the growth of concentration in the United States, while in chapter 3, David Skinner and Mike Gasher provide an overview of similar developments in Canada.

Case studies of corporate concentration and its impact on journalism follow in the second section. In chapter 4, Francisco McGee, Danielle Fairbairn, and Dorothy Kidd examine the ways in which Clear Channel's rapid rise to become one of the U.S.'s largest radio networks has impacted both the programming offered by the chain and the service its stations offer the communities in which they operate. In chapter 5, Leslie Regan Shade illustrates how CanWest Global's takeover of the Southam newspaper chain in Canada exemplifies the problems inherent in media concentration, including a diminution of journalistic freedom and integrity, devaluation of local content, and the decline of public-interest values. In chapter 6, Mark Cooper, director of Research at the Consumer Federation of America, provides an overview of the literature detailing the negative impacts that concentration of ownership has had on the practice of both print and broadcast journalism in the United States. And in chapter 7, Chris Paterson illustrates how the seeming abundance of news providers on the World Wide Web consists largely of cybermediaries for content recycled from the same major international news agencies, redistributing wire copy rather than producing original news dispatches.

The third part of the book considers instances of resistance, calls for reform, and attempts to construct alternatives to the mainstream news media. Debra Clarke turns the focus to audiences in chapter 8, illustrating how audience dissatisfaction with established television network news formats is leading some viewers to seek alternative news and alternative news media, such as on-line journalism and other Internet information sources. Chapters 9 and 10 chart the growing dimensions of public discontent with media consolidation in the United States, as Ben Scott draws upon his experience working in Washington, D.C., to illustrate sometimes arcane dimensions of the struggle to initiate media reform legislation, and Dorothy Kidd details the development of the media reform movement on the West Coast. In chapter 11, Jeanette McVicker argues that the larger social conditions that are precipitating change in journalism and news production also call for a change in the philosophy and practice of journalism education. In chapter 12, Michel Sénécal and Frédéric Dubois detail the ongoing struggle to establish alternative media on the margins of corporate media in Quebec. In chapter 13, Nick Dyer-Witheford illustrates how the developing cyber-network that underpins the digitization of news and information production is not simply fodder for creeping corporatization, but is also a site for: significant social dissent; the strengthening of existing independent and community media; and the development of new media alternatives. Finally, chapter 14 addresses the possibilities for media reform initiatives that might waylay the ongoing rationalization of journalism and news production, and the necessity of creating alternative forums of public communication.

In the opening lines of this introduction we asked: What is journalism for? If the chapters in this volume respond to that question each in their own way, the collection is nonetheless concurrent on the need to reappropriate journalism and reconnect both its structure and its practice to the needs of democracy.

NOTES

1. See for instance: Ted Magder, "Taking Culture Seriously: A Political Economy of Communications," in *The New Canadian Political Economy*. eds. Wallace Clement and Glen Williams, (Kingston and Montreal: McGill-Queen's University Press, 1989) 278–96; Manjunath Pendakur, "United States–Canada relations: Cultural Dependence and Conflict," in *Critical Communications Review. Volume II: Changing Patterns of Communications Control*, eds. Vincent Mosco and Janet Wasko (Norood, N. J.: Ablex Publishing, 1984), 165–84; Dallas Smythe, *Dependency Road: Communications, Capitalism, Consciousness and Canada* (Norwood, N.J.: Ablex Publishing Co., 1981).

2. *Canada, Our Cultural Sovereignty: The Second Century of Canadian Broadcasting. Report of the House of Commons Standing Committee on Canadian Heritage* (Ottawa: Communication Canada, 2003); Robert W. McChesney, *Rich Media, Poor Democracy* (New York: The New Press, 1999).

3. See for instance: Vincent Mosco and Janet Wasko, eds, *The Political Economy of Information*. (Madison: University of Wisconsin Press, 1988); McChesney, *Rich Media, Poor Democracy*, 1999. Dwayne Winseck, *Reconvergence: A Political Economy of Telecommunications in Canada* (Cresskill, N.J.: Hampton Press, 1998); Catherine Mckercher, *Newsworkers unite: labor, convergence, and North American newspapers* (Lanham, Md.: Rowman & Littlefield, 2002).

4. Marita Moll and Leslie Regan Shade, eds., *Seeking Convergence in Policy and Practice: Communications in the Public Interest* (Ottawa: Canadian Centre for Policy Alternatives, 2004); Dan Schiller and Vincent Mosco, eds., *Continental Order? Integrating North America for Cybercapitalism*. (Lanham, Md.: Rowman and Littlefield, 2001). A recent exception to this rule is Robert W. McChesney, *The Problem of the Media* (New York: Monthly Review Press, 2004).

5. Vincent Mosco, *The Political Economy of Communication* (Thousand Oaks, Calif.: Sage Publications, 1996), 82–93.

6. Integrated either directly through mergers or, in some cases, more flexibly through cross promotion and resource-sharing agreements.

7. Philip Napoli, *Foundations of Communications Policy: Principles and Process in the Regulation of Electronic Media* (Cresskill, N.J.: Hampton Press, 2001).

8. Mary Vipond, *The Mass Media in Canada* (Toronto: James Lorimer & Co., 1992); Robert Babe, *Telecommunications in Canada: Technology, Industry, and Government* (Toronto: University of Toronto Press, 1990); Robert Babe, *Canadian Television Broadcasting Structure, Performance and Regulation.* (Hull, Que.: Minister of Supply and Services, 1979).

9. Sotiron, Minko. *From Politics to Profit: The Commercialization of Canadian Daily Newspapers, 1890–1920* (Montreal: McGill-Queens University Press, 1997), 89–90.

10. Ben Bagdikian, *The Media Monopoly* (Boston: Beacon Press, 1992), 125.

11. Vipond, *Mass Media in Canada,* 68; Benjamin M. Compaine and Douglas Gomery. *Who Owns the Media?: Competition and Concentration in the Mass Media* (Mahwah, N.J.: L. Erlbaum Associates, 2000), 36–38.

12. McKercher, *Newsworkers Unite,* 18.

13. McKercher, *Newsworkers Unite,* 19.

14. Robert W. McChesney and Ben Scott, eds, *Our Unfree Press: 100 Years of Media Criticism* (New York: New Press, 2004), 125.

15. Susan Smulyan, *Selling Radio: The Commercialization of American Broadcasting 1920–1934* (Washington, D.C.: The Smithsonian Institution Press, 1994), 63–99.

16. Compaine and Gomery, *Who Owns the Media?* 3; William Leiss, Stephen Kline, and Sut Jhally, *Social Communication in Advertising: Persons, Products, & Images of Well-Being,* (Scarborough, Ont.: Nelson Canada, 1990), 91.

17. Fred Blevins, "The Hutchins Commission Turns 50: Recurring Themes in Today's Public and Civic Journalism," <http://mtprof.msun.edu/Fall1997/Blevins.html> (8 Dec. 2004).

18. Commission on Freedom of the Press, *A Free and Responsible Press: A General Report on Mass Communications—Newspapers, Radio, Motion Pictures, Magazines, and Books* (Chicago: University of Chicago Press, 1947), 92.

19. Stephen Bates, "Realigning Journalism with Democracy: The Hutchins Commission, Its Times, and Ours," <http://www.annenberg.northwestern.edu/pubs/hutchins/default.htm> (8 Dec. 2004).

20. Canada, Royal Commission on the Development of the Arts, Letters and Sciences, *Report* (Ottawa: King's Printer, 1951), 14.

21. Canada, Royal Commission on the Development of the Arts, Letters and Sciences. *Report* (Ottawa: King's Printer, 1951), 18.

22. Canada, Royal Commission on the Development of the Arts, Letters and Sciences. *Report* (Ottawa: King's Printer, 1951), 283.

23. Canada, Royal Commission on the Development of the Arts, Letters and Sciences. *Report* (Ottawa: King's Printer, 1951), 292.

24. Canada, Royal Commission on the Development of the Arts, Letters and Sciences. *Report* (Ottawa: King's Printer, 1951), 61.

25. Commission on the Free Press, *A Free and Responsible Press,* 97.

26. Robert Babe, "Empires in TV Land," *Search* (Spring 1979), 15.

27. Bagdikian, *Media Monopoly,* 96–97.

28. Bagdikian, *Media Monopoly,* 99.

29. Canada. Restrictive Trade Practices Commission. *Report: Concerning the Production and Supply of Newspapers in the City of Vancouver and Elsewhere in the Province of British Columbia* (Ottawa: 1960), 175.

30. Canada. Restrictive Trade Practices Commission. *Report,* 176.

31. While the Canadian Restrictive Trade Practices Commission generally conceded that high start-up costs mitigated against the appearance of new competitors in markets across North America, they also sought to block any further undermining of the independence of the papers through requesting the imposition of a judicial restraining order on the company to this effect.

However, no such action was ever taken. cf. Marc Edge, *Pacific Press: The Unauthorized Story of Vancouver's Newspaper Monopoly* (Vancouver: New Star Books, 2001), 62–63.

32. See Robert Horwitz, "On Media Concentration and the Diversity Question," <http://communication.ucsd.edu/people/ConcentrationpaperICA.htm> (6 December 2004).

33. Special Senate Committee on the Mass Media, *Vol. I: The Uncertain Mirror* (Ottawa: Queen's Printer, 1970), 111.

34. Compaine and Gomery, *Who Owns the Media?* 51.

35. Robert Everett and Frederic J. Fletcher, "The Mass Media and Political Communication in Canada," in *Communications in Canadian Society,* 5th ed., eds. Craig McKie and Benjamin D. Singer (Toronto: Thompson Educational Publishing Inc., 2001), 166.

36. Everett and Fletcher, "The Mass Media and Political Communication," 166.

37. Mosco and Schiller, *Continental Order?,* 12–13.

38. Bagdikian, *Media Monopoly,* 74.

39. Mosco and Schiller, *Continental Order?,* 13.

40. Ted Magder. "Franchising the Candy Store: Split-Run Magazines and a New International Regime for Trade in Culture," in *Canadian-American Public Policy.* 34 (April 1998), <http://www.alanalexandroff.com/Magder.htm> (10 Dec. 2004).

41. See Magder, "Franchising the Candy Store."

42. John Miller, *Yesterday's News: Why Canada's Daily Newspapers are Failing Us* (Halifax, N.S.: Fernwood Publishing, 1998).

43. Robert Horwitz, "On Media Concentration and the Diversity Question," <http://communication.ucsd.edu/people/ConcentrationpaperICA.htm> (5 Dec. 2004).

44. Lewis Lapham, "American Jihad," *Harper's Magazine,* no. 1820 (January 2002), p. 7.

45. James R. Compton, *The Integrated News Spectacle: A Political Economy of Cultural Performance* (New York: Peter Lang, 2004).

2

U.S. Media Policy Then and Now

Robert B. Horwitz

In June 2003 a closely divided U.S. Federal Communications Commission (FCC) voted to rescind several longstanding rules governing media ownership. Gone were the rules that prevented the cross-ownership of a daily newspaper and a television station in the same market; that limited an individual or corporation to the ownership of one television station in a market; and that restricted the overall ownership of television stations by a single individual or corporation to the number of stations that reach 35 percent of the national audience—raising that cap to 45 percent.[1] These are the most significant changes in the media ownership area in decades, changes that, if they stand, will greatly expand the reach of the nation's largest media companies. The FCC's actions unexpectedly galvanized widespread popular criticism across the political spectrum. In July, the U.S. House of Representatives voted 400 to 21 to roll back the commission's national television ownership rule; the Senate took a similar stand in September on a 55 to 40 vote. And in September, the Third U.S. Circuit Court of Appeals, siding with a coalition of media access groups that claimed its members could suffer irreparable harm if the rules went into effect as scheduled, issued an emergency stay of the new rules.[2] In June 2004 that court concluded that its stay of the FCC's decision remains in place until the FCC completes a remand of the court's decision. The court identified several provisions in which the commission fell short of its obligation to justify its decisions to retain, repeal, or modify its media ownership regulations with reasoned analysis.[3] Notwithstanding this public outcry and judicial remand, it is very likely that the FCC will return with very similar ownership policies but accompanied by a new set of explanations in an effort to satisfy the court's objections.

Why, when it seems that even as American media corporations are becoming larger and presumably more powerful, are ownership rules being changed to allow still greater concentration? After all, corporate mergers and the consolidation of ownership in the American communications arena have long been sources of great public concern. The perception of a direct relationship between democracy and a vibrant communications system of diverse sources and owners is near universal (or, at least, is given universal lipservice), as is, for the most part, the converse fear that a communications system which rests in just a few hands will corrupt the freedom of speech, impair the practice of democracy, and impress an ideological pall on society. In response to these concerns, Congress, the FCC, and the Justice Department put in place a series of regulations over the years to limit the control any single owner could exert over the mass media. These policies were pursued under the general rubric of a concept of a "diversity of owners" or "maintaining a diversity of voices." This chapter attempts to outline the development of media ownership and ownership policy in the United States, with particular attention paid to the effects of ownership on the news media. I will argue that the concept of diversity at the heart of the media concentration debate has become both more important yet more problematic in the aftermath of intertwined industry and legal developments.

THE OLD COMMUNICATIONS REGIME—A BRIEF OVERVIEW

U.S. media traditionally came under three distinct regulatory regimes, in large part dictated by medium and mode of delivery: print, broadcast, and common carrier. Print, protected by the First Amendment to the Constitution ("Congress shall make no law . . . abridging freedom of speech or of the press"), was most protected, but newspaper corporations were still subject to the antitrust laws with regard to ownership and business practices. The Supreme Court's reasoning in the 1945 case of *Associated Press v. United States* expresses the issue plainly.

In language that has since assumed a kind of talismanic status in discussions about the First Amendment and corporate power, the Court stated that:

The First Amendment rests on the assumption that the widest possible dissemination of information from diverse and antagonistic sources is essential to the welfare of the public, that a free press is a condition of a free society. Surely a command that the government itself shall not impede the free flow of ideas does not afford non-governmental combinations a refuge if they impose restraints upon that constitutionally guaranteed freedom. Freedom to publish means freedom for all and not for some. Freedom to publish is guaranteed by the Constitution, but freedom to combine to keep others from publishing is not. Freedom of the press from governmental interference under the First Amendment does not sanction repression by private interests.[4]

Because the press could itself stifle freedom of speech through its business practices (in this case via restrictive membership rules), the First Amendment did not preclude government from applying antitrust laws to that medium. A few years earlier in 1934, apprehension about private power in the then new medium of radio broadcasting saw Congress embed within the mandate of the Federal Communications Commission, broadcasting's new regulatory body, a general command to preserve competition in commerce in the broadcast medium and a specific directive to refuse a station license to any person adjudged guilty "of unlawfully monopolizing or attempting unlawfully to monopolize, radio communication." The FCC regulated broadcasting through its oversight of the electromagnetic spectrum, understood to be a scarce resource held in common by the people of the United States. Radio and television operators had to obtain licenses from the FCC and, because of the scarcity of the spectrum, broadcast licensees were considered public trustees with public-interest obligations that were not imposed on newspapers or magazines. Broadcasters were given time-bound permission to operate on certain frequencies to serve local communities. For sound economic reasons, broadcast licensees often affiliated themselves with national network organizations that provided prime-time programming.[5] Finally, telegraphy and telephony were considered common carriers, subject to FCC price and entry regulation and thus part of the New Deal commitment toward non-discriminatory and universal service. Historically, common carrier law permitted government regulation of infrastructure networks that stood, in the words of the famous 1877 railroad case of *Munn v. Illinois*, "in the very gateway of commerce."[6] The common carrier legal designation, as it was applied to the wired point-to-point communications infrastructure networks, not only permitted regulation over entry and pricing but largely precluded the carriers from the generation of communication content. Congressional fear of radio's potentially dangerous concentration of political power in part underlay the Communications Act's prohibition against any joint ownership of radio and wired systems.[7]

In the United States, of course, unlike most other countries, the historical pattern in communications was of privately owned service providers, oriented toward profits, but subject to some regulatory oversight organized around a general concept of the public interest. Traditionally, the dangers of ownership concentration in the communications industry were addressed by a combination of antitrust and regulatory policies that attempted to attend to the concentration of corporate power but, of course, did not question private power itself. Established policy separated communication industries from each other and restricted common ownership. One of the most important separations was that between content and conduit. A content provider, such as a broadcaster, could not also own the delivery system, such as the wired communications carrier that connected broadcast stations in a network. Likewise, the operator of a delivery system, such as a telephone company, could not also be a content provider. Industry separations were also maintained to prevent a dominant player in one part of the industry from dominating another; hence, for example, as cable television came on the scene in the 1960s, telephone companies were largely kept out of that medium.

At the root of such separations was a dual goal: to prevent the accumulation of property such that a powerful company might restrain trade and hence disrupt the economic market, and to maintain a diversity of voices—although the concept of diversity was never theorized very deeply. A diversity of viewpoints and perspectives was assumed naturally to follow a diversity of owners; yet, the powerful constraints and incentives produced by markets were barely acknowledged. In broadcasting, the FCC endeavored to foster diversity and forestall monopolization by a series of structural, content, and behavioral regulations. Broadcast licensees were supposed to serve their local communities. Structural regulations established ceilings on the number of broadcast stations an entity could own nationally. The commission promulgated the first of its multiple ownership rules in 1953 on the logic that the "fundamental purpose" of the rules was "to promote diversification of ownership in order to maximize diversification of program and service viewpoints."[8] A 1964 amendment to those rules stated that "the greater the diversity of ownership in a particular area, the less chance there is that a single person or group can have an inordinate effect in a . . . programming sense, on public opinion at the regional level."[9] Other structural regulations sought to prevent the dominance of a local market through cross-ownership restrictions and a rule that an individual or company could own just a single outlet in a local area. Another rule effectively dictated that broadcast networks be owned by different entities. The diversification of ownership was one of the comparative criteria used by the commission to assess applicants competing for a broadcast license.[10] In principle, regulations were designed to enhance competition and cultivate new programming, such as the Prime Time Access Rule, an FCC regulation that cleared out an hour of television prime time from network control so that local stations would air their own programming.[11] Content rules, such as the Fairness Doctrine and associated rules of section 315 of the Communications Act, were enacted to ensure that broadcasters would present issues of concern and controversy in their programming, guarantee access to stations by candidates for political office, and ensure that informational/editorial programming was aired with a degree of fairness and balance.[12] Other content rules included various regulations against indecent programming. The FCC also developed behavioral rules, such as requiring that broadcasters meet with community groups in their broadcast market to ascertain their concerns and interests.[13]

The public interest—understood in terms of the maintenance of diverse viewpoints, some degree of local control and local program orientation, the provision of news and information, a general balance of programming (what we now call format diversity, understood vertically, that is, within each broadcast outlet), and equitable treatment of political candidates—was the basis of oversight by the FCC. This set of interventions had its limits, of course. Government could not direct content. Indeed, the Fairness Doctrine, adopted in 1959 to formalize the expectation that broadcasters should air contrasting viewpoints, vested in the broadcaster the power to initiate debate and to select the mode for producing viewpoint balance. It was these fundamental limits on government that prompted the FCC to pursue its primary strategy for fostering diversity through ownership regulations. Diversity, along with localism and competition, was one of the three fundamental concepts that shaped FCC policy historically. But there are many aspects of the diversity concept: diversity of owners, diversity of sources, diversity of formats, diversity of workforce, diversity of viewpoints. The FCC did not work out what were the empirical relationships among these different aspects of diversity; most often it simply asserted their relationship. The train of logic went something like this: Putting a ceiling on the ownership of stations not only safeguarded the broadcast medium from being dominated by a single or a few owners, but also ensured the likelihood that different owners would have commitments to distinct broadcast formats and thus reach different audiences. The diversity of owners and formats would translate into a diversity of viewpoints. Similarly, the diversity of broadcast station workforces was expected somehow to infuse the content and viewpoint of broadcast stations.[14] This was understood as especially true in the case of minority groups, inasmuch as minority audiences, a series of FCC studies concluded, were not programmed to by traditional (white) station owners and their white employees.[15]

At the risk of oversimplification, the old communications system could be said to be limited but universally available, predominantly privately owned and commercially viable though regulated, and characterized by particular corporations confined to providing particular communication services. In broadcasting one could say that there was a vague commitment to liberal pluralism within a mainly private system of provision.

THE NEW REGIME

When new technologies came along, such as cable, satellite, microwaves, and computers, the FCC typically tried to squeeze them into the existing regulatory formulae governing broadcast and common carrier. This strategy had the short-term result of lending economic protection to the traditional service providers and technologies, whether AT&T or FM radio or VHF broadcasting, but also served to preserve the conceptions of the public interest that attached to those technologies. Over time, however, a combination of the growth of new technologies, administrative irrationalities, and tough corporate lobbying and legal challenges from large users and would-be entrants, prompted the FCC to relax some regulations and permit new communications services to blossom. In the beginning, these relaxations of rules were not undertaken as part of an ideological shift away from regulation and toward market solutions. But the emergence of new services and delivery options, in turn, highlighted policy contradictions and eventually underscored the inadequacy of existing communication law, policies, and regulatory formulae. These factors made communications an industry open to the ideology and practice of deregulation.[16] The 1982 Consent Decree that compelled the divestiture of AT&T was the first major break in the traditional regime, and the 1996 Telecommunications Act was the second.

The AT&T divestiture, which emanated from the courts, not from the FCC or Congress, reconfigured certain industry separations and hastened certain technological convergences. The old regulatory separations between content and conduit providers, between telephony and cable television, between local and long-distance telecommunications, between computers and telecommunications, finally seemed outmoded, especially with the technological developments of digitalization and compression. Regulating the old separations, especially as technology was effacing them, was increasingly difficult.

Attempts to rewrite the 1934 Communications Act had been before Congress for well over twenty years, but were always thwarted by industry groups unwilling to give up existing policy protections. By the mid-1990s things had changed. What would it take for the various big industry players to relinquish existing policy protections and face competition on their own turfs in order to expand into someone else's territory and invest in new areas? The widespread assumption was that constructing competitive communications networks would be high-risk, capital-intensive endeavors. It would require the resources of large and flexible corporations (whose needs and failures would also spur small businesses and entrepreneurs in budding and niche markets). The brokered compromises among major industry players and their congressional champions that constituted the Telecommunications Act of 1996 redrew the policy map. The act articulated a bold shift in the goals and mechanisms of policy and regulation. The broad change was that the public interest would be secured not by regulation but by competition. A key concept was regulatory forbearance: Regulation will be deployed only to the degree that it encourages a competitive telecommunications marketplace. The act eliminated the legal basis for protected monopoly in telecommunications and encouraged mergers and vertical integration as ways to facilitate what's termed "cross-platform" competition, that is, competition between previously separated industries to provide the same service. Ownership limits were lifted for radio and raised for television, and the regulatory oversight over broadcast stations, already limited from earlier deregulatory moves, was for all intents and purposes eradicated. The act thus created—by design—unprecedented conditions for competition *and* for the concentration of ownership.[17] Passage of the act unleashed a frenzy of mergers and acquisitions throughout the communications industry as corporations positioned themselves for expansion into new services and for the protection of their home turfs.

TRENDS IN NEWS MEDIA, ESPECIALLY IN THE AFTERMATH OF THE TELECOMMUNICATIONS ACT

Deregulation both accelerated some longstanding trends in media conglomeration and fostered novel dynamics in the news media in particular. The number of daily newspapers in the United States has been declining steadily since 1980. In 1979 there were 1,763 dailies; as of 2002, there were 1,457. Almost none face competition from other daily newspapers in their traditional urban market; in fact, only twenty-nine U.S. cities feature two or more daily newspapers with separate staffs.[18] As late as the 1960s, most daily newspapers were still privately owned by local proprietors. As newspaper founders died and the family faced burdens from inheritance taxes, the newspaper industry experienced sell-offs and consolidation. Some 587 family-owned papers were sold between 1960 and 1980. The 1990s was the busiest decade for newspaper transactions, with 856 deals. Today, group owners, such as Gannett or the Tribune Company, own approximately 80 percent of daily newspapers. Most of the chains are, or have become, publicly held corporations, ten of which own newspapers that account for more than 51 percent of the nation's weekday circulation.[19] Despite continual U.S. population growth, newspaper circulation has been declining since the 1980s. Circulation peaked in 1984 at 63.34 million newspapers sold daily and measured 55.19 million in 2002. Newspaper readership has experienced a corresponding decline. In 1970, 77.6 percent of the adult population reported that they read a daily newspaper. By 2002, that figure had dropped to 49 percent.[20] As the number of urban dailies has declined, there has been a rise in community or suburban nondaily newspapers, many of which have been bought recently by chain owners to create newspaper "clusters" that share administrative and printing functions and pool news coverage.[21] (See Appendix I: 20 of the Top U.S. Newspaper Companies by Circulation 2003).

Although there is much pessimism about the newspaper industry in the long term due to declining circulation and competition from other media sources, in the short term the daily newspaper business is highly profitable. Operating margins, historically in the 10- to 15-percent range, now range between 20 and 30 percent. This level of profit is two to three times that of the average industrial corporation. And these are averages. Some newspaper corporations do far better, such as the Tribune Company, which posted a profit margin of 29.2 percent in 1999.[22] Newspapers have become highly profitable properties for a number of reasons, but two stand out: first, a long-term trend of declining competition and emergence of single newspaper towns, effectively resulting in local monopolies;[23] second, a technological revolution that eventually computerized composition and platemaking in the 1970s and '80s and resulted not only in fewer workers needed to put out a newspaper but changed the balance of power between labor and management, because newspaper workers effectively lost the power to strike.[24] Together, these trends have allowed newspaper companies, increasingly consolidating through merger and acquisition under a publicly traded stock ownership model and intent on serving "shareholder value," to cut costs while charging advertisers more. Computerization not only eliminated entire classes of work at newspapers and reduced manning in general, it has also permitted enterprising newspaper companies to pursue profitable market segmentation and content specialization through intricately zoned suburban editions.[25] Conglomeration and computerization have allowed newspaper companies to attack their unions and effectively roll back wages. The average real hourly wage at U.S. newspapers dropped 25.7 percent between 1976 and 2000, from $18.58 to $13.81, a far steeper drop than the average decline of the average manufacturing real hourly wage (6.8 percent) during the same time period.[26] When all newspaper representation proceedings are considered since 1990, the percentage of union victories averaged only 23 percent.[27]

The result of these changes is mixed, but many scholars of the American press argue that, as newspapers become more a part of publicly traded corporations, they are reshaped and reoriented to realize "shareholder value" rather than traditional journalistic values. This is by no means a blanket assessment, of course. A few newspaper companies—primarily those with an ownership structure that maintains voting power in the founding family, such as the *New York Times* or *Washington Post*—are finer than ever, or, in the case of the papers owned by the A.H. Belo Corporation, have largely resisted the influence of stock analysts.[28] And there is evidence that takeover by a chain has rescued and improved some struggling independently owned newspapers. A study of the effects of Gannett's purchase of the *Louisville Courier-Journal*, for example, found that the paper devoted nearly 30 percent more space to news and 7 percent less space to advertising after Gannett took over the paper.[29]

At the same time, scholars and journalists find that publicly traded newspapers, as they have become more profitable in the last decade, have a tendency to become worse newspapers, reducing content, especially of politics, state government, and foreign affairs, cutting costs largely by reducing the quantity and quality of newsroom staff, and responding to the strict financial controls and profit expectations under which they operate by breaking down the old organizational separation between news and business.[30] Knight-Ridder and Gannett come in for particular condemnation in this regard, especially from veteran reporters and editors who have worked for those companies.[31] The publicly traded newspaper companies typically have been much more aggressively antiunion than have the companies that continue to be family owned.[32] Large newspaper corporations are keen to move into television in their local markets, and have strongly supported the FCC's rule change on newspaper-television cross-ownership. Still, this structural picture should not be overinterpreted. Of the 300 newspapers that have disappeared in the past twenty-plus years, few were distinguished. Moreover, the culture of newspaper journalism has evolved to a far higher level of professionalism than was true of earlier decades. Prior to Vietnam and Watergate, national news coverage was largely subservient to power in ways that even the most compliant journalists today would never accept.[33]

In the broadcast and cable arena, there has been a marked increase in the number of channels over the past twenty-five years. At the end of 1979, there were 8,748 radio stations and 1,008 television stations operating in the United States. At the end of 2001, those numbers had grown to 13,012 radio stations (83 percent of which were commercial and an increasing percentage owned by large group owners, particularly Clear Channel Communications) and 1,686 television stations (78 percent of which were commercial and most of which were network affiliated). The growth of cable television has been far more dramatic. At the end of 1979, there were 4,200 operating cable systems serving some 10,200 communities, reaching about 15.1 million subscribers with twelve channels. At the end of 2001 there were 11,800 operating cable systems serving some 34,000 communities, reaching approximately 69 million subscribers (which is 69 percent of the nation's TV households) with sixty or more channels. Direct broadcast satellite served another 16 million subscribers.[34] According to *TV Dimensions*, the average number of channels available in the American home in 2001 was 82.4—a quantum leap from the situation just ten years earlier, when U.S. television homes received an average of twenty-seven channels. The growth in the number of channels, accordingly, has important competitive consequences; the time spent per channel viewed weekly has dropped from 5.5 hours in 1990 to 3.5 hours in 2002, reflecting a significant fragmentation of the television audience.[35]

Thus, the interlinked forces of deregulation, growth of television outlets, and new forms of competition have transformed the traditional complexion of mass electronic media in the United States. Like newspapers of the pre-1960s era, the three historic television networks (NBC, CBS, ABC) were parts of media companies led by their founders. By the 1980s the founders had died and the networks were no longer parts of media companies; they became part of large publicly traded conglomerates. General Electric purchased NBC in 1986; ABC was bought by Capital Cities in the same year and was sold to Disney in 1996; a struggling CBS was bought by Wall Street investor Laurence Tisch, became part of Westinghouse in 1995 and then Viacom in 2000. In September 2003, GE/NBC, the network with the fewest nonbroadcast media holdings, purchased Vivendi's Universal media properties.

For decades, the network news divisions, and even local broadcast news operations, had a kind of privileged status. They were seen as fulfilling the public trustee mandate of broadcast licensees, thus serving, in effect, as insurance for FCC renewal of station licenses. The network news programs also acted as a signature of their networks, bestowing prestige on their corporate owner and providing a respectable cover for the highly profitable entertainment divisions. As such, paradoxically, network news and public affairs documentaries, generously budgeted and typically posting monetary losses, gave television journalists some freedom for the exercise of quality journalism without having to bow heavily to audience desires or ratings.[36] The old television system of limited choices also made this possible inasmuch as audiences unhappy with the news programming had few viewing alternatives.

The competition brought by the growth of broadcast television and cable outlets, combined with the waning of FCC regulation of broadcast licensees and a corresponding virtual automatic license renewal process, meant that news divisions no longer occupied a privileged position in the corporate hierarchy. The conglomerate owners forced their network news divisions to hew to the bottom line and imposed deep cuts in the 1980s, laying off thousands of staff, closing foreign bureaus, cutting documentaries and public-affairs programs, and requiring managers to pay close attention to ratings and audience desires.

Competition from cable had still other ramifications. The twenty-four-hour cable news channels, first CNN, then Fox News and MSNBC, though still rather small in audience compared with network television news, brought an up-to-the-minute headline service function to the medium with heavy reliance on news agency reporting from Associated Press and Reuters. Network news adapted by providing more background, context, and analysis. But as part of attending to ratings and the perception of audience desires, network news has also become somewhat softer in content, with less treatment of traditional hard news topics, especially foreign affairs, and greater focus on features, celebrity, health, and lifestyle.[37] The dynamic of celebrity increasingly pervades television news as a system, with anchors and star reporters serving as icons for the network brand. There is also less news, period. In 1983, for example, the half-hour CBS Evening News aired 23:10 minutes of news; in 2000 the half-hour broadcast aired 18:20 minutes of news, with the remaining 11:40 minutes taken up by advertising and promotional announcements, including announcements for the parent company's other media offerings.[38] In short, the new ethos of maximizing shareholder value now applies to television news. Whereas in the old days network news lost money, the NBC news division, for example, posted a $300 million profit in 2000.[39]

At the same time, local television news is flourishing, at least at the economic level. News has become the big money maker for local broadcast stations, and much time is cleared for it, as much as two to three hours a day in major markets. The average pre-tax profit margin expected of local television news is 40 percent; some major market stations reputedly have profit margins of 60 to 70 percent, which is why, when those stations go on the market, they sell for several hundred million dollars and may be approaching a billion dollars.[40] Better and cheaper technologies, including easy access to satellite feeds, has permitted local television news to cover issues outside the local vicinity. At the levels of content and quality, however, local television news is widely understood as nothing short of atrocious. Most local television news items come from the police scanner, scheduled events, or follow the lead stories of the daily newspaper. Local television newscasts rarely feature original material, as they typically do not organize their newsgathering into "beats" and hence do not cultivate reporters who know a beat and generate original or probing stories. The bulk of local newscasts consists of crime stories, disasters, weather, and sports. News directors report that advertisers try to tell them what to air and not to air. Market consultants typically advise station managers to cut government and political coverage for visually exciting live-action reports. Accordingly, the amount and incisiveness of political coverage is very low.[41] The Project for Excellence in Journalism maintains that, contrary to conventional wisdom, quality journalism in local television news builds market share and audience retention.[42] Still, anecdotally, local television stations that try to present more hard news content often find their ratings drop.[43]

The impact of the Telecommunications Act of 1996 on radio was dramatic. Radio had been the least concentrated and most locally rooted electronic mass medium, even after the FCC raised the national ownership ceiling in 1992 to thirty AM and thirty FM stations. The 1996 act removed national limits on the ownership of radio stations. The number of stations a company can own in a particular market depends on the size of the market (see footnote 1). Some companies moved rapidly to accumulate radio holdings. Clear Channel Communications is the leading radio conglomerate with nearly 1,300 radio stations, followed by Infinity Broadcasting, a division of the media giant Viacom, with more than 180.[44] Whereas radio had typically been local, both

Clear Channel and Infinity are pioneers in the centralized computerization of radio stations through voice tracking, the practice of creating brief, computer-assisted voice segments that attempt to deceive the listener into thinking that a program is locally produced, when in fact the same content is being broadcast to upwards of seventy-five stations nationwide from a central site. Clear Channel has been accused of practicing a new form of payola, among other things requiring musical acts and record companies to use its concert facilities in order to get radio play.[45] Infinity owns Westwood One and Metro Networks, the largest providers of turnkey newscasts and traffic information for radio, which provide the same news to its affiliates, even in the same market. In a 2003 Securities and Exchange Commission filing, Westwood One claimed to serve more than 7,700 radio stations, which means that 60 percent of U.S. radio stations relay news from a single source.[46] Seeing an opportunity in the decline of serious radio news, public broadcasting's National Public Radio stepped into the breach and expanded its programming. NPR claims to reach a growing audience of 21 million Americans each week via more than 730 public radio stations.[47]

Finally, the issue of synergy must be considered. As corporate owners agglomerate media and telecommunications properties, the idea is to cross-promote among co-owned or cooperating media and utilize content from one medium for another. Actual synergy may be more corporate buzz than reality, but its presumed efficiencies serve as legitimization for the conglomeration of media properties—especially given the 1996 Telecommunications Act's explicit encouragement of cross-platform competition. The cross-use of content may in principle provide additional news content for certain outlets and viewers, but the dynamics of synergy and competition also contribute to an erosion of the walls between news, entertainment, and advertising. Evidence for this erosion tends to be anecdotal but the accounts are worrisome. Local television news frequently pegs stories to the theme of the preceding network drama, a seemingly trivial practice, but a distorting one nonetheless. As noted above, television news directors report that big advertisers routinely tell them what stories to air; how much more pressure might be brought to bear if the television stations are themselves owned by large advertisers? Rupert Murdoch dropped the BBC from his Star satellite news service because the BBC was offensive to the Chinese government and for business reasons Murdoch's News Corp. needed to cozy up to the Chinese government. The *Los Angeles Times* entered into a conflict-of-interest promotional gambit with the Staples Arena whose exposure set off a grassroots uprising in the newsroom and eventually brought down the publisher. ABC devoted two hours of "Good Morning America" to the twenty-fifth anniversary of Disney World.

The above are but a few of the troubling stories. Synergy spawns an almost inevitable clash of values between the culture of the corporate owner and the culture of journalism. Synergy is about breaking down internal walls, cross-promotion, and publicity; journalism seeks to maintain those walls and the norms of objective reporting. The intersection of ownership consolidation and synergy increases the likelihood of business opportunities winning out over critical reporting. Because General Electric owns NBC, a question about whether stories critical of the military-industrial complex don't make it to NBC News always lurks in the background. The same, of course, is true of ABC News and the interests of its corporate parent, Disney, the news properties owned by AOL-Time-Warner, and so on down the corporate ownership list. Whether or not such stories are killed is hard to know—it is very difficult to perceive something that isn't there, an expose that didn't make it to print, a story that didn't air. But with fewer, larger, more conglomerated owners, this fear seems reasonable. A recent instance in June 2003 concerning CBS News and Jessica Lynch, the celebrated American soldier who was rescued from an Iraqi hospital during the Iraq war, highlights some of the lures and dangers of synergy. In exchange for a much sought-after interview with the celebrity soldier, CBS reputedly offered Lynch a combined two-hour documentary with ideas for possible tie-ins from various entertainment divisions of its corporate parent, Viacom Inc., including MTV, CBS, and book publisher Simon & Schuster.[48] The walls between news, entertainment, and advertising are made more permeable by the ability of media conglomerates to buy additional properties for purposes of synergy. Still, while there is good reason to be wary of ownership consolidation and synergy, the data do *not* support any conclusive judgment that consolidation is irretrievably damaging to diversity or that smallness and independence result in quality news. The data, to the extent that they exist, are decidedly mixed. For example, the Project for Excellence in Journalism's study of local television news found that smaller station groups and stations affiliated with, but not owned by, networks produced higher quality news. But the study also found that local ownership did not necessarily result in quality newscasts, and, most interesting, found that stations whose parent company owned a newspaper in the same market actually produced higher quality newscasts[49] (See Appendix II: Big Media).

WHERE THINGS ARE NOW

The Telecommunications Act of 1996 focused and accelerated a longer trend toward the deregulation of U.S. communications. Central to the trend is the view among policymakers that the U.S. communications environment has changed fundamentally due to technology and sectoral growth. The relevant institutional authorities—FCC, Justice Department, and federal courts—also

have now largely accepted the concept of "substitutes," that the product offered by, say, cable television, broadcast television, satellite television, and
video rentals, is essentially the same. Thus, companies previously understood as individual media segments operating in separate product markets
are now seen as competing with one another and therefore should be included in the same product market for purposes of antitrust analysis.[50] The
overall growth of media (including, now, the spectacular growth of the Internet) and the acceptance of the concept of substitutes have important
bearing on how policymakers now think about diversity and regulation. In
a limited media system, such as the old broadcast system, it might make
sense to regulate vertically, that is, require that any individual outlet to air a
broad and diverse mix of programming, including news; in an extensive
media system, doesn't it make sense to look at the diversity question horizontally, that is, across all substitutable outlets? If so, and that market shows
no troublesome concentration, government intervention is not needed and
is, in fact, pernicious. Simple vigilance on the antitrust front will safeguard
diversity.

In view of this changed environment, the federal appellate courts, increasingly skeptical of congressional or regulatory assertions of media concentration and the defense of old ownership rules, began insisting on a new
concentration metric based on "nonconjectural" empirical evidence of anticompetitive behavior and verification of the efficacy of regulatory remedies.
In a series of cases beginning in the 1990s, the courts expressed irritation at
what the judges saw as the FCC's unreflective, ritualistic invocation of diversity in defense of many of its longstanding structural rules on ownership.[51]
Of course, this change reflects not simply a changed communications environment. It also reflects a changed legal environment, to wit, the rise of a
conservative formalism in equal protection law largely as a result of the ap-
pointment of federal judgeships by Republican presidents in recent decades.
The jurisprudential change highlights the change in what diversity is understood to mean. Diversity analysis in mass media had always been a part of
the regulatory mandate of the FCC, albeit in a general way. Diversity analysis attained significantly more bite when, in the late 1960s, civil rights litigation provided diversity a much more specific definition. In the media ownership arena, diversity's star, as it were, got hitched to the success of the legal
logic of civil rights and affirmative action. After the 1960s, diversity in broadcasting and other communications industries under the authority of the FCC
was assessed essentially by how accessible media were to minority, particularly racial minority, participation. In general, the diversity rationale received
strong support in both judicial and congressional forums for the roughly
twenty years between 1970 and 1990. The link between the diversity of
viewpoints and a diversity of owners was assumed. In fact, the empirical ev-

idence of the relationship between the diversity of ownership and the diversity of content is weak, and an increasingly conservative, formalistic judiciary in effect has called the FCC's bluff.[52] Moreover, the 1996 Telecommunications Act instructed the FCC to review media ownership rules every two years and rescind those that it cannot demonstrate still are needed to promote the public interest.

These forces reveal the context that underscores the FCC's ownership rule changes of 2003. The new Bush administration FCC, under the chairmanship of Michael Powell, seems to have entered into a kind of alliance, even one-upmanship, with the Court of Appeals in paying obeisance to corporations' First Amendment rights and removing traditional ownership limitations. Because the social science data on the nexus between ownership policies and programming are weak, most ownership or structural regulations were being read as violations of the speech rights of corporations. Although the public and congressional tumult over the new rules is encouraging, there is no guarantee that any legislation restoring the old rules will survive a presidential veto, or more apropos to this chapter, the new judicially required standards of social scientific proof.

NOTES

1. The key rule changes are as follows:

   - Local TV multiple ownership limit: In markets with 5 or more TV stations, a company may own 2 stations, but only one of these can be among the top four in ratings. In markets with 18 or more TV stations, a company can own 3 TV stations. The FCC has a waiver process for markets with 11 or fewer stations in which 2 of the top 4 stations wish to merge.
   - National TV ownership limit: A company can own TV stations reaching no more than a 45 percent share of U.S. TV households (had been 35percent). The FCC maintains the historical UHF "discount": Stations in the UHF frequency band count only 50 percent for calculating the national television reach.
   - Continuation of local radio ownership limit, but a change in the methodology for defining a radio market (replacing the signal contour method with a geographic market approach): In markets with 45 or more radio stations, a company may own 8 stations; 30–44 stations: 7; 15–29 stations: 6; 14 or fewer: 5.
   - Cross-media limits: In markets with 3 or fewer TV stations, no cross-ownership is permitted among TV, radio, and newspapers. In markets with between 4 and 8 TV stations, combinations are limited to one of the following:
     A. A daily newspaper; one TV stations; and up to half of the radio station limit for that market;
     B. A daily newspaper; and up to the radio station limit for that market (no TV).
     C. Two TV stations; up to the radio station limit for that market (no newspapers).

FCC, Report and Order and Notice of Proposed Rulemaking, 2002 Biennial Regulatory Review—Review of the Commission's Broadcast Ownership Rules and Other Rules Adopted Pursuant to

Section 202 of the Telecommunications Act of 1996 (MB Docket 02-277). Adopted June 2, 2003; released July 2, 2003.

2. Prometheus Radio Project v. FCC, No. 03-3388, U.S. Court of Appeals, 3rd Cir., decided 3 Sept. 2003.

3. In the court's reasoning, the FCC's derivation of new cross-media limits, and its modification of the numerical limits on both television and radio station ownership in local markets, all have the same essential flaw: an unjustified assumption that media outlets of the same type make an equal contribution to diversity and competition in local markets. *Prometheus Radio Project v. FCC*, 373 F.3d 372 (3rd Cir. 2004).

4. *Associated Press v. United States*, 326 U.S. 1, 20 (1945).

5. The scarcity theory, that broadcast frequencies were inherently physically scarce and thus required government to assign them—the standard accepted constitutional basis for the regulation of broadcasting—has come under considerable fire in recent years. Many courts and commentators have cast doubt on the continued relevance of the scarcity rationale, particularly given the recent growth of the medium. But the rationale for the regulation of broadcasting was never premised simply on the basis of physical scarcity, but of scarcity ensconced within a problem of the commons and a fear of radio's potential to focus political power. As every standard history of American broadcasting recounts, before the licensing of frequencies in 1927, "chaos" ruled the airwaves. The limited availability of a valuable resource, combined with the absence of some form of governmental or social allocation of usage rights, resulted in overuse, making the resource worthless to everyone. Natural scarcity exists when there is no legal definition of rights. In the language of the Court of Appeals in *National Citizens Committee for Broadcasting v. FCC*, 555 F.2d 938, 948 (D.C. Cir. 1977), "The need for some regulation of the airwaves became clear in the 1920's when there was none. 'With everybody on the air, nobody could be heard' [quoting *National Broadcasting Co. v. FCC*]. In order to ensure the public's ability to hear some speakers, the rights of other potential speakers were curtailed. The hard choice was between forcing free speech to bend or watching it break." In other words, the private system of allocation was unable to solve the problem of the commons. The government responded with a licensing regime that, because licenses were given away without charge, inevitably created a second scarcity. Could/should the government have created a standard, exclusionary private property right in the spectrum? Again, as any standard broadcast history will tell, that possibility was recognized and rejected in 1927 as embedding a "right of selfishness" in the medium. The reasons for rejecting private property rights in the spectrum were unanimously affirmed by the Supreme Court in *Red Lion Broadcasting Corp. v. FCC*, 395 U.S. 367 (1969). Noting broadcasters' claim to have unlimited choice in respect to the use of their licenses, i.e., their ability to treat the license like private property, the *Red Lion* Court cited *Associated Press* that the "First Amendment does not sanction repression of that freedom by private interests." The Court rejected the print model of private First Amendment rights for broadcasting. And when presented an explicit opportunity in 1994 to repudiate the scarcity doctrine in *Turner Broadcasting v. FCC*, 512 U.S. 622, 638 (1994), the Court "declined to question its continuing validity." See C. Edwin Baker, "Turner Broadcasting: Content-Based Regulation of Persons and Presses," in *The Supreme Court Review 1994*, ed. Dennis J. Hutchinson, David A. Strauss and Geoffrey R. Stone (Chicago: University of Chicago Press, 1995), 57–128.

6. *Munn v. Illinois*, 94 U.S. 113 (1877).

7. Public L. – No. 416 – 73rd Congress; S. 3285; 47 C.F.R. § 314, 311.

8. Amendment of Sections 3.35, 3.240, and 3.636 of Rules and Regulations Relating to Multiple Ownership of AM, FM, and Television Broadcast Stations, Report and Order, 18 FCC 288, 291 (1953).

9. Amendment of Sections 73.35, 73.240, and 73.636 of Commission's Rules Relating to Multiple Ownership of AM, FM, and Television Broadcast Stations, Report and Order, 45 FCC 1476, 1477, 1482 (1964).

10. Policy Statement on Comparative Broadcast Hearings, 1 FCC 2d 393 (1965).

11. Prime Time Access Rule, 47 C.F.R. § 73.658(k).

12. 47 C.F.R. § 315.

13. Primer on Ascertainment of Community Problems by Broadcast Applicants, 27 FCC 2d 650 (1971).

14. Philip Napoli, "Deconstructing the Diversity Principle," *Journal of Communication* 49, no. 4 (Autumn 1999): 7–34.

15. See, for example, FCC, *Public Service Responsibility of Broadcast Licensees* (Washington, D.C.: FCC, 1946), which inaugurated this mode of analysis but did not focus on racial minorities.

16. It's important to see deregulation in the United States as a general *political* phenomenon, not confined to communications and not the particular consequence either of the technological revolution in communications or of some abstract notion of economic necessity. Deregulation in the United States affected particular kinds of industries under particular kinds of regulatory controls: infrastructure industries, such as airlines, trucking, telecommunications, broadcasting, banking, natural gas, electricity, all of which had been under price-and-entry regulation, where government determined the number of firms to provide service and set the prices the regulated firms could charge consumers for the services rendered. The success of price-and-entry regulation was dialectically the reason for its downfall. On the one side, the tight regulated system came subject to criticism in the 1960s by liberals and a thriving public interest movement as evidence of the "capture" of regulatory agencies by the industries under regulation. Regulators and large regulated industries were thought to be in bed with each other. On another side were academic economists who had been criticizing the efficiency of regulated industries for several years. They concluded that regulation was sometimes irrational, that monopolies thought to be "natural" were in fact maintained only through regulation, that regulation stifled innovation, and that regulation often was used as a means of cartel management. By the mid to late 1970s these criticisms found an audience in business, now suffering under the regulatory consequences of 1960s politics. This resulted in the clarion call to "get the government off the backs of the people." In short, these agencies and these regulated industries had earned the wrath of *both* liberals and conservatives. Each wing of a curious, heterodox political alliance of liberals and conservatives, of public interest movement leftists and free market ideologues, operating wholly within their own internal ideological logics of participatory democracy and free market economics, respectively, believed that the reform of price-and-entry regulation was in the public interest. See Robert Britt Horwitz, *The Irony of Regulatory Reform: The Deregulation of American Telecommunications* (New York: Oxford University Press, 1989).

17. See Patricia Aufderheide, *Communications Policy and the Public Interest: The Telecommunications Act of 1996* (New York: Guilford Press, 1999).

18. "Trends and Numbers," Newspaper Association of America www.naa.org/artpage .cfm?AID=1610&SID=1022 (2 Oct. 2003).

19. Howard Stanger, "Newspapers: Collective Bargaining Decline Amidst Technological Change," in *Collective Bargaining in the Private Sector*, ed. Paul F. Clark, John T. Delaney and Ann C. Frost (Champaign, Ill: Industrial Relations Research Association, 2002), 183–84; Gilbert Cranberg, Randall Bezanson, and John Soloski, *Taking Stock: Journalism and the Publicly Traded Newspaper Company* (Ames: Iowa State University Press, 2001), 26–27; Robert G. Picard, "The Economics of the Daily Newspaper Industry," in *Media Economics: Theory and Practice*, ed. Alison Alexander, James Owers, and Rodney Carveth (Mahwah, N.J.: Erlbaum, 1998), 111–30.

20. Newspaper Association of America, "Daily Newspaper Readership Trends," www.naa.org/artpage.cfm?AID=1613&SID=1022 (19 Sept. 2003); "U.S. Daily and Sunday/Weekend Newspaper Reading Audience," www.naa.org/info/facts00/02.html (19 Sept. 2003); www.naa.org/ marketscope/DSN2002/DSNAud2002Final.pdf (19 Sept. 2003); <http://www.naa.org/info/facts03/ 14_facts2003.html (17 Nov. 2003).

21. Jack Bass, "Newspaper Monopoly," in *Leaving Readers Behind: The Age of Corporate Newspapering*, ed. Gene Roberts, Thomas Kunkel, and Charles Layton (Fayetteville: University of

Arkansas Press, 2001), 109–53; Newspaper Association of America, "Total U.S. Non-Daily News-papers," www.naa.org/info/facts00/27.html>.

22. John Morton, Telephone interview with author, 14 Aug. 2003; idem, "Everything is Coming Up Profits for Papers," *American Journalism Review* (June 1999): 80; Geneva Overholser, "Editor, Inc.," in *Leaving Readers Behind*, 164.

23. See Leo Bogart, *Preserving the Press: How Daily Newspapers Mobilized to Keep Their Readers* (New York: Columbia University Press, 1991); Benjamin M. Compaine and Douglas Gomery, *Who Owns the Media? Competition and Concentration in the Mass Media Industry*, 3rd ed. (Mahwah, N.J.: Erlbaum, 2000); Cranberg, Bezanson and Soloski, *Taking Stock*.

24. Stephen R. Sleigh, *On Deadline: Labor Relations in Newspaper Publishing* (Bayside, N.Y.: Social Change Press, 1998); Catherine McKercher, *Newsworkers Unite: Labor, Convergence, and North American Newspapers* (Boulder, Colo.: Rowman & Littlefield, 2002); Richard Vigilante, *Strike: The Daily News War and the Future of American Labor* (New York: Simon & Schuster, 1994); Stanger, "Newspapers: Collective Bargaining Decline," 179–216.

25. See, among others, Leonard Downie, Jr. and Robert G. Kaiser, *The News about the News: American Journalism in Peril* (New York: Knopf, 2002); Roberts, Kunkel, and Layton, ed., *Leaving Readers Behind*.

26. U.S. Department of Labor, cited in Stanger, "Newspapers: Collective Bargaining Decline," 197.

27. Stanger, "Newspapers: Collective Bargaining Decline," 191.

28. Cranberg, Bezanson and Soloski, *Taking Stock*.

29. David C. Coulson and Anne Hanson, "The Louisville Courier-Journal's News Content After Purchase by Gannett," *Journalism & Mass Communication Quarterly* 72, no. 1 (Spring 1995): 205–15. Coulson and Hansen also found that after the purchase the average story length became shorter, the percentage of hard-news stories was smaller, and wire stories came to exceed staff-written stories.

30. Doug Underwood, *When MBAs Rule the Newsroom: How the Marketers and Managers Are Reshaping Today's Media* (New York: Columbia University Press, 1991); Cranberg, Bezanson, and Soloski, *Taking Stock*, 77–113; Downie and Kaiser, *The News about the News*.

31. Roberts, Kunkel, and Layton, 2001; Gene Roberts and Thomas Kunkel, *Breach of Faith: A Crisis of Coverage in the Age of Corporate Newspapering* (Fayetteville: University of Arkansas Press, 2002); Jay Harris, Luncheon Address to ASNE, 6 April 2001 (ASNE Reporter 2001), www.asne.org/index.cfm?id=1525 (22 Sept. 2003).

32. Vigilante, *Strike*; Stanger, "Newspapers: Collective Bargaining Decline."

33. See Michael Schudson, *The Sociology of News* (New York: Norton, 2003).

34. *Broadcasting Yearbook* (New York: Broadcasting, 1980), A-2; *Broadcasting & Cable Yearbook, 2002–2003* (New York: Broadcasting and Cable, 2003), xxxii.

35. *TV Dimensions 2003*, ed. Ed Papazian (New York: Media Dynamics, 2003), 24, 30.

36. See Michael Curtin, "Redeeming the Wasteland: Television Documentary and Cold War" *Politics* (New Brunswick, N.J.: Rutgers University Press, 1995).

37. James T. Hamilton, *All the News That's Fit to Sell: How the Market Transforms Information into News* (Princeton, N.J.: Princeton University Press, forthcoming 2004).

38. Downie and Kaiser, *The News about the News*, 113.

39. "NBC to Report Record Revenue," *Broadcasting & Cable* (4 Dec. 2000).

40. *Broadcasting & Cable Yearbook, 2002–2003* (New York: Broadcasting and Cable, 2003); Downie and Kaiser, *The News about the News*, 176.

41. John H. McManus, *Market-Driven Journalism: Let the Citizen Beware?* (Thousand Oaks, Calif.: Sage, 1994); Project for Excellence in Journalism, "Special Report: Local TV News," Supplement to *Columbia Journalism Review* (Nov./Dec. 2001); Downie and Kaiser, *The News about the News*.

42. Project for Excellence in Journalism, "Special Report: Local TV News."

43. See Michael Winerip, "Looking for an 11 O'Clock Fix," *New York Times Magazine* (11 Jan. 1998), 30–63.

44. Clear Channel, Inc., Webpage, www.clearchannel.com/company_history.php (14 Sept. 2003).

45. Jeff Perlstein, "Clear Channel: The Media Mammoth That Stole the Airwaves," *CorpWatch* (14 Nov. 2002), www.corpwatch.org/issues/PID.jsp?articleid=4808 (22 Sept. 2003); Eric Boehlert, "Radio's Big Bully," Salon.com, www.salon.com/ent/clear_channel/ (22 Sept. 2003).

46. Westwood One, Inc., SEC filing 8-K (5 Aug. 2003), www.sec.gov/Archives/edgar/data/771950/000077195003000033/0000771950-03-000033.txt (22 Sept. 2003).

47. National Public Radio Web site, www.npr.org/about/index.html?loc=topnav (25 Sept. 2003).

48. Jim Rutenberg, "To Interview Former P.O.W., CBS Offers Stardom," *New York Times* (16 June 2003), A1.

49. Project for Excellence in Journalism, "Special Report: Local TV News."

50. For instance, in *Cable Holdings of Georgia v. Home Video, Inc.*, the court of appeals upheld a merger between two cable companies under the logic that the relevant product market definition was that all "passive visual entertainment," including cable television, satellite television, video cassette recordings, and free broadcast television, were reasonable substitutes and hence constituted a single product market. 712 F. Supp. 1389 (N.D. Cal. 1989), *aff'd*, 903 F.2d 659 (9th Cir 1990).

51. See, among others, Justice O'Connor's dissenting opinion in *Metro Broadcasting v. FCC*, 497 U.S. 547 (1990); *Lamprecht v. FCC*, 958 F.2d 382 (D.C. Cir. 1992); *Lutheran Church-Missouri Synod v. FCC*, 141 F.3d 344 (D.C. Cir. 1998); *Time Warner v. FCC*, 240 F.3d 1126 (D.C. Cir. 2001); *Fox Television Stations v. FCC*, 280 F.3d 1027 (D.C. Cir. 2002). For further discussion of the diversity issue, see Robert B. Horwitz, "On Media Concentration and the Diversity Question," <http://www.communication.ucsd.edu/people/ConcentrationpaperICA.htm>.

52. For example, writing in 1970, Harvey J. Levin was largely critical of the claims made for the group ownership rule in terms of its effects on competition and diversity (though he admitted to a paucity of good data on content diversity). "Competition, Diversity, and the Television Group Ownership Rule," *Columbia Law Review* 70, no. 4 (May 1970): 791–835. J.C. Busterna found no significant relationship between the effects of TV/newspaper cross-ownership on the diversity of issues covered in the news. The slight negative relationship between cross-ownership and issue diversity, though not statistically significant, may still constitute enough evidence to suggest that prohibitions of future cross-ownership should continue, even if the findings are not strong enough to justify a policy move to break up existing cross-ownerships. "Television Station Ownership Effects on Programming and Idea Diversity: Baseline Data," *Journal of Media Economics* 1, no. 2 (Fall 1988): 63–74. Writing in 1985, Jacob Waklshlag and William Jenson Adams found that the introduction of the Prime Time Access Rule, enacted in 1970 by the FCC to encourage local production, was largely responsible for a sharp decline in network program diversity. "Trends in Program Variety and the Prime Time Access Rule," *Journal of Broadcasting & Electronic Media* 29, no. 1 (Winter 1985): 23–34. Most of the programming that replaced network shows in the 7 to 8 p.m. hour was cheap (and generally agreed as dreadful) game shows and animal shows. These findings seem to underscore the power of market conditions. The one area where regulations on ownership did have an effect on the diversity of program formats and primary audience was the FCC minority preference policies. See Congressional Research Service, *Statistical Analysis of FCC Survey Data: Minority Broadcast Station Ownership and Minority Broadcasting* (Washington, DC: U.S. Government Printing Office, 1988); Jeff Dubin and Matthew L. Spitzer, "Testing Minority Preferences in Broadcasting," *Southern California Law Review* 68, no. 4 (May 1995): 841–84.

Appendix I: 20 of the Top U.S. Newspaper Companies by Circulation 2003

Publisher	Number of Dailies	Daily Circulation	Share of Total Circulation 55,185,351[1]
[2]Gannett Co.	101	7,600,000	13.8
[3]Knight Ridder	31	3,863,000	7.00
[4]Tribune Co.	13	3,400,000	6.16
[5]Advance Publications Inc.	25	3,129,721	5.68
[6]Dow Jones and Co.	16	2,444,633	4.44
[7]The New York Times Co.	17	2,294,500	4.12
[8]Media News Group Inc	40	2,164,573	3.90
[9]The Hearst Corporation	12	1,668,587	3.02
[10]The McClatchy Co.	12	1,415,990	2.56
[11]The EW Scripps Co.	21	1,300,000	2.34
[12]Cox Newspapers Inc.	17	1,200,000	2.17
[13]Media General Inc	25	1,181,274	2.14
[14]Lee Enterprises	44	1,108,567	2.00
[15]Freedom Newspapers Inc.	27	1,003,417	1.82
[16]Community Newspape Holdings	87	950,000	1.72
[17]Belo	4	900,000	1.63
[18]The Washington Post Company	2	795,637	1.44
[19]The Copley Press	9	681,157	1.23
[20]Morris Communications Corp.	25	659,618	1.20
[21]Pulitzer Inc.	14	578,618	1.05
Percentage Share of Total			**69.42**

[1]"Editor & publisher international year book." Part 1: U.S., Newspaper and Foreign Dailies. New York: Editor and Publisher, 2004.
[2]www.gannett.com/map/gan007.htm.
[3]biz.yahoo.com/prnews/040322/sfm160_1.html.
[4]investor.tribune.com/EdgarDetail.cfm?CIK=726513&FID=1047469-04-5918&SID=04-00.
[5]Editor and Publisher, 2004—results of period ending September 30, 2003.
[6]www.dj.com/annualreports/2003/2003Annual.pdf.
[7]www.nytco.com/company-properties.html.
[8]www.medianewsgroup.com/AboutUs/default.asp.
[9]Editor and Publisher, 2004—results of period ending September 30, 2003.
[10]Editor and Publisher, 2004—results of period ending September 30, 2003.
[11]www.scripps.com/corporateoverview/businesses/index.shtml.
[12]coxnews.com/cox/news//cni/overview.html.
[13]Editor and Publisher, 2004—results of period ending September 30, 2003.
[14]www.lee.net/newspapers/.
[15]Editor and Publisher, 2004—results of period ending September 30, 2003.
[16]www.mediainfo.com/eandp/departments/business/article_display.jsp?vnu_content_id=1000479680.
[17]www.belo.com/companies/newsgroup.xml.
[18]ww.washpostco.com/business-newspapers.htm.
[19]Editor and Publisher, 2004—results of period ending September 30, 2003.
[20]Editor and Publisher, 2004—results of period ending September 30, 2003.
[21]media.corporate-ir.net/media_files/NYS/PTZ/reports/SBM11199_03_Complete.pdf.

Time Warner[1]	*News Corporation*[2]

Publishing

—7 book publishing companies with 27 book publishing imprints. Companies include: Little, Brown and Company Adult Trade Books, Little Brown and Company Books for Young Readers, Warner Books, Bilfinch Press, Warner Faith, Time Warner Audio Books, and Time Warner Book Group UK

—47 magazine publishing companies, with 164 titles. Popular magazines include: Time, Fortune, Sports Illustrated, People, Wallpaper, and many specialty magazines including *Ride BMX, Yachting Monthly,* and *Golf Magazine.*

Cable TV

—HBO (7 variations, 8 international joint-ventures), Cinemax (7 Variations), CNN (8 Variations), Court TV, Time Warner Cable, Road Runner, New York 1 News (24 hour news in NYC), Kablevision (Cable television in Hungary)

Film and TV Productions and Distribution

—12 domestic companies including Warner Bros., Hanna Barbera Cartoons, Castle Rock Entertainment, The WB Television Network, and Telepicture Productions.

—8 Turner Entertainment networks including TBS superstition and the Cartoon Network

—International television distribution and The Warner Channel in Latin America, Asia, Australia, and Germany)

—Warner Bros. International Theatres owns and operates in 12 different countries

Music

—47 Warner Music Group Recording Labels including The Atlantic Group, Elektra Entertainment Group, Warner Bros. Records, Maverick

—Other music related projects include the Warner Chappell Music (a publishing

Publishing

—3 book publishing companies with 29 imprints, including 6 children's labels. Companies include: HarperCollins Publishing, ReganBooks, and Zondervan

—More than 175 English Language papers worldwide, *New York Post* in the U.S.

—News America Marketing: a portfolio of consumer promotions media

—5 magazines including TV Guide, Smart Source, Inside Out, donna hay, and the Weekly Standard

Television and Film Production and Distribution

—Direct Broadcast Satellite Television: BskyB, FOXTEL, DirectV and Skyltalia

—Cable Networks, with nearly 300 million subscribers, include Fox News Channel, Fox Movie Channel, 7 Fox Sports channels, FX, and 2 National Geographic channels

—35 Fox television stations across the United States

—The Fox Entertainment Group produces and distributes film and television worldwide through Twentieth Century Fox Television, which produces entertainment shows that air on of News Corporation networks and through Twentieth Century Fox and Fox Searchlight Pictures, which produces and distributes motion pictures worldwide.

Others

—Owner of LA Dodgers and part owners of New York Rangers, New York Knicks, Los Angeles Kings, Los Angeles Lakers

—Part owner of Staples Center

—Owner of the Fox Sports Radio Network

—Owner of Festival and Mushroom Records

(continued)

Time Warner[1]	News Corporation[2]

company) Ivy Hill Corporation (printing and packaging company), and many joint ventures to produce direct marketing, Web sites, and music channels such as Columbia House (direct marketing project w/ Sony), Viva (German music video channel w/ Sony, PolyGram and EMI), and MusicNet (Online music with RealNetworks, BMG and EMI.)

Online Services

Websites and Web Services including AOL, CompuServe, ICQ, Mapquest.com, Moviefone and Netscape

Others

—Warner Bros. Consumer Products

—Warner Bros. Recreation Enterprise: owns and operates international theme parks

—3 Sports teams including Atlanta Braves, Atlanta Hawks and Atlanta Thrashers

—Classroom learning tools such as Turner Adventure Leaning which are electronic school field trips, and CNN Newsroom, which is a daily news program geared towards kids.

—Owner of NDS, a company that provides digital and pay TV solutions such as providing interactive applications, security broadband solutions, and personal TV.

—News Interactive: The third-largest online publisher in Australia

—News Outdoor Group: Leading outdoor advertiser in Eastern Europe

Viacom[3]	Disney[4]

Publishing

—1 book publishing Company, Simon & Shuster, with imprints including Pocket Books, Scribner, Free Press, Touchstone, Fireside, Archway, Minstrel, Pocket Pulse, and Washington Square Press

Television

—CBS Television Network: Viacom owns 16 CBS networks, and is affiliated with 185 more, producing news, entertainment and sports programming through CBS Productions, it in house producer.

—UPN Television Network: Viacom owns 18 UPN stations across the USA

—CBS Enterprises distributes CBS programming internationally

Publishing

—3 publishing companies: The Walt Disney Book Company, Hyperion Books, and Miramax Books

—5 Magazine publishing groups: ABD Publishing Group, Disney Publishing Group, Diversified Publications Group, Financial Services and Medical Group and Miller Publishing Company. Popular titles include: ESPN Magazine, Discover, U.S. Weekly, and Biography

Television

—ABC Television Network: Disney owns and operates 10 stations producing news, sports daytime and kids television

—Viacom produces and distributes programming domestically through Spelling Television, Big Ticket Television, and King World Productions

—Viacom owns and operates 15 cable channels including: MTV, MTV2, Nickelodeon, BET, Nick at Nite, TV Land, NOGGIN, VH1, Spike TV, CMT, Comedy Central, Showtime, The Movie Channel, Flix, Sundance Channel

Film

—Viacom produces and distributes films through Paramount Pictures.

—Viacom is a leading distributor of videos and DVD's from its motion picture producers and cable shows through Paramount Home Video Production.

Radio

—Viacom owns and operates 185 radio stations through Infinity Broadcasting, covering everything from news, modern rock, oldies, country, FM talk, classic rock and urban formats. Weekly, these stations attract more than 76 million listeners.

Others

—Viacom Outdoor is a leading out-of-home media company, with over 1 million display faces

—Viacom Interactive Ventures: Viacom works to create online business opportunities with companies such as iWin.com, MarketWatch.com, and MovieTickets.com

—Famous Music: A music publishing company with over 100,000 copyrights spanning 7 decades

—Viacom Consumer Products licenses brands names from films and television shows for product creation such as video games, apparel, and toys

—Blockbuster rental stores: 4,141 owned and 830 franchised in the U.S., 1,951 owned and 454 franchised internationally, and over 43,000,000 U.S. members

—12 cable channels including: ABC Family Channel, The Disney Channel, Toon Disney, SoapNet, ESPN Inc (6 Variations), Classic Sports Network, and E!

—Television Production assets include: Buena Vista Television, Touchstone Television, Walt Disney Television and Walt Disney Television Animation (owns production facilities in Canada, Australia, and Japan)

Film

—Distributes and produces films through 8 production companies including: Walt Disney Pictures, Touchstone Pictures, Hollywood Pictures, Caravan Pictures, Miramax Films, Buena Vista Home Video, Buena Vista Home Entertainment, Buena Vista International

Radio

—ABC Radio owns 72 stations across the US but provides programming to over 4,800 affiliates

—ABC News programming is syndicated to over 2,000 radio affiliates

—Radio Disney is broadcast in markets covering 61% of the United States

—ESPN Radio provides programming for over 700 affiliates, 238 of which are full time carriers of ESPN programming.

Music

—Produces music through 5 companies which include Buena Vista Music Group, Hollywood Records (producer of motion picture soundtracks), Mammoth Records, Walt Disney Records, and Lyric Street Records (country music label)

Multimedia

—Disney boasts over 38 million unique viewers per month to its Web sites, which include ABC.com, ANCNEWS.com, Oscar.com, Disney.Com, ESPN.Sportszone.com, NBA.com, and NASCAR.com.

(continued)

Viacom[3]	Disney[4]
—Famous Players movie theater chain with approximately 1700 screens in 13 countries —Paramount Parks: 5 amusement parks with over 13 million annual visitors	—Broadband subscription video-on-demand services allow online access to 24 hour news coverage online, including access to popular news shows such as World News Tonight with Peter Jennings —Through the labels ABC, Disney and ESPN, Disney offers over 30 wireless content service which include downloadable ring tones, games, and streaming news video. **Others** —Minority ownership in TV ventures in France, Germany, Japan, Spain and Scandinavia —Owns and operates themes parks (MGM studios, Disneyland, Epcot), cruise lines (Disney Cruise Line), sports centers (Disney World Sports Complex), zoos (Disney's Animal Kingdom) and themed dining (Disney Regional Entertainment in the U.S. as well as in France and Tokyo —Owner of the Anaheim Mighty Ducks —Theatrical productions including "The Lion King" and Beauty and the Beast —Partial investor in Sid. R. Bass, a crude petroleum and natural gas production —Retail store chain, The Disney Store —Partial interest in TiVo, a television recording device

Vivendi Universal[5]	Bertelsmann Media Inc.[6]
Publishing —Vivendi publishes educations books through its imprints Larousse, Nathan, Anaya, Coktel, Atica, Scipione, Bordas, and Retz, and they publish literature through its labels Robert Laffont, Plon-Perrin, Les Presses - Solar – Belfond, La Decouverte & Syros, Les Presses de la Renaissance, Pocket Jeuness, 10/18, and Fleuve Noir. **Television and Film** —NBC Universal is the result to a merger between General Electric and	**Publishing** —Random House is Bertelsmann's book publishing company, publishing over 8,000 new books each year, and owning over 50,000 blacklisted titles. With publishing houses in more than 16 countries, and using over 100 different imprints. U.S. imprints include Alfred A. Knopf, Ballantine, Broadway, Crown Publishing Group, Doubleday, and Pantheon —Random House uses the internet to reach readers through AtRandom.com, the

Vivendi Universal Entertainment (VUE) in October 2003 and is 20% owned by the shareholders of VUE. Assets include: The NBC Television Network, NBC Studios and Universal Television (international production and distribution of television programming), cable TV networks including USA network, Sci-Fi Channel, CNBC, MSNBC, Bravo and Trio, The NBC stations group with14 owned and operated stations, Spanish broadcaster Telemundo, and 15.

Telemundo stations reaching 91% of Hispanic homes in the U.S. and interest in 5 theme parks.

—Canal+ Group: Canal+ Group produces and distributes Pay-TV France and interactive services (4.9 million subscriptions), they produce over 20 themed channels in over 16 countries, they produce, co-produce, acquire, distribute and license products for American and European film and television programs through StudioCanal, and they market sports rights through SportFive, which has the exclusive rights to French Rugby Championships.

Music

—Universal Music Group (UMG) has 24.5% of the world market share. Their operations include:

—Recording and distributing music through their many labels including Interscope Geffen A&M, Island Def Jam Music Group, MCA Nashville, Mercury Record, Mercury Nashville. Lost Highway, Polydor, Barclay, Universal Motown Records Group, Decca, Deutsche Grammophon, Philips, ECM, and Verve Music Group

—Marketing, licensing, and selling music from its recorded music catalogue

—Music publishing through Universal Music Publishing Group

—Licensing and selling UMG music to online music distribution companies

—Concert promotion through Universal Concerts.

first e-book imprint where books can be downloaded online, Print-on-Demand, which supplies short print runs of backlist titles requested by booksellers and Fodors.com, which creates book communities online.

—Gruner+Jahr is Bertelsmann's newspaper and magazine publishers. They have 11 newspapers in Germany and Eastern Europe, and more than 25 magazine publications in more than 14 countries. U.S. publications include Family Circle, Fast Company, Inc., Parents, and YM.

Television, Radio and Production

—RTL Group is Bertelsmann's television and production group. They operate stations throughout Europe. Examples of stations include RTL, RTL II, SUPER RTL, VOX, n-tv, M6 , Five , RTL 4 , Yorin and RTL TV1. Theses stations all have interactive Web sites frequented many by viewers each day.

—RTL Group also operates radio stations throughout Europe that reach millions each day. Examples include RTL France and Radio Hamburg.

—RTL Group produces 260 programs in 39 different countries. They have the rights to over 17,500 hours or programming in 150 countries, making them the largest independent TV producer outside of the US. Their production companies include FreemantleMedia, SPORTFIVE, teamWorx, and UVA Film & TV Productions Broadway Books.

Music

—BMG is Bertelsmann's music company. They are involved in production, publishing, and distribution. They have 200 recording labels include Arista, RCA and Ariola and talent represented from over 40 countries.

—BMG Music Publishing helps songwriters market their work to record labels, film studios and other media. With the rights to over 700,000 songs, they are

(continued)

Vivendi Universal⁵ | *Bertelsmann Media Inc.⁶*

Others

Telecommunications: Subsidiaries of Vivendi Universal SFR Cegetel group is the number 2 provider of land line telephones (3.4 million) and mobile telephones (14.7 million, 35.3% of market share) in France. They also own over 21,000 km of fiber optic cable, making it the most extensive private telecommunications infrastructure in France.

—Vivendi Universal Games is a leading producer and distributor of PC, console-based and online games. Games are produced under the labels Black Label Games, Blizzard Entertainment, Fox Interactive, Knowledge Adventure, Sierra Entertainment, and Universal Interactive in North America, and Coktel, NDA Productions, and Massive Entertainment in Europe.

the world's third-largest music publishing companies.

—Click2Music is BMG's online counterpart, which operates 40 Web sites on five continents.

Others

—Arvato is Bertelsmann's media service company. They provide media services such as printing, logistics services, financial services, and information technology. A subsidiary of Arvato, Sonopress, produces storage technology, and is the world's second-largest CD producer.

—DirectGroup is Bertelsmann's direct-to-customer media commerce operation. Through their media communities like book and music clubs, available through direct-to customer sales through catalogues, shops, and online outlets, such as BeMusic and CDNow, they reach over 55 million customers in 20 countries.

---

[1]Information comes from "Who Owns What" from the Columbia School of Journalism Review, last updated 9/22/03: www.cjr.org/tools/owners/timewarner.asp - double checked/updated using information from Time Warner Website www.timewarner.com/companies/index.adp.

[2]Information comes from "Who Owns What" updated 07/21/03: www.cjr.org/tools/owners/newscorp.asp - information updated/double checked using information from News Corporation Website: www.newscorp.com/index2.html.

[3]Information comes from "Who Owns What" from the Columbia School of Journalism Review last updated 03/16/04 www.cjr.org/tools/owners/viacom.asp information updated/double checked on Viacom's corporate website.

[4]Information comes from "Who Owns What" from the Columbia School of Journalism Review, last updated 03/16/04, information updated/double checked on Disney's corporate website disney.go.com/corporate/investors/financials/annual/2003/i/fh/fh_int.html in "Key Businesses_section.

[5]Information comes from "Who Owns What" from the Columbia School of Journalism Review, last updated 08/27/03 www.cjr.org/tools/owners/vivendi.asp., information updated/double checked on Vivendi Universal's corporate website www.vivendiuniversal.com/vu/en/home/index.cfm.

[6]Information comes from "Who Owns What" from the Columbia School of Journalism Review, last updated 07/23/03 www.cjr.org/tools/owners/bertelsmann.asp, information updated/double checked on Bertelsmann's corporate website www.bertelsmann.com/bag/profile/profile.cfm.

3

So Much by So Few: Media Policy and Ownership in Canada

David Skinner and Mike Gasher

Ownership has been a longstanding concern in Canadian media policy. In Canada, the economic forces underlying concentration of ownership have been complicated by a range of government regulations that, on one hand, have tried to keep the ownership of Canadian media in Canadian hands, while on the other, have wrestled with the drawbacks and supposed benefits of large, privately owned media companies.

For decades, Canadian ownership and control of media properties has been viewed as key to cultural sovereignty and the only way to ensure that Canadian media represent the interests and perspectives of Canadian citizens. Canada presents a particular challenge to policymakers. Its land mass is the second-largest country in the world, yet it is sparsely populated. Eighty-five percent of its 31 million people live within 200 miles of the border with the United States, Canada's closest trading partner and a global media power. More than 60 percent of Canadians share a common language with their American neighbors, but Canada also has a sizable French-speaking population, which comprises almost one-quarter of the country's total population and four-fifths of the population in the province of Quebec.[1]

At first in broadcasting, and later in other fields, the federal government has seen communication systems as central to the development of a shared set of ideas and values, a sense of nationhood, a Canadian culture.[2] Historically, however, imported—mainly American—magazines, films, newspaper wire copy, music recordings, books, and television programs have provided the mainstay for many media outlets in English-speaking Canada. Simply put, the economies of scale inherent in these products—developed originally for the U.S. market, the richest in the world—make them much more lucrative than their Canadian counterparts, which are produced for a much

smaller market. In the face of these constraints, ownership and content regulations have been used to create an economics of Canadian production and
to prevent Canadian media companies and markets from becoming simple
extensions of their American cousins. In the broadcasting, cable, and
telecommunications industries, legislation imposes limits on foreign ownership. In the newspaper industry, tax policy ensures that newspapers stay in
Canadian hands.

At the same time, there has been public concern over the effects of concentration of ownership. Inquiries such as the 1970 Special Senate Committee on the Mass Media (Davey Committee) and the 1981 Royal Commission
on Newspapers (Kent Commission) have pointed to the ways in which concentration tends to narrow the perspectives found in the news media, as well
as raise the specter of owners manipulating news to suit their own corporate
or political agendas.

In spite of these warnings, however, the last decade has seen unprecedented consolidation in Canadian media markets. In the mid-1990s, Conrad
Black's Hollinger Corporation gained majority interest in the Southam newspaper chain and then went on to win control of almost 50 percent of daily
newspaper circulation in Canada.[3] More recently, a 1996 change in regulations that had been designed to keep newspaper, broadcasting, and telecommunications companies separate, paved the way for cross-media consolidations and, subsequently, three major cross-media ownership deals struck
during the year 2000 radically altered the Canadian mediascape.[4] CanWest,
owner of the Global Television Network, purchased the Southam newspaper
group and a 50-percent share in the *National Post*—one of Canada's two national newspapers—from Hollinger Corporation. Today, CanWest controls
one of Canada's two private English-language television networks and close
to 30 percent of the country's daily newspaper circulation.[5] In another deal,
Bell Canada Enterprises (BCE, Canada's largest telecommunications company) purchased the Canadian Television Network (CTV, the country's
largest private television network), and then struck an alliance with Thomson Newspapers (publisher of the *Globe and Mail*, Canada's principal national daily newspaper) to form Bell Globemedia. And in Quebec, Quebecor, one of Canada's largest newspaper groups, purchased Videotron, the
largest cable service provider in Quebec, and the private French-language
television network TVA. In Quebec, two companies—Quebecor and Power
Corp.—own all but one of the French-language daily newspapers in the
province (the exception is the small-circulation intellectual paper *Le Devoir*),
accounting for 97 percent of circulation.

Some would argue that there are now, thanks especially to the Internet
and specialty TV channels, more media outlets available in Canada than ever
before and, thus, concerns over concentration of ownership are without
foundation. The point, however, is not about the sheer number of outlets,

but the ways in which a small handful of corporations dominate the major markets for news and information. As University of Ottawa professor Marc-François Bernier told the 2003 Standing Committee on Canadian Heritage, "it is important not to confuse 'multiplicity' with diversity. When I talk about diversified information . . . I do not mean that we should have 12 Internet sites with the same information: that is multiplicity and not diversity."[6]

As tables 3.1 and 3.2 illustrate, converged media conglomerates like CanWest Global, Quebecor, BCE, and Rogers Communications are major players in several media industries and markets. This means that they can: aggregate audiences across media and thus increase their market power; reuse programming and editorial content in a number of platforms to increase efficiency, increase their potential ideological clout to decrease diversity and inhibit dissent; and build significant barriers to entry for new enterprises or competitors. CanWest Global, Quebecor, and BCE, specifically, are industry leaders in the supply of news and information, with significant holdings in television broadcasting, newspaper publishing and on-line news. In Vancouver, Canada's third-largest city, CanWest Global owns both daily newspapers, the leading TV news broadcaster, and the Internet portal canada.com. Similarly, in Regina, Saskatoon, and English-speaking Montreal, CanWest Global owns the lone daily newspaper and a TV news broadcaster.

Because of the debt burdens accrued by Canada's major media companies, the expansion in the quantity of their media properties has had a detrimental impact on the quality of their content as resource cutbacks and lay-offs

Table 3.1. Daily Newspaper Ownership Groups (November 2003)

Publisher	Number of Titles	Average Daily Circulation	Share of Daily Circulation
CanWest Publications	13	1,423,850	28.88
Quebecor/Sun Media	17	1,013,783	20.56
Torstar	4	661,017	13.41
Power Corp.	7	450,548	9.14
Bell Globemedia	1	327,665	6.65
Osprey Media	22	326,155	6.62
Groupe Transcontinental	11	157,357	3.19
F.P. CNLP	2	141,620	2.87
Brunswick News	3	106,233	2.15
Halifax Herald	2	103,784	2.10
Horizon Operations	5	89,312	1.81
Hollinger CNLP	10	58,005	1.18
Independents	4	52,394	1.06
Black Press	1	18,694	0.38
Totals	**102**	**4,930,417**	**100**

Source: Canadian Newspaper Association, www.cna-acj.ca (Accessed March 26, 2004).

Table 3.2. Canada's Converged Media Companies (March 2004)

	Quebecor	CanWest Global	BCE	Rogers
Film-TV		CanWest Entertainment Fireworks Entertainment Fireworks TV Fireworks Intnl Fireworks Pictures Fireworks TV USA		
New Media	Netgraphe CANOE Nurun Videotron Illico Interactive Progisia	Canada.com Infomart FP DataGroup	Bell Globemedia Interactive BCE Emergis	Rogers Hi-Speed Internet
Publishing	Sun newspapers magazines book publishers	CanWest Publications	Globe and Mail	Rogers Media
Radio		Jazz FM The Beat Cool FM More FM (NZ) Channel Z (NZ) Localworks (NZ) CanWest Radio (NZ)		Rogers Radio
Retail	Groupe Archambault SuperClub Videotron Select			Rogers Video
Telephony			Bell Canada Bell Mobility	Rogers Wireless
Television	Videotron cable Groupe TVA Canal nouvelles Illico	Global Television Network Ten (Aus) TV3, C4 (NZ) TV3 (Ireland) UTV (N. Ireland) specialty channels	CTV network Bell ExpressVu TQS specialty channels	Rogers Cable Rogers Media Television

Sources: www.quebecor.com; www.canwestglobal.com; www.bce.ca; www.rogers.com (Accessed March 29, 2004).

invariably follow takeovers. Since spending over $3 billion (Cdn) to buy the Southam newspaper chain in 2000, for example, CanWest Global has been trying to divest assets to ease a $3.8-billion (Cdn) debt load.[7] Its attention to reducing debt resulted in an increased share price in early 2004.[8] Similarly, Quebecor, "engulfed in debt problems" following its October 2000 purchase of cable company Videotron, was forced to sell more than $1 billion (Cdn) in holdings. Quebecor Media recently recovered from three years of cost cuts in every division, but still carries $1 billion (Cdn) in high-yield debt.[9] BCE, too, remains saddled with a debt of $17 billion (Cdn), which represents an onerous two-thirds of the company's market value.[10]

The argument in favor of big media is that size gives them audience reach, human resources, capital, and technological resources to invest in content, the durability to take chances and absorb short-term losses, promotional power and independence from parochial political and/or local advertiser concerns.[11] David Demers argues that in the specific case of newspapers, critics overstate "the adverse consequences of the corporate form of organization."[12] Based on U.S. survey data conducted during the mid-1990s, Demers concludes that as newspapers become "more corporatized," they place more emphasis on quality and less on profits, and their editorial content becomes more critical of the status quo.[13] This is because: their owners, managers, and journalists have weaker loyalties to the community; they are better insulated from special-interest groups, advertisers, governments, "even the owners"; and they are more likely to be located in "socially and economically complex communities," which increases the amount of social conflict in the community "and generates more criticism of mainstream groups and ideas," criticism which is reflected in news coverage.[14]

But, as the Standing Committee on Canadian Heritage noted, these hypothetical advantages are too rarely exploited for the purpose of diversifying and otherwise improving content. Citing the examples of CanWest Global and Bell Globemedia, the committee noted these companies' lack of investment in original Canadian television drama while remaining heavy importers of American prime-time programming. The committee also argued that CanWest's centralized newspaper editorial policy wrested independence from local publishers and editors, while at the same time establishing ideological boundaries on debate. The danger of corporate concentration, the committee noted, "is that too much power can fall into too few hands and it is power without accountability."[15] A number of Canadian studies provide concrete instances of corporate interference with news coverage.[16]

Patterns of consolidation in Canada are similar to those in the United States. Local media outlets and markets are being integrated into larger regional, national, and transnational units of production and consolidations are marked by layoffs and rationalization of production processes. For the moment, newspapers in Canada remain overwhelmingly Canadian in content, and ownership of Canadian television and newspaper corporations remains in Canadian hands. But this may not continue as highly placed members of industry and government are asking to relax foreign-ownership rules in Canadian media markets and there are no guarantees that further integration of Canadian media companies into the global mediascape will not occur.[17]

What's driving these changes? Shifting advertising revenues, technological convergence, and competition from new web-based media. All of these forces are seen as pushing media consolidation as companies try to forge new economies of scale and scope that will wring profits from this changing institutional context. Some of the key "synergies"—as the efficiencies gleaned from consolidation are commonly called—sought by these corporations are: reduced labor requirements, cross-promotion of media products, larger and more flexible advertising markets, the "repurposing" of content created for use in one medium for use in another, the integration of executive and administrative functions, and vastly increased barriers to entry for would-be competitors.[18]

With companies trying to capture cost savings through consolidating news production facilities from different media, the recent trend toward cross-media ownership has raised particular concerns. Integrating print, broadcast, and web newsrooms and personnel is seen as narrowing the range of perspectives and distinct voices available in the media, while new editorial policies and sanctions that are evolving through these changes are raising fears for editorial independence.[19]

Recent events like those outlined by Leslie Regan Shade (chapter 5 in this volume) have renewed old fears about the effects of concentration and several recent public inquiries have moved to address these concerns. But to better understand the context of these inquiries we need to consider the history of media regulation in this country.

EARLY HISTORY

While recent trends toward cross-media ownership and technological convergence may give the impression that media markets have been separate until recently, in Canada this has certainly not been the case. Distinctions between media markets developed out of a patchwork of regulations and corporate agreements. In Canada, the first regulatory separation of the publishing and carriage of information arose out of disputes between telegraph and newspaper companies. As newspapers moved to consolidate their appeal to mass audiences in the late nineteenth and early twentieth centuries, they became increasingly dependent upon news and wire copy supplied by the telegraph companies. In Canada, telegraph companies offered their clients the Associated Press service, other American reports, and a national summary of Canadian news.[20] However, in an effort to force newspapers to subscribe to both their news and telegraphic services, Canadian Pacific Telegraphs (CPT)—a subsidiary of the Canadian Pacific Railway, Canada's largest railway—bundled the two services and charged one rate for both. In many areas competition to CPT was weak or nonexistent and the company exploited this advantage. Rates for this service were a constant source of friction, and in 1910 the Board of Railway Commissioners ruled that they were indeed exorbitant and forced the company to establish separate pricing policies for the two services. Shortly thereafter, their advantage lost, the railways abandoned the news business. A division of responsibility between the production of information and its carriage was thus instituted in regulation and, as Robert Babe points out, "the era of the telecommunications common carrier began."[21] This regulatory distinction between different kinds of communication markets slowly became entrenched in the fabric of regulation. Eventually, it was written into the charters of telephone companies and helped inform the division between telephone, broadcast, and cable-TV markets. It wasn't until the 1980s that this sanction against the right of telephone companies to operate as "publishers" would again come under serious question.

In its early days, the broadcasting field, too, was the site of struggle between a number of competing communications interests. A 1922 agreement between AT&T's Canadian subsidiary, Bell Telephone, and the subsidiaries of General Electric, Westinghouse, the International Western Electric Company, and the Marconi Company divided the manufacturing sides of telephone and broadcasting markets between them, and appears to have discouraged Bell from holding broadcast licenses.[22] In the early 1930s, a plan by the CPR to establish a monopoly national radio broadcasting company was forestalled by the government's creation of the Canadian Radio Broadcasting Commission, the forerunner of today's Canadian Broadcasting Corporation.

While the content/carrier distinction worked to keep the newspaper and telecommunications markets separate, historically, newspaper companies often made investments in broadcast outlets. In the 1920s and '30s, newspapers invested in radio stations in an effort to forestall competition in news markets and use the stations as promotional vehicles for their papers. By 1929, eleven Canadian radio stations were owned by newspapers and a Canadian Newspaper Radio Association was formed in the early 1930s.[23] To cite just two examples, *La Presse* founded CKAC in Montreal in 1922 and CKCI was founded by Quebec City newspaper *Le Soleil* in 1924.[24] By the end of the 1930s, more than a third of private radio stations had ownership links with newspapers.[25] As advertising revenue picked up during that period, small chains of radio stations also became established.[26]

NEWSPAPERS AND THE POSTWAR EXPANSION

Newspaper markets are sometimes characterized as natural monopolies because of the economic advantages producers glean from economies of scale. The larger a newspaper's circulation, the lower the cost of each paper it produces. Size also affords newspaper chains competitive advantages in that they can cut costs through sharing editorial material, production and management facilities, and purchasing newsprint and other production materials in bulk. And by cross-subsidizing papers in competitive or poorly performing markets, chains are better able to weather the effects of competition and recession. Size can also be an advantage in the broadcast industry, where sharing everything from programming to technical facilities and administrative functions can yield cost savings.

Driven by these forces, concentration of ownership in the Canadian newspaper industry began as early as 1897 when the Southam family, proprietors of the *Hamilton Spectator*, set out to purchase the *Ottawa Citizen*.[27] The first half of the twentieth century was a period of considerable transformation as newspapers became mass media by shifting their allegiance from partisan causes—trade unions, church groups, political parties—to the marketplace. Social changes like urbanization and rising literacy rates expanded newspaper markets, technological innovations in news-gathering (transoceanic telegraph lines, photography) and publishing (faster and larger printing presses, automobiles to facilitate delivery) increased newspapers' capacity to serve those markets. And as their market power increased, newspapers became increasingly attractive to advertisers, who replaced subscribers as the principal source of revenue.[28] Economies of scale became increasingly important to newspaper production, as average daily circulation rose from 5,000 in 1901 to almost 40,000 by 1951.[29] Newspapers were increasingly concentrated in fewer hands; in 1930, 116 dailies were under the control of ninety-nine publishers, by 1953, eighty-nine dailies were controlled by just fifty-seven owners.[30]

The postwar period saw concentration grow steadily in both the newspaper and the broadcasting industries. In 1958 the three largest newspaper ownership groups controlled 25 percent of daily newspaper circulation. By 1970 the three largest groups accounted for 44.5 percent, and by 1980 two groups held 48 percent. In Quebec, chains controlled 90 percent of circulation by 1980. Although there were some attempts by regulators to check these forces in the broadcast field, through this period concentration of ownership also grew in the broadcast and cable industries. In 1968, 38 percent of television stations were group-owned, and by 1975 groups accounted for 56 percent of the total.[31] Almost two-thirds of radio stations were group-owned in 1968, rising to 81 percent by 1975.[32] In terms of cross-media ownership, in 1975 four of the top ten revenue-producing radio groups were also counted among the top ten revenue-producing television groups.[33] Moreover, by the early 1980s, a number of companies with large newspaper holdings—such as Southam, Maclean Hunter, and the Irving Group in New Brunswick—also held extensive interests in radio, television, and cable, often in the same cities.

However, the evolving structure of Canada's media industries was not simply driven by economics; political forces also shaped its form and direction.

The clearest statement about the importance of communications media to Canada's sense of nationhood came from the Royal Commission on National Development in the Arts, Letters and Sciences. Known as the Massey Commission, it equated commercialization with American cultural dominance, particularly in the fields of educational materials, magazines, film, and radio.[34] As the commission noted, "[i]t cannot be denied . . . that a vast and disproportionate amount of material coming from a single alien source may stifle rather than stimulate our own creative effort."[35] While the Massey Commission cited the example of CBC's national public radio system as a success in fostering "a national spirit," it lamented the dependence of Canadian newspapers on "foreign news services designed primarily to serve the United States" and the fact that Canadians were the only people in the world to read more foreign than local magazines.[36] The Massey Commission endorsed the expansion of the role of government in ensuring Canadian content in radio, the new medium of television, film, and magazine publishing.

COMMUNICATION, CULTURE, AND CONCENTRATION

Early in the 1960s, increasing friction between Canada's English- and French-language communities called for attention by the federal government. As it came to office in 1963, the Liberal Party struck the Royal Commission on Bilingualism and Biculturalism, which pointed to the direction this strategy would take.[37] "Culture"—broadly defined—would become the field for constructing a common national vision while at the same time increased federal funding and coordination of the public and private elements of that field would provide the vehicle. And, beginning in the mid-1960s, a series of somewhat tentative measures were taken to carry this project forward.

Framed by nationalist concerns for American domination of Canadian industry in general, the accent was on creating relations of production based upon Canadian private capital. One element of this strategy was policy measures designed to ensure that Canadian advertising revenues flowed to Canadian rather than American media companies.[38] Prompted by a crisis in the magazine industry, amendments to the Income Tax Act were introduced in 1965 to stem the flow of Canadian advertising revenues to popular American publications, which were dominating Canadian newsstands. Initially, however, circulation leaders *Time* and *Reader's Digest*, which together accounted for 56 percent of Canadian magazine ad spending in 1969, were exempted.[39] But the legislation was revised in 1976 (Bill C-58), eliminating the *Time* and *Reader's Digest* exemptions and disallowing tax deductibility for Canadian advertising on U.S. border television stations that were structured to explicitly tap into Canadian ad markets (e.g., in Detroit, Buffalo and Bellingham, Wash.). *Time* ceased its Canadian edition a few weeks later and

Reader's Digest reorganized its ownership structure in order to qualify as Canadian.[40] The legislation also worked to ensure that ownership of Canadian newspapers remained in Canadian hands. Through the 1970s and early 1980s, this logic of developing distinct Canadian markets for media and cultural products would gain momentum.

Another step involved the repatriation of foreign-controlled Canadian broadcast companies. Foreign, and particularly American, ownership of radio and television had been a concern since the advent of broadcasting and these concerns were given official voice in the 1958 Broadcasting Act. However, over the years a number of radio and television properties had found their way into foreign hands, and the quickly growing cable-TV system—beyond the purview of broadcast regulators until 1968—had a high degree of foreign ownership. So, in 1969, the federal government issued a directive to the newly appointed regulator, the Canadian Radio and Television Commission (CRTC), to ensure that as broadcast licenses came up for renewal, no more than 20 percent of voting shares of broadcast companies were held by non-Canadians. Over the next four years, the ensuing divestitures comprised 13 percent of radio, 16.3 percent of television, and 46.5 percent of the cable industry's assets.[41]

The repatriation of broadcasting licenses tended to accelerate already rising levels of concentration in that field. In the mid-1960s, large radio and television stations enjoyed extraordinary profits, while smaller stations often lost money. These smaller outlets were popular sources of investment for the larger companies. As well, in the face of concerns over Canadian frequencies being hijacked by U.S. companies, the regulator began licensing FM stations in Canada, although there was no clear demand for them at the time. These, too, became popular sources of investment for successful broadcast companies and most of the new FM licenses were granted to broadcasters who already had AM stations. However, the Board of Broadcast Governors, the broadcast regulator of the time, was not insensitive to growing concentration, and in 1966 the BBG formulated a network ownership policy that strove to ensure that no one person would be able to own shares in more than one station affiliated with the Canadian Television Network (CTV), Canada's only private television network at the time. This rule would later be adopted by the CRTC and can be seen as carrying through to today in that the CRTC continues to discourage ownership of more than one over-the-air station in one language in any given market.[42]

However, amidst these efforts to secure Canadian ownership of media properties, escalating concentration of ownership began to draw public attention and, in 1969, in the midst of the development of policies to capitalize Canada's cultural industries, the Special Senate Committee on Mass Media (Davey Committee) was struck to investigate "the impact and influence" of "ownership and control" of the mass media.

The Davey Committee cast its gaze across daily and weekly newspapers, magazines, the business and ethnic press, and broadcasting. Its report issued a litany of complaints over the fact that private media outlets of all stripes put the pursuit of profit ahead of the public interest. The committee was unable to find any direct evidence that chain ownership necessarily undermined editorial quality and diversity, and it noted that this form of ownership had a number of possible advantages, including the ability to hire better managers, greater mobility for staff, less susceptibility "to pressures from advertisers and special interest groups," and, perhaps most importantly in the face of growing market rationalization, it "tends to prevent more newspapers from dying."[43] But while the committee noted that "there is no such thing as a 'good' chain or a 'bad' chain—only good and bad owners," it also observed that chains can lead to "numbing journalistic conformity" of a kind characterized by the Thomson newspapers, one of the fastest-growing chains of the period.[44] However, the committee was far from sanguine on the issue, noting "this country should no longer tolerate a situation where the public interest in so vital a field as information is dependent on the greed or goodwill of an extremely privileged group of businessmen."[45] Moreover, conglomerate and "mixed media" holdings raised particular concern and were seen as a "Bad Thing, unless individual circumstances indicate(d) otherwise."[46]

Among the recommendations made were: (i) the institution of a Press Ownership Review Board to watch over future mergers and takeovers of publications; (ii) the establishment of a federal Publications Development Loan Fund; (iii) the request to industry to set up a press council to review public complaints; and (iv) the strengthening of income-tax provisions designed to keep Canadian advertising dollars in Canada. And although the committee recommended issuing the CRTC clearer guidelines to follow regarding concentration in the broadcast field, it rejected the "American practice" of a "rigid mathematical formula" which it described as "not applicable to Canadian conditions."[47]

Some of the report's strongest admonitions for action were to those who had the least control over the product: journalists and the public. For example, the report asked working journalists to "demand better newspapers and better broadcasting," and to "stop griping; start organizing." Similarly, the report encouraged members of the public to push for community press councils, to get involved in producing programming for community-access cable channels and to telephone or write owners, editors, and producers when they have a complaint.[48] In the end, few of the recommendations were followed upon, other than the establishment of provincial press councils in Ontario, Quebec, and Alberta, and the strengthening of the legislation that eventually became Bill C-58. Nevertheless, Davey put concerns over escalating concentration of ownership on the public agenda and set a precedent for concern over cross-media ownership.

Struggles around concentration of ownership continued through the 1970s. However, efforts to control concentration in the newspaper industry were dealt a blow by a 1976 Supreme Court ruling that K.C. Irving interests were not in violation of the law with Irving's acquisition of all five English-language newspapers in the province of New Brunswick.[49] Moreover, CRTC licensing decisions, while demonstrating that the commission favored separate control of newspaper and broadcast undertakings (including cable), were decided on a "case by case" basis and illustrated a clear lack of policy direction regarding concentration and cross-media ownership in general.[50]

In 1978, the Report of the Royal Commission on Corporate Concentration added fuel to concerns over concentration.[51] While the commission's mandate was to investigate the nature, role, and implications of corporate concentration in general in the Canadian economy, it focused special concern on the media, and particularly newspapers.[52] In the end, the commission found that strengthening competition law might prove to be a useful check on curbing concentration, and that the CRTC should be empowered to "prevent the owners of broadcasting stations from also owning newspapers and other print media that circulate in the same market."[53]

In February of 1979, the CRTC announced that it would hold a public hearing on its ownership policies and particularly cross-media ownership. But these meetings were cancelled and events in the newspaper industry eclipsed these efforts before a clear policy could be articulated.

In January of 1980, the Thomson newspaper chain acquired FP Publications. Among the papers acquired were some of the largest in the country and, with this merger, Thomson gained control of forty of Canada's 117 daily newspapers. Thomson's Canadian newspaper holdings were only a part of much larger international corporate holdings, however, which included seventy-one daily and five weekly newspapers in the United States, as well as holdings in a wide range of other businesses such as travel and tourism, oil and gas, trucking, and department stores. In August of 1980, the Southam and Thomson newspaper chains engaged in a series of newspaper closures and share sales that left Thomson as the owner of the only daily newspaper in the Winnipeg market, and Southam as the sole owner of the only English-language newspapers in Ottawa and Montreal, as well as Pacific Press, the publisher of Vancouver's two daily newspapers.[54] An investigation of these events was undertaken by the Department of Consumer and Corporate affairs and seven charges under the Combines Investigation Act were subsequently laid.

A mere six days after this shake-up, the federal government struck a royal commission to investigate conditions in the newspaper industry and their consequences for "the political, economic, social and intellectual vitality and cohesion of the nation as a whole."[55] Named after its chairman, Tom Kent, the commission conducted an exhaustive survey of the field, complete with numerous background studies and reports. The Kent Commission was unable to discover much evidence of direct editorial meddling by owners and found that, in terms of chain ownership, the attitude of the owners was the main determinant of the ratio of editorial expenditure to revenue. The commission concluded that chain-owned papers were not always worse editorially than independent papers. The commission had particular praise for the Southam newspaper chain, which it noted had a reputation for taking the "public service objective seriously."[56] (Although it also noted that the propensity of Southam to spend more on editorial than its rivals made it "vulnerable to takeover"—a point that would prove to be prophetic.)

However, given the possibilities of direct editorial interference afforded by chain ownership and the indirect control exercised through such things as hiring decisions, budgets, and editorial policy, the commission found: "The structure of the industry that has now been created, that existing law and public policy have permitted, is clearly and directly contrary to the public interest."[57] Moreover, the commission found that possible problems associated with chain ownership leading to lack of editorial diversity were exacerbated by cross-media ownership. And "conglomerate" ownership, by which a company has extensive business interests beyond newspapers, was seen as particularly problematic in that, in the words of the commission, "often, the newspaper is, for the conglomerate, a 'cash cow' . . . milked not only to buy other newspapers but also . . . to finance expansion into other ventures."[58]

Following its assertion that "freedom of the press is not a property right of owners," the commission made sweeping recommendations. Key among them was new legislation—the Canada Newspaper Act—that would "contain provision to prevent any further increase in concentration and to reduce the worst features of concentration that has hitherto been allowed."[59] Under the terms of its recommendations, for the most part companies would be allowed to keep their existing holdings, but there would be strong restrictions on future growth. To forestall the development of conglomerates, the legislation would prohibit companies from buying newspapers unless their total assets outside the newspaper industry were less than those of the proposed purchase. And to prevent the growth of more chains, companies would be limited to owning no more than five papers. With regard to cross-media ownership, the commission proposed that ownership of newspaper and broadcast outlets in the same geographic location be disallowed. Recommendations were also made to disallow common ownership of daily and weekly newspapers in the same region, and changes in organizational form that would restrict the abilities of owners to interfere with editorial policies were also urged. Tax measures to stimulate expenditures on editorial content were proposed and, to oversee the operation of the proposed act, the commission recommended that a Press Rights Panel be set up.[60]

Nine months after the commission reported, the government announced plans for legislation on the issue. However, mired in economic problems and amidst a storm of protest from the newspaper industry and its allies, the government proposed only small steps toward the commission's recommendations.[61] Among the legislation's highlights were: that individual chains not be allowed to control more than 20 percent of the daily newspaper market (although those already in that position would not be required to divest); that a publicly funded National Press Advisory Council be set up to field complaints and study ways to improve the performance of newspapers; that public funds be used to encourage the establishment of regional and international bureaus that would function to improve the quality of news.[62] While these proposals received some debate in the House of Commons, a national election brought a change in government before any legislation could be passed and the new government failed to reintroduce the legislation.

However, some attempts to address the situation were made. In an effort to head off further government regulation, the industry established press councils in British Columbia and the Atlantic provinces.[63] Moreover, following Kent's recommendations, the federal Cabinet did issue a directive to the CRTC designed to limit the cross-ownership of newspaper and broadcasting outlets in the same market. While the commission had no power over newspapers per se, it did have the right to refuse license renewals to broadcast companies that also had newspaper holdings. The CRTC subsequently identified 17 licenses held by eight different companies that fell under the jurisdiction of this directive, and proceeded to review them on a "case-by-case" basis. However, for a number of reasons, in all instances where hearings were held the licenses were renewed.[64]

Following on the heels of the election of a new government, this order was rescinded in 1985. The change in policy reflected a much broader program of deregulation issued by Brian Mulroney's Progressive Conservative government. And as Mulroney put his stamp on the mechanisms of government, he declared that Canada was "open for business" and began to dismantle the previous Liberal government's nationalist program.

THE SHIFTING ENVIRONMENT

By the mid-1980s, changes in both the political climate and technology had begun to press upon the structure of Canadian broadcast regulation. The footprints of U.S. broadcast satellites bled into Canada, sending the CRTC scrambling to find ways to keep Canadians tuned to Canadian broadcasters and maintain the integrity of Canadian advertising markets. While developing Canadian satellite services offered a stop-gap measure to forestall the collapse of these markets, the plethora of broadcast services promised by both new and emerging broadcast technologies threatened to overwhelm the structure of Canadian broadcast regulation. In the face of this threat, evolving cable TV systems were seen as providing some measure of control over development and cable became the "chosen instrument" of government policy in the broadcasting system.[65]

Meanwhile, in the face of the developing technological threat, the federal government struck a Task Force on Broadcasting Policy to make recommendations on "an industrial and cultural strategy to govern the future evolution of the Canadian broadcasting system." In the spirit of the new economic imperatives driving public policy, the Task Force's Terms of Reference noted that the strategy should take "full account of the overall social and economic goals of the government . . . including the need for fiscal restraint (and) increased reliance on private sector initiatives."[66]

Laying the ground for a new broadcasting act, the Task Force undertook a comprehensive review of broadcasting policy, of which ownership issues comprised only a small part. Contrasting Canadian broadcast regulation to that in the United States, the Task Force noted that in the United States "the number of radio or television stations any single company may own continues to be limited by the Federal Communications Commission (FCC)." But in Canada, "[n]o explicit rules have ever been set to limit the number of radio or television stations or cable systems any company may own."[67] In terms of recommending a strategy, the Task Force noted that "concentration in Canada must also be seen in the context of growing concentration in other countries" and that its recommendations reflected "an acceptance of more concentration."[68] At the same time, however, in terms of a "cultural strategy," the Task Force "shared the concern expressed . . . by the Davey Committee and in later reports that there be a diversity of sources of information, opinion and entertainment for Canadians and a number of alternative opportunities for journalists, creators and producers to pursue their work."[69] Consequently, the Task Force also recommended that "a more precise public policy must be developed and that there would indeed be merit in basing that policy in part on limits to the share of particular markets that an individual broadcaster or media owner might hold."[70]

No policy was forthcoming. But concerns over concentration in the broadcasting industry remained on the public agenda and were again voiced by the 1987 Standing Committee on Communications and Culture. The committee noted that "changes in CRTC policy dating from 1984 that relaxed rules restricting cross-media ownership had led directly to increased concentration."[71] Moreover, its final report argued that the "diversity principle is the fundamental principle in regulating broadcasting ownership" and that, "Policies to achieve financial strength in the private sector of the Canadian broadcasting system must be compatible with a clearly enunciated ownership policy, and guidelines on the limits of ownership. . . . These rules must protect the public interest in the free flow of information, opinion and entertainment from a diversity of independent sources."[72]

Meanwhile, the late 1980s and early 1990s were not kind to the newspaper industry in Canada. A recession in the early 1990s combined with shrinking readerships and shifts in the advertising market to put serious pressure on publishers' bottom lines. The changing economics of the industry precipitated shifting patterns of ownership, and in 1992 Southam became a takeover target as Conrad Black's Hollinger Corp. acquired a 22.6-percent share in the company. In 1993, Power Corp.—a Canadian conglomerate—purchased another 18.7 percent. In an October 1993 interview, Black indicated the direction the new shareholders wished to take the company: "Southam's newspaper division employed 7,500 people, clearly a third of whom shouldn't have been there . . . Restoration of profitability required a serious assault on costs above all other things."[73] The Kent Commission's observations about the vulnerability of the Southam chain had indeed proved prescient.

COURTING CONVERGENCE

The years leading up to the turn of the century saw a sea change in patterns of ownership in the industry. In 1994 Rogers Communications, Canada's largest cable-TV company, acquired Maclean Hunter Ltd. in a $3-billion (Cdn) deal which created a media conglomerate with holdings in radio broadcasting, newspaper and magazine publishing, and cellular telephony.[74] In 1995, Thomson began slowly to dispose of its more than 150 newspapers in Canada, Britain, and the United States, reinvesting in electronic and specialty publishing.[75] By February 2000, the company had put all of its Canadian newspapers up for sale, except the prestigious national daily, the *Globe and Mail*. In May of 1996, Hollinger acquired Power Corporation's share of Southam, giving it 41 percent of the company and effective control, and between 1995 and 1999, Hollinger acquired a large number of the Thomson papers as well as several other dailies. By 1999, Hollinger controlled in excess of 48 percent of the daily circulation of English-language newspapers in Canada. And like Thomson's newspaper holdings, Hollinger also had international properties, including the *London Daily Telegraph*, the *Chicago Sun-Times* and the *Jerusalem Post*. This was in marked contrast to Black's daily newspaper holdings at the time of the Kent Commission, which comprised eleven small dailies confined mainly to the interior of British Columbia.[76]

Canadian competition policy offered no remedy to this situation. Under the terms of the Competition Act, the Competition Bureau is only empowered to consider the potential impact consolidation might have on advertising markets, not on editorial diversity. Throughout the mergers of the 1990s there was only one instance in which the bureau ordered a rollback of ownership. This involved Southam's 1990 takeover of a number of weekly papers in the Vancouver area—most notably the *Courier*, the *North Shore News*, and the *Real Estate Weekly*—that had eaten into the Vancouver daily newspapers' advertising markets.[77] Southam fought the order, and after years of litigation, including an appeal to the Supreme Court of Canada, the dispute was resolved in favor of the bureau's initial ruling. Southam was ordered to sell either the *North Shore News* or the *Real Estate Weekly* because of a monopoly on real-estate advertising on the North Shore, and in September 1998, Southam divested itself of the *Real Estate Weekly* on the North Shore in an asset swap.[78]

In another case, the Council of Canadians—a nonprofit organization that provides a critical voice on national issues and public policy—set out to appeal the bureau's approval of Hollinger's takeover of Southam. The council argued that not only would the merger lessen competition in some advertising markets, but that it would also lessen competition among different points of view in the press, and that, read through elements of the Canadian Charter of Rights and Freedoms, the Competition Act charged the bureau with reviewing the merger in this light. The argument was never actually heard, however. The complaint was dismissed in Federal Court on the grounds that it was not brought within thirty days of the decision, as necessitated by regulation (a ruling later upheld on appeal). However, and most importantly, the federal court judge also noted that the applicants did not appear to have "legal standing" in the case, meaning that they were not "directly affected by the event at issue" and, therefore, did not have the legal right to challenge the ruling.[79] This latter point is of particular significance as it underscores the definition of the transaction in the courts as a simple transfer of property rights and not a matter to be measured in terms of some larger public interest. In other words, contrary to Kent's assertion that "Freedom of the press is not a property right of owners" in Canada, if pressed in court, this may in fact be the case.

While concentration was proceeding apace in the newspaper industry, the traditional regulatory boundaries between the telecommunications, broadcasting, and cable industries were being called into question. In the early 1990s, there appeared to be little chance of convergence between the telecommunications and broadcasting industry. New Broadcasting (1991) and Telecommunication Acts (1993) maintained traditional regulatory boundaries and allowed no opportunity for convergence between the two industries.[80]

However, late in 1993, following U.S. vice president Al Gore's promotion of the information highway, that began to change. Stentor, a now disbanded alliance of telephone companies, floated plans to build a Canadian version of this system. Stentor argued that the key to Canada's future competitiveness lay with the development of a national broadband communication network. The federal government was soon on board with the general plan and, in 1994, set in motion a number of initiatives to develop a Canadian information highway strategy. As noted in the government's 1996 report, *Building the Information Society,* keeping up with developments in the United States appeared to be a major motive for its enthusiasm. "If we fall behind our major trading partners in building our Information Highway, its worldwide counterpart will come to Canada—later—and not the way Canadians want to see it."[81] Moreover, after a decade of government cutbacks, the information highway was framed as a panacea for many of the ills plaguing Canadian society. It would create jobs, enhance education and health care, and make government more accessible and responsive.[82]

After several years of consultations, the government issued a Convergence Policy Statement in 1996. This document laid out the broad framework for developing cooperation between companies operating in the telecommunications and broadcasting systems. Key to the strategy was creating a technological environment that would allow capital more flexibility and encourage competition between different industrial sectors. The policy stated the terms for the entry of telecommunications and broadcasting companies into each others markets. Cable and telecommunications companies would be able to compete on each others turf, and telecommunications[83] companies would be able to provide broadcast programming services as long as the broadcast license was held by a structurally separate entity. Indeed, just as Horwitz points out, the 1996 Telecommunications Act created "unprecedented conditions for competition and for the concentration of ownership" in the United States (see chapter 2 in this volume), so too Ottawa's convergence policy set out similar conditions in Canada.

Opening another avenue to concentration of ownership, in 1999 the CRTC announced that it would not regulate Canadian sites on the Internet. In its *Report on New Media*, the CRTC concluded that the Internet was not subject to either the Telecommunications or the Broadcast Act, and for those services that did fall under the legal definition of broadcasting—digital audio and audiovisual signals—"the Commission has concluded that regulation is not necessary to achieve the objectives of the Broadcasting Act." The CRTC reported that, in terms of Canadian content, an estimated 5 percent of the world's Web sites were Canadian, and the commission determined that new media had no detrimental impact on radio or television advertising markets. Web sites specializing in "offensive and illegal content," such as pornography and hate messages, were already covered by Canada's Criminal Code.

It would take several years for the new convergence policies to meet with events in the newspaper industry, but when they did it would be with a vengeance.

CONVERGENCE REALIZED

The escalating series of mergers and takeovers in 2000 and 2001, described at the beginning of this chapter, brought together the country's major media organizations under a few corporate umbrellas, and while governments continue to study the consequences convergence may have on news and information content, none has yet given any indication that it has either the political appetite or the legislative means to curb this trend.

Of the three large cross-media companies created in 2000–2001, Quebecor has perhaps been the most successful at exploiting the financial possibilities of media convergence. In 2003, it launched the Quebec television ratings hit "Star Académie" on its TVA network. With the popular Julie Snyder as host and producer (not to mention girlfriend of Quebecor CEO Pierre-Karl Péladeau), the "reality television" series followed fourteen aspiring singers being trained for stardom. The series consisted of four thirty-minute weeknight "documentaries" and a ninety-minute special each Sunday night in prime time. The April 13 finale attracted three million viewers, close to half of the entire Quebec population. Quebecor promoted the show through its publications—most notably Montreal's most popular daily newspaper, *Le Journal de Montréal*, and the entertainment magazine *7 Jours*—and profited from audience members using either its Netgraphe Internet portal or the telephone to vote for their favorites. The Quebecor music company Select later produced a recording, which sold 500,000 copies and which were available in Quebecor's Archambault music and bookstores.[84]

Convergence, of course, does not always produce such happy endings. Quebecor prompted a media storm in April and May 2004 when the company suddenly fired comedian and writer Louis Morrissette, shortly after hiring him to host ten episodes of a new TVA reality show entitled "Pour le meilleur et pour le pire." According to newspaper reports—non-Quebecor newspapers *La Presse* and *Le Devoir* have taken up the story most enthusiastically—Morrissette was fired because of a New Year's Eve comedy sketch he had written for Radio-Canada television, a sketch which lampooned Péladeau, Snyder, and "Star Académie."[85]

While CanWest Gobal has undergone extensive reorganization of its properties in preparation for exploiting the supposed benefits of convergence—such as exploiting economies of scale and repurposing material created for one medium for use in others—it also incurred a huge debt; when CanWest will realize financial benefits from convergence is not clear.[86] Neither is its long-term commitment to the media business in Canada. Leonard Asper, CanWest's chief executive officer, recently called for the federal government to loosen foreign-ownership rules and open the broadcast sector to foreign ownership, a move that would surely increase the value of the company.[87] Asper has also been reported as considering turning all or part of the company's newspaper holdings into an income trust to help pay down debt.[88]

BCE has been drifting slowly away from its convergence strategy since 2002, and rumors of an asset sale have consumed the business press ever since. A champion of convergence under the leadership of Jean Monty, its

former chief executive officer, BCE took a significant loss on the telecommunications subsidiary Teleglobe Inc., which sought bankruptcy protection
and prompted Monty's resignation in April 2002. Michael Sabia, who replaced Monty, disbanded the board of directors of the Bell Globemedia television and newspaper company at the end of 2003, and was reported to be
waiting for an opportune moment to sell the CTV television network and the
Globe and Mail newspaper.[89]

Whether by coincidence or by design, the convergence trend has gone
hand in hand with increasingly interventionist owners. In contrast to Thomson Newspapers' singular interest in the bottom line and the Southam chain's
much-heralded respect for the editorial independence of its newspapers, the
new generation of owners has included people like Conrad Black and Izzy
Asper, who fancied themselves as journalists, even intellectuals, anxious to
shape public debate.

Black had written and published a 700-page biography of former Quebec
premier Maurice Duplessis in 1977 and his own autobiography in 1993.
Quick to expound his political views on Quebec separatism, labor unions,
"lazy" journalists, and Canada's ruling Liberal Party, he also contributed letters to the editor and the occasional book review when he owned the
Southam newspapers. Asper, the former Liberal Party leader of Manitoba and
a one-time syndicated columnist on finance and tax law, used his platform
as a media mogul to expound his views on the CBC, the state of Israel, and
the Liberal Party of Canada. Under the leadership of the Asper family, Can-
West overturned the longtime independence of the Southam newspapers by
imposing a centralized national editorial policy.

Meanwhile, concentrated ownership, the convergence of newspapers
with television networks and Internet sites, and the interventionist style of
the new generation of media owners have renewed government interest in
concentration issues. In Quebec, where two companies own all but one of
the French-language dailies, the provincial government conducted public
hearings on press concentration in February and March 2001. The result was
a rather timid report, released in November 2001, which asked newspaper
companies to publish both a statement of principles and whatever steps they
are taking to ensure editorial diversity.[90] The Quebec government followed
up by establishing a consultative committee on media quality and diversity,
which produced its report in February 2003. Among its twelve recommendations, the committee proposed: an Information Law requiring media owners to state publicly their operating principles, their code of ethics, and the
proportion of revenues they devote to editorial production; written contracts
ensuring the independence of newspaper editors; and regular public hearings on how media concentration affects the public's right to information.[91]

In 2003, the Canadian federal government joined the debate. In June, the
House of Commons Standing Committee on Canadian Heritage released the

first review of Canadian broadcasting since the adoption of the 1991 Broadcast Act.[92] In its chapter devoted to ownership, the committee identified three pressing issues—horizontal integration (chain ownership), vertical integration (of content producers and carriers), and cross-media ownership[93]—and made four specific recommendations. First, the committee recommended that the CRTC be directed to strengthen its policies on the separation of the newsroom activities of cross-owned media, to ensure editorial independence. Second, it recommended the CRTC monitor the editorial independence of broadcast operations. Third, it called for a federal government policy statement. And until the federal government makes that policy declaration, the committee recommended the CRTC postpone all decisions on new broadcast licenses where cross-media ownership is involved, and automatically extend the existing licenses of cross-media owners for between two and three years.[94, 95] Also in 2003, the Senate Committee on Transportation and Communications, chaired by former *Montreal Gazette* editor Joan Fraser, began a series of public hearings to examine the quality and diversity of news and information available to Canadians. This committee is due to submit its final report in late 2005.

CONCLUSION

Due in large part to its unique physical and demographic characteristics, Canada has a long tradition of market intervention and regulation, whereby the communications media have been perceived through a culturalist frame, as integral to Canadian nationhood, national culture, and national sovereignty. This regulatory tradition has foregrounded the ethic of public service—the 1991 Broadcasting Act, for example, defines the Canadian broadcasting system not as an industry but as "a public service." And while, as evidenced in the historical dimensions of the struggle and debate over concentration of ownership in Canada, concerns for public service have not always (or even often) won the day and dictated the direction of development, they have at least tempered commercial imperatives and provided a critical lens for evaluating and helping to curb creeping commercialism.

Today however, policy discussions are taking place in both a highly charged and a highly changed environment. Highly charged because of the increasing incidents in which media owners have used their economic power to interfere with, even restrict, the news and information content of their media properties. Highly changed because of technological innovations, which have enabled content sharing among different media and which have facilitated the expansion of audiences beyond national borders. Highly charged, too, because of a new political climate, which is characterized by deregulation, privatization, deficit reduction, and tax cuts.

Whether the ethic of public service will survive in this environment or finally succumb to market imperatives and the financial interests of a small group of shareholders remains to be seen.

NOTES

1. Statistics Canada, "Population by mother tongue, provinces and territories," <http://www.statcan.ca/english/Pgdb/demo_18b.htm> (22 March 2004); Central Intelligence Agency, *The World Fact Book: Canada*, <http://www.odci.gov/cia/publications/factbook/geos/ca.html> (22 March 2004).

2. Mike Gasher, "From Sacred Cows to White Elephants: Cultural Policy Under Siege," *Canadian Cultures and Globalization*, eds. Joy Cohnstaedt & Yves Frechette, (Montreal: Association for Canadian Studies, 1997), 13–29.

3. John Miller, *Yesterday's News: Why Canada's Daily Newspapers are Failing Us* (Halifax, N.S.: Fernwood Publishing, 1998), 61.

4. Canada, Information Highway Advisory Council. (IHAC) *Preparing Canada for a Digital World* (Ottawa: Industry Canada, 1997), 10–12.

5. Campaign for Press and Broadcast Freedom (CPBF), "Ownership Tables," <http://www.presscampaign.org> (5 March 2004)

6. Canada, Standing Committee on Canadian Heritage. *Our Cultural Sovereignty: The Second Century of Canadian Broadcasting*, p. 397 <www.parl.gc.ca/InfoComDoc/37/2/HERI/Studies/Reports/herirp02-e.htm> (18 June, 2003)

7. Canadian Press. "CanWest Global May Sell More Assets." *Charlottetown Guardian* (22 January, 2003), B11.

8. Stephen Edwards, "CanWest on Mission to Woo U.S. investors," *Vancouver Sun* (10 February, 2004), D7.

9. Sean Silcoff, "Peladeau: A Year of Redemption." *National Post* (23 December, 2003): FP7.

10. Rene Lewandowski, "Anger Management," *National Post Business Magazine* (1 July, 2003), 56.

11. One advantage of "big media" which is often cited is their ability to maintain their own foreign news bureaus, whereas smaller independents are forced to rely on international wire services. Yet Canadian news organizations' commitment to international coverage has dwindled remarkably in recent years. The three Canadian daily newspapers with the largest budgets for international news have all reduced their foreign coverage. Since the late 1980s, the *Globe and Mail* has closed eight overseas bureaus, and now has just six (two of them in the U.S.). The *Toronto Star* has cut its number of bureaus by half (from eight to four) and the *National Post* has just two foreign bureaus, both in the United States. See Adria Vasil, "World Domination," *Ryerson Review of Journalism*, 20/2 (2003): 56–61.

12. David Demers, "Corporate Newspaper Bashing: Is it Justified?" *Newspaper Research Journal*, 20/1 (Winter 1999): 83–97.

13. Demers, "Corporate Newspaper Bashing," pp. 96–97.

14. Demers, "Corporate Newspaper Bashing," pp. 94–95.

15. Canada, *Standing Committee on Canadian Heritage*, 404–405.

16. Robert A. Hackett and Richard Gruneau, *The Missing News* (Ottawa and Aurora, Ont.: Canadian Centre for Policy Alternatives and Garamond Press, 2000); Miller, *Yesterday's News*; TNG Canada. *Your Media* <http://www.yourmedia.ca> (26 March 2004); Canadian Journalists for Free Expression. *Not in the Newsroom! CanWest Global, Chain Editorials and Freedom of Expression in Canada*, <http:www.cjfe.org/specials/canwest/canwintro.html> (26 March 2004).

17. Simon Tuck, "CanWest Urges Removal of Ownership Limits," *Globe and Mail* (28 February 2003): B4.

18. See Canada, Canadian Radio Television and Telecommunications Commission (CRTC) Decision 2001-457 (2 August 2001) and Canada, (CRTC) Decision 2001-458 (2 August 2001). cf. Janet McFarland and Keith Damsell, "CanWest Unveils Management Shuffle," *Globe and Mail* (29 January 2003), B3 and Keith Damsell "CanWest Set to Launch News Hub," *Globe and Mail* (20 January 2003), B2l.

19. TNG Canada, *Your Media.*

20. Paul Rutherford, *The Making of the Canadian Media* (Toronto: McGraw-Hilll Ryerson, 1978), p. 54.

21. Robert Babe, *Telecommunications in Canada* (Toronto: University of Toronto Press, 1990), p. 59.

22. Babe, *Telecommunications in Canada*, 202–203.

23. Frank Peers, *The Politics of Canadian Broadcasting: 1920–1951* (Toronto: University of Toronto Press, 1969), pp. 27, 141.

24. Gilles Proulx, *L'aventure de la radio au Québec* (Montréal: La Presse, 1979).

25. Peers, *The Politics of Canadian Broadcasting*, p. 286.

26. Peers, *The Politics of Canadian Broadcasting*, p 287.

27. Minko Sotiron, *From Politics to Profit: The Commercialization of Canadian Daily Newspapers, 1890–1920* (Montreal: McGill-Queen's University Press, 1997).

28. Minko Sotiron, *From Politics to Profit*; Jean de Bonville, *La Presse québécoise de 1884 à 1914: genèse d'un media de masse* (Québec Presses de l'Université Laval, 1988); Pierre Godin, *la lutte pour l'information: Histoire de la presse écrite au Québec.* (Montréal: Le Jour, 1981).

29. Wilfred Kesterton and Roger Bird, "The Press in Canada: A Historical Overview," in *Communications in Canada*, ed. Benjamin D. Singer (Scarborough, Ont.: Nelson, 1991), p. 9.

30. Kesterton and Bird, "The Press in Canada," p. 9.

31. Paul Audley, *Canada's Cultural Industries* (Toronto: James Lorimer and Co., 1983), p. 290.

32. Audley, *Canada's Cultural Industries*, p. 204.

33. Audley, *Canada's Cultural Industries*, p. 204.

34. Canada, Royal Commission on the Development of the Arts, Letters and Sciences, *Report* (Ottawa: King's Printer, 1951), pp. 16–18.

35. Canada, Royal Commission on the Development of the Arts, Letters and Sciences, *Report*, p. 18

36. Canada, Royal Commission on the Development of the Arts, Letters and Sciences, *Report*, pp. 28, 62, 64.

37. Ted Magder, *Canada's Hollywood: The Canadian State and Feature Films* (Toronto: University of Toronto Press, 1993), pp. 118–19.

38. These measures touched upon a number of media industries and included a range of policy instruments and, to a large extent, they paralleled government actions in other areas of production, as it struggled to gain control over an increasingly fickle economy (Howlett and Ramesh, 1992: 203, 219–21, 248–52).

39. Mary Vipond, *The Mass Media in Canada*, (Toronto: James Lorimer & Co., 2000), pp. 56–57.

40. Vipond, *The Mass Media in Canada*, pp. 57–58.

41. Canadian Radio-Television and Telecommunications Commission, Canadian Ownership of Broadcasting (Ottawa: Minister of Supply and Services, 1974), p. 42.

42. See for instance Public Notice, Canadian Radio-Television and Telecommunications Commission, 1999–97.

43. Canada, Special Senate Committee on the Mass Media, *Vol. I: The Uncertain Mirror* (Ottawa: Queen's Printer, 1970), pp. 68–69.

44. Canada, Special Senate Committee on the Mass Media, p. 69.

45. Canada, Special Senate Committee on the Mass Media, p. 67.

46. Canada, Special Senate Committee on the Mass Media, p. 67.

47. Canada, Special Senate Committee on the Mass Media, p. 223.

48. Canada, Special Senate Committee on the Mass Media, pp. 258–59.

49. Audley, *Canada's Cultural Industries*, p. 20.

50. See for instance: CRTC Decision 74-44; CRTC, Decision 72-16; CRTC, Decision 71-104; CRTC Decision 75-78.

51. Canada, Royal Commission on Corporate Concentration, *Report* (Ottawa: Minister of Supply and Services Canada, 1978).

52. The commission was prompted by Power Corp.'s bid—ultimately unsuccessful—for control of Argus Corp. in March–April 1975 (xix). Aside from the more general concern about the market power of such an amalgamated conglomerate, a particular concern was the "significant concentration of ownership of media interests" in Canada at that time (178). Power Corp.'s communications company, Gesca, already owned five Quebec daily newspapers accounting for more than half of French-language circulation in the province, as well as weekly newspapers and radio stations. Argus had ownership interests in radio and television broadcasting. "We see no advantage to the public interest in the common ownership of the Power-Argus communications interests, and there is a potential detriment to the public interest if enough important instruments of communication, in different media fields, are owned or controlled by one person or group" (179).

53. Canada, Royal Commission on Corporate Concentration, *Report*, p. 411.

54. Marc Edge, *Pacific Press: The Unauthorized Story of Vancouver's Newspaper Monopoly* (Vancouver: New Star Books, 2001), pp. 284–85.

55. Canada, *Royal Commission on Newspapers* (Ottawa: Minister of Supply and Services, 1981), p. 299.

56. Canada, *Royal Commission on Newspapers*, p. 102.

57. Canada, *Royal Commission on Newspapers*, p. 225.

58. Canada, *Royal Commission on Newspapers*, p. 102. As mentioned above, Thomson Newspapers Ltd. was part of a much larger multinational conglomerate with subsidiaries involved in real estate, oil and gas, insurance, travel and tourism, financial and management services, and trucking. Its partners were the Hudson's Bay Co., International Thomson Organization Ltd., and Scottish and York Holdings (90–91). The Power Corp. of Canada included among its subsidiaries and affiliates The Investors Group, Great West Life Assurance, Montreal Trust, and Consolidated Bathurst (94–95). The Irving family had interests in transportation, pulp and paper, mining, and petroleum (95).

59. Canada. *Royal Commission on Newspapers*, p. 238.

60. Canada. *Royal Commission on Newspapers*, pp. 237–55.

61. Tom Kent, "The Times and Significance of the Kent Commission" in *Seeing Ourselves: Media Power and Policy in Canada* (Toronto: Harcourt, Brace, Jovanovich, 1992).

62. See the proposed "Canadian Daily Newspaper Act," in Tom Kent, "The Times and Significance of the Kent Commission."

63. As John Miller illustrates in *Yesterday's News* (Halifax, N.S.: Fernwood Publishing, 1998. p. 42–43), these press councils are a "pale shadow of what Davey envisioned." They have a very low rate of public participation, limited powers and, because they are run by the industry, rarely find themselves guilty or responsible in the claims made against them.

64. A series of decisions by the Canadian Radio-television Commission (CRTC) illustrate this point. See CRTC, Decision, 83-773; CRTC, Decision, 83-656; CRTC, Decision, 83-676.

65. Canada, Task Force on Broadcasting Policy, *Report* (Ottawa: Minister of Supply and Services, 1986), pp. 545, 569, 577–80.

66. Canada, Task Force on Broadcasting Policy, *Report*, p. 703.

67. Canada, Task Force on Broadcasting Policy, *Report*, p. 639.

68. Canada, Task Force on Broadcasting Policy, *Report*, pp. 645–46.

69. Canada, Task Force on Broadcasting Policy, *Report*, p. 646.

70. Canada, Task Force on Broadcasting Policy, *Report*, p. 646.

71. Based on the recommendations of the Davey, Bryce, and Kent Commission reports, the federal government had instructed the CRTC in 1982 not to issue or renew licences to applicants who also owned a daily newspaper in the same market. But this directive was rescinded three years later by a Mulroney government with a strong private-enterprise orientation (Canada, *Our Cultural Sovereignty*, p. 387).

72. Canada, Department of Heritage. *Media Studies: Concentration of Ownership in the Media Part I*, (2001), p. 10. Source: www.pch.gc.ca/culture/convergence/pch/isspap1.html.

73. *Globe and Mail* (21 October 1993): B 9.

74. Bertrand Marotte, "Rogers Creates Multi-Media Giant with Maclean Hunter Takeover," *Ottawa Citizen* (9 March, 1994), C1.

75. Marcia Berss, "Greener Pastures," *Forbes* (23 October 1995), 56–60.

76. Canada, *Royal Commis Competiton on Newspapers*, p. 94.

77. Canada, Competition Bureau. "Competition Tribunal Issues Revised Divestiture Order in Southam Inc., Lower Mainland Publishing Ltd. et al. Case" <http://cb-bc.gc.ca/epic/internet/incb-bc.nsf/en/ct01324e.html> (15 Dec. 2004).

78. Rod Nutt. "Southam Gives Up North Shore's Real Estate Weekly in Swap of Assets," *Vancouver Sun* (15 September, 1998): D4.

79. See Federal Court of Canada. Council of Canadians v. Director of Investigation and Research. Court No. T-2096-96. <http://decisions.fct-cf.gc.ca/fct/1996/t-2096-96.html> (20 Feb. 2004) and Council of Canadians c. Director of Investigation and Research, (1997-04-09) CAF A-1034-96 Source: http://canlii.org/ca/jug/caf/1997/1997caf10273.html. (20 Feb. 2004). Canada. Department of Heritage. *Media Studies*, pp 18–24.

80. Dwayne Winseck, *Reconvergence: A Political Economy of Telecommunications in Canada* (Cresskill, N.J.: Hampton Press, 1998) p. 265

81. Canada, *Building the Information Society: Moving Canada into the 21st Century* (Ottawa: Minister of Supply and Services, 1996), p. 3.

82. Canada, *Building the Information Society*, p 3.

83. Canada, Industry Canada, "Convergence Policy Statement," <http://strategis.ic.gc.ca/epic/internet/insmt-gst.nsf/en/sf05265e.html> (12 Dec. 2004).

84. Hélène Baril, "Quebecor engranger les profits de Star Académie," *La Presse* (9 May 2003), D1.

85. Hugo Dumas, "Congédiement arbitraire de TVA," *La Presse* (1 May 2004), A1.

86. See, for instance, Janet McFarland and Keith Damsell. "CanWest Unveils Management Shuffle," *Globe and Mail* (29 January 2003), B3; Keith Damsell, "CanWest Set to Launch News Hub," *Globe and Mail* (20 January 2003): B2l; and Neco Cockburn. "CanWest Plans Book Unit," *Toronto Star* (1 April 2004), D3.

87. Richard Blackwell, "Asper Wants Martin to Back Foreign Control," *Globe and Mail* (14 November 2003), B3.

88. Andre Willis, "An Income Trust Would Cure What's Ailing Asper's CanWest," *Globe and Mail* (4 November 2004), B21.

89. Barbara Shecter, "BCE Loses Interest in Prized Media Assets," *The National Post* (January 10 2004): FP1.

90. Quebec, Secrétariat des commissions, *Mandat d'initiative portent sur La concentration de la presse*. <www.assnat.qc.ca/fra/publications/rapports/rapcc3.html> (22 March 2004).

91. Québec, Comité conseil sur la qualité et la diversité l'information, *Les effets de la concentration des medias au Quebec: problématique, recherces et consultations*. Janvier 2003 <http://www.mcc.gouv.gc.ca/publications/rapportst-jenatome_2.pdf>

92. Canada, *Our Cultural Sovereignty*.

93. Canada, *Our Cultural Sovereignty*, pp. 410–11.

94. A report by the Ministry of Canadian Heritage (2000) stated: "The Commission's view is that concentration of ownership, including cross-media ownership, is not in and of itself a concern provided that there continues to be an effective degree of diversity of programming

sources to ensure that the objectives of the Broadcasting Act are met. The CRTC allows broadcasting entities to also own newspapers in the same market provided that there is a degree of overall diversity of programming sources and that certain safeguards are implemented such as requiring that the two entities operate independently of each other." See Canada, Ministry of Canadian Heritage, "Diversity and Concentration of Ownership in the Cultural Sector, <http://www.pch.gc.ca/prpgrs/ac-ca/progs/esm-ms/divers2_e.cfm> (10 March 2004).

　　95. Canada, *Our Cultural Sovereignty*, pp. 410–11.

4

Clear Channel: The Poster Child for Everything That's Wrong with Consolidation

Dorothy Kidd, Francisco McGee, and Danielle Fairbairn

Clear Channel Communications epitomizes a new model of corporate media. From a handful of radio stations in the mid-1990s, they now rank among the top ten U.S. global media conglomerates, combining a radio chain of more than 1,200 radio stations, the No. 1 position in the indoor and outdoor U.S. entertainment market, and other cross-media holdings.[1] In 2003, they had a profit of $1.15 billion (U.S.) profit, through their delivery to advertisers of several different audience niches in sixty-six countries. In the United States, the company claims to reach over half of the adult population and 75 percent of the nation's people of Hispanic descent via conventional and satellite radio, entertainment venues with everything from rock concerts to monster truck polls to Broadway shows, promotion, outdoor advertising, television stations, television, film and TV production, and athlete management.[2] Clear Channel has also expanded into sixty-five countries, bulking up vertically and horizontally in the transnational entertainment industries with the purchase of dozens of entertainment agencies, 135 concert venues, mega-musicals and major tours, radio stations, and 775,00 advertising sites (billboards, taxi tops, mobile truck panels, bus, train, shopping mall, and airport displays, and assorted street furniture).

Clear Channel is not the only media firm to grow during the latest wave of mega-mergers. However, the conglomerate stands out because of its monopoly-style business practices in several interconnected media and entertainment industries, right-wing political interventions, and, most critically, the large number of constituencies it has angered and helped to mobilize. Best known for its brazen policies in support of the Bush regime's war in Iraq, it has distinguished itself from the older established media conglomerates, which pay lip service to journalistic neutrality and public service because of a lack of ambiguity about its capitalist goals. As Founder Lowry Mays has proclaimed, "We are not in the business of providing music, news or information. We're not in the business of providing well-researched music. We're simply in the business of selling our customers products."[3]

Clear Channel has helped catalyze the formation of a nascent media reform movement across a wide swath of the political spectrum. Musicians and cultural workers, African-American and Hispanic radio station owners, independent music promoters, Democratic and Republican politicians, and youth, environmental, aboriginal, peace, and labor activists have all been variously enraged by Clear Channel's exploitation of cultural workers, homogenization of music, right-wing political interventions, slashing of jobs, or gutting of local news. These groups have prompted congressional and Federal Communications Commission (FCC) hearings, and antitrust investigations, lawsuits, boycotts, strikes, demonstrations, and counterinformation campaigns. The organizing and outcry also played a critical part in the national campaign to halt further deregulation of media ownership rules, prompting company executive John Hogan to say, "Clear Channel is the poster child of the perceived ills of consolidation."[4] (See chapter 10 in this volume.)

To understand the poster child, we draw on two schools of media theory—critical political economy and autonomist Marxism. We begin by relating changes in media corporations and economics with the larger historical trends in political, social, and cultural institutions and daily life.[5] Our inquiry goes beyond the Clear Channel owners, to interrogate the larger political, economic, social, and cultural factors that led to the company to become so big and such an object of derision and anger. We argue that Clear Channel can best be understood by not only following the money trail but also uncovering the stories of the social actors in conflict with them.

Behind every corporate media account is a set of other narratives, in which creative personnel, technical crews, creative managers, and engaged audiences have combined their creativity, technical innovation, cooperation, and organizational skills to create dynamic cultural wellsprings. Most global media corporations have tended to concede much more autonomy to these networks of cultural producers, content to let them take the risks, and skim the profit at the level of circulation, in marketing and distribution.[6] Teasing out an analytical framework from autonomous Marxism, we argue that the Clear Channel story underscores a new composition, or conjuncture of relations of power, among symbol creators, corporate and state players, and audience subcultures and social change organizations.[7]

Clear Channel also describes its role as a retailer of audiences to its primary clients, the advertisers, and not as a producer. However, as we describe below, a major part of its corporate growth has involved strategies, as one radio station owner puts it, to "go head to head,"[8] with every group of social actors in the cultural production, distribution, and circulation process. While the company has, to a large degree, been successful in capitalizing on the historic weaknesses and divisions of and among cultural workers,[9] we point out that Clear Channel's consolidation of corporate power in the music promotion industries has in fact led to a convergence of politics, if not yet of political actors.

WITH A LITTLE HELP FROM THEIR FRIENDS

How did a little Texas-based radio chain get to be so big? One explanation often given is that Bush blood runs thicker than oil at Clear Channel. Charles Goyette, a Clear Channel DJ, spelled out the tightly knit relationship in "How to Lose Your Job in Talk Radio" in the magazine *American Conservative*, edited by Pat Buchanan:

> The principals of Clear Channel, a Texas-based company, have been substantial contributors to George W. Bush's fortunes since before he became president. In fact, Texas billionaire Tom Hicks can be said to be the man who made Bush a millionaire when he purchased the future president's baseball team, the Texas Rangers. Tom Hicks is now vice chairman of Clear Channel.[10]

The sale of the Texas Rangers netted George W. Bush $15 million (U.S.).

The family of Lowry Mays, Clear Channel's chairman of the board, continues to be one of George W. Bush's biggest supporters, providing large sums to his campaigns and to those of other Republican candidates.[11] Between 2000 and 2004, Clear Channel campaign contributions totalled over $1.2 million (U.S.), with approximately three-quarters going to Republican candidates.[12] In return, Clear Channel can count on strong representation within the Bush administration. For example, Charles James represented Clear Channel's bid for regulatory approval when the company purchased AMFM in 2000, and vaulted to the top spot among radio chains with 898 stations; James is now the current antitrust chief in the Justice Department.[13]

While its Bush connections go way back, it wasn't until 2002 that Clear Channel set up an official lobbying office in Washington, D.C. It is staffed by former aides from both political parties, and has the capacity to reach politicians from the municipal level to the White House. In the first year, with the FCC ownership rules at stake, Clear Channel increased its lobbying expenditures more than tenfold, from $68,675 to $700,000 (U.S.).[14] In 2003, in a year in which they were the main target of FCC fines against obscenity, they paid $2.28 million (U.S.) in lobbying fees.[15]

Clear Channel's establishment of a Washington office is not unusual for an industry which outdoes most others in political lobbying. In 2003, broadcasters, cable networks, and telecommunications companies spent $169.2 million, in contrast to the $59.4 million spent by the much larger oil and gas industry.[16] Nor does the size of Clear Channel's budget set it apart. In the same year, Fox News spent $3.9 million.[17] Instead, Clear Channel is unusual for ideological reasons; instead of following the usual pattern and sharing its money between the parties, Clear Channel gives the majority of its money to Republicans, and, until very recently, the bias of its programming has been consistently to the right.

Clear Channel began to attract notoriety for its lock-step support of the Bush regime, after September 11, 2001. First, the company advised program directors to avoid songs about "sensitive" issues such as peace in a list that included John Lennon's *Imagine*, Cat Stevens's *Peace Train*, and everything by Rage Against the Machine.[18] Then in 2003, several Clear Channel stations banned the Dixie Chicks after singer Natalie Maines told British fans that she was ashamed to be from the same state as President Bush. It is only fair to note that rival radio chain Cumulus Media also banned the Dixie Chicks; Cumulus's Louisiana station, KRMD, organized the rally at which a 33,000-pound bulldozer obliterated Dixie Chicks's CDs and other merchandise.[19] These decisions led to criticism inside and outside the industry, from musicians Tom Petty, Michael Stipe, and former Pink Floyd manager Peter James to socially responsible investment firms.[20]

Clear Channel further raised the ire of critics, when it, like Cumulus, promoted pro-war rallies around the country on its radio stations in 2003.[21] While the size and number of pro-war rallies paled in comparison to the peace rallies, the direct organizational involvement was unique among media conglomerates, and Clear Channel's name began to appear regularly on antiwar signs, and in rallies against the commercial media coverage of the war. On May 29, 2003, a number of national peace organizations and consumer groups in a dozen cities, including New York, Philadelphia, Washington, Charlotte, N.C., Salt Lake City, and San Francisco held protests at Clear Channel stations against further media consolidation in general and the upcoming decision of the FCC on media ownership rules, in particular. Their message: "No more Clear Channels, stop the FCC!"[22]

Clear Channel has also wrangled with the environmental and aboriginal movements. In early 2003, Clear Channel reneged on a contract it had signed with the Sierra Club in Phoenix for billboard space to promote the campaign to save Zuni Salt Lake in western New Mexico from strip mining. The lake is the only natural source of salt in the Southwest, and considered a no-war sanctuary for aboriginal peoples. The mining company, the Salt Lake Project, had previously rented billboard space to promote its countermessage and was also leasing the land to Clear Channel. As Clear Channel Outdoor national president and chief executive officer Paul Meyer said, "I would be disappointed in any of our division presidents that put up copy that is offensive to a good client of ours or to someone from whom we lease land for our billboards. Any other policy would be bad business."[23]

Of course, Clear Channel's most important contribution to messaging is its radio programming. Through its subsidiary, Premiere Radio, Clear Channel broadcasts 100 syndicated programs to 7,800 stations nationwide, reaching over 180 million listeners weekly. They feature Rush Limbaugh, Michael Savage, Dr. Laura Schlessinger, and Michael Regan, among other conservative pundits. Until recently, they also carried Howard Stern's show on six stations, but suspended the contract in early 2004. Stern contended that he was not dropped because of his routinely obscene programming but instead his opposition to the Bush reelection.[24]

NEOLIBERAL COAT TAILS

The larger explanation for Clear Channel's growth is not about Texas conspiracies, but the result of political endorsement from both major parties for the consolidation of the commercial media. J.H. Snider has argued that the broadcasting industry is one of the most protected and subsidized industries in the United States, benefiting from a "welter of copyright, zoning, tax, and airwaves use laws designed to bolster the profitability of their business."[25] Clear Channel Radio's first growth spurt coincided with a major paradigm shift away from the longstanding social compact between media corporations and the U.S. public. The U.S. Communications Act of 1934 had privileged the corporate commercial networks to the detriment of public and amateur broadcasters.[26] However, the 1934 act opened a small loophole with its promotion of the "public service" paradigm, in which broadcasters were granted stewardship of the public airwaves in return for meeting a set of obligations to the public in the local community for which they were licensed. Succeeding generations of media reform groups used this "public interest" wedge to force more accountability from commercial broadcasters and to open up the spectrum for national public radio, local community and low-power FM, and for ownership by excluded groups, including African-Americans, Native and Hispanic-Americans, and women.

After a very strong decade of media reform efforts in the 1970s, the pendulum swung back suddenly.[27] Following the neoliberal move to "market rule," begun during the Ford administration and continued through the Reagan era, the FCC began to eliminate the public-service regulations of broadcasters in the early 1980s. Its longstanding antitrust rule, which had capped radio chains at seven AM and seven FM stations, was lifted.[28] As well, the FCC removed the content regulations requiring broadcasters to produce local news and public-affairs programming, and which provided a modicum of public transparency and accountability. During Clear Channel's first growth spurt, there were few measures regulating its expansion, or requiring the company to provide local public-service programming.[29]

By the mid-1990s, Clear Channel had grown to a radio chain of forty stations. Much like its bigger network rivals Viacom/CBS and Disney/ABC, Clear Channel benefited by the Telecommunications Act of 1996. The act eliminated the national forty-station ownership cap and allowed media companies to own up to eight stations in large markets and five in small markets (up from two).[30] In the five years after the ownership caps were relaxed, the number of radio station owners shrank from 5,100 to 3,800. The top three networks assumed control of at least 60 percent of the stations in the top 110 markets in the United States.[31]

Clear Channel picked up almost 1,000 stations, in all sizes of markets throughout the country. While it only controls 11 percent of all stations, it reaches 27 percent of all radio listeners and makes a quarter of all U.S. radio industry revenues. This is still a much less consolidated industry than during the heydays of radio in the 1940s, when the four major networks reached over 95 percent of the audience. However, in thirty-seven of the top 300 markets, Clear Channel's strategy of purchasing clusters of stations means that its market share ranges between 50 and 99 percent. In many small markets it has a greater impact, often owning eight or more stations, taking it over the FCC ownership cap in several communities.[32]

Clear Channel has combined the power of the horizontal radio chain, with vertical integration of music and entertainment promotion, and global exhibition opportunities across media in music, theater and sports venues, national and international tours, outdoor advertising, and television.[33] As a result, the company can exploit economies of scale in selling to its primary clients, advertisers. Few companies have such global and convergent media holdings, allowing them to woo advertisers with "cluster" sales of ads across multiple media platforms, geographic areas, or station music formats.[34] Clear Channel can also lower advertising prices below what its smaller competitors can offer, forcing them out of business, or to sell to Clear Channel.

FROM THE GARAGE BAND TO THE RADIO

The profitability of commercial radio in the United States has always been due to music. Broadcasters in the United States, unlike those in Europe and seventy-five other countries, pay no performance rights for sound recordings on radio. "Broadcasters are allowed," a coalition of musicians' groups recently stated "to build their business by selling to advertisers the fans that our recordings attract, and yet the broadcasters do not pay compensation for broadcasting the recording. This means neither the record company who invests, nor the performing artists who play instruments or sing and bring the song to life, receive compensation when their recordings are broadcast."[35]

While radio remains one of the most important ways to promote pop music, musicians have had to seek other income streams, through recording sales, song-writing income, live concert fees, and concert sales of t-shirts and other merchandise. Musicians' careers have followed a well-worn route, from gradual exposure in local clubs and concert halls to the various regional and national touring circuits. Until the 1990s, the live music industry comprised a highly fragmented network of artists, artist representatives, local venue operators, independent promoters, record producers, and technical crews, who engaged in complex negotiations depending on their knowledge of artistic content, the production and aesthetic capacities of the local venues, and the tastes of the local community.

Building and sustaining musical communities requires long-term commitments, differing amounts of sacrifice, and a high level of collaboration and cooperation by everyone in the network.[36] For artists, "paying their dues" means insecure working conditions and wages, and subsidizing their artistic activities with other jobs. Creative managers, promoters, venue operators, and independent recording companies, in turn, often invest in the development of newer, and less profitable artists by cross-subsidizing them with more popular ones.[37] Since the beginnings of radio and the recording industry, musicians have worked within consolidated environments; however, the major radio networks were usually content to allow musicians to operate outside of their direct control. After all, it has been the succeeding generations of subcultures of production and consumption who have borne the major costs of conception and development, with a disproportionate number from working-class, African-American and Hispanic communities.[38]

This relative autonomy of the music production community began to change, in the 1990s, when radio station owner Robert Sillerman started SFX Entertainment. He quickly assembled concert promoters and venues in nearly thirty states, spending $2 billion (U.S.) on consolidation. While SFX went deeply into debt, it gained control of the booming concert industry, generating $1.6 billion (U.S.) in revenue in 2000.[39] "SFX swallowed local promotions businesses and reinvented the concert industry around national tour packages."[40] Many knowledgeable local promoters were forced out of the business, and the development of local talent was undermined. As well, the focus on national, commercially sponsored tours in big arenas led to higher ticket prices and the subjection of audiences to more corporate branding.[41]

In 2000, Clear Channel bought out SFX, garnering immediate new possibilities for cross-promotion. Clear Channel's radio networks and other media could promote concerts, and the concerts would give the stations live content, and make them more visible among fans. As well, vertical integration of the concert and radio industries allowed Clear Channel to coordinate the promotion and advertising of artists across all its platforms. For all these financial strengths, its strategy is short-lived. "The wise people in the business will tell you that you have to have a way of assuring the next generation of creative talent. . . . You've got to have a farm team. Clear Channel isn't in that business," said entertainment consultant Larry Moulter.[42]

Clear Channel's greater market power also allowed it to challenge the power of local creative managers. According to Tim Weber, general manager of Mississippi Nights Concert venue in St. Louis, independent producers have been forced to raise their payments to artists, and their ticket prices to fans, in order to compete; for example, he paid Willie Nelson $25,000 (U.S.) when the club normally pays $6,000 to $8,000 (U.S.) for an act.[43] Since Clear Channel's purchase of SFX, the average ticket price has risen by a third, partly as a result of Clear Channel driving up the price of acts and passing on the cost to fans.[44] Clear Channel executive Brian Becker justifies the price hikes by arguing that fans are getting more with improved seat locations or "something special," such as meeting the band.[45] However, small promoters like Weber cannot always offer or afford those kinds of perks and often end up losing the competition for both artists and fans.

Denver-based independent promotion company, Nobody in Particular, filed a lawsuit against Clear Channel in 2001, charging the company with violating antitrust laws, and exercising predatory pricing and anticompetitive business practices to edge out the competition. Nobody in Particular asserted that Clear Channel prohibited other promoters from operating by overpaying artists. In April 2004, U.S. District Court judge Edward Nottingham ruled that there was enough of a case on the monopoly charges to go forward.[46] Then, in July, shortly before it was scheduled to go to trial, Nobody in Particular settled with Clear Channel, agreeing to keep the terms of the agreement confidential. Clear Channel still faces suits from at least three other promoters.[47]

Nobody in Particular also charged that Clear Channel penalized its artists by keeping them off Clear Channel–owned radio stations. As DJ and ex–Clear Channel employee Davey D Cook has testified, "It's not just sour grapes. It's a systemic problem." Clear Channel not only leverages its oligopoly power in music promotion to coerce artists to work exclusively for Clear Channel, but to refrain from criticizing the company. In testimony at the Monterey FCC hearing on localism, in July 2004, Cook described how artists are afraid to be interviewed, in case they say something that may lead to them being boycotted on the radio network, the Clear Channel venues or any of its other holdings.[48]

Not all the artists have been silenced. On January 19, 2001, the Detroit Hip-Hop Coalition, a multicultural organization of hip-hop artists, promoters, DJs, magazines, designers, entrepreneurs, and their supporters staged a protest and boycott of WJLB FM, a Clear Channel station. They were outraged with the station's refusal to play top independent artists from the local area, while "simultaneously profiting from local concerts," a complaint also voiced in Chicago, Seattle, New York, and San Francisco.[49] While unsuccessful in the short term, this attempt is but one in which the hip-hop community has worked to overcome its divisions, and leverage its power.

THE TWIN MUSIC BOTTLENECKS

The consolidation of the music industry, in which Clear Channel has played an integral part, has attacked the autonomy of the creative community. It has also provided bridges between artists and their allies, in the hip hop community and in the rock and independent music scenes. Independent musicians Jenny Toomey and Kristin Thompson transcended the organizational limits of the musicians' unions and "star" based lobbying groups, when they formed Future of Music in Washington, D.C. in 2000 with Michael Bracy from the low-power FM coalition, Walter McDonough, a recording artist representative and entertainment lawyer, and Brian Zisk, a digital technology entrepreneur. They describe themselves as a "not-for-profit think tank that strives for the creation of a musicians' middle class."[50] They are building collaborations between unionized and independent musicians, Internet-savvy techies, media policy advocates, and those working to challenge the corporate domination of intellectual property regimes.

Beyond their new composition, their goals are also more expansive; educating the media, policymakers and the public; developing creative technological solutions for music; promoting innovative business models that will help independent musicians benefit from new technologies; and helping mobilize underrepresented musicians on issues that impact the value of their labor.[51] Their oft-quoted 2002 report, "Radio Deregulation: Has It Served Citizens and Musicians?" documents how the radio and recording industry oligopolies hurt both musicians and citizens. Four radio oligopolies control "almost every geographic market" and "virtually every music format,"[52] and program 80 to 100 percent of the radio charts with songs from the five major labels. This "twin bottleneck" makes access to the airwaves exceedingly difficult for musicians—and reduces choice for citizens."[53]

Future of Music also played an important lobby role in Washington, challenging the orthodoxies of the market paradigm, especially during the deliberations over the FCC media ownership rules. Working with other public-interest advocacy groups, they helped convince the two Democratic Party FCC commissioners to conduct field hearings around the nation. With the support of unionized and nonunionized musicians groups, they testified before the influential Senate Commerce Committee Hearing, on January 30, 2003.[54] Chaired by Republican senator John McCain, this special session on media ownership quickly became an inquiry into Clear Channel's practices.

Toomey and Future of Music debunked one of the pillars of the corporate media argument, that consolidation would benefit consumers. The radio industry had claimed that consolidation provided consumers with an increase in the varieties of music formats. At first glance, this appeared to be the case; between 1996 and 2000 there was an increase of 28 percent in self-reported format diversity in both large and small markets. Yet, Future of Music pointed out that the effect was nominal; there was no corresponding increase in choice of content within those formats. The new formats were mostly subclassifications of existing formats, such as adding Hot AC, Rock AC, Urban AC, Mix AC, Soft AC, Light AC, Bright AC to the category Adult Contemporary (AC). They did not necessarily feature a different set of songs, but overlapped by as much as 76 percent between formats.[55] "In the U.S. you have a number of corporations all competing with the exact same formats to attract the exact same demographics," said Toomey.[56] In addition to this "faux-mat" variety, Future of Music argued that consolidation had narrowed what was available, as the large networks such as Clear Channel routinely operated two or more stations in the same community with the same format.

PAY FOR PLAY

At the hearing, Democratic senator Russ Feingold from Wisconsin spoke about the deleterious impact of consolidation on independent radio station owners, promoters, and consumers.

> Play lists are no longer based on quality—subjective as that is—but are sold to the highest bidder instead . . . in the past, if you couldn't get a DJ to play your song in Cleveland, perhaps you could try in Pittsburgh, and if the song was a hit in Pittsburgh, the Cleveland DJ would probably hear about it . . . that doesn't happen any more. It really can't. The same companies own stations in both markets. If they don't want to play a song, they don't—anywhere. Opportunities for artists to try their music somewhere else just doesn't exist.[57]

Senator Feingold introduced the Competition in Radio and Concert Industries Act to redress these problems.[58]

Both Feingold and Toomey pinpointed Clear Channel's practice of "pay-for-play," in reducing opportunities for musicians and to musical homogeneity. After the first "payola" scandal in the late 1950s, in which recording companies paid radio stations directly for airplay, the practice was deemed illegal because of the unfair advantage it gave to the major labels over unrepresented artists or smaller independent companies.[59] However, pay-for-play works slightly differently. Rather than paying stations directly to play specific songs, record labels pay middlemen, or independent promoters called "indies," who promote the label's songs via media ads on television and magazines. The indies also "align themselves with certain radio stations by promising the stations "promotional payments" in the six figures. Then, every time the radio station adds a Shaggy or Madonna or Janet Jackson song to its playlist, the indie gets paid by the record label."[60]

Journalist Eric Boehlert estimated that indies pay at least $100,000 (U.S.) per station, and as much as $400,000 (U.S.) in major markets; "a minimum $3 million worth of indie invoices [are] sent out *each week* [his emphasis]." Technically, this isn't considered illegal payola under current law, because indies don't pay stations to play *specific* songs, but instead reward stations when they play songs from the indies' repertoire. The indies get paid regardless of which particular songs the station's management chooses to play.[61] In April 2003, after the Senate investigation, and harsh criticism from within and outside the industry, Clear Channel publicly severed its deals with indies.[62] Soon after, there were allegations that Clear Channel had not severed all its ties with independent promoters.[63]

Future of Music and its allies are more concerned about whether the structural basis for pay for play is really gone. In a joint statement, in May 2003, they contended that Clear Channel's new "group-wide" promotional strategy will "very likely program from a centralized location and focus on artists with group-wide, i.e., national, appeal at the expense of artists with local appeal. This practice ignores the FCC principle that individual radio stations in radio groups are licensed to serve local communities. Furthermore, this practice, if implemented, will continue to harm local artists, making it nearly impossible for them to use their local popularity to garner local airtime and denying even the most successful local artists legitimate access to a local audience."[64]

Raising its voice about Clear Channel and the problems of media consolidation in general, Future of Music heralds a recomposition of creative workers, who are not content to be limited by craft structures or resign themselves to the margins of "indy-hood." Claiming autonomy from business interests, they have positioned themselves to take advantage of the new digital technologies, which " are loosening the stranglehold of major labels, major media, and chain-store monopolies . . . to distribute their music with minimal manufacturing and distribution costs, with immediate access to an international audience." At the front of their agenda is action on another long-term collective problem of musicians, their loss of control over their intellectual property.

JIM CROW ECONOMICS

Clear Channel's strategy has also involved exploiting the market vulnerabilities of the smaller independent radio stations. For the African-American and

Hispanic-owned stations, this expropriation is nothing new, but follows a re-curring theme in U.S. entertainment history.[65] So often the creative managers in these communities have taken the greater risks to develop their cultural capital and audiences, only to see them expropriated by the white-dominated entertainment industry. Most African-American and Hispanic-owned radio stations have not been around very long.[66] The systemic exclusion of peoples of color from ownership and broadcast jobs was not overturned until the late 1960s, during the civil rights movement.[67] In the 1970s, an informal network of African-American media advocacy groups, including The National Associ-ation of Black Owned Broadcasters (NABOB), the National Black Media Coalition (NBMC) and the Communications Brain Trust, helped push the FCC to increase minority ownership in radio.[68] From 1978 to 1995, the numbers of "minority-owned" stations grew from forty to 350.[69] Many built strong loyal followings. While they survived through advertising, most derived and ori-ented their music, public affairs, and debate to their local communities, coun-tering the trend of the big chains toward targeting consumers with nationally syndicated talk and musical play lists.[70]

These stations had to survive with two economic strikes against them. Ad-vertising capital discriminated, as the best ad rates were given to Top 40 sta-tions that served the white audiences, a premium of 29 percent more rev-enue per listener for the white firms.[71] The independents also found it much more difficult to recruit advertisers when Clear Channel and other large chains could offer greater promotional premiums and cheaper cross-media packages.[72] Robert Short Jr., the president of Short Broadcasting, appeared at the Senate Commerce hearing. He testified that he sold his station, WRDS in Syracuse, New York, in 2000 when he was unable to compete with Clear Channel's seven-station cluster, which controlled 50 percent of ad revenue. As a result, the Syracuse African-American community lost local news and public-affairs programming, and an outlet for a community voice that other media ignored.[73]

Banks have also been unwilling to finance independent and/or African-American and Hispanic-owned stations, meaning many owners were forced to seek private equity funds where capital is much more expensive and of-ten requires giving up a substantial ownership stake.[74] Florida-based Span-ish Broadcasting System (SBS), the nation's largest Hispanic-owned radio operator, alleged in a suit in federal court in 2003 that Clear Channel at-tempted to induce investors to withdraw financial support. Clear Channel is a major investor in SBS's competitor, Hispanic Broadcasting Corporation. The suit was dismissed but is being appealed.[75]

Clear Channel's rapid expansion has masked the greater plunder, the expropriation of cultural capital. As Robert Short testified, Clear Channel used its national advertising clout to compete head to head with the African-American stations such as WRDS. These "urban" stations played a major role in the 1980s in fronting hip hop, today's most profitable music genre. As DJ, and one-time Clear Channel employee, Davey D describes, once hip hop became profitable, and the white Top 40 stations started to play it, they were backed with far greater resources from both the advertisers and the major record companies.[76] Then, after Clear Channel and the other dominant chains commandeered the bulk of the advertising and promotional dollars, making the independents even more financially vulnerable, they bought out the stations that were left.

It was not only the music that began to suffer as program directors cut out local artists and more political ones in favor of gangster and bling-bling styles to entice their white suburban audiences to the advertisers. The expansion of white-dominated radio also led to the loss of the electronic billboards in the Black and Latino communities. Imitative entertainment programming has been expanded at the expense of local news and public affairs, which have been cut to news bites or relegated to 7 am slots on weekends.[77] As well, the political autonomy, especially of the Black DJs, has been severed. One of the FCC's own studies showed a clear connection between minority ownership and diversity in programming content and staffing; minority stations were far more likely to hire minority staff, produce live broadcasts of community events, and programs of concern to senior citizens and women.[78] As William Saunders, who owns WPAL AM in Charleston, South Carolina told *Black Enterprise*, "Now we have people at urban stations that don't know anyone in the community. [They] just play music and come up with new ways to make money."[79]

While losing ground, the independent stations have continued to organize through their networks and trade associations, and through public discussions, lawsuits, and political lobbying. The National Association of Black Broadcasters spoke at the Senate Hearings on Clear Channel, and in the FCC Review on Media Ownership. For the first time, journalists of color from the California Chicano News Media Association, the Association of Black Journalists, UNITY: Journalists of Color, chimed in to challenge the public process of the FCC review.[80]

WORKING FOR CHEAP CHANNEL

Clear Channel has also gone head-to-head with the creative and technical personnel within its radio and entertainment empire. Adopting a neo-Taylorist strategy, the company uses computer-driven technologies to automatically program several stations from one location; and to substitute prerecorded voice tracks and program elements for live talent.[81] As a result, Clear Channel has laid off hundreds of workers from technical, sales and management, and programming positions. Entire news teams have been replaced with taped feeds from CNN or other national agencies. This became apparent on September 11, 2001, when the Pentagon was attacked and Clear Channel had no news team to cover it. In another well-publicized incident, after a chemical spill in Minot, North Dakota, in January 2002, there was no one to respond to the call from Emergency Services at KCJB, the designated emergency broadcaster. While Clear Channel owns all six radio stations there, it employs just one full-time news employee, who rips and reads the newscasts from state and national wire services.[82]

Operations have been consolidated by market, and by format, merging, for example, the two sports-format stations, XTRA/AM of San Diego and KXTA/AM of Los Angeles.[83] Brad Johnson worked as a radio engineer for two different companies in Modesto, California, for over a decade until both were bought by Clear Channel.

> I kept very busy for a few years after the Telecommunications Act of 1996, breaking down long-time local stations and moving them into the corporate building. Maybe everyone else was busy too—too busy to ask why we built five stations in one building without a newsroom.
> Since CC and other large broadcasters began buying up what were once local and independent radio stations all over the country, it's now hard to find a job in radio without having to work for Cheap Channel, and that's if they even have any new job openings. Typically, those new stations that are freshly corporatized employ a salary and a hiring freeze.[84]

Like Johnson, the remaining employees are expected to work at lower salaries, as Clear Channel has successfully forced wages down throughout the industry. Most remaining employees must also multitask; for example, four people staff the remaining eight Washington-Baltimore stations, with one program director for two entirely different formats, rock and roll and bluegrass.[85] In San Antonio, TV sportscaster Don Harris also hosts an afternoon radio show, while TV meteorologist Jennifer Broome broadcasts on radio as well.[86] In response to the restructuring, dozens of employees have filed suits, claiming violation of overtime labor laws, discrimination against women, racism, and questionable sales ethics and Unfair Labor Practice charges with the National Labor Relations Board.[87]

Only 5 to 10 percent of Clear Channel employees are unionized, scattered in fifteen different craft unions, which bargain separately from one another. However, individual employees such as Johnson have spoken out and the unions are beginning to recognize the importance of challenging Clear Channel's economic and political power. In February, 2004, the American Federation of Labor (AFL) released *The Clear Picture on Clear Channel Communications, Inc: A Corporate Profile*, advocating a more coordinated strategy for the labor movement. The AFL launched its campaign in San Antonio, Clear Channel's headquarters, during the FCC Forum on Localism in January 2004.

The report notes the advantage of union concentration in major markets. For example, while there are only thirty-five unionized radio stations, the American Federation of Television and Radio Artists contract covers well-known announcers and radio personalities, which gave additional clout in appeals to members and the public during the most recent contract campaign in New York.[88] On Broadway, Clear Channel, following Disney's lead, has moved into the transnational mega-entertainment industry.[89] The two conglomerates are not signatories to the master union agreements, but are both trying to keep wages down, and reduce the numbers of live musicians through automation. In 2003, a union coalition supported the strike of the American Federation of Musicians (AFM) in New York to defeat two such proposals. In Baltimore and Pittsburgh, two International Alliance of Theatrical Stage Employees (IATSE) locals, including Clear Channel employees, went on strike over the same issues.[90]

DJs and on-air personalities, who commanded a great deal of autonomy during the early days of FM radio, have been some of the most obvious targets of Clear Channel's neo-Taylorism. Clear Channel has replaced its live programs with "voice-tracking." For example, millions of Americans in forty-eight cities listen to Kiss FM DJ's Rick Dees and Sean Valentine chat about local news, or promote concerts in local amphitheaters owned by Clear Channel. However, their voices, and other program elements were prerecorded in Los Angeles and cut and spliced to sound as if they were originating down the street. In the local KISS station in Des Moines, or Jacksonville, board operators play the recorded elements for as little as $6 per hour.[91]

Clear Channel has not been able to control all of its DJs. Charles Goyette lost his prime afternoon drive-time slot at KFYI-AM in Phoenix after opposing the war in Iraq and questioning the competency of Donald Rumsfeld on air. Goyette has written that the only thing protecting him from being fired was his well-drafted contract. However, instead of suffering unemployment, he was vilified and ridiculed by radio hosts at his own station, effectively shriveling his listener base. Roxanne Cordonier, a former radio personality at WMYI, in South Carolina, filed suit claiming she was also belittled by colleagues on and off air for her opposition to the war, and forced to participate in pro-war rallies.[92]

CALLING FOR COMMUNITY ACCOUNTABILITY

Clear Channel's aggressive actions and attacks on creative workers' autonomy have galvanized some of the most difficult to organize groups of cultural workers. They've also been successful in bringing together an even more motley group: fans. On October 1, 2001, Davey D Cook was fired from his position as community affairs director at KMEL FM. Davey D hosted the popular "Street Soldiers" program that was aimed at youths of color. His termination took place not long after he aired the antiwar song of Coup's Boots Riley and hosted a program with Democratic congresswoman Barbara Lee from Oakland, the sole dissenting voice in the first congressional vote to attack Afghanistan.[93] Clear Channel denies that Cook's severance was related to these two incidents. However, it catapulted Davey D to the front of a community campaign to make KMEL and Clear Channel more accountable. Somewhat reluctantly, he began to speak out about the problems of Clear Channel, and the larger problems of independent hip-hop artists trying to survive within the bottlenecks of the music industry.

A leading urban music station during the late 1980s and 1990s, KMEL called itself the "People's Station," and had developed a strong and loyal following. Its programs were often cutting edge, engaging its young audiences of color with fresh and local music, and talk programming which addressed the social issues of the hip-hop generation. The station was also very successful in the local market. When Clear Channel bought KMEL and its rival station in 1999, KMEL began to broadcast a shorter play list of no risk-taking tunes, removed the local community-driven music and talk programming, and replaced some of the DJs with digitally preprogrammed tapes.

After Cook was fired, several groups of young people of color formed the Community Coalition for Media Accountability. They approached the station, demanding redress for the firing of Davey and another popular host, the cutting of hip-hop programs of social issues, and the replacement of local music by preprogrammed "top hits." When their concerns were not addressed by Clear Channel, they researched and published a content analysis of the programming. Their report, *Is KMEL the People's Station? A Community Assessment of 106.1*, found that KMEL "routinely excludes the voices of youth organizers and local artists, neglects discussion of policy debates affecting youth and people of color, focuses disproportionately on crime and violence and has no clear avenues for listeners to hold the station accountable."[94]

Their work led to some concessions from the station. KMEL added a new local music program.[95] In June 2003, the station agreed to co-host a community forum, featuring young people talking about community solutions to street violence with Let's Get Free, one of the coalition partners. Live coverage of "360° of Violence," broadcast young activists "speaking out against racism, the criminal 'injustice' system and the oppressive, abusive dangers of concentrated corporate media."[96] In 2004, KMEL began to add more local music and a greater range to its play lists. While management argues its decision is due to greater availability of quality music, it must also reflect the direct community pressure, the short-lived competition of a hip-hop station in Oakland, which had aimed to capitalize on those who felt disenfranchised by Clear Channel,[97] and the widespread dissatisfaction with restricted programming.[98]

CHANNELING CLEAR CHANNEL

By 2003, Clear Channel was facing opposition from several different constituencies. The company had to deal with lawsuits from radio station owners,[99] promoters and employees, Senate investigations, and local and national protests. In addition to Senator Feingold's bill, Democratic representative Howard Berman of California sponsored an investigation of Clear Channel's coercion of artists, and its use of third parties to park, or hold the title for, radio licenses in markets where it exceeded the FCC caps. Three federal Department of Justice investigations focused on Clear Channel.[100] The florida attorney general fined the company $80,000 (U.S.) when its use of voice-tracking misled listeners into thinking that a national contest was local.[101] Then, in the fall of 2003, Essential Information, a D.C.-based nonprofit organization started by Ralph Nader, initiated a new citizen-driven strategy. It petitioned the FCC to deny license renewal to sixty-three of Clear Channel's stations in Washington D.C., Virginia, West Virginia, and Maryland.[102]

At the same time, the larger media regulation environment was shifting. On June 4, 2003, the FCC Republican majority voted to pass the new rules deregulating media ownership even further. However, the outcry over Clear Channel helped stop the further deregulation of radio. In fact, the FCC rewrote the parameters for defining markets, leaving eighty-two Clear Channel stations out of compliance. Clear Channel was required to divest sixteen of them, and also may be required to give up those stations where it "provides programming to or sells advertising on stations it does not own."[103]

The FCC decision released a cascade of more organizing, moving outside the music and entertainment, social justice movement and media activist communities to more established constituencies across the political spectrum. As a result, Michael Powell, the chairman of the FCC, reversed his position on public participation and set up a Localism Task Force that would host public hearings. At the first hearing in San Antonio, in January 2004, many of the 500 in attendance focused their criticism on the hometown-based Clear Channel, raising placards saying "Clear Channel Blurs the Truth" and "We're not one country under Clear Channel."[104] Then, in June 2004, the Third Circuit Court of Appeals in Philadelphia rejected the FCC's decision.

Clear Channel has changed some of its tactics and polished others. Facing a slew of obscenity fines from the FCC, the company tried to cut some of its losses by suspending its contract with Bubba the Love Sponge and Howard Stern. Stern counterattacked, claiming that he was dropped because of his opposition to Clear Channel ally, George Bush. Stern's primary broadcaster and Clear Channel competitor, Viacom's Infinity Radio, are still involved in legal arguments; Stern himself has jumped to the new medium of digital radio. More sparks flew in July 2004, when Clear Channel tried to back out of a contract in New York City with Project Billboard, an antiwar group. Surprisingly, after only a few days of bad publicity in the mainstream and alternative press, Clear Channel reached a compromise.[105]

On another programming front, after the localism hearings, Clear Channel provided more election news coverage and public affairs programming during the national elections of 2004, an initiative that begins to redress its statutory commitment to its local communities. Clear Channel also cut the number of ads per hour, partly to satisfy advertisers who fear the clutter is preventing them from reaching their declining audiences, who are fleeing the sameness of chain radio for Satellite and Internet radio, and their own self-programming via Internet downloads. Cutting the number of ads per hour will also allow Clear Channel to raise its ad rates. Clear Channel is making all these tactical moves in a period when radio sales are down once again, and its wide-sweeping acquisitions still find the company financially vulnerable, with $8.8 billion (U.S.) in acquired debt.[106]

Clear Channel's new programming initiatives are certainly surprising; at the localism hearing in Monterey, California, Davy D called them "smoke and mirrors." If the conglomerate is responding to public pressure about its programming, we need only look a few steps behind our backs to see the continuity in its macrostrategies, in which Clear Channel continues to capitalize on the cultural capital developed by others. The company is counting on winning more of the growing number of ad dollars targeting Spanish speakers, and will convert twenty-five of its stations to Spanish-language formats.[107] It has also contracted for the syndicated liberal program "Air America" in communities with sizable niches of liberal audiences, in Santa Barbara, San Diego, Ann Arbor, Miami, and Portland. Clear Channel is also increasing its transnational theatre investments, including a major new hall in Dublin and a planned production of a Bob Marley mega-musical in London.[108]

Clear Channel, like many other global conglomerates, has attracted international attention and criticism because of its rapid consolidation and its negative impact on local creative communities and cultures. Fortunately, the company's restructuring efforts, in which it has tried to break down the existing power base of musicians, promoters, independent station owners, recording labels, fans, and political movements, has led to a whole new composition of creative labor. As well, a series of bridges have opened up between older social movements and a whole new set of creative organizers, whose collective energy for a renewed media reform movement is only just emerging.

NOTES

1. Maria Figueroa, Damone Richardson, and Pam Whitefield, *The Clear Picture on Clear Channel Communications,Inc: A Corporate Profile* (Ithaca, N.Y.: Cornell University, AFLCIO, 28 January 2004), p. 3. David Kaplan. "Concert Promoter Louis Messina Sees World of Opportunity as Noncompete Clause with Old Boss Expires." *The Houston Chronicle,* 8 August 2003, Business p. 1.

2. Clear Channel Inc. <http://www.clearchannel.com/out_about.php.> (8 November 2004). L.A. Lorek, "Changing of Clear Channel: SA Based Radio Group Looks at Ways to Continue its Success," *San Antonio Express-News,* 25 July 2004, Business p. 1L.

3. Christine Y. Chen, "The Bad Boys of Radio." *Fortune,* 3 March 2003, 119.

4. Jeremy Egner, "The Static over Station Ownership Comes to SXSW. Are the Radio Giants too Big?" *The Austin American Statesman,* 15 March 2003, p. 1.

5. See David Hesmondhalgh, *The Cultural Industries* (London: Sage Publications, 2002) for an excellent overview of political economy of cultural industries.

6. Hesmondhalgh, *The Cultural Industries,* p. 6.

7. There are very few autonomist Marxist analyses of cultural industries. We draw on Nick Dyer-Witheford, *Cyber-Marx,* (Urbana and Chicago: University of Illinois Press, 1999); and Dorothy Kidd, "Talking the Walk: The Communications Commons Amidst the Media Enclosures," unpublished Ph.D. dissertation: Simon Fraser University. 1998.

8. Federal News Service. "Hearing of the Senate Commerce, Science, and Transportation Committee: Hearing on Media Ownership," Federal News Service, Inc. (30 January 2003).

9. Drawing on Miège, Hesmondhalgh describes contic competition among them because of an oversupply of artistic labor, and the historic failure of cultural workers to come together. As we shall see, we must also add the exploitation of gendered and racialized divisions. Hesmondhalgh, *The Cultural Industries,* p. 57.

10. Charles Goyette, "How to Lose Your Job in Talk Radio: Clear Channel Gags an Anti-war Conservative," *American Conservative,* 2 February 2004. www.amconmag.com/1_19_04/article3 .html

11. In 1998, Lowry Mays, Clear Channel's chairman of the board, gave Bush's gubernatorial campaign $51,000, while his family have donated $160,000 for political action between 1999 and 2002. See Figueroa et al., *The Clear Picture on Clear Channel Communications, Inc: A Corporate Profile,* p.60.

12. Mary Boyle, *Clear Channels of Influence: Where the Money Goes,* <http://www .commoncause.org/action/printable.cfm?ArtID=175&topicid=11.> (28 September 2004). Figueroa et al., *The Clear Picture on Clear Channel Communications,Inc: A Corporate Profile,* p. 8.

13. After approving the AMFM-Clear Channel merger, the Department of Justice, citing "antitrust concerns," forced Clear Channel to divest 99 radio stations in 27 markets. Department of Justice, see "Justice Department Requires Clear Channel and AMFM to Divest 99 stations in 27 Markets: Required Sale Is Largest Radio Divestiture Ever." <http://www.usdoj.gov/opa/pr/2000/ July/415at.htm> (20 July 2003).

14. Figueroa et al., *The Clear Picture on Clear Channel Communications,Inc: A Corporate Profile,* p. 59.

15. Mark Glassman, "Broadcast Industry Increases Lobbying Budget, Study Says," *New York Times,* 1 November, 2004, C7.

16. Glassman, "Broadcast Industry Increases . . . .," C7.

17. Glassman, "Broadcast Industry Increases . . . .," C 7.

18. See <http://www.counterpunch.org/chang2.html>

19. Associated Press, "Clear Channel Growth the result of 1996 Deregulation." *Salt Lake Tribune*. <http://www.sltrib.com/2003/Sep/09212003/business/94315.asp> (21 September 2003); P. Krugman, "Channels of influence," *New York Times*, 25 March 2003, A17.

20. Michael Fitzgerald, "Dixie Chicks Axed by Clear Channel." <http://jacksonville.bizjournals.com/jacksonville/stories/2003/03/17/daily14.html.> (18 March, 2003). In late April 2003, Trillium Assets Management, a socially responsible investment firm, sent a letter to Clear Channel raising concerns about the blacklisting. See William Baue, "Blacklisting, Vocietracking, and Payola: Clear Channel and the Effects of Media Consolidation." SocialFunds. com. <http://www.socialfunds.com/news/article.cgi/1130.html>

21. They assisted syndicated radio talk show host Glen Beck in organizing eighteen pro-military rallies in fourteen states, primarily in the South, co-sponsoring and promoting most of them on their stations and via their company Web site. See W. Barrett, "Bush's Voice of America," *Village Voice*, 8 April 2003, 22; Aria Seilgmann, "De-Reg Demons: Clear Channel Builds Conservative Airwave Monopoly," *Eugene Weekly*, 22, no. 17, 14 (2003): 12.

22. Andrea Buffa, "Clear Channel Feels the Heat," *Media File*, 22, no. 2 (Fall 3003). <http://www.mediaalliance.org/article.php?story=20031028000337860&query=Clear+Channel> (21 January 2004).

23. J. Dougherty, "Indian Ruin: The Zuni Tribes Plans for Phoenix Billboards Were Abruptly Canceled by Clear Channel," *Phoenix New Times*. 6 February 2003.

24. Eric Boehlert, "The Passion of Howard Stern." Salon.com. 4 March, 2004. <http:www.salon.com/news/feature/2004/03/04/stern/print.html>

25. J. H. Snider, "The Decline . . ." p. 1.

26. R. W. McChesney, *Telecommunications, Mass Media, and Democracy: The Battle for the Control of U.S. Broadcasting, 1928–1935* (New York: Oxford University Press. 1993).

27. Milton Mueller, Brendan Kuerbis, and Christiane Pagé, "Reinventing Media Activism: Public Interest Advocacy in the Making of U.S. Communication-Information Policy, 1960–2002," The Convergence Center, School of Information Studies, Syracuse University. <http://www.dcc.syr.edu/ford/rma/reinventing.pdf.> (16 July, 2004). Juan Gonzalez and Joseph Torres, "How Long Must We Wait: The Fight for Racial and Ethnic Equality in the American News Media," Case Study for Race and Public Policy: A Proactive Agenda for 2005 and Beyond. <http://RAPP@arc.org/downloads/casestudies/HowLong.pdf> p 8–10.

28. J. H. Snider, Matt Barranca, and Papia Debroy, "The Decline of Broadcasters' Public Interest Obligations," New America Foundation. 29 March 2004. <http://www.newamerica.net/Download_Docs/pdfs/Pub_File_1518_1/pdf>

29. In 1984, the FCC raised the ownership ceiling to twelve AM and twelve FM stations nationally.

30. Table 1: **Local Radio Station Ownership Rules According to the 1996 Telecom Act**

In a market with . . .	A single entity can control . . .
. . .45 or more stations	. . . up to 8, no more than 5 in same band (AM or FM)
. . . 30–44 stations	. . . up to 7, no more than 4 in same band
. . . 15–29 stations	. . . up to 6, no m ore than 4 in same band
. . . 14 or fewer stations	. . . up to 5, no more than 3 in same band

Source: Dicola and Thomson. *Radio Deregulation,* 11.

31. Eric Boehlert, "Pay for Play." <http://www.salon.com> (14 March 2001).

32. In Boston, Clear Channel owns or controls 9 stations; in Louisville, Ky., 10; in Atlanta, 9; in New York, 10; in Columbus, Ohio, 11. Of 17 stations in Mansfield, Ohio, Clear Channel owns

11; in Corvallis, Oregon, 7 of 13; in Casper, Wyo., 6 of 12. John Dunbar and Aron Pilhofer, "Big Radio Rules in Small Markets." See The Center for Public Integrity, <http://www.openairwaves.org/telecom/report.aspx?aid=63>

33. For a more general discussion of the importance of theatrical production within "ever-more convergent " transnational entertainment corporations (TECs), see Jonathan Burston, "Spectacle, Synergy and Megamusicals," in *Media Organisations in Society*. ed. James Curran (London: Arnold, 2000), 72.

34. Lynnley Browning, "Making Waves on Air: Big Radio's Bad Boy," *New York Time,*. 19 June 2002, C1.

35. Future of Music, American Federation of Television and Radio Artists (AFTRA), American Federation of Musicians (AFM). "Joint Comments at the Federal Communications Commission on the Transition to Digital Broadcasting Digital Audio Broadcasting Systems and Their Impact on the Terrestrial Radio Broadcast Service," MM Docket No. 99-325, 16 June 2004.

36. David Hesmondhalgh, "Alternative Media, Alternative Texts? Rethinking Democratization in the Cultural Industries," in *Media Organisations in Society*, James Curran, 111–12.

37. Adam J. Van Alstyne, "Clear Control: An Anti-trust Analysis of Clear Channel's Radio and Concert Empire," *Minnesota Law Review*, February 2004, 13.

38. Hesmondhalgh. *Cultural Industries*, 74.

39. Van Alstyne, "Clear Control," 9.

40. Van Alstyne, "Clear Control," 9–10.

41. Van Alstyne, "Clear Control," 13.

42. Maureen Dezell, "Is Bigger Better? In the Entertainment Business Clear Channel Is Every-where, and Critics Say That Is the Problem," *Boston Globe*. 27 January 2002, L1.p. 3.

43. K.C. Johnson, "Promoter," *St. Louis Post-Dispatch*, 25 January 2004, F1.

44. ABC News, "Rock 'N' Roll Rip-Off? Fans Angry Over Soaring Ticket Prices."<http://abcnews.go.com/sections/2020/Entertainment/2020_concertgreed030314.html> (15 March 2003).

45. R. Waddell, "A Q&A with Brian Becker," *Billboard*. 6 December 2003, 66.

46. Entertainment Law Reporter, "Clear Channel Communications Settles Case." *Entertainment Law Reporter*, October 2004, (Lode Date: 9 November 2004).

47. Chicago's Jam Sports and the New York region's Metropolitan Talent are alleging anti-competition violations, among other issues, while the third dispute is with longtime promoters Greg Perloff and Sherry Wasserman of the legendary Bill Graham Company, now controlled by Clear Channel. See Ray Waddell, "Promoters Prep for More CC Court Cases." *Billboard*, 19 June 2004.

48. See also Eric Arnold and Chris Thompson, "Fighting the Power: Upstart Rap Station Power 92.7 Had Its Eyes on Big, Bad KMEL, but Didn't Watch Its Back." *East Bay Express*, 6–12 October 2004, 16.

49. Davey D, "Detroit Hip Hoppers to Boycott WJLB" <www.daveyd.com> (1 December 2001).

50. Future of Music, "Frequently Asked Questions." http://www.futureofmusic.org/about/faq.cfm, (11November, 2004).

51. Future of Music,"Our Mission." <http://www.futureofmusic.org/mission.cfm.>

52. Dicola and Thomson, *Radio Deregulation*, 3.

53. Dicola and Thomson, *Radio Deregulation*, 4.

54. Jenny Toomey, "Radio Deregulation: Has It Served Citizens and Musicians?"Testimony submitted by the Future of Music Coalition for "Media Ownership: Radio" Hearings before the Senate Committee on Commerce, Science and Transportation, <www.futureofmusic.org/news/senatecommercetestimony.cfm.> (30 January 2003).

55. Dicola Thomson. *Radio Deregulation*, 4.

56. Robert Wilonsky, "What's Left of the Dial; One Nonprofit Helped Save Radio. Sort of. For now," *Dallas Observer*, 23, no. 25 (19 June 2003): 1.

57. Media Ownership: Radio Hearings, Senate Committee on Commerce, Science and Transportation, 30 January 2003.

58. Russ Feingold, "Feingold Introduces Competition in Radio and Concert Industries Act," <http://feingold.senate.gov/~feingold/releases/03/01/2003128910.html> (28 January 2003).

59. Jack Kapica, "Edison's Noisy Children," *Digital Journal.com*, http://www.digitaljournal .com/news/?articleID=3630&page=3, July 2003. "Announcement of payment for broadcast," 47 C.F.R. § 317, Subchapter Iii - Special Provisions Relating To Radio. Part I - General Provisions U* Communications Act Of 1934. Chapter 5 - Wire Or Radio Communication.

60. Eric Boehlert, "Pay for Play," *Salon.com* (14 March 2001).

61. Eric Boehlert, "Is Pay-for-Play Finally Finished?" *Salon.com*, <http://www.salon.com/ent/ music/feature/2003/02/20/pay_for_play/index.html.> (20 Feb. 2003.)

62. Susan Crabtree and Justin Oppelaar, "Clear Channel Snips Indie Promo Ties," *Daily Variety*, 10 April 2003.

63. Unknown author, "What Effect Will CC's Indie Policy Have?" *Airplay Monitor, 2* May 2003.

64. "Joint Statement on Current Issues in Radio," <http://futureofmusic.org/news/radio issuesstatement03.cfm.> (8 October 2003).

65. William Barlow, *Voice: The Making of Black Radio* (Philadelphia: Temple University Press, 1999), 22.

66. Juan González and Joseph Torres, "How Long Must We Wait: The Fight for Racial and Ethnic Equality in the American News Media," Case Study for Race and Public Policy: A Proactive Agenda for 2005 and Beyond. <http://RAPP@arc.org/downloads/casestudies/HowLong.pdf.> pp. 8–10.

67. The major civil rights media initiative was in Jackson, Mississippi. The initiative, started by the United Church of Christ, years of organizing against the racism of local white-owned stations, and the refusal of the FCC to intervene finally led to the revoking of the station's license by an appeals panel in 1969. Mark Lloyd. "Communications Policy is a Civil Rights Issue." *Civil Rights Forum on Communications Policy* <http://www.civilrightsforum.org/foundations.html.> (4 August 1997). Carrie Solages. *The Crisis.* Baltimore. Vol. 110, Issue 5, Sept/October 2003, 20.

68. William Barlow,*Voice,* 251.

69. Juan González and Joseph Torres. "How Long," 13–14.

70. William Barlow, *Voice,* 296. Gilbert Garcia. "When Latino Doesn't Mean Latino. Real-Deal Minority Broadcasters Face the Threat of Big Media." *San Antonio Current.* 22 January 2004. http://www.zwire.com/site/news.cfm?newsid=10848009&BRD=2318&PAG=461&dept_id=4840 45&rfi=8.

71. Davey D. Cook, "Ultimate Battle Race, <http://www.daveyd.com/FullArticles%5Carticle N1370.asp> (4 October 2004); Minority Media and Telecommunications Council, "Frequently Asked Questions." http://mmtconline.org/FAQ_s/rtb/index.shtml. (11 November 2004).

72. M. Dellinger, "It's O.K. I'm with Clear Channel." *New York Times,* 29 June, 2003, 31. Brentin Mock, "Station Identification:WAMO, the City's Historic Black Radio Station, Once Had the Community to Itself. Now It's Counting on That Sense of Community to Compete Against Monoliths." *Pittsburgh City Paper,* 15, no. 29 (July 2003): 10.

73. Federal News Service, "Hearing of the Senate Commerce, Science and Transportation Committee: Hearing on Media OwnershipService, Inc. (30 January 2003).03).: Hearing on

74. Walter Dawkins and Mathew Scott, "Battle for the Airwaves!" *Black Enterprise,* New York, 33, no. 10 (May 2003): 64–70. National Association of Black Owned Broadcasters and the Rainbow Push Coalition. "Petition for Reconsideration." Before the Federal Communications Commission. In the Matter of the 2002 Biennial Review of the Commission's Broadcast Ownership Rules. 4 September 2003, 10. http://www.nabob.org/Press_Releases/9_4_2003-Petition.pdf.

75. Dawkins and Scott, "Battle for the Airwaves!" 55.

76. Davey D Cook, "Ultimate Battle Race," www.daveyd.com/articleaultimatebattlerace.html (4 October 2004).

77. University of San Francisco Media Research Group, "San Francisco Hearing on Local Ownership, April 26, 2003". Unpublished Transcripts, 17.

78. González and Torres, "How Long," 15.

79. Mock, "Station identification:WAMO."

80. Juan González and Joseph Torres, "How Long," 17.

81. Figueroa et al., *The Clear Picture*, 6.

82. Jennifer Lee, "On Minot, N.D., Radio, A Single Corporate Voice," *New York Times*, 31 March 2003, C7.

83. Figueroa et al., *The Clear Picture*, 29.

84. Brad Johnson. FCC Hearings, City Hall, San Francisco, 26 April 2003.

85. Figueroa et al., *The Clear Picture*, 18.

86. Figueroa et al., *The Clear Picture*, 15.

87. Figueroa, *The Clear Picture*, 66. C. Yezbak, "Media Giant Clear Channel Sued for Policy of Working Employees Off-the-Clock without Pay," <http://www.usnewswire.com/topnews/qtr1_2003/0331-125.html> (31 March 2003). John Nova Lomax, "Static on the Dial; Shady Ethics and Racism behind the Scenes at Clear Channel Radio? That's What Ex-employee June Garcia Sherman Is Claiming in a Lawsuit," *Houston Press*, 15, no. 27 (July 3, 2003).

88. Figueroa et al., *The Clear Picture*, 31.

89. Jonathan Burston, "Spectacle, Synergy and Megamusicals," in Curran, *Media Organisations in Society*, 72.

90. Figueroa et al., *The Clear Picture*, 39.

91. Figueroa et al., *The Clear Picture*, 65.

92. Figueroa et al., *The Clear Picture*, 57.

93. Jeff Chang, "Urban Radio Rage," *Bay Guardian*. <http://www.sfbg.com/37/18/cover_kmel.html.> (22 January 2003).

94. Youth Media Council, "Is KMEL the People's Station? A Community Assessment of 106.1 KMEL," Fall 2002, <http://www.youthmediacouncil.org/pdfs/BuildAPeoplesStation.pdf.>

95. Chang, "Urban Radio Rage."

96. Aliza Dichter, "U.S. Media Activism and the Search for Constituency." *Media Development*. February 26, 2004. http://www.wacc.org.uk/modulesΩ.php?name=News&file=article&sid=1487.

97. Eric Arnold and Chris Thompson, "Fighting the Power," *East Bay Express*, 6–12 October 2004.

98. Paul Weideman, "Radio America: They're not Playing Our Song," *Santa Fe New Mexican*, 31 January 2003.

99. In San Diego, they faced another antitrust lawsuit from Jefferson Pilot Communications. See Jeff Leeds, "Firm Skirts Radio Caps in San Diego," *Los Angeles Times*, 4 October 2002, California Metro; Part 2; Page 1; Metro Desk.

100. One suit resulted in a consent decree, requiring Clear Channel to sell stations and interests in Lamar Broadcasting. See Figueroa et al., *The Clear Picture*, 56–57. A second "concerned more allegations that Clear Channel uses its market dominance to coerce recording artists into using its concert promotion business in return for better radio airplay. See L.A. Lorek, "Clear Channel Sweetens Its Profit Despite Sour Economy," *San Antonio Express-News*, 30 July 2003, 6E. A third Justice Department investigation was looking at their San Diego cluster's use of cross-border stations in Tijuana, to avoid the ownership cap. See Rachel Laing, "FCC Rules Signal Confusion for Cross-Border Broadcasting; Clear Channel's Stations in Mexico May Cross the Line." *The San Diego Union-Tribune*, 15 July 2003.

101. Figueroa et al., *The Clear Picture*, 54.

102. See essential information. <http://www.essentialinformation.org/features/clearchannel.html>.

103. Figueroa et al., *The Clear Picture*, 53.

104. Bill McConnell, "The Public Is Interested; In Heart of Texas, FCC Panel Gets an Earful over Lack of Localism," *Broadcasting and Cable*, 2 February 2004, 2.

105. Project Billboard had leased a Times Square billboard site to post an image of a red, white, and blue bomb captioned "Democracy Is Best Taught by Example, Not by War." The compromise was that the bomb image was changed to a dove and Project Billboard would received more space for a billboard that says "Total Cost of Iraq War" with the dollar-changing ticker. Lisa Stein, "Battle of The Boards. Clear Channel Communications Did Not Approve of a Political Billboard," *U.S. News and World Report*.

106. Figueroa, Richardson and Whitefield, *The Clear Picture, p. 6*

107. Katy Bachman. "Tuning in Hispanic: Clear Channel to Grow Spanish-language Format Stations in All-Sized Markets," *Business Media*, 16 September, 2004.

108. Presumably Clear Channel will be able to leverage the value of the 'Bob Marley' and other musical brand across their media holdings. Jonathan Burston, "Spectacle, Synergy and Megamusicals," In James Curran, ed., *Media Organisations in Society* (London: Arnold, 2000), p. 72.

5

Aspergate: Concentration, Convergence, and Censorship in Canadian Media

Leslie Regan Shade

This chapter provides a case study of CanWest Global Communication as an exemplar of many of the structural problems inherent in media concentration in an era of media convergence, such as diminution of journalistic freedom and integrity, shrinking of local content, and the decline of public-interest values. With CanWest's $3.5-billion (Cdn) purchase of the Southam newspaper chain in July 2000, and its completed purchase of *The National Post* in 2002, it is now the largest daily newspaper provider in Canada; its holdings include thirteen major metropolitan daily newspapers and more than 100 weekly and community newspapers. In the last few years, CanWest has come under intense criticism from local citizens, and national and international newspaper unions, for its centralization of content (particularly a national editorial policy) reflecting an autocratic attitude toward journalists—and revealing, for many, a disturbing pattern of censorship. Specific examples will be discussed, including the furor over national editorial policies, which attracted international coverage; and the dismissal of *Ottawa Citizen* publisher Russell Mills for printing an editorial critical of then prime minister Jean Chrétien, which galvanized local citizens to debate the notion of editorial freedom and media democracy.

This case study will be illustrated as part of broader historical trends in Canada, including the Davey Committee and the Kent Commission of 1970 and 1980, respectively, which were concerned with media ownership concentration, specifically within the newspaper industry. Debates over media concentration, particularly that of cross-media ownership and convergence strategies in Canada, have continued with the Canadian Heritage Standing Committee on Broadcasting and an ongoing Senate Committee on Transport and Communications.

These debates have animated the Canadian public, which has expressed, in polls and public forums, dissatisfaction with the current levels of media concentration, and a concomitant call for widespread public debate and policy on media concentration and convergence, including suggestions for initiation of a government inquiry into media cross-ownership.

MILLS GETS SACKED

Mary Lou Finlay: Ms. Howard, how many people were there at your protest last night?
Karin Howard: Well, the estimates were from 200 to 500. I didn't take time to count. But frankly, they were solid, respectable, concerned, and committed and you know, to me that's what's important.
MLF: Who were they—were they other journalists?
KH: A few came out of the *Citizen* building—bravely—but mostly people who were available on short notice, because there wasn't much notice about this. It was basically announced on CFRA radio, and you know, 45 minutes notice for a rally in a town that takes half an hour to drive anywhere . . . we think it was a great turnout . . .[1]

Karin Howard, a former attorney and local politician, now an importer and retailer of antique Chinese furniture, also a wife, mother, and concerned Ottawa citizen, heard about the firing of *Ottawa Citizen* publisher Russell Mills on local radio and decided she had to do something. In the space of a few short hours, she organized a demonstration outside the *Citizen* building to protest what she and many others considered to be a blow to democracy, justice, and freedom of speech.

MLF: Did you come out primarily in support of Russell Mills himself, or because of what his firing says itself about editorial freedom in the country?
KH: Personally for me, the big issue is the freedoms that are related to the muzzling of the press. So, I think for the group, however, the issues were intertwined, because he's basically a local hero, he's done good, he's everywhere when he's needed . . . for charities . . . he truly cares about the community.[2]

In June 2002, Mills was fired from the *Ottawa Citizen* by David Asper, chairman of CanWest Global Corporation's publications committee, for failing to seek approval of the publication of an editorial that called for the resignation of then prime minister Chrétien over his role in "Shawinigate," a controversy over whether or not Chrétien lied about selling his shares in a golf club before he became prime minister. According to Mills himself, CanWest "offered me a financial settlement that was only available if I would portray my departure as a retirement and sign an agreement not to discuss the situation. I refused. I said that I had not spent 30 years in journalism attempting to pursue the truth in order to leave on a lie."[3]

The public furor over Mills's firing was remarkably swift, vociferous, and widespread. Howard's demonstration coalesced into a coalition of local citizens, the Ottawa City Council unanimously passed a motion demanding Mills's reinstatement as publisher, and, within forty-eight hours, over 500 *Citizen* readers had cancelled their subscriptions. The issue dominated parliamentary debate, with questions about the relationship between the prime minister and the Asper family that owned CanWest. Said former New Democratic Party leader Alexa McDonough: "Russell Mills was fired because the Prime Minister's buddy [CanWest founder Israel Asper] happened to be his boss . . . that is downright dangerous to democracy. We need a full public inquiry into media concentration, ownership and convergence."[4]

These allegations were dismissed by CanWest president Leonard Asper, who asserted that Mills was fired for violating a "'basic principle of diversity' in the paper . . . 'there was too much homogeneity in coverage of events in Ottawa.'"[5] Furthermore, Asper argued, running the editorial critical of Chrétien violated "a company 'code of conduct'" that required all local editorials to be vetted by CanWest's Winnipeg head office prior to publication.

The media storm—e.g., CBC Radio host Michael Enright hosted a live, town-hall forum on the issue in Ottawa—galvanized the journalistic community.[6] Journalists decried the action and publicly voiced concerns about their own fears of reprisal and possible chill. As many commented, Russell Mills was a corporate player, and if someone like Mills could be fired, then every journalist should be worried. Said *Toronto Sun* columnist Greg Weston, Mills "spent most of his career playing what one of his former editors aptly described as the perfect corporate bureaucrat, deftly surviving changes in newspaper ownership from the Southam family to Conrad Black to the Asper clan."[7] Christie Blatchford of the *National Post* echoed this sentiment: "[I]f the amiable likes of Mr. Mills can so annoy Israel Asper and the CanWest media group that he is fired, who indeed is safe?"[8] In an editorial, the *Globe and Mail* wrote:

> In writing this, we are conscious of being CanWest's competitor, and our views may be considered in that light. But as journalists, we are alarmed at the ease with which the Aspers are brushing aside the editorial independence of their individual newspapers. And as believers in freedom of the press, we worry that CanWest's trampling of its editorial vineyards will spark yet another attempt to have the federal government become the guarantor of a free press.[9]

Within the first week of the furor, it was reported that more than 5,000 *Citizen* readers had cancelled their subscriptions.[10] International coverage of the incident was also scathing, with the International Press Institute, a global network of media editors, journalists, and executives, calling the Mills incident "an attack on press freedom by an unholy coalition between politics and big business."[11]

But the Mills firing was only the latest manifestation of CanWest's insistence on asserting centralized, corporate, and heavy-handed control over its newly acquired daily newspaper operations. That control was first signaled by the company's December 2001 announcement that it was directing each of its dailies to publish "national editorials" three times a week—regardless of whether local publishers agreed with their positions—and was reinforced by the company's disciplining of employees who dared to criticize head-office decisions. These newspapers had previously enjoyed a longstanding policy of editorial independence under the ownership of Southam Inc.

Former Southam editors and directors, in fact, published a one-page declaration in the *Globe and Mail*, paid for by descendents of Southam's founder William Southam, under the organization Diversity of Voices. Titled "Is Freedom of the Press Being Lost, One Newsroom at a Time?" the declaration emphasized the crucial role of publishers and editors in understanding and bringing into focus community concerns and diverse opinions and voices. Diversity of Voices called for CanWest to review its editorial policy, for citizens, press councils, universities and colleges to debate and share publicly their concerns, and for policymakers to consider strategies to encourage independent newsrooms, such as tax incentives for media corporations that meet such objective criteria.[12] Six months later, CanWest dropped the name of Southam Newspaper Group and renamed it CanWest Publications. Said chairman Izzy Asper: "We couldn't find any reason to keep the name and we wanted to put our stamp on the company."[13]

Newspaper unions reacted predictably, with many of their arguments reiterating concerns over the imposition of national editorials by CanWest management. *Halifax Daily News* columnist Stephen Kimber resigned in protest after his opinion piece criticizing CanWest and its recent editorial policy was pulled. *Montreal Gazette* reporters drew attention to the national editorials by removing their bylines and creating a Web site to contest the national editorial policy.[14] The site was subsequently ordered shut down by *Gazette* management, who threatened to dismiss employees who continued to criticize CanWest, but the site was quickly reestablished by the Professional Federation of Quebec Journalists.[15] *Gazette* journalists assumed a leadership role in the criticism of CanWest in large part because the *Gazette* is the only English-language daily in Montreal. As Gasher comments, "While not all Montreal anglophones are happy with this, readers nonetheless depend on the *Gazette* to offer an anglophone perspective on current events. *Gazette* editorials, columns and op-ed articles have a particularly important role to play in this regard, something *Gazette* journalists clearly comprehend and which explains their commitment to local editorial independence."[16] Presciently, Michael Goldbloom had resigned as publisher of the *Gazette* a few months before CanWest's announcement, telling his staff that "CanWest has a more centralized approach to its management, and there are some aspects of the operations where we have had different perspectives." Some cited the "different perspectives" as coverage of the Middle East.[17]

The national editorial policy escalated an international debate within the media about the concentration of media ownership in Canada, corporate censorship, and journalistic autonomy.[18] The concern over national editorials was expressed well by John Miller, a professor of journalism at Toronto's Ryerson University, who argued that a sustainable democracy must include a free press that is host to a diversity of opinions, representative of regional sensitivities, and upholds the right to freedom of expression.[19] Some CanWest columnists either quit the chain or revealed that some of their columns were pulled because of the views they expressed. Doug Cuthand, an Aboriginal columnist with the *Saskatoon Star-Phoenix*, wrote an opinion piece comparing the treatment of Native Canadians and Palestines. The column was pulled and Cuthand resigned.[20] Conservative columnist Peter Worthington had his column criticizing CanWest's editorial policies dropped from the *Windsor Star*.[21]

Critics contend that the CanWest case exemplifies the danger of such intense corporate concentration of the media, particularly related to journalistic freedom and integrity. The International Federation of Journalists (the largest journalists group, comprising 500,000 members in 106 countries) lent support to its Canadian affiliate TNG Canada-CWA in its campaign, writing that "corporate control of editorial policy proves how dangerous concentration of ownership is to media pluralism."[22] The Newspaper Guild/CWA called on CanWest to uphold principles of journalistic integrity through "The Public Trust," signed by 200 delegates representing more than 36,000 newspaper and other media workers across North America:

THE PUBLIC TRUST

An informed citizenry is the cornerstone of a democratic society. Recognizing this, the 2002 Sector Conference of The Newspaper Guild-CWA calls on Can-West Global Communications Corp., the largest player in the Canadian media industry, to formally and fully commit itself to the following principles:

That each newspaper within its chain of holdings retain full autonomy in the choice and formulation of its editorial opinions, specifically those expressed on its editorial pages;

That columnists at all newspapers within that chain retain the freedom to express their opinions fully and without prior restraint, especially by CanWest Global's corporate headquarters. Editing of columns should take place within the newspaper of origin, and be limited to issues of factual accuracy, grammar and style—not the opinions that a columnist puts forward;

That the appropriate editors at each newspaper rely on their news judgment in making story and photo assignments, story and photo selections, and relative placement of layout elements, not on the dictates of CanWest Global;

That the primary and overriding responsibility of any journalist, and of any journalistic enterprise, is to the reader, listener or viewer. All have a right to full and accurate reporting of news within their community, country and world and to a range of viewpoints that will stimulate—not stifle—the healthy debate that is the foundation of democratic choice.

The rigorous adherence to these principles by both journalists and management is not only a public trust, but a precondition for the credibility that is any media outlet's core asset and the only reliable foundation for its financial success.[23]

For its part, CanWest argued that its promotion of national editorials was only meant to spark national debate on salient issues, and that the policy "in no way limits others from expressing contrary views in our papers."[24] In an annual shareholder meeting, Izzy Asper, when challenged on its editorial policy inhibiting the notion of a free press, declared that "as publishers-in-chief, we are responsible for every word which appears in the papers we own, and therefore, on national and international key issues we should have one, not 14, editorial positions."[25] At the time of writing, CanWest has revamped its policy, announcing that it will print only one national editorial per week.[26]

Critics were not appeased. Commenting on the rationale given by the Aspers for the national editorials, Michael Cobden, a former *Toronto Star* editorial writer and the Maclean Hunter Professor of Journalism at King's College in Halifax, wrote that its "purpose is to justify the company's shuddering ambitions to make millions of Canadians across the country see the world as Israel Asper and his sons see it. That's why people are worried."[27]

With the January 2003 CanWest announcement of the creation of a centralized news desk in Winnipeg, featuring an Internet-based editorial calendar, more concerns over journalistic autonomy and employee layoffs were raised. And, the resignation of journalist Patricia Pearson of the CanWest-owned *National Post* made many Canadians even more worried. According to Pearson, under Asper rule she began to exercise self-censorship to stifle her liberal sensibilities. With the Iraq war and the *Post*'s pro-war sentiments, Pearson, a self-acknowledged Canadian nationalist, found the hawkish editorials and biased coverage intolerable:

I cannot sit back and watch this nation attacked, relentlessly and viciously, by a newspaper that would trash so much of what we believe in, from tolerant social values to international law, belittling us for having our beliefs, while turning around and saying that what makes America great is Americans' ardor in defending their beliefs.[28]

A year later, another controversy erupted when CBC News reported that CanWest's *National Post* and other newspapers were inappropriately inserting the word "terrorist" into Reuters and Associated Press news copy on the Middle East, particularly on stories about the Iraq war and the Israeli-Palestinian conflict. The *Ottawa Citizen* admitted that its editors had inserted "terrorist" seven times into an AP story about the conflict in Fallujah, the site of intense Iraqi insurgent conflict. Editor Scott Anderson admitted that Fallujah insurgents were not terrorists, but that CanWest policy was to rename some groups as terrorists.[29] Its internal style guide suggests that CanWest journalists should consult the Canadian government's official list of terrorist organizations before adopting the term, but because "violent sub-national groups appear and reappear all the time with new names," some flexibility in usage is warranted. This raised the ire of the National Council on Canada-Arab Relations and the Canadian Arab Foundation, who called for an investigation on biased reporting in CanWest.[30]

THE ASCENT OF THE ASPERS

CanWest Global Corporation is owned by the Asper family of Winnipeg. Father Israel ("Izzy"), who died in 2003, was the leader of the Manitoba Liberal party for five years in the 1970s when he also established CanWest Capital Corporation, receiving a broadcast license for independent television station CKND. In 1974, Asper rescued Toronto-based Global Television Network, setting up the cornerstone for the Global Television system. Over the next ten years, Asper acquired Western regional television stations, and in 1989 the remaining interest in Global. Their first forays into international acquisitions began with a 20 percent interest in New Zealand's TV3, followed by a 57.5 percent interest in Australia's Network Ten, expansion in the UK through an interest in Talk Radio UK Network, further acquisitions in Australia, and later an agreement with an Irish consortium for the first private sector national television service, TV3. In the 1990s, Global expanded into the Ontario market via the licensing of five rebroadcasters. The CRTC approved CanWest's licensing of new cable network Prime TV in 1996, and an English Quebec-wide network, Global Television Network (Quebec) in 1997.[31]

Besides the Global Television Network, CanWest is best known for CanWest Entertainment and CanWest Interactive. It also owns Canadian specialty television channels (Prime, MenTV, Mystery, DejaView, Lonestar, Fox Sports-World Canada, Extreme Sports). Broadcast holdings are international in scope, and other major holdings include the Canada.com Internet portal and the on-line magazine dose.ca.

In 2000, CanWest purchased from Hollinger Inc. the *National Post* and 135 other newspapers for $3.5 billion (Cdn), thus consolidating itself as one of the major media players in Canada. CanWest has the second-highest concentration of newspaper interests in the Western world (behind Rupert Murdoch's News Corporation). According to Canada's broadcast regulator, the Canadian Radio-Television and Telecommunications Commission (CRTC), CanWest's combined newspaper and TV reach is a potential 97.6 percent of English-speaking Canadians. Recent initiatives include the launching of a jazz radio station in Winnipeg, which, along with billboards and outdoor advertising, are key acquisition targets for the company's portfolio.[32] Leonard Asper has stated that one of their next goals is to penetrate the U.S. market.[33]

In the 1990s, control of CanWest Global passed to Asper's children, with Leonard serving as president and chief executive officer. CanWest's Asper Foundation and Global Foundation reflect the personal ideologies of the Aspers (staunch Liberal supporters and pro-Israel), with a strong commitment to supporting Winnipeg projects, including the Asper Jewish Community Campus, the Aspercenter for Entrepreneurship at the University of Manitoba, CanWest Global Center for Performing Arts, and the I.H. Asper Clinical Research Center at the St. Boniface Hospital. They have also supported various cultural events and institutions and millions have been donated to Canadian universities and colleges, including a $1-million (Cdn) gift to McMaster University for the creation of the Global Television Network chair in communications.[34]

CanWest is illustrative of trends in vertical integration, wherein a firm in one industry acquires a subsidiary in another stage of the same industry. This is exemplified through CanWest's acquisition of Mobile Video Production Inc., a firm that provides mobile production facilities for sporting, entertainment, and news events. CanWest also represents cross-media ownership trends, wherein a firm in one media industry acquires a firm from another industry—illustrated by CanWest's acquisition of newspapers. But, as will be discussed below, the convergence strategies of the large Canadian media behemoths, including CanWest's, have neither been lucrative nor popular with consumers.

NEWSPAPER CONCENTRATION IN CANADA: THIRTY YEARS OF THE SAME DEBATE

The Asper case raises many ethical issues and questions. CanWest exemplifies both the dangers of media concentration, wherein a few powerful corporations control the majority of the media fare the public receives, and of media convergence, which calls for content-sharing across distinct media owned by one company operating in the same community. Media concentration and convergence, rather than expanding the media fare the public receives, restrict the access available to diverse voices. This is particularly significant when it comes to community and regional news and viewpoints, as the autonomy of local community content vanishes. Centralization of media content, as in the policy of national editorials, diminishes local perspectives. Editorial freedom becomes a contentious issue: will journalists be pressured to comply with the views of their owners? For instance, because the Aspers are avowedly pro-Israel, does this mean that editorials can't be printed which support the perspective of Palestinians, or which are perceived to be critical of Israel?[35]

Journalistic integrity and the rights of journalists can also be severely curtailed and censored, as the CanWest case illustrates. The role of newspapers as a public trust, reflecting the news and views of a diverse and often fractious public, has been significantly weakened under the Asper thumb.

Take away the names of CanWest Global Corporation and the Aspers, rewind thirty and then twenty years, and we find that the same issues were being debated in Canada as they are today. In 1969, the Special Senate Committee on Mass Media,[36] known as the Davey Committee, was mandated to look at the concentration of all media in Canada. Ten years later, the Kent Commission looked solely at the concentration of newspaper ownership.[37] As discussed in chapter 3, these serve as useful and interesting historical reference points for present-day debates on media concentration.[38]

Twenty years after the commission, Tom Kent, responding to the Standing Committee on Canadian Heritage, urged the government to reconsider the granting of broadcast licenses to newspaper owners, through directive to the CRTC. Newspapers, Kent said, "have abandoned their previously cherished independence from government. Their owners have made themselves financially beholden to politicians."[39]

CONVERGENCE: IN THE PUBLIC INTEREST?

A newspaper is worth more as a business the less its proprietor is concerned with serving the public interest by comprehensive, accurate, fair reporting of the news. Profit can be maximized by cutting editorial costs to a minimal level. Newspapers can then be milked for most attractive cash flows with which to build expanding business empires.[40]

Tom Kent was referring to the fortunes of the Thomson Corporation in the early 1980s, and its forays into North Sea oil, international media holdings, and retail acquisitions. But, twenty years later, he could easily have been referring to the Aspers. It wasn't called convergence then, but as many noted,[41] media firms began to be part of the corporate mergers and acquisitions frenzy, with holdings running the gamut from an extension of media properties to entirely unrelated holdings.

Convergence is a touted yet nebulous strategy by the major media players, heavily promoted in the 1990s, wherein the ownership of cross-media platforms and assets, particularly with the integration of digital technologies, aims to produce both vertical and horizontally integrated conglomerates. Convergence was promoted as a way for consumers to reap the benefits of "one-stop" shopping; media behemoths would be providers of information and entertainment, content and distribution, telephone and cable, subscriptions and advertisements. Fueled by the domestic growth of Internet services, particularly the deployment of broadband services in Canada, convergence, as Ellis described it, "is the artful combination of text, images and time-based media (sound and motion video) on a single digital platform, delivered for interactive use by consumers—typically via the Web."[42]

In Canada, some of the mergers that characterized convergence included Bell Globemedia, the result of a merger between Bell Canada (its phone company, Internet portal Sympatico-Lycos, satellite distributor Bell ExpressVu) and CTV (the Canadian Television Network, and the *Globe and Mail* newspaper); Rogers Communications (cable TV, cell phones, and radio stations) which bought Maclean Hunter Publishing, and Astral Media (specialty and pay-per-view TV, radio, outdoor advertising, and the Toronto Blue Jays baseball team); Shaw Communications (cable and the satellite company Star Choice TV) which bought cable TV owner Moffat Communication, now dominating Western Canada; and Quebecor (a newspaper and printing group) which purchased Sun Media (newspapers), TVA (French-language television network), and Videotron (cable TV, Internet services).

CanWest Global Communications, through its acquisition of Global TV, the television properties of Western International Communications, Southam newspapers, Hollinger's Canadian Internet properties, and the *National Post*, has become one of the largest media corporations in Canada. Its ascent was not without concern. In 2001, when the CRTC renewed Global's television licenses, it issued a strong statement regarding cross-ownership issues and concerns over journalistic practices:

The Commission considers that Global's position in newspapers and television raises concerns related to cross-media ownership in the markets that it serves, and that safeguards are required. Specifically, the Commission considers that Global must, as a minimum, maintain news management for its television stations that is separate from news management of the newspapers affiliated to Global. The Commission has therefore set out, in Appendix 1 to this document, a *Statement of Principles and Practices* that it is imposing on Global as a condition of license. The Commission will monitor developments with respect to news and information programming over the upcoming license term to determine if other action is necessary.[43]

The *Statement of Principles and Practices* required CanWest to maintain both separate and independent news management and presentation structures for Global television operations and "any Global affiliated newspaper."[44] Separation of news management functions was mandated, but not newsgathering activities; thus, cross-promotion and "some cooperation" between the television stations and newspapers is permissible.

In its defense, CanWest argued that collaboration between its newspapers and television stations would be in the public interest because it could potentially increase the quality, variety, and depth of news coverage, as well as realize cost savings. In media parlance this is "synergy"—a rationale for media firms to acquire more holdings because business dictates keeping a competitive edge, and, according to media executives, consumers themselves demand more integrated content.

However, in the wake of recent economic downturns in the telecommunications and Internet sectors, many Canadian companies have found their convergence strategies to be less lucrative than originally anticipated. With television ratings sinking and stale newspaper circulation, many media companies are selling their holdings to reduce debt. In order to alleviate the debt that accrued with its purchase of the Southam chain of newspapers and the *National Post*, CanWest has cut jobs, several sections of the *National Post*, and reduced bulk sales. In January 2003, CanWest sold four dailies in southern Ontario ("non-strategic assets") to Osprey Media as part of a $193.5-million (Cdn) cash deal.[45] In May 2003, Murdoch Davis, CanWest's vice president responsible for the national editorials, resigned, while *Montreal Gazette* employees were encouraged to take voluntary buy-outs.[46]

In an interview with a trade publication, Leonard Asper described their convergence strategy as creating "better content, better news product, better information programming, even better entertainment programming" from the acquisition and generation of multimedia content and integration, and in penetrating the U.S. market.[47] According to Asper, "no content is thrown out . . . All of our content will be kept stored, repurposed, and will be generating new revenue streams for no cost."[48] But, in 2001, when asked by a reporter for a definition of convergence, he quipped "it's kind of like pornography. You know it when you see it."[49]

CONCLUSION: WHITHER THE PUBLIC TRUST?

Since the Kent Commission, Canadians have consistently voiced concern about media concentration. In reviewing media concentration issues following Conrad Black's acquisitions for Hollinger Inc. in the 1990s, the Council of Canadians recommended limiting and reversing ownership concentration. The council specifically recommended that the total number of daily newspapers, radio and TV stations owned by one company in any market should not exceed 50 percent, and that no one company or individual should directly or indirectly control more than 25 percent of the circulation of daily newspapers in Canada.[50]

Days after Russell Mills was fired by the Aspers, the Communications, Energy and Paperworkers Union of Canada conducted a survey to determine the opinion of the Canadian public about media concentration. Overwhelmingly, respondents expressed concerns. When asked if media owners exercise too much control over the content of news and opinion in Canadian newspapers, radio and television stations, the majority of respondents said yes. A large majority also responded that media owners should not limit freedom of speech in what their journalists are reporting or commenting on in news and current events, and that legal protection should be accorded to journalists to cover news as they see fit. When asked if there is too much concentration of media ownership in Canada, 48.5 percent strongly agreed, and 25.6 percent responded they somewhat agreed. Further, 34.6 percent strongly agreed that media concentration is a serious problem and the Canadian government should do something, while another 31.7 percent somewhat agreed. Given the statement: "Freedom of expression in media is a cornerstone of Canadian democracy. However, a small number of companies owning too large a part of Canada's newspapers, radio, and television stations, has undermined freedom of expression in the Canadian media," 42.2 percent of respondents strongly agreed and 32.5 percent somewhat agreed.[51]

In June 2003, the Canadian Heritage Standing Committee on Broadcasting released its report. The mandate of the Standing Committee was to provide an in-depth study of the Canadian broadcasting system in meeting the objectives of the Broadcasting Act of 1991, paying particular attention to cultural diversity, technological developments, globalization of media and information, and new trends in convergence and conglomeration. Commenting on the concerns of cross-media ownership, the committee acknowledged the intense concentration of ownership since 2000, and created four specific recommendations to ensure citizen access to a plurality of viewpoints, without jeopardizing the financial stability of Canadian media industries.

Addressing the issue of corporate concentration in the media industries, specifically related to broadcasters, the committee wrote, "while the Committee recognizes that size does matter in terms of achieving economies of scale and that Canadian broadcasters need the capacity to compete against giant foreign conglomerates, it sees journalistic independence as being critical to the health and safeguarding of our democratic system."[52]

RECOMMENDATION 11.1:

The Committee recommends that the CRTC be directed to strengthen its policies on the separation of newsroom activities in cross-media ownership situations to ensure that editorial independence is upheld.

RECOMMENDATION 11.2:

The Committee recommends that the CRTC put in place a mechanism to ensure the editorial independence of broadcasting operations. A report to Parliament should be made by an appropriate authority (e.g., the Canadian broadcasting monitor) on an annual basis.

Cross-media ownership issues are potentially so vexatious, the Standing Committee wrote that "the time has come for the federal government to issue a clear and unequivocal policy on this matter before 30 June 2004."[53] Until that time, Recommendation 11.4 urges the CRTC to "postpone all decisions concerning the awarding of new broadcast licenses in cases where cross-media ownership is involved" and to extend automatically all existing license renewals "for a minimum of two years and a maximum of three years."

The Senate Committee on Transport and Communications is currently conducting an investigation into the future of media in Canada. The first phase of its work includes hearings from media experts—practitioners, academics, and researchers. Reprising his role twenty years ago, Tom Kent was the first witness to address the committee. Calling for a ban on broadcast licenses for companies that also own newspapers, Kent reiterated the need for government action: "The growing complexity of our society isn't a reason for a more concentrated, one-size-fits-all media . . . on the contrary, it makes the old principles of liberty and freedom of information and diversity of discussion more essential than ever."[54]

When queried about potential ethical issues owing to media concentration, the Aspers have tended to respond glibly. In his submission to the House of Commons Standing Committee on Canadian Heritage, Leonard Asper argued that media concentration was not an issue: "Canadian media are more fragmented and less concentrated than ever before . . . I submit that people who believe otherwise are not looking at the facts and they also probably believe Elvis is still alive."[55] Asper argued that the proliferation of specialty channels, satellite services, and other digital media offerings have led to a dilution of ownership within the Canadian media, despite cross-media ownership trends. Asper further reiterated his company's pleas for more government funding for the production of Canadian films and television programs, and for a diminution of support for the Canadian Broadcasting Corporation; the CBC, he said, is "unfairly competing with private broadcasters" and should cease news production because the public broadcaster is not meeting Canadian needs.[56]

Elvis may be dead, but there are thousands of Elvis impersonators and a veritable industry of Elvis impersonator agencies. The King thus lives on, in sequined verisimilitudes and hip-thrusting gyrations. As with media convergence and concentration, the Aspers would have us think that the public interest is being met by the creation of new, unbridled cross-platform content.

But as CanWest has demonstrated, through its control of editorial content and its attitude toward journalists, this is a chimera. Media convergence and concentration have eroded the ideal of a newspaper as a "distinctly local enterprise."[57] Indeed, many international mega-media corporations, such as Rupert Murdoch's News Corporation, have shifted the concept back to journalism as a partisan business, and they have been aided in this endeavor by the neoliberal and deregulatory nature of institutions such as the Federal Communications Commission under Michael Powell. But, as in Canada, the FCC's June 2003 ruling on media ownership policy reexamination has not been without contentious public debate and congressional rancor.[58]

The Canadian public has reacted, calling the Aspers' actions an affront to democracy in a free society. Supporters of the Aspers argue that the newspaper industry is a business, and that owners can decree whatever they want. But given the quarrels and discords expressed by the Canadian public, in public forums, media, and in demonstrations, if newspapers are meant to embody the public trust, then the Aspers have broken that trust.

Thanks to Pierre Belanger for his comments on an earlier version of this chapter.

NOTES

1. CBC Radio transcript, As It Happens, 19 June 2002, <www.cbc.ca/stories/2002/06/18/citizen.reac02061>
2. As It Happens, 19 June 2002.
3. Russell Mills, "Under the Asper thumb," *Globe and Mail* (June 19, 2002): A15.
4. Shawn McCarthy and Jeff Sallot, "Publisher's Firing Sets Off Storm," *Globe and Mail* (June 18, 2002). <http://friendscb.ca/articles/GlobeandMail/globe020618-2.htm>
5. McCarthy and Sallot, "Publisher's Firing Sets Off Storm."
6. David McKie, "First word: What Were They Thinking?" *Media Magazine* (Summer 2002). <http://www.caj.ca/mediamag/summer2002/firstword.html>
7. Greg Weston, "Freezing the Free Press; the Firing of Russell Mills Will Make Any Journalist Covering Politics Think Twice before Printing the Truth—It's an Incredible Opportunity for the PM," *Toronto Sun* (June 20, 2002). <http://www.montrealnewspaperguild.com/canwestlinks.htm>
8. Christie Blatchford, "The Curious Trust We Share with Readers," *National Post* (June 20, 2002). <http://www.montrealnewspaperguild.com/canwestlinks.htm>
9. "Let's Press for Press Freedom," *Globe and Mail* (April 19, 2002): A13. [editorial]
10. Newspaper Guild of Canada, "Citizen Asper: Publisher, Fired for Editorial, Fires Back with Libel Lawsuit." (July 12, 2002) <http://www.newsguild.org/gr/gr_display.php?storyID=849>
11. International Press Institute, "IPI Condemns Firing of Canadian Publisher." (June 18, 2002).<http://www.orbicom.uqam.ca/in_focus/news/archives/2002_juin/2002_juin_18_b.html>
12. Diversity of Voices, "Is Freedom of the Press Being Lost, One Newsroom at a Time?" *Globe and Mail* (June 6, 2002): A7. [advertisement for www.DiversityOfVoices.ca]
13. "CanWest Is Dropping the Historic Name of Its Southam Newspapers Group, Founded by the Southam Family 126 Years Ago and Purchased by CanWest from Hollinger Inc. Three Years Ago," *Canadian-Press-Newswire*, 28 January 2003.
14. T. T. Ha, "Sparks Fly in Quebec over Changes at Gazette," *Globe and Mail* (December 21, 2001): A7.

15. See <http://www.fpjq.org/canwest>.

16. Mike Gasher, "Point of View: Does CanWest Know What All the Fuss Is About?" *Media Magazine* (Winter 2002). <http://www.caj.ca/mediamag/winter2002/pov.html>

17. Gasher, "Point of View," 6.

18. T. Grant, "Media Spat: Profit vs. Free Speech," *Christian Science Monitor* (February 15, 2002). <http://www.csmonitor.com/2002/0215/p06s01-woam.htm>

19. John Miller, "Do Editorials Matter?" *Straight Goods* (17 February 2002), <http://www.straightgoods.ca/ViewFeature.cfm?REF=264>

20. Ha, "Sparks Fly,"14.

21. DeNeen L. Brown, "Journalists Feel Shackled by New Owner," *International Herald Tribune*, (31 January 2002). <http://www.iht.com/articles/46496.html>

22. International Federation of Journalists, "Corporate Control of Editorial Policy in Canada Threatens Press Freedom Says IFJ" (20 December 2001). [Press release]. <http://www.ifj.org/publications/press/pr/281.html>

23. Newspaper Guild of Canada, "The Newspaper Guild Calls on CanWest Global to Change Policies in Name of Public Trust", (20 February 2002). [press release]. <http://www.montreal newspaperguild.com/News/pr-feb202002.htm>

24. B Schecter, "Editorial Policy 'Mischaracterized,'" *National Post* (31 January 2002). <http://www.nationalpost.com/home/story.html?f=/stories/20020131/1294510.html>

25. Peter Kennedy, "Asper Blasts Critics of Editorial Policy," *Globe and Mail* (31 January 2002): A6.

26. Keith Damsell, "CanWest Scales Back Policy," *Globe and Mail* (12 February 2002): B8.

27. Michael Cobden, "The Danger of CanWest's National Editorials," *Globe and Mail* (30 January 2002): B15.

28. See Keith Damsell, "CanWest Set to Launch News Hub," *Globe and Mail* (20 January 20 2003) and Patricia Pearson, "See no evil, no more," *Globe and Mail* (19. April 2003: A19).

29. "Newspaper accused of misusing the term terrorist", *CBC News* (17 September 2004). <http://www.friends.ca/News/Friends_News/archives/articles09170401.asp>

30. See James Adams, "CanWest Editing Questioned," *Globe and Mail* (18 September 2004). <http://www.yourmedia.ca/modules/canwest/040918_gm_cwg-terrorist.html>

31. See CanWest Global Communication Corporation Homepage at <http://www.canwest global.com/> and "CanWest Global Milestones." *Broadcaster* 62(1), January 2003.

32. Keith Damsell, "CanWest Wins License to Launch Jazz Radio," *Globe and Mail*. (August 9, 2002). URL: <http://www.friendscb.org/articles/GlobeandMail/globe020809.htm>

33. "Taking It to the Next Level: Leonard Asper Reveals His Convergence Strategy." *Broadcaster* 62(1) (January 2003).

34. "Making a Difference: Giving Back to the Community Remains a Top Priority at CanWest." *Broadcaster* 62(1) (January 2003).

35. According to *Montreal Gazette* investigative reporter Bill Marsden, "They do not want to see any criticism of Israel. We do not run in our newspaper op-ed pieces that express criticism of Israel and what it is doing in the Middle East. We even had an incident where a fellow, a professor wrote an op-ed piece for us criticising the anti-terrorism law and elements of civil rights. Now that professor happens to be a Muslim and happens to have an Arab name. We got a call from headquarters demanding to know why we had printed this." See Gully Craig, "Corporate censorship: CanWest muzzles staff", *Index on Censorship*. (18 April 2002). URL: <http://www.indexonline.org/news/20020418_Canada.shtml> And, journalist Robert Fisk has another journalist to raise critical questions about the Asper's pro-Israeli slant. He took to task an editorial by Izzy Asper, published in the *National Post*, where he accused his own journalists of being "lazy, sloppy or stupid" in their coverage of Israel, and of being "biased or anti-Semitic". See Robert Fisk, "Journalists are under fire for telling the truth," *The Independent*, 18 December 2002, <http://argument.independent.co.uk/low_res/story.jsp?story=362545&host=6&dir=140>

36. Canada, Special Senate Committee on Mass Media [Davey Committee]. *Uncertain Mirror: Report of the Special Senate Committee on Mass Media. Vol. 1* (Ottawa: Queen's Printer, 1970).

37. Canada, Royal Commission on Newspapers [Kent Commission]. *Report* (Ottawa: Supply and Services Canada, 1981).

38. Marie-Hélène Lavoie and Chris Dornan, under the direction of Florian Sauvageau, Center d'études sur les medias. *Concentration of newspaper ownership: An 'old' and still unresolved problem*. Ottawa: Department of Canadian Heritage, 2001. <http://www.pch.gc.ca/progs/ac-ca/progs/esm-ms/prob1_e.cfm>

39. Tom Kent, "Concentration with Convergence—Goodbye, Freedom of the Press," *Policy Options/Options Politiques* (October 2002): 26–28.

40. Tom Kent, "The Times and Significance of the Kent Commission," in *Seeing Ourselves: Media Power and Policy in Canada*, edited by H. Holmes and D. Taras (Toronto: Harcourt Brace Jovanovich Canada Inc, 1992), 21–39.

41. Ben H. Bagdikian, *The Media Monopoly*. Boston: Beacon, 1983. (Subsequent editions were published in 1987, 1990, 1992, and 1997).

42. John Ellis, "Why the Pirates Will Win: Television May Hurt, Rather than Help, the New Media Moguls as They Work to Make Convergence a Reality." *Marketing* 106(8) (February 26, 2001): 25.

43. Canadian Radio-Television and Telecommunications Commission. Decision CRTC 2001-458. Ottawa (2 August 2001). Licence renewals for the television stations controlled by Global. <http://www.crtc.gc.ca/archive/ENG/Decisions/2001/DB2001-458.htm>

44. Decision CRTC 2001-458, 122.

45. "CanWest Selling Ontario Newspapers to Osprey Media." *CBC News*, 27 January 2003. <http://www.cbc.ca/stories/2003/01/27/canwest_030127>

46. "Davis Leaves CanWest Global." *CNews Media News*. (16 May 2003). <http://cnews.canoe.ca/CNEWS/MediaNews/2003/05/16/89119-cp.html>

47. Adams, "CanWest Editing Questioned."

48. Richard Blackwell, "Asper Wants Martin to Back Foreign Control," *Globe and Mail* (14 November 2003).

49. R. Robin, "Mixed-up media: CanWest Is Hyping the Benefits of Convergence. Trouble Is, No One knows What It Actually Means," *Canadian Business* 74(19) (October 15, 2001): 65–66.

50. The Campaign for Press and Broadcasting Freedom, "Media Reform," 2003 and The Council of Canadians, Campaign for Press and Broadcasting Freedom. "Policies for a Democratic Media: Confronting the Problem of Media Ownership Concentration in Canada," Spring 1997.

51. See <www.cepmedia.ca/files/mediademocracy_e.html> and <http://www.presscampaign.org/news2.htm>.

52. Canadian Heritage Standing Committee. *Our Cultural Sovereignty: The Second Century of Canadian Broadcasting*. Ottawa: Canadian Government Publishing, 2003. <http://www.parl.gc.ca/InfoComDoc/37/2/HERI/Studies/Reports/herirp02-e.htm>, p. 14.

53. Canadian Heritage Standing Committee, *Our Cultural Sovereignty*, 411.

54. Joe Paraskevas, "Kent Takes Aim at Media Convergence: Senate Hearings Begin: Ex-commissioner's Views Dismissed as 'Old-Fashioned,'" *Financial-Post-National-Post* (30 April 2003): 4.

55. Krista Foss, "CanWest Presses Ottawa on Media Legislation," *Globe and Mail* (2 March 2002): B4.

56. Foss, "CanWest presses Ottawa on media legislation."

57. Catherine McKercher, *Newsworkers Unite: Labor, Convergence, and North American Newspapers* (Lanham, Md.: Rowman & Littlfield Publishers, Inc., 2002).

58. Stephen Labaton, "A Media Rule by the FCC Is in Jeopardy in the House," *New York Times* (23 July 2003). <http://query.nytimes.com/gst/abstract.html?res=F20A16FB3F5B0C708EDDAE0894DB404482>

6

Hyper-Commercialism and the Media: The Threat to Journalism and Democratic Discourse

Mark Cooper

Concern about the deterioration of journalism and its impact on democracy are perennial topics in the United States,[1] but the decibel level of debate at the turn of the century was off the charts. The din was caused by the intersection of two choruses: one made up of loud, name-calling conservative and liberal journalists butting heads over bias in the media,[2] the other made up of academic voices raising an alarm over escalating concentration of ownership and declining journalistic values.[3]

This chapter argues that the heightened concern is well justified. Reviewing the empirical evidence in the social science and professional literatures, it demonstrates that powerful forces of hyper-commercialism—namely, the interaction of commercialism, concentration, consolidation, and conglomeration—are undermining the ability of the print and broadcast news media to act as a fourth estate. We are in danger of losing, in the words of Downie and Kaiser, "independent, aggressive journalism [which] strengthens American democracy, improves the lives of its citizens, checks the abuses of powerful people, supports the weakest members of society," and, ultimately, "connects us all to one another."[4]

Many media critics across the political spectrum argue that the dictates of hyper-commercialism deeply affect political news reporting in ways that may be undermining the fabric of democratic discourse. With more television outlets needing to fill more space[5] and attract more viewers to be profitable, the media's schedule and perpetual news cycle become a force emphasizing speed, simplicity, and routinization.[6] But print journalism is not immune from these pressures as a growing series of scandals about erroneous and poorly sourced reporting have mounted.[7] Hyper-commercialism is pushing toward a "worrisome conclusion: that the citizens of television societies may be rapidly losing their faculties of political judgment as a result of . . . stage-managed, entertainment oriented presentation of events."[8]

The central purpose of this chapter is to describe the problems that the economic characteristics of mass media at the end of the twentieth century pose for media "performance." It considers the issues in the context of both print and television and includes a brief discussion of the Internet as well. The conclusion outlines the types of solutions that are needed.

OVERVIEW OF THE THREAT TO THE FOURTH ESTATE

Given the technologies and cost structure of commercial mass media in the twentieth century, pursuit of efficiency through economies of scale and scope has pushed media industries toward oligopoly or monopoly.[9] Such concentrated markets fail to meet the information needs of society in a number of ways.

Weak competition in media markets allows owners to pursue personal agendas and serve the interest of the parent corporation.[10] The influence is pervasive, affecting advertising, the selection and presentation of content, reporting, and editorial position.[11] The chilling effect need not be conscious or overt. Powerful media owners tend to be very visible figures in their political and policy preferences.[12] Employees and institutions instinctively toe the line and self-censor for the sake of self-preservation, dampening antagonism in the media.[13] The incongruous dynamic between editors (bottom-line) and reporters (integrity) tends to produce stories that are unbalanced.

The potential for abuse of influence grows as media markets become more concentrated and cross-media conglomerates control local media outlets.[14] These abuses range from favorable newspaper reviews of a broadcaster's programming to loss of coverage to positive editorials/opinion articles about the business interests of a broadcaster or politician.[15] Moreover, left unrestrained, the marketplace will produce fewer watchdog activities conducted by less rigorous institutions, making abuses less likely to be uncovered and more likely to occur because the deterrent of the threat of exposure will be diminished.[16]

Advertising as a determinant of demand reinforces the disconnect between what citizens need and what the market produces.[17] Because advertisers account for such a large share of mass media revenue, the market produces what advertisers want as much as, if not more than, what consumers want. The tendency to avoid controversy and seek a lowest common denominator is augmented by the preferences of advertisers.[18] Because advertising and the media revolve around influencing people's choices, there is a sense in which the industry creates its own demand.[19] As a result, the dictates of mass audiences create a largest market share/lowest common denominator ethic that undercuts the ability to deliver culturally diverse,[20] locally oriented,[21] and public interest content.[22]

Extensive econometric evidence confirms this "tyranny of the majority."[23] The tyranny of the majority in media markets is linked to the tyranny of the majority in politics because the media are the central means of political communication. As Waldfogel puts it, "Electoral competition leads candidates to propose policies that are supported by proportionately larger groups and that members of these groups are more likely to turn out if they find the proposed policies more appealing. In addition . . . candidates find it easier to direct campaign efforts at larger groups because many existing media outlets cater to this audience."[24]

Extensive evidence illustrates that the failure of commercial mass media to meet the needs of citizens is nowhere more evident than in minority communities.[25] These groups express strong preferences for specific types of programming or content or have needs that are different from larger aggregate audiences. With high fixed costs and strong group preferences, media owners must decide to whom to target their content. Given the profit maximizing incentive to recover the high costs from the larger audience, the minority audience is less well served.

Concentration of media ownership compounds the problem. Greater concentration results in less diversity of ownership,[26] and diversity of ownership—across geographic, ethnic, and gender lines—is correlated with diversity of programming. Simply, minority owners are more likely to present minority points of view[27] just as females are more likely to present female points of view[28] in the speakers, formats, and content they put forward.[29]

The important role of the media in informing citizens about local affairs is well documented,[30] but concentration of national and local markets into national chains reinforces the tendencies of media owners to ignore local needs.[31] The impact of this reduction of local coverage can be severe as the primary referent for identity and community has traditionally been, and remains, significantly local[32] and the coverage that disappears tends to deal with schools, localized government affairs, and other community-strengthening material.[33]

PRINT JOURNALISM

Commercialism

Over the past few decades large newspaper companies have shown a growing interest in profit-maximizing business practices. As Roberts et al. point out, "News has become secondary, even incidental, to markets and revenues and margins and advertisers and consumer preferences."[34] This is due, in part, to the makeup of the corporate boards that run newspaper companies, which "draw heavily from industry, finance and law for outside directors."[35] Without dedicated newspaper people involved in the highest level of management, the publicly traded newspaper becomes a stock market entity like any other and the product, news, becomes an expendable commodity that is "altered to fit tastes" and used to drive shareholder value up, without regard for journalistic integrity.[36]

A survey of CEOs of some of these companies found a common commitment to shareholders and stock value, not news and readers. William Burleigh of Scripps Howard points to a "suitable return" as his obligation, while Robert Jelenic of Journal Register Co. says his "mandate from the board is to produce longtime shareholder value."[37] The simple omission of news and readers as motivation speaks to how these papers are run, assembled and presented to the public—as money-making machines that subvert their "primary purpose of gathering and distributing news and opinion [in order] to serve the general welfare."[38] As Bartholomew Sparrow, quoting former journalist Harold Evans, writes, "The challenge before the American media 'is not to stay in business—it is to stay in journalism.'"[39]

Consider the contrast between journalistic values and the image presented by Tribune Company executives describing how the *Chicago Tribune* and Chicago television station WGN, among other media properties, view their business:

> Tribune had a story to tell—and it was just the story Wall Street wanted to hear. . . . It was a well-scripted, well-rehearsed performance, thorough and thoroughly upbeat. And the word 'journalism' was never uttered, once.
>
> The editor's gaze is fixed on the future, on new-zoned sections, multimedia desks, meetings with the business side, focus group research on extending the brand, or opening new beachheads in affluent suburbs. 'I am not the editor of a newspaper,' says Howard Tyner, 54, whose official resume identifies him as vice president and editor of the Chicago Tribune. 'I am the manager of a content company. That's what I do. I don't do newspapers alone. We gather content.'[40]

In addition to being one of the nation's largest newspaper owners, the Tribune Company is one of the largest owners of television stations.

Editors at papers big and small describe the stress caused by newspaper corporations bearing down on their news operations, enforcing a bottom-line principle, and, ultimately, infringing on their editorial role and the newspaper's output. Ninety percent of editors in one survey affirmed that they felt pressure from the bottom line, many adding that they felt "resignation" and "resentment" because of this pressure.[41] Geneva Overholser found that "ownership by public corporations has fundamentally and permanently transformed the role of editor," noting that of the seventy-seven editors surveyed, half said they spent a third or more of their time on "matters other than news."[42] *The News about the News* explains that editors who once "spent their days working with reporters . . . now spend more of their time in meetings with the paper's business-side executives, plotting marketing strategies or cost-cutting campaigns."[43]

In order to accomplish this, the corporations often hire analysts to determine how much of their newsroom staff and resources they can cut. At the *Winston-Salem Journal* in North Carolina, owned by Media General, consultants analyzed how efficiently the paper's staff was operating by having reporters keep "precise diaries on how they spent their time over three weeks. A 'grid' was created describing how much time various journalistic endeavors should take."[44] Based on the placement of a story within the paper, the analysis suggested how much time should be spent working the story (down to the tenth of an hour), whether or not a press release should be used, how many and which types of sources should be used and, of course, how long the story should be. It took three months for the editors to convince the owners that "creative work like journalism cannot be governed by such arbitrary formulas."[45] Nonetheless, Media General laid off 20 percent of its workforce by the time the consultation was completed.

Instances of staff cutting by corporate companies are common. When Gannett bought the *Asbury Park Press* (boosting its and Newhouse's combined share of New Jersey's circulation to a whopping 73 percent), it immediately liquidated one-quarter of the newsroom staff.[46] Next, the news hole was reduced, bleeding out niche local coverage that was vital to a highly subdivided area with many townships and districts. The *Press* had trained itself to adequately serve its varied readership, setting up localized bureaus and printing five zoned editions. Gannett swiftly dropped the *Press* to four zoned editions and in a final swipe at the newsroom staff, the chain increased workloads and took away overtime pay.

Putting circulation quality over circulation quantity is the other major tactic corporate papers use to cut costs and boost profits. This means that newspapers determine the value of a region with respect to its attractiveness to advertisers. Advertisers are not interested in pitching their products to economic and social groups they do not normally attract or who fall into unwanted demographics, so they put pressure on the papers to get their ads to the "right" people for the smallest price.

Another survey found that 90 percent of editors felt pressure from the bottom line, which subverts "their primary purpose of gathering and distributing news and opinion to serve the general welfare."[47] Corporate takeovers have also resulted in the 'softening' of news to appease advertisers who want buoyant, happy readers perusing their ads. Avoiding content that some advertisers find boring (mainly government, especially state and local government) or unlikely to give readers the zest they need to buy, has become commonplace.

The pressure on commercial mass media is to produce high volumes of "happy" or sensationalized news with the fewest number of reporters.[48]

Although the chain-owned newspapers may add content, in order to make room given shrunken budgets, other content has to be cut, and it almost always comes from hard news. This means that Gannett can easily and profitably remove hard-news reporters, load up on AP story releases, shrink hard-news story lengths, and add low-cost sections like "Whatever," a teen beat section, and "Critters," a pet section which includes pet obituaries that cost readers at least $50 and sometimes $300 (U.S.) to print.[49]

Papers remove hard news to add "reader-friendly" content, as Gannett calls it.[50] Their aforementioned *Asbury Park Press* reporters were told that "there will be no bad news in the 'Day in the Life' stories," and "no aggressive reporting or attempts to expose problems or wrongdoing." Former editor Mark Silverman criticized Gannett's *Courier-Journal* in Rockford, Illinois, for emphasizing "hard-news subjects" and suggested the paper consider "more how-to stories, stories that show how a person or a group of people accomplished something, question-and-answer columns, 'ask the experts' call-in hot lines, and even first-person stories by readers."

The chains do a significant amount of the cutting in the state government bureaus. In 1998, only 513 reporters nationwide were covering all state governments full-time.[51] Over 3,000 media credentials were issued for that year's Super Bowl.[52] The corporate departure from state government coverage has come with little or no regard for journalistic integrity or the benefits the public receives from this coverage. Bureaus at hundreds of papers across the country have been slashed.

While the phenomenon is most prevalent in smaller markets, it also afflicts some of the largest newspapers, including *USA Today*,[53] the *Washington Post*,[54] and the *New York Times*.[55] In order to maintain advertiser relationships, coverage is undermined.

Concentration and Consolidation

In *Taking Stock*, Cranberg, Bezanson, and Soloski argue that if any one thing is to blame for the deterioration of American newspapers it is the over-concentration of the marketplace.[56] Chains own 80 percent of America's newspapers and content-sharing has become pervasive.[57] The efforts of the large newspaper corporations to monopolize regions and their respective voices has led to a profit-driven business model that has deprioritized product quality and debilitated most news operations' ability to fully serve a free press.[58]

Many public companies have begun to seek advantages by grouping papers into dominant metropolitan and regional chains and then combining aspects of the news operations, sharing news among nominally separate papers.[59] This has an immediate impact on the local news consumer who is fed a generic dose of coverage that does not likely inform about what is going on in his neighborhood.

Examples can be found all over the country.[60] In Wisconsin, Gannett purchased Thomson's central holdings (eight dailies and six weeklies) to add to the two it already owned, effectively monopolizing the area. Thousands of subscribers lost their local coverage. CNHI bought eight Thomson dailies in Indiana, adding to the four it already owned. Gannett and CNHI now account for 40 percent of Indiana's daily circulation. In the Southeast, Knight Ridder shares content among three of its papers, the *Charlotte* (N.C.) *Observer*, the *State* (Columbia, S.C.) and the *Sun News* (Myrtle Beach, S.C.), which are at least one hundred miles away from each other and span two states. In Baltimore, Times Mirror Co. bought a chain of thirteen weeklies in the Baltimore suburbs even though it owns the *Baltimore Sun*. The purchase cut citizens' access to any competing dialogue being offered by the thirteen weeklies.

Family-operated papers are being swallowed up by corporate papers.[61] In Hartford, Times Mirror Co. bought the *Hartford Advocate*, a weekly created for the sole purpose of competing with the Times Mirror-owned *Hartford Courant*, the dominant daily.[62] In Montana, Lee Enterprises bought the *Hungry Horse Tribune* and the *Whitefish Pilot* and began running identical editorials as if the two communities had the same concerns.[63] In Westchester County, New York, Gannett combined ten papers it owned and created one, the *Journal News*, sacrificing successful, respected papers such as the *Tarrytown Daily News*.[64]

Underserving Commercially Unattractive Audiences

According to *Taking Stock*, "the practice of cutting circulation has increased in the past two decades, with papers halting circulation to areas where readers don't interest advertisers."[65] The lowest circulation penetration is found "in areas with high concentrations of both low-income and minority populations."[66] This leaves minority and low-income populations underserved by the press, with fewer opportunities to access the valuable daily news and entertainment with which people in higher "quality" socio-economic groups are supplied.

As Cranberg et al. go on to illustrate, "competition for socio-economically defined market segments increasingly takes the form of altering the subject matter and shape of news content, delivering the types and forms of information that persons in the socio-economically defined market prefer."[67] Not only are the chain papers not delivering papers to certain social groups, but they are slanting the news they do print to please the readers advertisers want pleased. Low-income and minority populations are doubly deserted.

The "deliberate industry strategy to pursue a more upscale readership" is shown by a survey of the ninety largest U.S. dailies:

> Interviews . . . made it evident that lower-income neighborhoods were being disadvantaged by such tactics as requiring payment in advance, refusing to deliver to public housing, door-to-door sales efforts only on days of the month when government checks were due, and denial of discounts. Combined with "aggressive pricing"—that is, charging more—the practices amount to writing off a whole class of potential readers.[68]

These tendencies are reinforced by a relative absence of minorities in newsrooms. Vanessa Williams weaves together the relationship between communities, journalists, news organizations, reporting, and democracy that I have highlighted throughout this analysis:

> News organizations' continued inability to integrate African-Americans and other journalists of color into their newsrooms and to more accurately and fairly represent racial and ethnic communities threatens the credibility and viability of daily general-circulation newspapers. How can a newspaper claim to be a journal of record for a given city or region if it routinely ignores or misrepresents large segments of the population in the geographic area it covers?
>
> Our greatest concern about the industry's failure to grasp the gravity of its diversity deficit should be the potential harm to society. Many Americans continue to operate out of misinformation and misunderstanding when it comes to perceptions and relationships between racial groups, between religious groups, between men and women, straight and gay people, young and old people, middle-class and working-class people. The press, by failing to provide more accurate, thorough, and balanced coverage of our increasingly diverse communities, has abdicated its responsibility to foster an exchange of information and perspectives that is necessary in a democracy.[69]

Cross-Media Ownership: TV-Newspaper Mergers

For the last quarter of the twentieth century, broadcasters were forbidden from owning newspapers in a market in which they held a TV license. A wide range of literature illustrates that there is a complex relationship between newspapers and TV and that the antagonism between the two media types is an important element of promoting civic discourse.[70] At the same time, the operation of newspaper newsrooms produces many stories, especially local, that become input for TV news.[71] Consumers turn to the newspaper for in-depth follow-up of the news headlines that they encounter in broadcast. Without the much more intensive and in-depth newsgathering done by newspapers, the news product space would be reduced.

This complex relationship gives rise to several negative effects of TV station–newspaper mergers that justify keeping the two media separate: The dictates of video delivery would alter the nature of newspaper reporting and commitment to investigative journalism. Conglomeration of different types of media in larger enterprises could reduce journalistic activity to a profit center that is driven by the larger economic goals of the parent. Combining the two activities within one entity diminishes the antagonism between print and audiovisual media. Moreover, the basic activity of gathering news as an input for distribution is very similar in the print and television media. Consequently, to the extent that large entities control a substantial part of the news production in an area, these mergers can create market power.

Industry commentators in Federal Communications Commission proceedings have made part of the argument by complaining that partnerships in joint ventures that preserve journalistic independence do not capture economic efficiencies because independent entities in joint ventures are too difficult to keep in line. As Lisa Rabasca points out, "You can't rely on orders from a common owner to work through issues that arise."[72] It is exactly that antagonism that the forum for civic discourse needs but would lose with cross-ownership because "news decisions for all these outlets are made in a coordinated way, sometimes in the same meeting. In effect the same group of minds decides what 'news' is, in every conceivable way that people can get their local news."[73] Management makes no bones about the goal: "We want to place a high value on experimental risk taking, rather than on the tried and true journalism story."[74]

In Tampa, Media General, Inc. owns both the *Tampa Tribune* and WFLA-TV. As a key player in the most vigorous effort to create convergence put it: "The single greatest challenge we have is to overcome our [work] cultural differences."[75] Media General's decision to co-locate the two media outlets led to a loss of editorial and journalistic integrity even before the actual move. "*Tribune* TV writer Walter Belcher offered a chilling example, saying editors forced him to lay off criticism of WFLA for nearly a year prior to the opening of the News Center supposedly to avoid ill will between the staffs."[76] This was not the only example of chilling of free speech in a newsroom in Tampa. Nor is the problem limited to Tampa. A.H. Belo Corporation, owner of the *Dallas Morning News* and WFAA-TV, made the decision that the *Morning News* should cease any TV criticism in order to stay away from critical reporting about its sister station.[77]

A substantial part of the economies that are sought by companies that are pushing hard for cross-ownership results from using reporters to repurpose or repackage their output for use in both TV and newspapers. As Strupp notes, reporters caught in the convergence frenzy bristle under the heavy-handed efforts to merge the media:

Kathleen Gallagher, a Milwaukee Journal Sentinel investment writer, who often does live 45-second interviews from the newsroom, finds the TV piece 'disconcerting.' [TV anchors] spend all this time thinking about their product and how they present themselves, and you're interrupting the writing of your story to do [the interview] quickly.[78]

'The last newspaper story I wrote, I wrote on my own time," says veteran WFLA reporter Lance Williams. "But the fun part of it is there are no restrictions on my story. It is hard to write a minute and thirty-second story. But writing for the newspaper is freeing.'[79]

While mergers tend to starve the enterprise of the resources necessary to uphold journalistic values, in the drive to produce profits for the merged entity, the multitasking[80] and cross-selling[81] that typifies combination mergers pose a special threat. They are intended specifically to homogenize the media. Moreover, because professional lines are breached, it is quite problematic to define activities and preserve professional ethics.[82] As McConnell points out, these pressures are heightened because the "fear is that corporate bean counters see convergence simply as a way to 'thin the herd' of reporters rather than using the huge reporting teams fielded by papers to greatly broaden the scope of broadcast stories."[83]

TELEVISION AND THE QUALITY OF DEMOCRATIC DISCOURSE

Television is one of the dominant means of political communication in the United States and serves a crucial role in providing information and affecting pubic opinion. Visual images are important in *priming* the audience.[84] Television impacts not only news coverage but also, and perhaps even more importantly, advertising and the interaction between advertising and news.[85] The impact of television is particularly important during elections,[86] and how such election news is relayed on local television is increasingly important in our political system. Studies highlight the importance of TV advertising during elections and the huge amounts spent on TV advertising by candidates attest to its importance. Campaign consultants believe that television advertising is pivotal to winning state-level campaigns.

Commercialism in the Production of News

The criticism of the impact of television on the political process adds another important layer to concern about escalating commercialism and the role of mass media in the erosion of democratic processes. Early on, the profit potential of the burgeoning electronic media industry led to a takeover by advertisers and large bureaucratic and corporate institutions, and that takeover has in turn resulted in an increase in the entertainment quotient and a decrease in the community-serving quotient.[87] Viewership has been boosted and, as Mosco notes, advertisers are able to "reach huge audiences regularly, and in receptive settings, with messages about products and, generally through those products, with messages about consumption as the centerpiece of the American Way of Life."[88]

With media conglomerates clawing at consumers' tastes by careful observation of their interests and ever more intensive targeting of marketing, they have gained strength in controlling public attitudes and action.[89] The electronic media "are mainly employed to measure and monitor information transactions and to package and repackage information products many times over."[90] The underlying logic of this "market research" effectively dictates the dimensions of the marketplace.[91] As the most profitable products (information or otherwise) are made exponentially available since they are safe money-makers, the set of genuine choices narrows. As Levy argues, one result of this commercial logic is to dull citizens' hunger for new information by force-feeding them what they already know how to digest.[92]

The power of commercialism is so great that it overwhelms other possible functions of the media, particularly political functions. [93] As Meyer argues in *Media Democracy*, "Media rules on capturing audience attention and thus eventually market shares dominate the business almost to the exclusion of all other principles, and are put into effect without any thought being given to the democratic or cultural standards of communication."[94]

Media critics from across the political spectrum argue that hyper-commercialism combined with the expansion of media outlets deeply affects the reporting process. Tight schedules and competition for attention put their stamp on newsgathering and reporting.[95] Reporting becomes selective and highly condensed.[96] Short pieces require extreme simplification. Stories become stylized so they can be easily conveyed. Time pressures create a tendency to not only run quickly with a story but to uncritically pass through manufactured news.[97] Entertainment and aesthetic values dictate the nature of the picture; getting good video images becomes a critical need.[98] Staging gives the news the predictability it needs, but results in typecasting and posing.[99] As Gans argues, "The problems stem largely from the very nature of commercially supplied news in a big country. News organizations are responsible for supplying an always-new product to large numbers of people, regularly and on time. As a result, news must be mass-produced, virtually requiring an industrial process that takes place on a kind of assembly line."[100]

The search to capture and maintain the audience's attention drives the media toward exaggeration and emotionalism at the expense of analysis.[101] Critics point to four types of news that are ideally suited to perform this function. *Celebrity personalities* become the centerpiece because of the easy point of focus on highly visible individuals.[102] *Scandal* attracts audiences. The personal travails of prominent figures in titillating scandals are grist for the media mill, attracting attention without threatening the audience. This news may not be happy, but it fills the preference for happy news because it involves someone else's troubles of no direct relevance to public policy or the public's welfare. The *horse race and hoopla*—the game—are another easy way to frame the news and to produce constant updating of who is ahead.[103] Who wins and who loses is much easier to portray than the complexity of what is at stake. *Verbal duels*[104] and loud, often one-sided arguments find audiences[105] more easily than reasoned, balanced debates. Talk-show pundits grab attention with extreme positions, usually negative attacks on targets that are not in the room to defend themselves. Both journalism and politics suffer as a result of this process.

A recent study of television news by the Project for Excellence in Journalism provides powerful evidence of the impact of concentration on programming, noting that "overall the data strongly suggest regulatory changes that encourage heavy concentration of ownership in local television by a few large corporations will erode the quality of news Americans receive."[106] The growing impact of homogenization in the TV industry, stimulated by the lifting of national ownership limits and restrictions on vertical integration is clear.[107] Local programming is restricted or eliminated. Stories of local importance are driven out of the high visibility hours or off the air. Pooled news services reduce the ability of local stations to present local stories and eventually erode the capability to produce them.

Distortion of Democratic Dialogue

Pressure applied by corporate ownership has forced news and entertainment to submit to heavy profit-maximizing strategies.[108] Politicians and corporations conform and cater to the demands of the media and leverage their ability to manipulate their public image. As Levine points out, "There has been an enormous increase in expenditure on public relations by both government and business. . . . These powerful institutions subsidize the cost of gathering and processing the news in order to influence positively the way they are reported."[109] Their interaction with the media becomes a form of extracted publicity in which they strive to be placed in the most favorable theatrical light. Journalism degenerates into a photo-op dance[110] between reporters and political handlers in which handlers have the upper hand. At the same time, politics has been forced to submit to the media's dictatorship over the depiction of its major parties and personalities, creating a "house of mirrors, in which both politics and the media recognize only images of themselves, thereby losing sight of the real world."[111]

Political handlers become gatekeepers who can punish or reward with access to politicians and who control the scheduling of events. They can stonewall some or give exclusives to others. As a result, "top-down news turns journalists into messengers of the very political, governmental, and other leaders who are . . . felt to be untrustworthy and unresponsive by significant numbers of poll respondents."[112] Hence, journalistic values are marred.[113] Dependence on well-connected sources and pressures to get a story out first short-circuit the application of traditional standards of reporting.[114] Discourse degenerates into a stream of stage-managed, entertainment-oriented, issueless events.[115] The media produce a blend of news and free advertising for the candidates[116] and, as with much advertising, the point may be to give a misimpression rather than convey accurate information.[117]

Whether or not the politicians themselves are largely responsible for allowing the emergence of media-run democracy, they acquiesce in a Faustian bargain.[118] As Meyer points out, "In exchange for their 'tactical' submission to the media rules, political actors gain a well-founded expectation that they will be invited to help shape the way the media portray them."[119] This clearly undermines the political process and changes the relative weight of parties and how they function to achieve goals.[120] Citizens are presented with an illusion of policy in election campaigns.[121] Concentration of ownership, with its attendant reuse and repurposing of material, complicates this problem.

As Curran points out, corporate pressures in this heavily commercialized environment point reporters toward covering mainly "prestige institutions as an economical and effective way of gathering the news."[122] This severely hampers the public's knowledge of the overall democratic landscape and widens the gap between elite and less visible groups in society, supporting the power structure while stigmatizing dissent as extreme and rare.[123] The watchdog function is short-circuited by the close relationships.[124] Parties and ordinary group affiliation recede, as individuals and lead institutions become the center of attention."[125] Without an ongoing dialogue of the conditions that enable the reported events to take place, the public cannot adequately formulate opinions; hence, they cannot act or mobilize in an educated manner and the critical elements of responsibility, causality, and connectedness between events are lost.

Public involvement in policy formation suffers not only because of the shift in focus fostered by the media, but also because of the short time-frame demanded by the media, which highlights the troubling difference between the media's timeline and the timeline necessary for political agendas to be carried out. The media's need for decisive headlines encourages quick, extreme stances to be taken. As Meyer observes, "Abbreviating the time interval normally demanded by the political process down to what the media's production schedule permits means abridging the entire process by deleting the procedural components that qualify it as democratic."[126] Insisting that politicians rush to get their views to their constituents before they can be swayed in an opposing direction eliminates thoughtful deliberation. The rapid-fire sequence of simple, emotional snap shots staged to increase popularity replaces discourse as the basis of politics.[127] "The traditional model of a political party that reaches consensus via extended discussions with many centers of influence in civil society, that allows decisions and programs to mature gradually, has become practically an anachronism."[128]

There are certainly many reasons for the declining participation in elections, but as Patterson and others argue, the media circus has played an important part.[129] Journalistic consideration and portrayal of candidates rests often on meaningless probing (someone's five o'clock shadow, misspoken words during speeches, candidates' pasts) and moral power plays, leaving the issues of the election unattended. The issues themselves are not given sufficient care by the candidates, according to Patterson, who find it easier to speak vaguely and play the public opinion charade. Voters are forced to choose a candidate whom they least dislike, based on nonsubstantive grounds, which we can easily link to disenchantment and a rapid trickle-down effect of squashing voter turnout.

HOPE AND HYPE VERSUS REALITY: THE ROLE OF THE INTERNET

Many hoped that the Internet would deliver on the promise of electronic mass media to educate, motivate, and mobilize the great body of citizens to participate in political discourse in a constructive way.[130] Internet optimists had hoped for a hyper-connected populace, capable of reaching out to anybody and anything with a simple set of keystrokes. They predicted intensified participation in the democratic process given a new outlet to access and spread information, which would allegedly make it easier to be heard.[131] True electronic democracy would be created by "the possibilities for interactive and collective communication offered by cyberspace to encourage the expression and elaboration of urban problems by local citizens themselves."[132] If the architecture of the Internet was geared toward democracy, we might begin to conquer space by connecting citizens to each other "in ways that extend the developmental benefits of civic participation beyond those immediately present."[133] An active, informed citizenry would spark self-organization and participation, two benchmarks of the counter-culturalist dream. Democracy would benefit greatly if we were "encouraging the collective and continuous elaboration of problems and their cooperative, concrete resolutions by those affected."[134]

After three decades of existence and two decades of presence in civil society, the Internet has not lived up to its hope or hype. It has become more of an extension of the dominant, twentieth-century communications media than a revolutionary twenty-first-century technology, as huge corporate media giants harness its ability to "push" their commercial messages on the public. The one-to-many broadcast function has been quickly exploited for its commercial value. The Internet has also become an extension of the telephone, a "pull" medium. One-to-one communications have been rapidly exploited (e-mail and chat), while the unique, many-to-many potential of the Internet is lagging behind, particularly as a political vehicle.

Because the Internet is being cited as a justification to allow further concentration in the commercial mass media, it is particularly important to debunk the myth that the Internet has significantly altered or diminished the influence of the powerful push broadcast media on politics. To date, the Internet's ability to create a more vibrant forum for democratic discourse has been limited by a number of factors, some inherent in the technology, others the result of public policy, and there is growing concern that the Internet will not fundamentally enhance the quality of civic discourse.[135]

Commercialism

By the late 1980s, the Internet had emerged as a new media alternative,[136] but governments in the nations with a leading role in developing the Internet and related technologies were committed to free market economics, which led, willy-nilly, to a resurgence of commercial interests on the Internet.[137] Symbolically, the network itself was handed over to Sprint, MCI, WorldCom, PSINet and GTE.[138] Shortly thereafter, corporate dominance of the Internet was reinforced when a decision was made to allow the leading technology for delivering high-speed Internet services to consumers to be operated on a closed, proprietary basis.[139] Cable companies were allowed to choose which high-speed Internet services flow over their wires.[140] Telephone companies were later allowed to follow the same path.

With commercialism as the guiding principle, the extremely powerful commercial thrust of the new medium reinforces the central concern of media public policy.[141] New technologies do not alter underlying economic relationships because the mass-market audience orientation of the business takes precedence.[142] Because the new media markets have moved quickly to vertical integration by dominant incumbents from the old media, the problems that afflict the old media persist[143] and the circumstances surrounding the production and delivery of information inhibit its utility to expand political participation and enhance social and cultural consciousness.[144]

The Internet has become the logical conclusion to the development of electronic media. The economic relationships that have taken over the mass media have been transferred to the Internet, frustrating the hoped for increase in diversity, pluralism, and opportunities for entry. After seventy years of titillating public tastes through advertising, electronic media could now provide instant e-commerce, to buy on the spot. The Internet can deliver immediate consumption and instant gratification. E-commerce is "direct mail on steroids," pumped up by the ability of viewers to click through digitally inserted advertising for purchases.[145] High-powered advertising is targeted at demographically compatible viewers identified by detailed information created by the two-way network on viewing patterns and past purchases,[146] leading to growing concerns that certain groups are not likely to have fair access to the opportunities of cyberspace.[147] New services may be expensive to deliver because of the cost of appliances, production equipment necessary to produce programming that takes advantage of the new appliance, and the infrastructure necessary to deliver interactive services.[148] This stacks the odds against small groups and individuals, as the bulk of users are directed through corporate portals, which are made attractive by glitzy visuals and distractions. Likewise, "some search engines are commercial ventures in which sites must pay for inclusion in their database,"[149] further deprioritizing small organizations and individuals who could never match large, corporate offerings. As Levine observes:

> Under these conditions, citizens who try to operate their own sites for democratic purposes will become increasingly discouraged, since few visitors will be able to find their work and they will be legally barred from using the patented production techniques employed on commercial sites. Thus the Internet will begin to look like the next generation of cable television instead of a decentralized, participatory medium. Most non-profit sites will be as marginal as public-access television stations today.[150]

The Qualitative Weaknesses of the Internet

Ironically, the Internet suffers inherent weaknesses that the other mass media have developed over time. It lacks the qualitative connection between persons and places that traditional media have lost as a result of consolidation. While the hometown paper and local TV stations have lost their local flavor, the Internet was born without it.

The Internet's characteristic impersonality keeps discussion and action on-line from achieving what discussion and action face-to-face have achieved in the past. On-line forums have not achieved a breakthrough in democratic deliberation,[151] and on-line newspapers look like the cyber-versions of the physical world counterparts from which they are a spin-off.[152] It is still early and the possibility for new forms of communications emerging cannot be discounted[153] since "people who participate in typical on-line activities sometimes initiate political discussions and organize political actions."[154] But we must be cautious because "participants tend to be distributed across jurisdictions which makes political organizing difficult," particularly at the local level.[155]

In fact, critics argue that the time spent in political discussions on-line may be detrimental because it cuts into the amount of time individuals spend face-to-face, which has proven functionality and promise. It becomes difficult to put faith in on-line relationships and the time spent promoting ideas[156] because the mechanisms for developing trust and bonds are weak.[157] These are crucial to driving political organizations and communities. In face-to-face political discussions there is a better understanding of how the people involved will be affected, which informs their motivations and intentions.

Similarly, the ease of exit on the Internet undercuts its role as a political platform.[158] In most respects the Internet is a highly selective tool where individuals seek out what they already know or are interested in proliferating. Attempting to change the "prevailing norms" of an on-line space is particularly difficult because the receivers one encounters will be different every time and the sender will never have any knowledge of its audience at any given moment. On-line, people can cleanse their world of all interactions outside of those they explicitly choose, isolating themselves from other ideologies and avoiding "uncomfortable perspectives and stories that might shake their prejudices."[159] Though self-segregation does exist in the physical world, its opposite also exists in abundance. On the Internet, "there is no common space, mass audience or means of addressing people who don't seek out the speaker."[160]

While being involved in discussion on-line makes an individual more socially active at any given moment, there is concern that over time social and political activity will decrease, weaken, and become atomized as a result of the Internet. As Levine argues, "The search functions on the Internet make selection too easy and threaten to tip the balance toward hyperspecialization,"[161] furthering the digital divide and enabling "intellectual stratification as experts are able to talk only among themselves and ignore the rest of the public."[162]

The end point of this could be weaker communities where mutual obligation to the consequences and decisions of groups will be nonexistent. Volunteering locally has always resulted from the desire to have an impact in the local setting. On the Internet it is difficult to gauge the impact one will have since reliance on other on-line members and participants is risky and uncertain. Hence, the speed and "access" which promoters of the Internet cite as beneficial is "unlikely to raise the level of participation"[163] because strong, motivating community ties have not subsisted and users are not convinced their work will yield results.

In the shopping mall quality of the Internet, we have relearned the "lesson of media history that, in an unregulated or lightly regulated regime, what gets transmitted is primarily what is profitable rather than what is in the public interest."[164] Pretending that the technology will accomplish the goals without active guidance has allowed the Internet to amplify "the passive spectator-democracy of sound-bites and photo-opportunities rather than encouraging real participation."[165]

CONCLUSION

The challenge of hyper-commercialism to the role of the news media in democracy is formidable. The response must be multifaceted. We need a critical mass and mix of independent outlets—local/national, commercial/noncommercial, professional/partisan—to ensure the media's role in democratic discourse, but there is no simple formula. The ultimate goal is for "the dissemination of information from diverse and antagonistic sources"[166] to become a self-disciplining process. Public policy has a major influence on the contours of the mass media and their ability to promote this democratic discourse.

Public policy sets the limits on concentration in the media, particularly in the broadcast space. It has allowed a smaller and smaller number of corporations to have a larger and larger reach and control across the media. It has allowed economic interest to dominate democratic discourse. The trend can be reversed if a commitment to independent ownership of outlets is restored because independent ownership of outlets fosters antagonism in viewpoints. The more numerous the independent outlets, the more likely they are to pursue investigative journalism and to be local, but that is not uniformly so. To capitalize on the reach of commercial media in promoting civic discourse, public policy can also strengthen the obligations and incentives to air public-interest programming.

Institutional independence, particularly the separation of print and broadcast outlets, is critical and can be preserved through public policy. Institutional diversity involves not only different points of view but, more importantly, different structures of media presentation—different business models, journalistic culture, and tradition. It supports the special expertise and culture of certain media, such as the newspaper tradition of in-depth investigative journalism. The quality of investigative reporting and the accessibility of different types of institutions to leaders and the public are promoted by institutional diversity.

One of the key aspects of institutional diversity is to promote noncommercial media. Commercial interests have dominated the airwaves since their initial exploitation as a means of communication, but the possibility exists for both professional and partisan interests to have a space in the spectrum. Noncommercial alternatives can play a large role in adding diversity to democratic discourse. Community media based in low-power radio and television can play a significant role in providing local perspective and greater access, but only if public policy allows them to do so. The national noncommercial media—PBS and, in some respects, NPR—can play a much larger investigative and informational role, as does the CBC in Canada, but only if public policy provides the resources.

New technologies may open new possibilities for access to information distribution (e.g. the Internet and potential for unlicensed use of the spectrum) and new organizational form for information production (e.g., peer-to-peer, and other cooperative, many-to-many arrangements). Public policy will determine the space in which these new institutions and approaches are allowed to exist and thrive.

There is a long way to go. The first step is to recognize the adverse consequences of unfettered hyper-commercialism on the political processes of our democracy and reaffirm our commitment to a simple, but fundamental idea articulated by the founders of the United States, that a well-functioning system of free expression [is] the "only effective guardian . . . of every other right."[167]

NOTES

1. For example, Ben Bagdikian, *The Media Monopoly* (Boston: Beacon Press, 2000), which described the concentration of media, was first published in 1983 and Martin Esslin, *The Age of Television* (New Brunswick, N.J.: Transaction, 2002), which raised concerns about the impact of television on civic and political functions, was first published in 1982.

2. Eric Alterman, *What Liberal Media: The Truth about Bias and the News* (New York: Basic Books, 2002); Kristina Borjesson, *Into the BUZZSAW* (Amherst, N.Y.: Prometheus Books, 2002); Bernard Goldberg, *Bias* (Washington, D.C.: Regnery, 2002), 190; Bob Woodward, *Bush at War* (New York: Simon & Shuster, 2002), 207; Michael Kelly, "Left Everlasting," *Washington Post*, 11 December 2002, A-33; Paul Klugman, "In Media Res," *New York Times*, 29 November 2002, A 39, which Ailes disputed (see Lloyd Grove, "The Reliable Source," *Washington Post*, 19 November 2002, C3); Seth Ackerman, *The Most Biased Name in News* (New York: Fairness & Accuracy in Reporting, August 2002), *Cable News Wars: Interviews* (PBS, Online Newshour, March 2002), 2; S. Robert Lichter, "Depends on How You Define 'Bias'," *Washington Post*, 18 December 2002, A-19. Peter Phillips and Project Censored, *Censored 2003* (New York: Seven Stories, 2002).

3. Marion R. Just, Ann N. Crigler, Dean F. Alger, Timothy E. Cook, Montague Kern, and Darrell M. West, *Crosstalk: Citizens, Candidates and the Media in a Presidential Campaign* (Chicago: University of Chicago Press, 1996); Doris Graber, *Mass Media and American Politics* (Washington, D.C.: Congressional Quarterly, 1997); David L. Paletz, *The Media in American Politics: Contents and Consequences* (New York: Longman, 1999); Kim Fridkin Kahn and Patrick J. Kenney, *The Spectacle of U.S. Senate Campaign* (Chicago: University of Chicago Press, 1999); Doris Graber, *Processing Politics* (Chicago: University of Chicago Press, 2001); Herbert J. Gans, *Democracy and the News* (Oxford: Oxford University Press, 2003).

4. Leonard Downie, Jr. and Robert Kaiser, *The News about the News* (New York: Alfred A. Knopf, 2002), 13.

5. Bill Kovach and Tom Rosenstiel, *Warp Speed: America in the Age of Mixed Media* (New York: The Century Foundation Press, 1999).

6. Gans, *Democracy*, 50.

7. John Hanchette, "'USA Today' Editors Should Not Emerge Unscathed," Says Pulitzer Winner," *Editor and Publisher*, 22 March 2003; Gregg Mitchell, "Keller Defends Judith Miller in Statement," *Editor and Publisher*, 28 March 2004; "Reporter Apologizes for Iraq Coverage," *Editor and Publisher*, 29 March 2004.

8. Thomas Meyer, *Media Democracy* (Cambridge: Polity Press, 2002), citing B.R. Barber, *Jihad v. McWorld* (New York: Ballentine, 1996), 88–99, and Neil Postman, *Amusing Ourselves to Death: Public Discourse in the Age of Show Business* (New York: Viking, 1985).

9. Yochai Benkler, "Intellectual Property and the Organization of Information Production," *International Review of Law and Economics* 22, no. 1 (2002); Carl Shapiro and Hal R. Varian, *Information Rules: A Strategic Guide to the Network Economy* (Boston: Harvard Business School Press, 1999).

10. John McManus, "How Objective Is Local Television News?" *Mass Communications Review*, 1991; James Snider and Benjamin I. Page, "Does Media Ownership Affect Media Stands? The Case of the Telecommunications Act of 1996" (paper delivered at the Annual Meeting of the Midwest Political Science Association, April 1997); C. Edwin Baker, *Media, Markets, and Democracy* (Cambridge: Cambridge University Press, 2002), 43–44.

11. Sue Carter, Frederick Fico, and Joycelyn A. McCabe, "Partisan and Structural Balance in Local Television Election Coverage," *Journalism and Mass Communications Quarterly*, 79 (2002); Kim Fridkin Kahn and Patrick J. Kenny, "The Slant of News: How Editorial Endorsements Influence Campaign Coverage and Citizens' Views of Candidates," *American Political Science Review*, 96 (2002): 381; Benjamin I. Page, *Who Deliberates* (Chicago: University of Chicago Press, 1996); McManus, "How Objective Is Local Television News?"; Edward Rowse, *Slanted News: A Case Study of the Nixon and Stevenson Fund Stories* (Boston: Beacon, 1957).

12. C. Edwin Baker, "Giving Up on Democracy: The Legal Regulation of Media Ownership," Attachment C, *Comments of Consumers Union, Consumer Federation of America, Civil Rights Forum, Center for Digital Democracy, Leadership Conference on Civil Rights and Media Access Project* (before the Federal Communications Commission, In the Matter of Cross Ownership of Broadcast Station and Newspaper/Radio Cross-Ownership Waiver Policy, MM Docket No. 01-235, 96-197, 3 December 2001), 43; Ronald J. Krotoszynski, Jr. and A. Richard M. Blaiklock, "Enhancing the Spectrum: Media Power, Democracy, and the Marketplace of Ideas," *University of Illinois Law Review* (2000): 875.

13. Krotoszynski and Blaiklock, "Enhancing the Spectrum," 867.

14. The effort of a dominant media conglomerate in Canada to dictate content was chronicled in comments filed in the proceedings at the Federal Communications Commission. See *Comments of Consumers Union, Consumer Federation of America, Civil Rights Forum, Center for Digital Democracy, Leadership Conference on Civil Rights and Media Access Project* (before the Federal Communications Commission, In the Matter of Cross Ownership of Broadcast Station and Newspaper/Radio Cross-Ownership Waiver Policy, MM Docket No. 01-235, 96-197, 3 December 2001)

15. Albert Karr, "Television News Tunes Out Airwaves Auction Battle," *Wall Street Journal*, 1 May 1996, B1; Joe Strupp, "Three Point Play," *Editor and Publisher*, 21 August 2000, 23; Lucia Moses, "TV or Not TV? Few Newspapers Are Camera Shy, but Sometimes Two into One Just Doesn't Go," *Editor and Cable*, 21 August 2000, 22; Gene Roberts, Thomas Kunkel, and Charles Clayton, eds., *Leaving Readers Behind* (Fayetteville: University of Arkansas Press, 2001), 10; Bill McConnell, "The National Acquirers: Whether Better for News or Fatter Profits, Media Companies Want in on TV/Newspaper Cross-Ownership," *Broadcasting and Cable*, December 10, 2001.

16. Baker, "Democracy;" Cass Sunstein, "Television and the Public Interest," *California Law Review*, 8 (2002): 517; Neil Netanal, "Is the Commercial Mass Media Necessary, or Even Desirable, for Liberal Democracy" (paper presented at Telecommunications Policy Research Conference on Information, Communications, and Internet Policy, October 2001), 20–24.

17. C. Edwin Baker, *Advertising and a Democratic Press* (Princeton, N.J.: Princeton University Press, 1994). C. Edwin Baker, 1997, "Giving the Audience What It Wants," *Ohio State Law Journal*, 58.

18. Baker, *Democratic Press*; Krotoszynski and Blaiklock, "Enhancing the Spectrum," 831.

19. Cass Sunstein, *Republic.com* (Princeton, N.J.: Princeton University Press, 2001), 108–109.

20. Vernon A. Stone, "Deregulation Felt Mainly in Large-Market Radio and Independent TV," *Communicator* (April 1987): 12; Patricia Aufderheide, "After the Fairness Doctrine: Controversial Broadcast Programming and the Public Interest," *Journal of Communication* (1990): 50–51; Michael L. McKean and Vernon A. Stone, "Why Stations Don't Do News," *Communicator* (1991):

23–4; Vernon A. Stone, "New Staffs Change Little in Radio, Take Cuts in Major Markets TV," *RT-NDA Communicator* (1988); Karen L. Slattery and Ernest A. Hakanen, "Sensationalism versus Public Affairs Content of Local TV News: Pennsylvania Revisited," *Journal of Broadcasting and Electronic Media* (1994); James M. Bernstein and Stephen Lacy, "Contextual Coverage of Government by Local Television News," *Journalism Quarterly* 67 (1992); Raymond L. Carroll, "Market Size and TV News Values," *Journalism Quarterly* (1989); David K. Scott and Robert H. Gobetz, "Hard News/Soft News Content of the National Broadcast Networks: 1972–1987," *Journalism Quarterly* (1992); V. E. Ferrall, "The Impact of Television Deregulation," *Journal of Communication* (1992).

21. Karen L. Slattery, Ernest A. Hakanen, and Mark Doremus, "The Expression of Localism: Local TV News Coverage in the New Video Marketplace," *Journal of Broadcasting and Electronic Media*, 40 (1996); Raymond L. Carroll and C.A. Tuggle, "The World Outside: Local TV News Treatment of Imported News," *Journalism and Mass Communications Quarterly*, 74, no. 1 (Spring 1997); Charles Fairchild, "Deterritorializing Radio: Deregulation and the Continuing Triumph of the Corporatist Perspective in the USA," *Media, Culture & Society* 21, no. 4 (1999); Charles Layton and Jennifer Dorroh, "Sad State," *American Journalism Review* (June 2002); Kathryn Olson, "Exploiting the Tension between the New Media's 'Objective' and Adversarial Roles: The Role Imbalance Attach and Its Use of the Implied Audience," *Communications Quarterly* 42, no. 1 (1994): 40–41; Alan G. Stavitsky, "The Changing Conception of Localism in U.S. Public Radio," *Journal of Broadcasting and Electronic Media* (1994).

22. Peter Clarke and Eric Fredin, "Newspapers, Television, and Political Reasoning," *Public Opinion Quarterly*, 42, no. 2 (1978); Michael Pfau, "A Channel Approach to Television Influence," *Journal of Broadcasting and Electronic Media* 34, no. 2 (1990); Donald T. Cundy, "Political Commercials and Candidate Image," in *New Perspectives on Political Advertising*, ed. Lynda Lee Kaid, Dan D. Nimmo and Keith R. Sanders (Carbondale, Ill.: Southern Illinois University Press, 1986); Garrett J. O'Keefe, "Political Malaise and Reliance on the Media," *Journalism Quarterly* (1980); S. Becker and H. C. Choi, "Media Use, Issue/Image Discrimination," *Communications Research* (1987); J. P. Robinson and D. K. Davis, "Television News and the Informed Public: An Information Process Approach," *Journal of Communication* 40, no. 3 (1990); Paul S. Voakes, Jack Kapfer, David Kurpius, and David Shano-yeon Chern, "Diversity in the News: A Conceptual and Methodological Framework," *Journalism and Mass Communications Quarterly* (Autumn 1996); Ronald Bishop and Ernest A. Hakanen, "In the Public Interest? The State of Local Television Programming Fifteen Years After Deregulation," *Journal of Communications Inquiry* 26 (2002).

23. Joel Waldfogel, *Who Benefits Whom in Local Television Markets?* (Philadelphia: The Wharton School, November 2001). Other papers in the series of studies of "preference externalities" were made a part of the record in conjunction with Joel Waldfogel's appearance at the FCC Roundtable, including *Preference Externalities: An Empirical Study of Who Benefits Whom in Differentiated Product Markets*, NBER Working Paper 7391 (Cambridge: National Bureau of Economic Research, 1999); Peter Siegelman and Joel Waldfogel, "Race and Radio: Preference Externalities, Minority Ownership and the Provision of Programming to Minorities," *Advances in Applied Microeconomics* 10 (2001); Felix Oberholzer-Gee and Joel Waldfogel, *Electoral Acceleration: The Effect of Minority Population on Minority Voter Turnout*, NBER Working Paper 8252 (Cambridge: National Bureau of Economic Research, 2001); Joel Waldfogel and Lisa George, *Who Benefits Whom in Daily Newspaper Markets?* NBER Working Paper 7944 (Cambridge: National Bureau of Economic Research, 2000); Joel Waldfogel, *Comments on Consolidation and Localism*, Federal Communications Commission, Roundtable on Media Ownership (29 October 2001); Joel Waldfogel and Felix Oberholzer-Gee, *Tiebout Acceleration: Political Participation in Heterogeneous Jurisdictions* (2001).

24. Oberholzer-Gee and Waldfogel, *Political Participation*, 36–37.

25. Philip Napoli, "Audience Valuation and Minority Media: An Analysis of the Determinants of the Value of Radio Audiences," *Journal of Broadcasting and Electronic Media* 46 (2002):

180–81. The author notes agreement with Kofi A. Ofori, *When Being No. 1 Is Not Enough: The Impact of Advertising Practices on Minority-Owned and Minority-Targeted Broadcast Stations* (Civil Rights Forum on Communications Policy, 1999); James G. Webster and Patricia F. Phalen, *The Mass Audience: Rediscovering the Dominant Model* (Mahwah, N.J.: Erlbaum, 1997); Bruce Owen and Steven Wildman, *Video Economics* (Cambridge: Harvard University Press, 1992); Baker, *Advertising*; James T. Hamilton, *Channeling Violence: The Economic Market for Violent Television Programming* (Princeton, N.J.: Princeton University Press, 1998); Steven Wildman, "One-way Flows and the Economics of Audience Making," in *Audiencemaking: How the Media Create the Audience*, ed. James S. Ettema and Whitney D. Charles (Thousand Oaks, Calif.: Sage Publications, 1994); Steven S. Wildman and Theomary Karamanis, "The Economics of Minority Programming," in *Investing in Diversity: Advancing Opportunities for Minorities in Media*, ed. Amy Korzick Garner (Washington, D.C.: Aspen Institute, 1998).

26. William D. Bradford, "Discrimination in Capital Markets, Broadcast/Wireless Spectrum Service Providers and Auction Outcomes," (University of Washington, School of Business Administration, 5 December 2000).

27. Empirical studies demonstrating the link between minority presence in the media and minority-oriented programming include Marilyn D. Fife, *The Impact of Minority Ownership on Broadcast Program Content: A Case Study of WGPR-TV's Local News Content* (Washington, D.C.: National Association of Broadcasters, 1979); Marilyn D. Fife, *The Impact of Minority Ownership on Broadcast Program Content: A Multi-Market Study* (Washington, D.C.: National Association of Broadcasters, 1986); Congressional Research Service, *Minority Broadcast Station Ownership and Broadcast Programming: Is There a Nexus?* (Washington, D.C.: Library of Congress, 1988); T. A. Hart, Jr., "The Case for Minority Broadcast Ownership," Gannet Center Journal (1988); Kurt A. Wimmer, "Deregulation and the Future of Pluralism in the Mass Media: The Prospects for Positive Policy Reform," *Mass Communications Review* (1988); Akousa Barthewell Evans, "Are Minority Preferences Necessary? Another Look at the Radio Broadcasting Industry," *Yale Law and Policy Review* 8 (1990); Jeff Dubin and Matthew L. Spitzer, "Testing Minority Preferences in Broadcasting," *Southern California Law Review* 68 (1995); Christine Bachen, Allen Hammond, Laurie Mason, and Stephanie Craft, *Diversity of Programming in the Broadcast Spectrum: Is There a Link between Owner Race or Ethnicity and News and Public Affairs Programming?* (Santa Clara University, December 1999); Laurie Mason, Christine M. Bachen, and Stephanie L. Craft, "Support for FCC Minority Ownership Policy: How Broadcast Station Owner Race or Ethnicity Affects News and Public Affairs Programming Diversity," *Comm. Law Policy* 6 (2001).

28. See Stephen Lacy, Mary Alice Shaver, and Charles St. Cyr, "The Effects of Public Ownership and Newspaper Competition on the Financial Performance of Newspaper Corporation: A Replication and Extension," *Journalism and Mass Communications Quarterly* (Summer 1996); T. G. Gauger, "The Constitutionality of the FCC's Use of Race and Sex in Granting Broadcast Licenses," *Northwestern Law Review* 83 (1989); Howard Klieman, "Content Diversity and the FCC's Minority and Gender Licensing Policies," *Journal of Broadcasting and Electronic Media* (Fall 1991); Lori A. Collins-Jarvis, "Gender Representation in an Electronic City Hall: Female Adoption of Santa Monica's PEN System," *Journal of Broadcasting and Electronic Media* 37, no. 1 (1993); Martha M. Lauzen and David Dozier, "Making a Difference in Prime Time: Women on Screen and Behind the Scenes in 1995–1996 Television Season," *Journal of Broadcasting and Electronic Media* (Winter 1999); Patrick B. O'Sullivan, *The Nexus between Broadcast Licensing Gender Preferences and Programming Diversity: What Does the Social Scientific Evidence Say?* (University of California at Santa Barbara, Department of Communication, 2000).

29. Harvey J. Levin, "Program Duplication, Diversity, and Effective Viewer Choices: Some Empirical Findings," *American Economic Review* 61, no. 2 (1971); Stephen Lacy, "A Model of Demand for News: Impact of Competition on Newspaper Content," *Journalism Quarterly* 66 (1989); Thomas J. Johnson and Wayne Wanta, "Newspaper Circulation and Message Diversity in an Urban Market," *Mass Communications Review* (1993); William R. Davie and Jung-Sook Lee, "Television News Technology: Do More Sources Mean Less Diversity?" *Journal of Broadcasting and*

Electronic Media, 37, no. 4 (1993): 455; Wayne Wanta and Thomas J. Johnson, "Content Changes in the St. Louis Post-Dispatch during Different Market Situations," *Journal of Media Economics* (1994); David C. Coulson, "Impact of Ownership on Newspaper Quality," *Journalism Quarterly* (Summer 1994); David C. Coulson and Anne Hansen, "The Louisville Courier-Journal's News Content After Purchase by Gannet," *Journalism and Mass Communications Quarterly* (Spring 1995); Petros Iosifides, "Diversity versus Concentration in the Deregulated Mass Media," *Journalism and Mass Communications Quarterly* (Spring 1999); Stephen Lacy and Todd F. Simon, "Competition in the Newspaper Industry," in *The Economics and Regulation of United States Newspapers,* ed. Stephen Lacy and Todd F. Simon (Norwood, N.J.: Ablex, 1999).

30. Baker, *Media, Markets,* "Democracy," 16; Sunstein, *Republic,* 46–47.

31. Krotoszynski and Blaiklock, "Enhancing the Spectrum," 871 . . . 875–876; Waldfogel, "Local Television Markets;" Waldfogel and George, "Daily Newspaper Markets;" as well as Waldfogel, *Consolidation and Localism.*

32. The connection to grounded in self-definition (see Jeremy Rifkin, *The Age of Access* [New York: J.P. Tarcher, 2001], 7–9; Robert D. Putnam, *Bowling Alone the Collapse and Revival of American Community* [New York: Simon and Schuster, 2000]) and links to political involvement (James G. Gimpel, *Separate Destinations: Migration, Immigration and the Politics of Places* [Ann Arbor: University of Michigan Press, 1999], Robert Huckfeldt and John Sprague, "Political Parties and Electoral Mobilization: Political Structure, Social Structure, and the Party Canvas," *American Political Science Review* 86 [1992]), which is reinforced by the fact that political units are local for purposes of representation (e.g. single member districts, see John Mark Hanson, "The Majoritarian Impulse and the Declining Significance of Place, in *The Future of American Democratic Politics,* eds. Gerald M Pomper and Marc D. Weiner [New Brunswick, N.J.: Rutgers University Press, 2003]) as well as services (e.g. school districts, fire, police, etc.).

33. Jack Bass, "Newspaper Monopoly," in Roberts, Kunkel, and Clayton, *Leaving Readers Behind;* Pat Gish and Tom Gish, "We Still Scream: The Perils and Pleasures of Running a Small-Town Newspaper, and E.R. Shipp, "Excuses, Excuses. How Editors and Reporters Justify Ignoring Stories," in *The Business of Journalism,* ed. William Serrin (New York: New Press, 2000). Complaints about the failure to cover larger national and international stories also abound (see Phillips, *Censored 200;* Borjesson, *BUZZSAW*).

34. Gene Roberts, Thomas Kunkel, and Charles Clayton, 2001, "Leaving Readers Behind," in Roberts, Kunkel, and Clayton, *Leaving Readers Behind,* 2.

35. Gilbert Cranberg, Randall Bezanson, and John Soloski, *Taking Stock: Journalism and the Publicly Traded Newspaper Company* (Ames: Iowa State Press, 2001), 42.

36. Cranberg, Bezanson, and Soloski, *Taking Stock,* 108.

37. Cranberg, Bezanson, and Soloski, *Taking Stock,* 64.

38. Cranberg, Bezanson, and Soloski, *Taking Stock,* 86.

39. Bartholomew H. Sparrow, *Uncertain Guardians* (Baltimore: Johns Hopkins University Press, 1999), 103.

40. Ken Auletta, "The State of the American Newspaper," *American Journalism Review,* June 1998.

41. Cranberg, Bezanson, and Soloski, *Taking Stock,* 89; *The Business of News, The News About Business,* Neiman Reports, Summer 1999.

42. Downie and Kaiser, *The News about the* News, 93.

43. Downie and Kaiser, *The News about the* News, 68, Charles Layton, "What Do Readers Really Want?" *American Journalism Review* (March 1999).

44. Downie and Kaiser, *The News about the* News, 97.

45. Downie and Kaiser, *The News about the* News, 109.

46. Layton, "What Readers Really Want," 143.

47. Cranberg, Bezanson and Soloski, *Taking Stock,* 86.

48. Randal A. Beam, "What It Means to Be a Market-Oriented Newspaper," *Newspaper Research Journal* 16, (1995); Randal A. Beam, "Size of Corporate Parent Drives Market Orientation,"

140   *Mark Cooper*

Newspaper Research Journal 23 (2002); Sharyn Vane, "Taking Care of Business," *American Journalism Review*, March 2002; *The Business of News*.

49. Bass, "Newspaper Monopoly," 145.

50. Downie and Kaiser, *The News about the* News, 87–91.

51. Mary Walton and Charles Layton, "Missing the Story at the Statehouse," in *Breach of Faith: A Crisis of Coverage in the Age of Corporate Newspapering*, ed., Gene Roberts and Thomas Kunkel (Fayetteville: University of Arkansas Press, 2002), 14.

52. Roberts, Kunkel and Clayton, *Leaving Readers Behind*, 10.

53. Arthur E. Rowse, *Drive-By Journalism* (Monroe, Maine: Common Courage Press, 2000), 163.

54. Rowse, *Drive-by Journalism*, 49.

55. John Street, *Mass Media, Politics, and Democracy* (New York: Palgrave, 2001), 141; Rowse, *Drive-By Journalism*, 162.

56. Cranberg, Bezanson, and Soloski, *Taking Stock*.

57. Downie and Kaiser, *The News about the* News, 68.

58. Cranberg, Bezanson, and Soloski, *Taking Stock*, cite Gene Roberts, "Corporatism vs. Journalism," *The Press-Enterprise Lecture Series* 31, 12 February 1996; for recent discussions see also Ronald Dugger, "The Corporate Domination of Journalism," in *The Business of Journalism*, ed., William Serrin (New York: New Press, 2000); Sparrow, *Uncertain Guardians*, Chapter 4.

59. Cranberg, Bezanson, and Soloski, *Taking Stock*, 11.

60. Bass, "Newspaper Monopoly," 111.

61. Downie and Kaiser, *The News about the* News, 76.

62. Buzz Bissinger, "The End of Innocence," in Roberts, Kunkel, and Layton, *Leaving Readers Behind*, 83.

63. Bissinger, "The End of Innocence," 103.

64. Roberts, Kunkel, and Clayton, *Leaving Readers Behind*, 5.

65. Cranberg, Bezanson, and Soloski, *Taking Stock*, 93.

66. Cranberg, Bezanson, and Soloski, *Taking Stock*, 96.

67. Cranberg, Bezanson, and Soloski, *Taking Stock*, 10.

68. Cranberg, Bezanson, and Soloski, *Taking Stock*, 95.

69. Vanessa Williams, "Black and White and Red All Over: The Ongoing Struggle to Integrate America's Newsrooms," in Serrin, *The Business of Journalism*, 100.

70. Clarke and Fredin, "Political Reasoning;" John P. Robinson and Mark R. Levy, "New Media Use and the Informed Public: A 1990s Update," *Journal of Communications* (spring 1996); Alan B. Albarran and John W. Dimmick, "An Assessment of Utility and Competitive Superiority of in the Video Entertainment Industries," *Journal of Media Economics* 6 (1993); W. Lance Bennett and Regina G. Lawrence, "News Icons and the Mainstreaming of Social Change," *Journal of Communication* 45 (1995); Douglas M. McLeod, "Communicating Deviance: The Effects of Television News Coverage of Social Protests," *Journal of Broadcasting & Electronic Media* 39 (1995); John B. Dimmick, "The Theory of the Niche and Spending on Mass Media: The Case of the Video Revolution," *Journal of Media Economics* 10 (1997); Glenn G. Sparks, Marianne Pellechia, and Chris Irvine, "Does Television News about UFOs Affect Viewers' UFO Beliefs?: An Experimental Investigation," *Communication Quarterly* 46 (1998); Juliette H. Walma Van der Molen and Tom H. A. Van der Voort, "The Impact of Television, Print, and Audio on Children's Recall of the News," *Human Communication Research* 26 (2000); Dan Berkowitz and David Pritchard, "Political Knowledge and Communication Resources," *Journalism Quarterly* 66 (1989); Steven H. Chaffee, Xinshu Zhao, and Glenn Leshner, "Political Knowledge and the Campaign Media of 1992," *Communications Research* 21 (1994); Dan Drew and David Weaver, "Voter Learning in the 1988 Presidential Election: Did the Media Matter?" *Journalism Quarterly* 68 (1991).

71. Carl Sessions Stepp, "Whatever Happened to Competition," *American Journalism Review* (June 2001); David C. Coulson and Stephen Lacy, "Newspapers and Joint Operating Agree-

ments," in *Contemporary Media Issues*, ed. E. David Sloan and Emily Erickson Hoff (Northport, Ala.: Vision Press, 1998); Stephen Lacy, David C. Coulson, and Charles St. Cyr, "The Impact of Beat Competition on City Hall Coverage," *Journalism & Mass Communication Quarterly* 76 (1999).

72. Lisa Rabasca, "Benefits, Costs and Convergence," *Presstime*, 3 (2001).

73. Thomas Kunkel and Gene Roberts, "Leaving Readers Behind: The Age of Corporate Newspapering," *American Journalism Review* (May 2001).

74. Aly Colon, "The Multimedia Newsroom," *Columbia Journalism Review* 26 (June 2000).

75. Al Tompkins and Aly Colon, "NAB 2000: The Convergence Marketplace," *Broadcast and Cable*, 10 April 2000, 48, quoting WFLA news director Bradley.

76. Tompkins and Colon, "NAB 2000," 48.

77. Moses, "TV or not TV?" 22.

78. Rabasca, "Benefits, Costs and Convergence," 2.

79. Strupp, "Three Point Play," 21.

80. Rabasca, "Benefits, Costs and Convergence," 4.

81. Rabasca, "Benefits, Costs and Convergence," 4; Tompkins and Colon, "NAB 2000," 50; Bill Mitchell, "Media Collaborations," *Broadcasting and Cable* (10 April 2000).

82. Moses, "TV or Not TV," 23.

83. McConnell, "The National Acquirers."

84. Sei-Hill Kim, Dietram A. Scheufele, and James Shanahan, "Think about It This Way: Attribute Agenda Setting Function of the Press and the Public's Evaluation of a Local Issue," *Journalism and Mass Communications Quarterly* 79 (2002), 381; Graber, *Mass Media*; Paletz, *The Media in American Politics*; Just, Crigler, Alger, Cook, Kern and West, *Crosstalk*; Kahn and Kenney, *U.S. Senate Campaign*; Shanto Iyengar and Donald R. Kinder, *News That Matters* (Chicago: University of Illinois Press, 1987); Maxwell E. McCombs and Donald Shaw, "The Agenda-Setting Function of the Mass Media," *Public Opinion Quarterly* 36 (1972). David Domke, David Perlmutter, and Meg Spratt, "The Primes of Our Times? An Examination of the 'Power' of Visual Images," *Journalism* 3 (2002): 131; Jon A. Krosnick and Donald R. Kinder, "Altering the Foundation of Support for the President through Priming," *American Political Science Review* 84 (1990); Zhongdang Pan and Gerald M. Kosicki, "Priming and Media Impact on the Evaluation the President's Performance," *Communications Research* 24 (1997); Marion R. Just, Ann N. Crigler, and W. Russell Neuman, "Cognitive and Affective Dimensions of Political Conceptualization," in *The Psychology of Political Communications*, ed. Ann N. Crigler (Ann Arbor: University of Michigan Press, 1996).

85. Gregory W. Gwiasda, "Network News Coverage of Campaign Advertisements: Media's Ability to Reinforce Campaign Messages," *American Politics Research* 29 (2001): 461; Lynda Lee Kaid et al., "Television News and Presidential Campaigns: The Legitimation of Televised Political Advertising," *Social Science Quarterly* 74 (1993); Stephen Ansolabehere and Shanto Iyengar, "Riding the Wave and Claiming Ownership Over Issues: The Joint Effect of Advertising and News Coverage in Campaigns," *Public Opinion Quarterly* 58 (1995); James B. Lemert, William R. Elliott and James M. Bernstein, *News Verdicts, the Debates, and Presidential Campaigns* (New York: Praeger, 1991); Glenn J. Hansen and William Benoit, "Presidential Television Advertising and Public Policy Priorities, 1952–2002," *Communications Studies* 53 (2002): 284. John R. Zaller, *The Nature and Origins of Mass Opinion* (New York: Cambridge University Press, 1992) is cited as the origin of the hypothesis on effect (see also Mark R. Joslyn and Steve Cecolli, "Attentiveness to Television News and Opinion Change in the Fall of 1992 Election Campaign," *Political Behavior*, 18 (1996); William L. Benoit and Glenn Hansen, "Issue Adaptation of Presidential Television Spots and Debates to Primary and General Audiences," *Communications Research Reports* 19 (2002).

86. Domke, Perlmutter, and Spratt, "The Primes of Our Times?" 131. The authors present a detailed social psychological and even neurological discussion of the reasons why and ways in which visual images have a greater impact.

87. Vincent Mosco, *The Pay-Per Society: Computers & Communications in the Information Age* (Norwood, N.J.: Ablex, 1989), chap. 2; Pierre Levy, *Cyberculture* (Minneapolis: University of Minnesota, 2001), 109; Peter Levine, *The Internet and Civil Society,* Report from the University of Maryland, Institute for Philosophy & Public Policy 20, no. 4 (Fall 2000): 3; National Council for Civil Liberties, *Liberating Cyberspace* (London: Pluto Press, 1999), chap. 8.

88. Mosco, *The Pay-Per Society,* 43.

89. Peter Levine, "Can the Internet Rescue Democracy? Toward an On-line Commons," in *Democracy's Moment: Reforming the American Political System for the 21st Century,* ed., Ronald Hayuk and Kevin Mattson (Lanham, Md.: Rowman and Littlefield, 2002); Levine, *The Internet,* 3.

90. Mosco, *The Pay-Per Society,* 11.

91. Meyer, *Media Democracy,* 37–38; McManus, 1994.

92. Levy, *Cyberculture,* 197.

93. Street, *Mass Media,* citations to Jurgen Habermas, *The Structural Transformation of the Public* (Cambridge: Polity Press, 1989), *Between Facts and Norms* (Cambridge: Polity Press, 1996).

94. Meyer, *Media Democracy,* 38.

95. Gans, *Democracy,* 50; Kovach and Rosentsteil, *Warp Speed,* 6; Street, *Mass Media,* 36–52.

96. Graber, *Processing Politics,* 113–14.

97. Kovach and Rosentsteil, *Warp Speed,* 21, 44.

98. Meyer, *Media Democracy,* 32–35.

99. Meyer, *Media Democracy,* 67; Graber, 112–14; Nicholas Jones, *Soundbites and Spindoctors: How Politicians Manipulate the Media—and Visa Versa* (London: Cassel, 1995).

100. Gans, *Democracy,* 49.

101. Kovach and Rosentsteil, *Warp Speed,* 7–8.

102. Street, *Mass Media,* 47–49; Joel Meyerowitz, *No Sense of Place: The Effect of Electronic Media on Social Behavior* (New York: Oxford, 1985).

103. Street, *Mass Media,* 47; Graber, 111–12; Todd Gitlin, "Bites and Blips: Chunk News, Savvy Talk and the Bifurcation of American Politics," in *Communications and Citizenship: Journalism and the Public Sphere,* ed. Peter Dahlgren and Colin Sparks (London: Routledge, 1991), 119–136.

104. Meyer, *Media Democracy,* 35; Kovach and Rosenstiel, *Warp Speed,* chap. 7; Street, *Mass Media,* 44.

105. David C. Barker, *Rushed to Judgment* (New York: Columbia University Press, 2002).

106. Project for Excellence in Journalism, *Does Ownership Matter in Local Television News: A Five-Year Study of Ownership and Quality* (Washington, D.C., February 17, 2003), executive summary.

107. Slattery, Hakanen and Doremus, "The Expression of Localism;" Carroll and Tuggle, "The World Outside;" Fairchild, "Deterritorializing Radio;" Layton and Dorroh, "Sad State;" Olson, "Exploiting the Tension," 40–41; Stavitsky, "The Changing Conception of Localism."

108. Mosco, *The Pay-Per Society,* 26.

109. Levine, Can, 124.

110. Sparrow, *Uncertain Guardians,* 28–38.

111. Meyer, *Media Democracy,* 133; Gans, *Democracy,* 47–48.

112. Gans, *Democracy,* 49.

113. Graber, 88.

114. Kovach and Rosentstiel, *Warp Speed,* chaps. 4, 5.

115. Gans, *Democracy,* 50–51.

116. Meyer, *Media Democracy,* 53; Andreas Dorner, *Politainment* (Frankfurt/Main: Surhkamp, 2001).

117. Graber, 84.

118. Street, *Mass Media*, 57–58, 83, 90; Gans, *Democracy*, 83; Timothy E. Cook, *Governing with the New: The News Media as a Political Institution* (Chicago: University of Chicago Press, 1998).

119. Meyer, *Media Democracy*, 58.

120. Meyer, *Media Democracy*, xi.

121. Meyer, *Media Democracy*, 15.

122. James Curran, *Media and Power* (London: Routledge, 2002), 150.

123. Curran, *Media and Power*, 138.

124. Gans, *Democracy*, 45–46, 79–80; Curran, *Media and Power*, 220.

125. Curran, *Media and Power*, 138.

126. Meyer, *Media Democracy*, 106.

127. Meyer, *Media Democracy*, 104.

128. Meyer, *Media Democracy*, 24.

129. Thomas E. Patterson, *The Vanishing Voter* (New York: Alfred A. Knopf, 2002); Matthew A. Crenson and Benjamin Ginsberg, *Downsizing Democracy* (Baltimore: Johns Hopkins University Press, 2002).

130. Bruce Bimber, "The Internet and Political Transformation: Populism, Community and Accelerated Pluralism," *Polity* 31 (1998); Lawrence Grossman, *The Electronic Republic: Reshaping Democracy in the Information Age* (New York: Penguin, 1996); Tracy Weston, "Can Technology Save Democracy," *National Civic Review* 87 (1998).

131. Richard Wise, *Multimedia: A Critical Introduction* (London: Routledge, 2000), 26; Levy, *Cyberculture*, 106.

132. Levy, *Cyberculture*, 166.

133. Diana Saco, *Cybering Democracy* (Minneapolis: University of Minnesota Press, 2002), 44.

134. Levy, *Cyberculture*, 176.

135. Levine, *Can*.

136. National Council for Civic Liberties, *Liberating*, Introduction.

137. Mosco, *The Pay-Per Society*, chaps. 2 and 4; Wise, *Multimedia*, 5.

138. Wise, *Multimedia*, 126; Steven E. Miller, *Civilizing Cyberspace* (New York: ACM Press, 1998), chap. 2

139. Lawrence Lessig, *Code and the Future of Ideas: The Fate of the Commons in a Connected World* (New York: Random House, 2001).

140. Mark N. Cooper, *Cable Mergers and Monopolies: Market Power, Digital Media and Communications Networks,* (Washington, D.C.: Economic Policy Institute, 2002).

141. Charles M. Firestone and Jorge M. Schement, 1995, *Toward an Information Bill of Rights and Responsibilities* (Washington, D.C.: Aspen Institute), 45; Guido H. Stempell, III and Thomas Hargrove, "Mass Media Audiences in a Changing Media Environment," *Journalism and Mass Communications Quarterly* (Autumn 1996); Albert C. Gunther, "The Persuasive Press Inference: Effects of Mass Media on Perceived Public Opinion," *Communications Research* (October 1998); *American Civil Liberties Union v. Janet Reno*, 929 F. Supp. 824 (E. D. Pa. 1996), 117 S. Ct. 2329 (1997); Iosifides, "Diversity versus Concentration."

142. K. C. Loudon, "Promise versus Performance of Cable," in *Wired Cities: Shaping the Future of Communications* ed., William H. Dutton, Jay G. Blumler, and Kenneth L. Kraemer (Boston: K. G. Hall, 1987); D. LeDuc, *Beyond Broadcasting* (New York: Longman, 1987); Thomas Streeter, "The Cable Fable Revisited; Discourse, Policy, and the Making of Cable Television," *Critical Studies in Mass Communications* (1987); B. Winston, "Rejecting the Jehovah's Witness Gambit," *Intermedia* (1990); N. M. Sine et al., "Current Issues in Cable Television: A Rebalancing to Protect the Consumer," *Cardozo Arts & Entertainment Law Journal* (1990); Robert H. Wicks and Montague Kern, "Factors Influencing Decisions by Local Television News Directors to Develop New Reporting Strategies during the 1992 Political Campaign," *Communications Research* (1995); Massimo Motta and Michele Polo, "Concentration and Public Policies in

the Broadcasting Industry," *Communications Law and Policy* (Spring 1997); Richard Lubunski, "The First Amendment at the Crossroads: Free Expression and New Media Technology," *Communications Law and Policy* (Spring 1997); Sylvia Chan-Olmsted and Jung Suk Park, "From On-Air to Online World: Examining the Content and Structures of Broadcast TV Stations' Web Sites," *Journalism & Mass Communication Quarterly* 77, (2000).

143. Ofori, *When Being No. 1 Is Not Enough,* asserts a bias in advertising rates. Bradford, "Discrimination in Capital Markets," asserts a bias in capital markets.

144. Tim Jordan, *Cyberpower* (London: Routledge, 1998), chap. 5

145. Bob Van Orden, "Top Five Interactive Digital-TV Applications," *Multichannel News,* 21 June 1999, 143; Kearney, chap. 4.

146. Bill Menezes, "Replay, TiVo Get Cash for Consumer Push," *Multichannel News,* 5 April 1999, 48.

147. Mark N. Cooper, "Inequality in Digital Society," *Cardozo Journal on Media and the Arts* 73 (2002).

148. "Profile with Bob Wright: The Agony Before the Ecstasy of Digital TV," *Digital Television* (April 1999): 40; Kim Maxwell, *Residential Broadband: An Insider's Guide to the Battle for the Last Mile* (New York: John Wiley, 1999), 9–10.

149. Peter Levine, *Building the Electronic Commons* (College Park, Md., Democracy Collaborative, April 5, 2002), 17.

150. Levine, Can, 135.

151. Lincoln Dahlberg, "The Internet and Democratic Discourse," *Information, Communications and Society,* 4 (2001).

152. Hsiang Iris Chyi and Dominic L. Lasora, "An Exploratory Study on the Market Relation between Online and Print Newspapers," *Journal of Media Economics* 15 (2002).

153. Kirsten A. Foot and Steven M. Schneider, "Online Action in Campaign 2000: An Exploratory Analysis of the U.S. Political Web Sphere," *Journal of Broadcasting and Electronic Media* 46 (2002).

154. Levine, Can, 125.

155. Levine, Can, 125.

156. Jordan, *Cyberpower,* chaps. 3 and 4.

157. Levine, The Internet, 2.

158. Levine, Can, 127.

159. Levine, Can, 23.

160. Levine, The Internet, 8.

161. Levine, The Internet, 7.

162. Levine, Can, 127.

163. Levine, Can, 127.

164. Wise, *Multimedia,* 197.

165. Wise, *Multimedia,* 202.

166. *Associated Press v. United States,* 326 U.S. 1, 20 (1945).

167. Sunstein, *Republic.com.*

7

News Agency Dominance in International News on the Internet

Chris Paterson

Do media convergence and the migration of news consumers to the Internet democratize information flow as conventional wisdom suggests, or only disguise a steady reduction in information diversity? Through analysis of the international news agency sector, this chapter posits the latter, alarming, possibility. Comparative Internet content research indicates that as Web news providers increase in quantity and scope, the original sources of consequential international news stories are few. Global multimedia information conglomerates Associated Press and Reuters dominate Internet news, but do so in mostly inconspicuous ways.[1]

In their analysis of Internet commerce, Sarkar et al. propose that contrary to predictions that reduced transactional costs afforded by electronic networks will lead to direct consumer-producer links, bypassing intermediary information processors (termed "disintermediation"), Internet growth is reinforcing the strength of traditional intermediaries and resulting in the development of a new kind of intermediary (which they label "cybermediaries").[2] News agencies remain mostly in the background, but extend their influence, for most cybermediaries merely relay agency content.

This chapter presents an analysis and quantification of these phenomena in the context of news agency political economy, and attempts to bridge traditional divides in the study of international news. Hjarvard posits these as micro- and macro-research approaches[3] and the perspectives of news construction (emphasizing the storytelling routines of journalists) versus news selection (emphasizing, in the tradition of White,[4] the journalist as selector of news, rather than creator of it).

Here, a mostly micro-level view of news selection in the gate-keeping tradition is situated in the macro-level context of media imperialism and media political economy. While it echoes 1970s concern about media and cultural imperialism (defined most effectively by Boyd-Barrett and Schiller, respectively),[5] and shifts antiquated critiques of news flow[6] to the cyberspace arena, I wish to suggest the problem identified here should be viewed as a manifestation of our globalized and converged age, and not merely as a continuation of the news agency influence over international news which has existed for nearly a century and a half (which it also is).[7]

Comparative analysis of international news stories from major news Web sites with wire stories reveals a dearth of original journalism (or even copy-editing) and near total dependence by major Web news providers (like MSNBC, CNN, Yahoo, and others) on wire service reporting and writing. The multitude of on-line information providers evidence burgeoning "cybermediation" of a limited diet of news, rather than the outright disintermediation evidenced in other cyberspace sectors.

Most Internet users go to just a few news sources. In 2001, it was reported that fully one-third of the time U.S. net users spent on-line was with AOL Time Warner Web sites. When confined to home, versus business, use, the number rose to 75 percent.[8] So, despite the vast amount of choice the Web offers, Disney, MSNBC, and Time Warner (which dropped AOL from its name in 2003), with a few other giants, provide most on-line news. This study shows that most of the international news they provide comes from just two sources.

To continue with an economic framework, I am defining Internet-based journalism as a transactional relationship between news producers and news consumers, which takes place through electronic networks. It need not be a monetary transaction; any provision of news on the Internet by a journalist who profits in some way by doing so can be categorized as such a transaction. Such relationships of information exchange form a subset of electronic commerce (e-commerce), so for this discussion, we term this subset "e-journalism."[9] E-journalism depends upon many of the same processes and channels of networked communication as do other sectors of e-commerce, but given the unique role of journalism in social relations and the formation of public consciousness,[10] it must be addressed as a special case.

Technological convergence and corporate consolidation during the past decade has resulted in an e-journalism sector in which the production of information is more highly concentrated than before the Internet age, and in which information delivery is becoming increasing concentrated. Such a hypothesis is at odds with popular perceptions of the Internet as a pluralist and democratizing environment, a mythology reviewed in its early stages by Aufderheide.[11]

NEWS IN CYBERSPACE

A few main forms of e-journalism are now common. Most news consumers go either to the Web sites of leading television networks or newspapers, or gateway/portal sites and the leading search engines. Most of the latter have news pages reproducing, under license, the news output of a few large news organizations. Formerly, all-purpose portals like Yahoo were distinguished from those more fully dedicated to searching, like Google; but in recent years, Google and other leading search engines have added news sections of their own, blurring such distinction. For both the portals and the search services, international news content is typically from one or two secondary producers like Reuters news agency (occasionally, with links provided for any given story to additional news producers). That is, news content is not created originally for the site, but it may be selected and presented by an editorial staff.

As stated in a commentary by the BBC, the "World Wide Web, widely thought of as an endless myriad of choice, appears to be shrinking."[12] That is, fewer major news providers are informing more people and (the BBC fails to note) doing so from fewer sources. And the dominance of global multimedia news providers Associated Press and Reuters appears to be growing. To demonstrate this phenomenon, I narrow the focus to the intersection of news agency political economy and cyberspace information exchange.

Industry research continues to show that news consumers are making less use of television and more use of the Internet. A 1998 survey reported that 76 percent of U.S. news consumers still "turn to broadcast or cable TV for information on breaking news," but that 12 percent go to the Internet, 9 percent to the radio, and 2 percent wait for the next edition of their newspaper.[13] A more recent, though less well evidenced, report based on survey data indicates that by 2000, 23 percent of Americans reported on-line news was their main news source, a figure which increased ten percentage points in two years.[14] That report also indicated that 18 percent of survey respondents who use on-line news say they are going to other sources less often, which is nearly double the number who made that claim two years earlier.[15] Pew later found that, "those who have searched for political news and information on-line grew by 57 percent between 2000 and 2002."[16] Data are inconsistent, though, with another frequently cited survey reporting that after September 11, 2001, the percentage of U.S. Web users "who say the Internet is their primary news source" increased from 3 percent to 8 percent.[17]

Some industry research contradicts a hypothesis of this study: that e-journalism is largely unoriginal. Major newspaper and magazine sites provided substantially more original content in 1998 than they had in previous years, and reported that more than half of U.S. newspapers have merged their print and on-line newsrooms.[18] Newspapers are reported to be increasingly breaking new stories on-line rather than waiting for the next edition, as has been the tradition from the outset of Internet journalism.[19] Based upon their survey, Ross and Middleberg declare: "1998 marks a historic moment—news organizations have now clearly broken away from their tendency to use on-line technology (Web sites usually, but not always) as a distribution device more than as a new medium."

There is little evidence of such a trend amongst broadcaster-run sites, however, and Burden found in a study of the BBC On-Line newsroom that content remains closely tied to broadcast output and that only minimal use is made of the interactive capabilities of the Internet medium.[20] McChesney is even more critical, with his insistence that "the trend of on-line journalism is to accentuate the worst synergistic and profit hungry attributes of commercial journalism, with it is emphasis on trivia, celebrities, and consumer news."[21] Tremayne found indications of genuine interactivity—the chief advantage of the new media—in many major sites, but does not demonstrate that any are substantial.[22]

Despite recent evidence that only the major sites draw large audiences, more and more forms of e-journalism constantly come on line. Major news sites continue to grow. That growth, however, is largely due to acquisition of smaller Internet sites by the few largest ones, and by the massive subsidization of Internet ventures by the major conglomerates, which are willing to lose $200–300 million (U.S.) yearly in order to dominate the Internet.[23] According to the European Journalism Centre, CNN reaches more people over the Internet than through broadcasting.[24]

Popular Internet news sites typically become immensely more so when a single news event is receiving saturation coverage from all media. Such was the case during the Iraq/U.S. war, on September 11, 2001, and in the United States in April 1999, when following the Colorado high school shootings Internet news sites saw as much as a 70 percent increase in traffic (in the case of the AP.org).[25]

Among Internet news consumers, national and international news is preferred over local content. An industry study reports that 61 percent of Internet users read national and international news on-line, while just 26 percent do so for local news.[26] Indeed, a U.S. survey indicated that news consumers are dissatisfied with the quality of local news available on the Internet, and that users prefer to get their national and international news from major news sites rather than their local newspaper.[27]

And in what may be an even more telling trend, industry researcher MediaMetrix reports that although the number of published Web sites continues to rise, Web users are spending more of their time with fewer sites. Most of these are the major news/gateway sites. The company reports that U.S. Web users "now spend almost 20 percent of their time on the Web visiting only the top ten sites," up from 16 percent one year earlier. Further, "the amount of time spent at the top 50 and 100 sites has risen even more since 1998."[28]

As of 2004, the top U.S. sites had changed little since the 1999 BBC report, but show an even greater degree of control by the leading media conglomerates. With non-news providing mega-sites Ebay, Amazon, Infospace, About/Primedia, and CNET removed, the following are the leading organizations providing e-journalism. The major news brands of each are indicated. European and other non-U.S. rankings generally show the same dominant conglomerates, occasionally using different brand names, and occasionally supplemented by the Web news offerings of local media (as with the popular BBC, ITN, and Guardian newspaper sites in the UK).[29]

1. Yahoo! Sites, with key news channel, news.yahoo.com
2. MSN-Microsoft Sites, with news channels MSNBC (in partnership with General Electric), and CNBC
3. Time Warner Network (with American Online), with news brands AOL, CNN, Time, Netscape News (cnn.netscape.cnn.com)
4. Google, with news brand news.google.com
5. Terra Lycos, with news channel news.lycos.com
6. Excite Network, with news channel news.excite.com
7. Walt Disney Internet Group (WDIG), with news channels ABCnews.com, Go, and others
8. Viacom Online, with news channel cbsnews.cbs.com

Closer examination of these top cybermediaries shows the news source concentration alluded to at the outset. When inspected for this research, the AOL (America On-Line) site provided only unedited Associated Press stories for international news, and only unedited Reuters stories for U.S. domestic news. Disney's GO Network portal site offered mostly unedited international news from Reuters, with some stories by ABC news mixed in. However, as noted below, ABC's on-line stories appear to be mostly minimally edited AP and Reuters stories. Such curious alliances as this, by which GO offers ABC, which offers barely reworked news wires, evidences the complex layers of mediation in e-journalism, especially with regard to international news provision. The processes of information concentration resulting from structural convergence are evidenced by the links between Microsoft products and General Electric (NBC) produced news, as well as other cases.

The Lycos portal offers a mix of AP and Reuters international stories, provided in essentially the same format and order as the agency stories provided by Yahoo. Excite formerly offered only Reuters stories, and later only AP stories (with a link to Reuters stories). Excite also selects almost exactly the same international stories, and presents them in almost exactly the same order of prominence, as do Yahoo and Lycos, for they are each depending on the editorial decisions of Reuters and Associated Press to determine what in the world is important on any given day. In 2001, the *New York Times* also began distributing its content through Yahoo, in addition to its own popular Web site.[30]

In the U.K., the BBC offers the most popular news site with BBC On-line, but as shown below, despite its extensive resources, much of its international content is news agency provided. It is therefore evident that unlike the fading, but still kicking, phenomenon of public-service broadcasting, public service Web-casting, especially in the arena of international news, has almost no popular foothold (the BBC is the only significant global example), and where it does exist, its content remains substantially commercially determined.[31]

Web users are fed the limited agency diet of international news in other ways. The same content providers discussed here often offer tailored news "pushed" to a user's computer screen. Yahoo and other services offer an e-mail alert service, which will send subscribers—at no cost—e-mail with news stories on selected topics of interest. Such services are increasingly migrating to wireless communications services, with a number of new alliances between news content providers and cellular telephone companies. These are the latest manifestations of "create your own newspaper" technologies that encourage the news audience to consume only the type of news stories that most gratify them (termed "the daily me" by Harper).[32] As of this writing, these have not emerged as significant channels of news delivery, and so do not feature in this analysis.

Your computer may also direct you to news agency content with little encouragement on your part. Netscape.com, which is the portal site directly linked to the most popular browser software, offers a news menu of mostly Reuters international stories, with some Associated Press stories. Microsoft's portal site, of course, links news junkies directly to MSNBC, which Microsoft co-owns with General Electric. Disney and Time-Warner have also arranged with Microsoft (along with Netscape and PointCast) to have their Web brands listed in the premier positions in built-in browser directories and buttons.[33]

Microsoft faced legal action in the United States and Europe for integrating its Explorer browser and various direct links to Microsoft Web sites into its Windows operating systems. Its news service is MSNBC, which provides international stories. Such stories (according to the present study), unless they happen near one of the few international NBC bureaus, will be written almost entirely by Reuters and the Associated Press. The increasingly popular Web sites operated directly by Reuters and by Associated Press, of course, provide exclusively the content generated by each company. AP, however, as a means of protecting the print media which own it, only provides links to its content through the Web sites of member newspapers.

Convoluted layers of mediation and distribution agreements often lead to contention within the cyberjournalism industry. For example, the BBC, which is mixing news agency content with the work of its own staff, posts news to its own bbc.co.uk Web site, the most popular site in the United Kingdom. Most of the funding for the service comes from Britons who pay license fees, not advertising. But Yahoo and other commercial providers, to the advantage of themselves and the BBC, repost the publicly funded BBC's news. Commercially funded British e-journalism organizations, such as Independent Television News (ITN), have felt so threatened by this as to complain to British regulators.[34]

But the story is more complex than that. With the BBC's international content consisting partially of unchanged wire service content (and, more abstractly, wire service story framing), the British television license holder is effectively paying for Yahoo (and others) to profit by displaying wire service stories with the valuable BBC byline (or "brand logo").

NEWS AGENCIES AND CYBERSPACE

Through many layers of mediation, the news product and news perspectives of major wire services are reproduced directly and indirectly in the Web content of cybernews providers, often despite claims of editorial independence by the major cybermediaries of e-journalism, like MSNBC, CNN, Yahoo, the BBC, and a few others. The process of on-line news production has received little close examination through comprehensive research in newsrooms. It is known that journalists specializing in the on-line distribution of their news product have had to develop numerous strategies to adapt to this new form of journalism.

Some researchers have argued that new forms of highly interactive journalism are emerging[35] but the evidence offered here suggests that the dominant Internet news sites do little more than redistribute the work of other—mostly news agency—journalists, with a minimum of editing or reinterpretation. To date, only a few small studies have actually detailed the news production environment of on-line journalists, and in these cases, they have depended more on survey and interview questions than newsroom observation.[36] The extensive dialogue about on-line journalism and the information content of cyberspace cannot be fully informed until substantial ethnographic analyses of on-line news production have been undertaken

There is some indication that journalism as a whole is coming to depend more and more on e-journalism for ideas and source material, and that the Internet sources preferred by journalists are the same ones dependent on news agency content. For example, Ross and Middleberg found that journalists heavily use the major Web portal sites both to navigate the Web and to read news, and the majority of these prefer the Reuters-dependent Yahoo news site.[37] While we know journalists' intake of information is shifting, there is little research on the impact.

Dependence on news agency content is not always the result of a desire for perceived high content quality at little cost, but is also a function of brand association. Web sites seek to draw users through association with well-known brands, especially those with strong positive associations for the user. Dependence on AP or Reuters provides these, for each is (at the time of this writing) a vaguely known brand name with no negative associations in the public mind, for the mass audience has little direct experience with them which could create such associations. Professional journalists, on the other hand, are quick to recite the many pros and cons of each. It is also important for populist Web sites to be seen by their users as reliable providers of what is widely regarded as the important news of the day, and the only way to demonstrate that to the mass audience is to provide the same news as other major media are providing.

Industry consultants are pressuring news providers to reduce the depth of news analysis they provide on-line, and instead to use editorial resources to "develop stories around headline stories" (which tend to be those selected by wire services).[38] This advice is based on usage data indicating that, on average, just ten minutes is spent by consumers in each on-line news session (ibid.).

This author's previous research has supplemented the earlier work of Boyd-Barrett, and others, describing how increasing concentration of control over the global wholesale news system has made the major news agencies more influential than they have ever been.[39] That is mostly the result of major television networks of the wealthiest nations dramatically curtailing their own international reporting since the 1980s, and relying more on agencies as a result; that, in turn, was mostly the result of the determination of new corporate owners like Disney and General Electric that news divisions should pay their own way. Disney's lack of interest in news also helped to consolidate the agency sector, when the company sold Worldwide Television News—the video agency with the longest history—to its new rival, Associated Press Television in 1997, leaving just AP and Reuters in the business of large-scale multimedia international news delivery.

News agencies, in their desire to please all of their clients, all of the time, must work even harder than their client journalists to create the appearance of objectivity and neutrality. In so doing, they manufacture an ideologically distinctive and homogeneous view of the world; stories challenging the ideological positions of the dominant political players on the world scene (in agency eyes, the United States and U.K.) receive little attention.

But the news agency role is crucial for additional reasons. News agencies set the agenda for what international stories other media choose to carry. This is done through the choice of stories they distribute to clients, the amount of visuals provided (moving for TV, still for newspapers and magazines, and both for Webcasters), and in the case of agency-provided TV pictures, the nature and amount of accompanying audio and textual information. In television, broadcasters write their stories around the video these organizations offer, and if they are not offered video images, they will not report, or will minimize, an international story. Various studies of television newsrooms have shown that the availability of visual images is an important factor in determining whether a foreign news story is carried.[40]

Global and regional news agencies are crucial due to their agenda-setting influence on other media, but are now even more crucial since they so effectively bypass or control the intermediary processors of news in cyberspace, enabling them to reach directly—for the first time—a large portion of the mass news audience (and potentially cultivate a new audience uninterested in traditional media).

News agencies have historically sought to minimize their public exposure, for their success had previously rested largely with their ability to make news audiences believe that their local media outlet—not an international agency—had brought them the news of the world. Now, agencies depend on the popular appeal of their brand names for audience loyalty in cyberspace, and so market their names aggressively.

The major wire services were ideally positioned to capitalize on both the technological and the structural aspects of convergence. Each has a 150-year history—more or less—of generating a great deal of textual content for delivery over wired networks. Digital and structural convergence now permit them to provide their product directly to a mass audience.

This project presumes that a diversity of information is a necessary prerequisite of democracy and a desirable goal, so it is not necessary to specifically indicate fault with the news content provided by the wire services. This is to argue, in effect, that the central weakness of the international wire services is their success—their ubiquity is the problem.

Former APTN chief executive Stephen Claypoole stated that the "Associated Press believes that its future in the next century depends on the ability to provide all the components of multi-media."[41] With Reuters, AP has been tremendously successful at doing so, and has skillfully exploited every new production and delivery option afforded by digital convergence. The importance of the Internet to Reuters is evidenced by its announcement that it would be creating a position of Web strategist at the corporate board level and putting the head of its highly profitable Trading Systems Division in that post.[42]

Reuters's head of television and visuals, Tony Donovan, clarified the evolving Reuters strategy in November 2000:

Perhaps more controversial, is the whole issue of channels. . . . Our history has always been that we have provided material to the channels (whether the channel has been a newspaper, magazine, or a TV channel). We have been a provider without ever actually being involved in running those channels. That, I believe, will change.[43]

The limited diet of international news provided mostly by a few organizations suggests that e-journalism follows a distribution model more closely akin to broadcasting than other aspects of cyberspace. That is, in the provision of international news on-line, a few large concerns generate and broadcast—with essentially no feedback loop—most of the content for most of the audience. Further, it is a very limited and homogenous content dictated by the ideological, structural, and cultural nature of these organizations.[44]

It is a view of the world as seen mostly through London, where international news providers are centered.[45] London is the home of Reuters, and despite on-again, off-again attempts to decentralize, its London headquarters continues to closely control news selection and provide much content and most editorial control for most of the world. For Associated Press, content is mostly shaped from New York, with considerable influence from the London bureau of the wire service and the London headquarters of the corporation's television arm, APTN.

Throughout their long histories, news agencies have been under pressure to localize their output by giving greater voice, and greater editorial power, to local, more expert, bureaus; but they have always resisted because their strength lies in their ability to process masses of news—in many forms—through their London and New York news factories. Doing so conveniently allows them to speak with "one voice" (though few agency journalists would admit a story could have multiple interpretations). We should also wonder about the impact of a small and culturally homogenous group of news professionals shaping the news of all the world's affairs—but that is beyond the scope of this chapter.

It makes economic sense that the two leading news agencies should dominate international news delivery in cyberspace, for as in any open and unregulated market, the strongest producers with the lowest unit costs will thrive. Such is the case for the major wire services, which each have a century and a half of experience in developing production processes which generate massive amounts of news. Digital technologies have made all aspects on news agency production more efficient, and their (technological) convergence has permitted easy access into new markets through the creation of news products tailored to new media, but built from the same agency words and pictures upon which traditional media have long depended.

Through processes of digital convergence and industrial alliances, news is gathered in various forms (words, sounds, moving and still pictures) but its various textual, visual, and aural components may typically be combined and transmitted digitally to a central newsroom (normally in London) for processing and distribution. A news agency can digitize and compress textual descriptions, still pictures, video, and sound at the scene of a news event and transmit these to headquarters, all at once via the same laptop computer and satellite telephone.[46] There, different news agency departments confer on the construction of the news and share each of these elements in the construction of stories for various audiences. Finally, the news consumer in cyberspace is reached through any of several processes of mediation, simplified by the convergence of digital distribution mechanisms.

At the level of news distribution, the primary cybermediaries in e-journalism take two forms: on-line media which consist of popular sites relaying agency content to audiences (gateways/ portals/ malls/ search services), and content producing on-line media (content producers), which tend to combine original content with agency content. The latter category includes mostly traditional media like the BBC or the *New York Times*, but also news companies which began on the Web (the now defunct *Nando Times* is the best known example). Since much of the Web content of these organizations is barely reconstructed agency material (mostly in the case of the former), the agencies reach a large secondary audience as part of the 'original' content of these services.

Since agencies also serve their traditional clients like newspapers and television broadcasters, and much of the content designed for those media is simply transferred to the World Wide Web, the agencies reach an additional secondary on-line audience through these traditional media, serving in a cybermediary role.

ANALYSIS OF CONTENT

The nature of news agency content has received relatively little scrutiny. Hjarvard,[47] Malik,[48] and Paterson[49] have described television news agency and television news exchange content in some detail, while a few studies have examined the textual output of the wires services at the international[50] and regional[51] levels, and have looked at wire service coverage of specific events.[52]

Reuters and AP output has typically been found to address a limited range of news frames and deal with a highly proscribed range of news actors.[53] In a study for Fairness and Accuracy in Reporting (FAIR), Amster-Burton and Amster-Burton found "consistent official and male bias" in Reuters stories provided by Yahoo.[54] They quote Yahoo as claiming that their Reuters content was then "by far the most popular on-line news service."

Of sixty-nine Reuters stories analyzed in a late 1996, week-long, sample, only 6 percent of news sources were women. Few other studies of gender bias in agency output are apparent, but in a study of television news agency output Paterson determined that where a main actor could be coded in internationally distributed television news agency stories, only 13 percent were female.[55] And that statistic was intriguingly generated from stories appearing during the week of the 1995 United Nations Women's Conference. Mainstream news services—and agencies are the most mainstream—also privilege official sources, as Tuchman and many others have chronicled.[56]

Amster-Burton and Amster-Burton found that the Reuters content they analyzed was comprised of 91 percent official governmental and corporate sources. Such data are similar to those of numerous other content studies of major international news services.

To date, social critics have taken note of news agency dominance in e-journalism, but detailed quantification is sparse. For instance, in a 1997 essay, Magid observed,

> Surf the Web long enough and you begin to notice some patterns. Wire services, like Reuters and Associated Press, sell the same stories to the Web sites of multiple publications. So do the major newspaper syndicates. Surf long enough and you're bound to find the same articles again and again. . . . You can change the channel, but it's a lot harder to change the story or even the perspective.[57]

As Magid notes, Web sites buy agency content directly from the agencies, even if their parent company—like CNN Interactive's parent CNN—are also agency clients. So while there is some indication that broadcast and newspaper Web sites do recycle a great deal of traditional media content from their sister organization in cyberspace, they also draw directly and extensively from a full range of news agency material. The EJC reports that "at MSNBC . . . the editors select the news, but do not write it," adding somewhat questionably—at least according to the data offered here—that "the 400 MSNBC journalist repackage what 1200 NBC journalists produce."[58] Langfield, in an apparent attempt to replicate this author's research, conducted a search for source dependence among major news sites in 2002 and similarly concluded that "most are extremely slow on breaking news and highly dependent on wire coverage."[59]

CONTENT COMPARISON

News agency dependency in international stories is demonstrated by the following small study, which compares wire service copy with the news content of major cybermediaries for a range of international news stories. Boyd-Barrett and Rantanen point out that as early as 1953, large studies were conducted by both the International Press Institute and UNESCO to measure the amount of news agency material in newspaper stories around the world.[60] Those early studies encouraged the focus on news agencies within the New World Information Order debates, led by UNESCO, in the 1970s.

The influential UNESCO/IAMCR study of international news flow in the early 1980s repeated such measurement, and confirmed extensive news agency dependence, especially among newspapers in developing nations.[61] This author similarly found in 1995 that less wealthy, developing world television broadcasters used a large percentage of news agency–supplied images in their international reporting (three-quarters or more), and, interestingly, the major American networks examined (CNN and ABC) did the same.[62] As Boyd-Barrett and Rantanen (2004) also note that all such studies—and this is true of the current project—are likely to underreport actual news agency content and influence, given the challenge of identifying everything with news agency origins.[63]

A pilot study was conducted with a single story in 1999, giving rise to the current project.[64] For that initial analysis, a single, relatively fast-breaking, and relatively major (in the sense of gaining worldwide coverage) news story was selected. The story was the escalation of violent student rioting in Tehran on the morning of July 12, 1999. Over a period of just a few hours, the text of stories being published on-line by each of the following were copied and electronically stored: Reuters, Associated Press, Agence France Presse, Yahoo, MSNBC, ABC On-line, CNN Interactive, and BBC On-line. Other sources, which might typically be used by journalists on such a story, were also retrieved and stored, including U.S. State Department statements, the relevant output of the Iran News Agency, and the statements of a London-based Iranian dissident group.

Since there is normally a small amount of rewriting of news agency copy, it is difficult to precisely quantify news agency use. It was easy to demonstrate, however, that these major services produced almost no original journalism in this case, and published stories that were almost entirely barely edited wire service material. Of course, in the case of Yahoo and other major sites that simply relay wire services' stories, the material is identical to the wire-service output. In the pilot study, for almost every paragraph of each sample of e-journalism service, there is an identical or nearly identical paragraph provided a few hours earlier by a wire service. Analysis of the CNN, BBC and MSNBC data, revealed that less than five paragraphs from the three services combined were not close or exact duplications of wire service paragraphs. Of thirty-eight nearly duplicated wire paragraphs in this small sample,[65] 37 percent (n=14) of such paragraphs are by Reuters, 58 percent (n=22) by Associated Press, and 5 percent (n=2) by AFP. The large dependency on AP in this sample is likely due to the fact that two of the three on-line services are U.S. based, and U.S. media typically make heavier use of AP than Reuters.

Some interesting news production procedures by on-line journalists could also be seen in this initial research. The choice of specific story frames by the on-line journalists is evident, as when MSNBC opens its story with mostly AP copy, but prefers the Reuters framing (main focus) of the story (in this case, marches in Tehran in defiance of government bans). Limited attempts to localize wire copy for an American audience were clear, especially in the opening paragraphs of the CNN and MSNBC stories. MSNBC, for example, turns the news agency phrase "marched" into "took to the streets;" "hard-liners who have thwarted efforts to institute reforms" become "hard line clerics."

CNN Interactive editors can be seen making numerous attempts to sensationalize wire copy, but not paying great attention to the process. In their on-line story, they insert a sub-headline reading "Women reportedly assaulted," when this gets the briefest mention in the agency coverage and isn't mentioned at all in the CNN story, and change the AP's reference to "leading newspapers" to "leading medias" (sic).

To provide a more comprehensive test of these results, the author worked with undergraduate assistants through the first six months of 2001 to identify and collect data for a series of international stories. The sample included all of the following news sources (although insufficient data were ultimately available for several of these): Reuters, AP, AFP, CNN, MSNBC, BBC, ABC, *New York Times*, *Nando Times*, Yahoo, AOL, Lycos, AltaVista, Excite, Sky (UK), and Yahoo (UK).

Story selection was purposeful, within some limitations; that is, selection was limited by student data-gatherer availability, but within the six-month period, stories were identified which met the following criteria: they were new to the international news menu, not ongoing stories; they took place outside the United States or other 'news elite' nations which receive heavy Western news coverage and are often host representatives of a wide range of news media;[66] they were receiving coverage from both Reuters and the Associated Press—and from at least a few of the other services—during the hours examined. With few exceptions, on-line news story text was collected from each of the news services above, if they covered the given story. In some cases, different versions of a story from a single news service were collected, if that service's story changed significantly during the (typically) three-to-six-hour data-gathering period.

Ultimately, fifteen stories were used (and a version of each story by each of the news providers was obtained). Unlike in the pilot study, where a manual comparison was conducted, the researcher compared the texts of this larger data set using a simple text comparison software called "Copyfind," developed by Professor Lou Bloomfield of the University of Virginia, to detect plagiarism, and made available through his Web site.[67] Many other such programs are now available, and recent editions of Microsoft Word contain text comparison features.

The software indicates strings of text in one document that are copied from another document. The user can set the parameters of what constitutes "copying." In this case, we asked the program to provide the number of words copied where copying was the duplication of a string of five or more words. After several trial runs, this appeared the best compromise to avoid the counting of names or common expressions (i.e. "appeared to be"), but to catch short sentences, or significant portions of sentences, copied directly from wire service copy without alteration.[68]

Comparisons were made between each wire service (AFP was later discarded from the sample for lack of use by the news services) and the story published (on the Web) on each topic by each of the news services in the sample. A total word count was also made (using a word processor) for each sample of news text. A typical result, for a 642-word CNN story on UN troops in the Congo, was that 553 words existed in phrases (strings of five words or more) copied from Reuters, and twenty-nine words existed in phrases copied from AP. This was, in other words, a virtually unchanged Reuters story published by CNN. Finally, some limited analysis of the resulting quantitative data has been undertaken for this paper, but more substantive analysis is ongoing.

The portals (here, Yahoo, Lycos, Excite, and AOL) showed no substantial mediation of agency content, with their text duplicating news agency text for an average of 85 percent of the content studied (the overall average of the average amount of duplication for each service). It is unclear if the remaining 15 percent accounts for actual changes made by Web portal editorial staff to agency stories, variations in identifying text or unrelated portions of the Web page, which were not edited out when the original texts were gathered, or slight changes in the versions of the wire service story compared. It is most likely a combination of those factors.

Of more consequence are the results for the original content producers, which typically claim editorial independence. These demonstrate verbatim use of agency text in 43 percent of their content.[69] That ranges from 53 percent in the international on-line stories of ABC (ironically, regarded in recent years as the best on-line news service by U.S. Web users)[70] to 33 percent in the international stories of CNN Interactive. The BBC has not been included in this analysis, since, to its credit, it demonstrated substantially less agency reliance than its U.S. counterparts.[71]

While depending on an imperfect methodology and small sample, these data provide some empirical evidence of a far more substantial dependence on wire service reporting than major American on-line media typically admit. Many of the stories analyzed were credited to one or more wire services, but it is more characteristically suggested at the top or bottom of a story that "Reuters and the Associated Press contributed to this report," or no mention of the wire services is made at all. These services, of course, have every right to use the news agencies in this way; however, they limit the diversity of information on global affairs when they choose to do so.

CONCLUSION

From this research, and the other work reviewed in this chapter, a number of misconceptions about e-journalism are suggested. Most crucially, while the multitude of on-line information providers evidence increasing "cybermediation" of news, it is a limited diet of news.

But other trends are apparent. For example, it is likely that e-journalism is not especially interactive,[72] and by extension, not more accountable to audiences than traditional media;[73] that it is rarely diverse or pluralist,[74] and by extension, not ideologically alternative; that is not terribly original in content (as shown in the present study, with 43 to 60 percent of "original" content actually originating in the newsrooms of AP and Reuters); and from examples studied for this research, rarely in-depth or nonlinear, although researchers are finding it increasingly so;[75] and finally, that it is not more localized or more relevant than traditional media.

The apparent concentration of international news in the on-line environment is mirrored by similar, and closely related, tendencies in other, traditional, media. Thus, through a lack of any international regulatory controls, market forces of convergence have resulted in a comfortable situation for media conglomerates Reuters and Associated Press, but an uncomfortable one for the public at large.

If further empirical analyses support the hypothesis of agency dependency and high concentration of information provision, provided here, it begins to seem that the diversity of information offered by the Internet is a mythical aspect of information globalization and convergence. Discourse on international events of consequence within the global public sphere—to the extent one exists—is substantially determined by the production practices and institutional priorities of two information services.

NOTES

1. This chapter updates a study originally published as Chris Paterson, "Media Imperialism Revisited: The Global Public Sphere and the News Agency Agenda," in *News in a Globalized Society*, ed. Stig Hjarvard (Göteborg: NORDICOM, 2001), 77–92.

2. M Sarker, B. Butler, and C. Steinfield, "Intermediaries and Cybermediaries: A Continuing Role for Mediating Players in the Electronic Marketplace," *Journal of Computer-Mediated Communication.* 54 (1995) <www.ascusc.org/jcmc/vol1/issue3/sarker.html>

3. Stig Hjarvard, "TV News Flow Studies Revisited," *Electronic Journal of Communication* 5, 2 (1995), 24–38.

4. David M. White, "The 'Gate Keeper': A Case Study in the Selection of News, " *Journalism Quarterly* 27 (1950) 383–90.

5. Oliver Boyd-Barrett, "Media Imperialism: towards an international framework for the analysis of media systems." in *Mass Communication and Society*, ed. James Curran, Michael Gurevitch, and Janet Woollacott (London: Edward Arnold, 1977), 116–35, and Herbert Schiller, *Communication and Cultural Domination* (White Plains, N.Y.: International Arts and Sciences Press, 1976).

6. Bernard Cohen, *The Press and Foreign Policy* (Princeton, N.J.: Princeton University Press, 1963); Johan Galtung and Mari Holmboe Ruge, "The Structure of Foreign News," *Journal of Peace Research* 2 (1965) 64–91; Annabelle Sreberny-Mohammadi, Kaarle Nordenstreng, Robert Stevenson, and Frank Ugboajah. *Foreign News in the Media: International News Reporting in 29 Countries.* Reports and Papers in Mass Communication, no. 93 (Paris: UNESCO, 1985).

7. Donald Read, *The Power of News: The History of Reuters 1849–1989* (Oxford: Oxford University Press,1992); Oliver Boyd-Barrett *The International News Agencies* (London: Constable, 1980).

8. Leslie Walker, "AOL Time Warner Sites Dominate Data," *Washington Post* (27 February 2001).

9. The term "e-journalism" was coined by the author for an early presentation of the current research project: Chris Paterson, "Internet News: Source Concentration and Cybermediation," EURICOM Colloquium on the Political Economy of Convergence, London, 1999.

10. See for instance Peter Berger and Thomas Luckmann, *The Social Construction of Reality; A Treatise in the Sociology of Knowledge* (Garden City, N.Y.: Anchor Books 1966). This is a relationship investors in e-journalism rarely acknowledge, because of the added responsibility such acknowledgment would bring.

11. Pat Aufderheide, "Niche-Market Culture, Off and On Line," in *The Electronic Grapevine: Rumor, Reputation, and Reporting in the New On-Line Environment*, ed. Diane Borden and Kerric Harvey (Mahwah, N.J.: Lawrence Erlbaum Associates, 1998) 43–57.

12. BBC On-line, "Web Is 'Shrinking'," 1999, *BBC On-line*, <news2.thls.bbc.co.uk/hi/english/sci/tech/newsid%5F428000/428999.stm>

13. Jupiter Communications, "Internet a Growing News Provider" *NUA Internet Surveys* <http://www.Nua.com> (9 December 1998),

14. Pew Research Center for the People and the Press "Internet News: More Log On, Tune Out" <http://people-press.org> (11 June 2001)

15. Pew, 2001.

16. Pew Internet & American Life Project "America's Online Pursuits" (December 22, 2003): iv, also available at <www.pewinternet.org>

17. HarrisInteractive, "Harris Interactive Survey Shows Internet's Growth as Primary Source of News and Information in Weeks Following September 11Attacks" (2001) <www.harrisinteractive.com/news/allnewsbydate.asp?NewsID=371>

18. Don Middleberg and Steven Ross (1998) "Media in Cyberspace Study 5th Annual National Survey," (unpublished report, formerly available at www.middleberg.com)

19. Christopher Hanson "The Dark Side of On-Line Scoops," *Columbia Journalism Review* (May/June 1997).

20. Peter Burden, "Interactivity and On-line News at the BBC" (Unpublished Masters Dissertation, CMCR, University of Leicester, 1999).

21. Robert McChesney "The Titanic Sails On: Why the Internet Won't Sink the Media Giants," *Extra!* (March/April 2000).

22. Mark Tremayne, "Internet: Is the Medium the Message?" (unpublished Paper, University of Texas: Department of Journalism, 1997).

23. Robert McChesney, 2000.

24. European Journalism Centre, *The Future of the Printed Press: Challenges in a Digital World* 1998 <www.ejc.nl/hp/fpp/execsum.html>

25. Media Metrix "Heavy News Week Drives Traffic at Web Sites," via *NUA Internet Surveys* (1999) <www.nua.ie/surveys>

26. Jupiter Communications, 1998.

27. Joe Strupp, "Local News Wins Popularity Contest on Newspaper Web Sites," *Editor and Publisher* (30 June 1999).

28. BBC On-line, 1999

29. Based on Nielsen//NetRatings, November 2003; MediaMetrix web ratings, 2001–2003, and other sources.

30. BBC On-line,"Yahoo links with *New York Times*," 2001, BBC On-line, <news.bbc.co.uk/1/low/business/1168993.stm>

31. Hills and Michalis explore the online migration of public service broadcasters at far greater depth than space permits in this chapter. See Jill Hills and Maria Michalis. "The Internet: A Challenge to Public Service Broadcasting?" *Gazette* 62, no.6 (2000).

32. Christopher Harper, "The Daily Me," *American Journalism Review* (April 1997): 40–44.

33. Robert McChesney, 2000.

34. Georgina Lipscomb, "BBC Online Put Under Scrutiny," *Broadcast* (January 2001).

35. For example Eric Fedlin, "Rethinking the News Story for the Internet: Hyperstory Prototypes and a Model of the User," *Journalism Monographs* 163 (1997).

36. See Ann Brill, "Way New Journalism: How Pioneers Are Doing," *Electronic Journal of Communication* 7, no. 2. (1997); Carol Christopher, "Technology and Journalism in the On-Line Newsroom," in *The Electronic Grapevine: Rumor, Reputation, and Reporting in the New On-Line Environment*, ed. Diane Borden and Kerric Harvey (Mahwah, N.J.: Lawrence Erlbaum Associates, 1998), 123–141; Burden, 1999.

37. Don Middleberg and Steven Ross, 1999.

38. Jupiter Communications, 1998.

39. See Paterson 1998, 1996; Boyd-Barrett 1998. Analysis of news agencies remains sparse, and the wire service production process poorly understood. To date, there is only limited large-scale ethnographic research on news agencies, although its focus is only the television side of these institutions (Paterson, 1996). There have been several smaller ethnographic projects and important works on agencies employing other methodologies (Hjarvard, 1995b; Read, 1992; Boyd-Barrett and Thussu, 1992; Fenby, 1986; Boyd-Barrett, 1980).

40. Cohen et al., 1996; Helland, 1995; Rodriguez, 1996; Molina, 1990; Schlesinger, 1987.

41. Paterson, 1996.

42. Reuters, press release, July, 1999 available at <Reuters.com>

43. Tvnewsweb, news story, originally posted November 18, 2001.

44. See especially the study by this researcher: Paterson 1996; also Cohen, et al., 1996; Hjarvard, 1995; Wallis & Baran, 1990.

45. Steve Clarke, "London: International News Capital," *Variety* (18 December 1995).

46. For a insider's review of news agency technology see Nigel Baker, "Invisible Giants. Quiet Revolution," in *International News the Twenty-First Century* ed. Chris Paterson and Annabelle Sreberny (Eastleigh, UK: John Libbey Press, 2004), 63–78.

47. Stig Hjarvard, *Internationale TV-nyheder. En historisk analyze af det europeiske system for udveksling af internationale TV-nyheder* (Copenhagen: Akademisk Forlag, 1995)

48. Rex Malik, "The Global News Agenda" *Intermedia*, 20, 1 (1992).

49. Paterson, 1996.

50. Frederick Schiff, "The Associated Press: Its Worldwide Bureaus and American Interests," *International Communications Bulletin* 31, 1 (1996), 7–19.

51. Lutz Hagen, "Foreign News in German Media in 1979 and in 1995" Paper for the IAMCR Annual Conference, Sydney, 1996.

52. Paterson, 1996; Anthony Giffard and Nancy Rivenburgh, "News Agencies, National Images, and Global Media Events" Paper for the IAMCR Annual Conference, Glasgow, 1998.

53. Schiff, 1996.

54. Mathew Amster-Burton and Laurie Amster-Burton, 1997.

55. Paterson, 1996.

56. Gaye Tuchman, *Making News: A Study in the Construction of Reality* (New York: Free Press, 1978).

57. Lawrence Magid. 1997. "All Roads Lead to Reuters," formerly published at *Currents.net*

58. European Journalism Centre. *The Future of the Printed Press: Challenges in a Digital World*. 1998. <www.ejc.nl/hp/fpp/execsum.html>

59. See Amy Langfield, "Net News Lethargy Most Sites Fail to Make Use of the Medium's Main Strength-Speed," *Online Journalism Review* (2002) <www.ojr.org/ojr/reviews/1017864558.php>; content analysis of on-line news media remains rare, and there is to date little empirical evidence to test the hypothesis of news agency dependency offered here—apart from the very limited original analysis of content provided below and the other small studies reviewed.

60. Oliver Boyd-Barrett and Terhi Rantanen. "News Agencies as News Sources: A Re-evaluation" in *International News the Twenty-First Century*, ed. Chris Paterson and Annabelle Sreberny (Eastleigh, UK: John Libbey Press, 2004), 31–46.

61. Annabelle Sreberny-Mohammadi, Kaarle Nordenstreng, Robert Stevenson, and Frank Ugboajah. *Foreign News in the Media: International News Reporting in 29 Countries*. Reports and Papers in Mass Communication, No. 93, Paris: UNESCO, 1985.

62. Chris Paterson, "An Exploratory Analysis of the Transference of Frames in Global Television," in *Framing in the New Media Landscape*, ed. S. Reese, A. Grant, and O. Gandy (Mahwah, N.J.: Erlbaum, 2001), 337–53.

63. Boyd-Barrett and Rantanen (2004), 34.

64. Texts were compared visually in a simple side-by-side comparison, where text from each of three major e-journalism sites was placed next to identical (or nearly identical) sentences in wire service copy. The author can furnish further detail of the study.

65. "Nearly duplicated," in the pilot research, meant a news agency sentence or paragraph is not reproduced verbatim, but is reproduced with only a few words altered.

66. The exception here are two stories from the Israel/Palestine conflict, which were included to provide some indication of agency dependence in the case of the leading ongoing international story. While this may bias the sample somewhat, it would likely only decrease the amount of agency use indicated (since most major services have their own correspondents in the region).

67. See <http://www.plagiarism.phys.virginia.edu>.

68. The system is still far from perfect. Among the problems encountered were when lengthy names were used together in similar ways from story to story (i.e. "Judge Juan Guzman charged General Pinochet"), adding, erroneously, to the total of copied words.

69. Given that the 85 percent average for the portals is closer to 100 percent when allowing for the factors listed in the preceding paragraph, it may be reasonable to presume the 43 percent figure for the major content providers is more realistically 55–60 percent.

70. American Customer Satisfaction Index data cited by NUA Internet Surveys. "US Net Users Most Happy with News and Info," August 21, 2002, <www.nua.ie/surveys/?f=VS&art_id=905358292&rel=true>

71. The full data set is available from the author.

72. Peter Burden, 1999; Shannon Martin, "How News Gets from Paper to Its Online Counterpart" *Newspaper Research Journal* 19 (Spring, 1998): 64–73; Ray Niekamp, "Television Station Web Sties: Interactivity in News Stories," Paper for the Association for Education in Journalism and Mass Communication annual meeting, 1997; also available <list.msu.edu/cgi-bin/wa?A2=ind9710A&L=aejmc&P=R63984>

73. European Journalism Centre,1998.

74. BBC On-line, Web Is 'Shrinking', 1999, BBC On-line, <news2.thls.bbc.co.uk/hi/english/sci/tech/newsid%5F428000/428999.stm>

75. Don Middleberg and Steven Ross, 1999; and Mark Tremayne, "Internet: Is the Medium the Message?" (unpublished Paper, University of Texas: Department of Journalism, 1997).

8

Bourdieu's "Show and Hide" Paradox Reconsidered: Audience Experiences of Convergence in the Canadian Mediascape

Debra Clarke

During his so-called campaign against television journalism,[1] Bourdieu discussed a set of mechanisms which enable television journalism to wield what he described as "a particularly pernicious form of symbolic violence," one that enjoys tacit complicity between its victims and its agents in the sense that "both remain unconscious of submitting to or wielding it."[2] As he pointed out, it is the task of sociology, as it is of every science, to reveal that which is hidden. In this way, sociology may help to minimize the symbolic violence within social relations and, in particular, within the relations of communication. The profound paradox is that "television can hide by showing. That is, it can hide things by showing something other than what would be shown if television did what it is supposed to do, provide information."[3] As it continues to be the primary news source, television is expected to provide the information that all citizens require in order to exercise their democratic rights. In reality, however, the production of television news and the provision of information are oxymoronic. By virtue of the very way in which "news" is conceptualized and defined by television news producers, it is intrinsically unable to inform citizens about the world. The world, as it is, including all of its history and all of the intricate social relations that configure it, must be taken as a given. It can serve only as the incidental backdrop or stage upon which the events of television news occur. From a journalistic perspective, what is "news" is not the world itself but rather what is "new" about it; namely, events that have occurred within a very recent time span, preferably dramatic events that can be highlighted with strongly evocative imagery.

Television journalism places these seemingly random and disconnected events on stage, accompanied by forceful images. Indeed, the ordinariness of "the world as it is" directly contravenes the most fundamental journalistic principles of newsworthiness; it is necessarily excluded from the domain of all that may be potentially "covered." In the words of Bourdieu, "there is nothing more difficult to convey than reality in all its ordinariness."[4] Journalists are invariably led to seek out that which is extraordinary and, together with the exceptional force of televisual imagery, the results can be captivating and compelling. The structural need to *capture* audiences, a need shared by private and public broadcasters alike, ensures that these features of a potential television news story are among the most highly valued. Unfortunately, there is no comparably powerful structural incentive to *inform* audiences.

Is the symbolic violence of television journalism truly an "unconscious" experience on the part of both its agents and its victims? Are television news producers oblivious to the informational limitations of their programs? Are news viewers oblivious to television's inability to inform? In this chapter, it is suggested that most agents and victims are fully cognizant of their complicity in the ongoing process whereby television journalism "hides while it shows"—there is, after all, a necessarily intrinsic relationship between production and reception, albeit one that has remained largely uncharted in the absence of much research that has connected the two. Nevertheless, one should not be surprised to find that the limitations of television news production invariably lead to restricted experiences of television news reception. The entire range of constraints operative in these interrelated processes can only be summarized here and, in accordance with the central themes of the collection, a principal focus of the discussion of reception will be to present highlights of audience responses to the consequences of ownership convergence in particular. These shall be derived from preliminary results of a recent analysis of news audiences in a medium-sized central Canadian city, one that utilized questionnaires, news diaries, and extensive field sessions conducted in private households. The tremendous extent of dissatisfaction with established news production practices became richly evident through the course of the analysis. It will be seen that, where reception outcomes are considered in the light of production practices, political economy can contribute useful insights into the former at the same time as it provides powerful explanations of the latter. In other words, a prerequisite consideration of the relations of news production can very effectively assist to explain the complexities and peculiarities of news reception.

THE CONSTRAINTS OF NEWS PRODUCTION

The subtleties of the process whereby the raw events of the world are transformed into a completed hegemonic news product long eluded the attention of most Marxist analyses of televisual communication which, until the 1970s, were largely content with a crude orthodoxy that linked media control to class relations as follows: media control by capitalist interests leads to the reproduction of bourgeois ideology which in turn leads to mystification and false consciousness and therewith the reproduction of existent relations of production.[5] Chibnall was among the first to point out that the transformation of the social world in fact occurs quite systematically through a process that exhibits "patterned regularities governed by a consistent set of interests, practices, and professional relationships."[6] These remained to be untangled and documented in later analyses of news production that were able to elaborate the process with a greater degree of comprehensiveness. The crux of these investigations centered around the forces and relations of news production, above all the constraints imposed upon television news reportage by the means in which production is organized, routinized, and rationalized in line with the imperatives of the capitalist mode of production. Broad *similarities* across networks and across capitalist societies assumed greater significance than the relatively inconsequential differences that were often the object of non-Marxist comparative analyses.

Golding and Elliott, for example, demonstrated the fundamental global uniformity of news practices and news programs by means of their three-nation observation of production in Ireland, Nigeria, and Sweden.[7] Their description of the successive stages of broadcast news production disclosed some of the more tacit restrictions upon reportage. Original newsgathering was found to be sharply limited by time constraints, by the demand for visual accompaniment, as well as by the inherently passive nature of broadcast journalism itself, a trait that arises inescapably out of the labor and other resources required to process news stories. The resultant dependence upon and extensive use of news agencies poses numerous constraints that are operative during the selection stage. News agencies become a critical source of foreign news, in that it is clearly impractical, at least for most news organizations, to field more than a few of their own foreign correspondents. It also contributes to a global uniformity of news definitions whereby the relative significance of news events is effectively predetermined by a limited number of dominant international news agencies. Moreover, where the organization's own journalists are assigned to cover foreign stories, agency items and line-ups alert the newsrooms to these stories, at least initially, and thereby effectively set the agenda of stories likely to be covered. The dependence of many news organizations upon the dominant international news agencies in fact represents a well-entrenched form of convergence that has long resulted in the cross-media content duplication of international news. Among Canadian news organizations, extensive use of the Canadian Press (CP) news agency as a historically pivotal source has assured the same results in the production of national news.[8]

Just as convergence is by no means a new phenomenon, neither are the multiple production constraints that have been identified throughout the extensive number of production studies that have been conducted since the 1970s. In the Canadian case, two interrelated phenomena transformed the character of the news industry during the latter part of the nineteenth century: economic consolidation and the professionalization of journalism. In fact, economic consolidation contributed directly to the consolidation of journalistic practices, organized around the newly imposed need for a consistently "professional" and "objective" news supply. The "Great Depression" of the 1880s and 1890s occasioned the large-scale consolidation of capital into a smaller number of larger hands. Markets became monopolized, and the form of economic organization shifted from the small entrepreneurial firm to the large corporation. The press was not spared either the economic or political consequences of corporate consolidation. Economically, consolidation meant the need to create mass markets as increasing dependency upon advertising revenues dictated the need for expansion and growth.[9]

Freely competitive partisan journalism fell victim to these momentous economic and political forces, overcome by the need to generate mass markets and replaced by a new mass-produced press. The overall effect was to centralize and homogenize the process of news production, including its infrastructural distribution system and the practices and ideologies of its producers. The foundations of contemporary Canadian journalism were consolidated at this crucial historical stage, and the roots of modern journalistic ideologies, couched within a philosophy of social responsibility and embodied in the principle of objectivity, trace directly to the dynamics of the political economy of the period. Outwardly manifest in a shift from "partisan" to "objective" journalism, these developments reflected the propelling force of economic consolidation which, first in the newspaper industry, assumed the decisive form of horizontal integration, chain ownership, or a dimension of what is more contemporarily discussed as "corporate convergence."

One can trace, therefore, a sequence of historical developments along which changes in journalistic practices have responded to correspondent changes in the political economy. Closely tied to these developments was the foundation of CP, the national news agency which proved to be a successful market tool geared to the restriction of competition. CP was and is a monopolistic device that assured the death of the competitive press in the 1920s. The small group of dominant newspaper owners assumed and exercised control of the agency from its outset, populated its board of directors, formulated the rules of its operation, and thereby achieved an almost impenetrable control of the supply and distribution of Canadian news. CP's directors constructed a web of policy entanglements that effectively denied access to the news supply system by any aspiring new publishers who posed a competitive threat. Through their judgments, all such threats to the established news monopoly were quickly extinguished.[10]

The rise of the mass-produced press and the increasingly specialized division of labor within the news industry meant that its different organizations were forced to develop and distribute a common, marketable product. Similarly, at the international level, the key counterpart to these developments was the rise of the international news agencies. Following the First World War, once the international cartel was formally broken, these agencies were required to service subscribers who not only represented different political perspectives and policies but also different national allegiances.[11] By formalizing a distinction between "news" as fact and "opinion" as ideology, the new style of journalism offered a product that could be successfully dispensed to large and diversified markets at the local, national, and international levels.

Three concurrent developments, then, result from the economic consolidation first underway at the close of the nineteenth century: the practical and professional shift from partisan to "objective" journalism, the formation of a centralized system of news supply and distribution in the form of CP at the national level, and the ascendancy of the dominant news supply and distribution agencies at the international level, which forged the global infrastructure of news production that continues to support much of the contemporary news industry. As these supply and distribution relationships crystallized into a worldwide network of interdependence, the need to package news in the form of sheer and straightforward "fact," a form that appeared to transcend the specialized interests and inputs of particular classes and nations, became all the more imperative. At the same time, the emergence of journalism as a distinctive profession under the control of large media monopolies was perfectly congruent with the claim of objective practice. As Knight has argued, the commitment to objectivity served a dual purpose in that "on the one hand it enabled owners to fend off potential political interference on the grounds that press monopolies contravened freedom of speech; on the other hand it enabled employee journalists to fend off editorial interference on the grounds that objectivity meant professionalism, and professionalism meant self-control."[12] In the contemporary period, however, two key developments have rendered both owners and journalists vulnerable to "interference"—the rapid acceleration of cross-media ownership convergence to the point where only a few multimedia enterprises control the major news outlets in Canada and, second, a notable decline in the sanctity of professional journalistic "objectivity" alongside the spread of tabloid journalism as well as political punditry in its various (explicit and implicit) journalistic forms. These developments, much more the former than the latter, have placed issues of press freedom and democratic communication within the realm of contemporary debate.

The forces that underlie the progression of broadcast journalism and the emergence of the current news production system can now be summarized. The capital investment required to serve mass markets made it more and more essential that journalism should produce a common, predictable, and marketable commodity. In contrast to earlier periods in which a small staff shared all of the work required to write and publish a newspaper, the contemporary journalist is part of a much more complex division of labor, assigned to perform much more specialized tasks oriented to the short- and long-range objectives of a large-scale organization. That division of labor extends from single organizations to the entire international newsgathering and processing system. The elaboration of the global system through supply agencies, syndication, and satellite distribution had also served to make news a routine and predictable product.[13] To ensure that the system is properly coordinated and efficient, it is essential that all those who contribute to it and work within it share common criteria by which to judge and process its final product. These criteria must include not just measures of newsworthiness but a shared set of fully formulated practices that guide the production of the news commodity from start to finish.

Such forces, then, can be called upon to account for the global uniformity of news practices as well as the historical specificity of professional journalistic principles such as objectivity. The international division of labor with respect to news production and distribution is the backdrop against which one must comprehend both the nature of news practices in Canada and the nature of the news production system in Canada, which could be perceived as a system of auxiliary news *distribution*. In view of its particular location within the international division of labor, one should not expect otherwise. The effects upon the actual substance of Canadian information programming, however, are somewhat less predictable; it could be argued that it creates a most peculiarly "passive" style of journalism here.

There are at least three significant dimensions to the dependence upon international and national supply agencies.[14] First, despite the occasional incompatibility of their stories and the criticisms of journalists and others, the agencies are absolutely crucial sources of international and national news, due entirely to the economics of newsgathering. The cost of foreign correspondents is astronomical compared to the cost of agency subscriptions, just as the capital required to support a network of national correspondents far exceeds that required to plug into CP's ready-made supply of domestic Canadian news. These practicalities impose powerful limits upon the amount of original news collection that can be reasonably undertaken in a country that, in terms of total land area, ranks second largest in the world. "Even" the publicly owned Canadian Broadcasting Corporation (CBC) is increasingly forced to restrict its activities to the reproduction of agency-produced news rather than the production of original news stories, a requirement all the more compulsory at smaller news enterprises.[15] Another dimension of agency dependence is that it leads to a global uniformity of news definitions, to a widely and commonly shared set of available news stories, and ultimately to a homogeneity of news content across the whole spectrum of "competing" news organizations. Globally, that uniformity is inevitable if one considers that no more than one or two agencies, notably Associated Press (AP) and Reuters, provide the basis of foreign news coverage in every newsroom of the world. Nationally, it is manifest in the "pack journalism" about which many Canadian news editors protest. Their protests reflect the third dimension of news agency dependence; namely, the limitations that the agencies impose upon the autonomy of individual newsrooms. As discussed, the choice of which stories will be covered by a newsroom's own reporters is strongly influenced by the sheer authority of the agencies. Even at the network level, agency line-ups alert the central newsrooms to international and national events, and hence the line-ups of the network newscasts are largely constructed upon the early "stock-of-knowledge" provided by their key suppliers.

These are but a few of the implications for news practices and news content, implications that are most evident to audiences in the homogeneous form that news tends to assume across all print, broadcast, and on-line media and in the extensive cross-media duplication of the substantive content of news stories. Indeed, in the absence of network identification logos and other emblematic indicators, news viewers would undoubtedly find it even more difficult to distinguish between their news sources. Their frequent observations of the homogeneity of news form and content are also appropriate reflections of the similarities in production practices between, for example, the CBC's English-language television network and the privately owned CTV network, whose newscasts were seen by the viewers in the audience research to be discussed shortly. In contrast to most other program genres, television news program formats and production practices sustain themselves amidst long years of change and struggle in the social world around them. As discussed, observational studies of television news production in Ireland, Nigeria, and Sweden,[16] the United Kingdom,[17] the United States,[18] and elsewhere have all pointed to the strongly patterned regularities and routines that characterize the news production process and to the professional ideologies that steer decisions about form and content. Barring minor variations in detail, all of their observations are generally applicable to the organization of newswork at the two oldest Canadian networks as well.

Many of the production constraints endemic within the news operations of CBC and CTV parallel those found recurrently elsewhere. Tracey's early identification of the constraints of time, money, and technology[19] enumerated the short-term, logistical constraints of production. All three tend to interact with each other and to congeal in their consequences for production and thereby in their consequences for the news text. Monetary and temporal constraints in turn reinforce the prevalent tendency to shy away from stories with poor visual potential and to otherwise conform to established production practices. As a CBC news producer once observed:

> Editors shy away from them too. There are minefields that are very tough to get into because people have failed at them so often in the past . . . in terms of *daily* news people who've been commissioned to do *daily* news coverage with short turn-arounds and Canada-limited production budgets, you tend to go for the tried-and-true rather than to break new ground, particularly if it's on a project that may not work and that may end up costing an awful lot in terms of crew time or material costs or per diems or travel time or just straight salary time.[20]

The monetary constraint is unquestionably the most critical, apparent in the *absence* of lengthy documentary productions, of extensive travel, of elaborate facilities, and of the specialized investigative labor required to do "bare-knuckled" reporting. In short, the economics of production constrain all facets of newsgathering and story assemblage, more notably at CTV where the budgetary allocation is smaller, yet also at the public network.

Inevitably, and importantly, production constraints are constraints by virtue of the way in which these features of the news production process shape the nature of the news text that results. In the case of CBC and CTV, previous research demonstrated that the dependent relationships between the networks and their external suppliers in fact serve to structure their respective newscasts into stories of accordingly different formats and lengths. The textual consequences were more marked at CTV where more than 80 percent of stories were found to be externally supplied.[21] Well beyond story formats and lengths, the full spectrum of production constraints, including the interactions between them, serves to powerfully shape the form and content of television journalism, to the extent that it is clearly the process that produces the news audiences see, not the producers. Indeed, news producers themselves tend to be keenly aware of the limitations intrinsic to the process; not, as Bourdieu theorized, "unconscious" of their submission to these limitations and the fundamental failure to inform that is their outcome.

Time constraints in the form of limited production periods and limited program and story lengths underlie the "event" orientation of television journalism, the decontextualization of those events, the focus upon actions and individuals rather than processes and structures, as well as the customary ahistoricism of the genre. Monetary constraints in the form of limited facilities and resources, including human labor power and technological resources, exert widespread effects upon the quantity, form, and content of stories. Technological constraints impose economic and logistical restrictions upon story form and content. Even more profound in their impact upon the ways in which audiences receive news are constraints that arise out of the division of journalistic labor, including a structured, unequal access to entire nations and regions (hence the limited story geography) and a structured, unequal access to subjects who might potentially appear in news stories (hence, among other ramifications, limited conceptualizations of "politics" and of "power"). Production values generally reinforce the limited criteria of story selection and impose a limited set of guidelines regarding the presentation of stories. Specific production values regarding the selection of subjects and the use of official spokespersons act in conjunction with the division of labor, time constraints, limited research resources, and a dependence upon official information suppliers to ensure that official definitions of social reality are most prominently espoused. Legal constraints and the *fear* of legal repercussions create a climate of "libel chill" that effectively deflects critical attention away from private-sector power-holders and confines it largely to those within the public arena of formal governmental institutions.[22]

These are but a few of the ways in which the dynamics of the production process shape the form and substance of the news text.[23] In turn, these invariably shape the reception experiences of news audiences. The phenomenon of libel chill may also help to explain why audiences are inclined to be more familiar with the textual consequences of ownership convergence—such as the degree of intermedia dependence, the homogeneity of form and content, and the limited extent of original news collection—than with the full extent of ownership convergence itself. The "show and hide" paradox thus extends to the ways in which convergence is experienced; television journalism shows all of the ramifications of convergence at the same time that it hides the highly converged informational infrastructure which feeds it. While there appears to be a multiplicity of diverse print, broadcast, and on-line news sources available to audiences in the much-celebrated "information age," the nexus of corporate interrelationships between these media, which ensures that news originates from a remarkably limited number of sources, remains largely hidden. The question of how audiences have accommodated these developments within their everyday news usage routines therefore acquires heightened interest.

FROM PRODUCTION TO RECEPTION

Historically, Canadians have been exceptionally voracious consumers of news and other media. Indeed, Canadian households are among the best-equipped in the world with information and communication technologies; currently, Canada is tied with Sweden as one of the two most "wired" nations in the world. Furthermore, the national average of more than 21 hours of television viewing weekly exceeds that of virtually all other nations across the globe.[24] Despite these outstanding consumption patterns, Canadian communication scholars have thus far been reticent to undertake any comprehensive ethnographic studies of audiences, probably due at least in part to the various epistemological issues and methodological challenges associated with such research.[25] Among other difficulties, the necessarily limited sample sizes seem to predetermine a substantial loss of generalizability. Research conducted elsewhere suggests that audiences are not only resistant to news texts, yet also resistant to any rigorous efforts at classification and generalization.[26] Such resistance must be anticipated among Canadian audiences, who represent a population characterized by a high degree of sociodemographic diversity.

While poststructuralists and others continue to dispute the merits of ethnographic audience research, Alasuutari has encouraged a means to proceed beyond the perceived epistemological "crisis" that has plagued the scholarly study of audiences.[27] The "new agenda" to which he pointed is a constructionist approach that seeks to reclaim the meaning of ethnography through extensive firsthand fieldwork and multiple modes of data collection. In pursuit of that agenda, the current research is part of a larger analysis that calls upon in-person observations and personally conducted in-depth interviews in 100 private households with a total of 167 adults resident in a medium-sized central Canadian city during the period September 2001 to September 2003. Adult members of each household were interviewed extensively before, during, and after their viewing of CBC and CTV network newscasts. The interviews were extended over a two-year period in order to examine responses to news coverage of a broad spectrum of developments. Household members also completed structured questionnaires, and unstructured one-week news diaries were completed on a voluntary basis. Beyond the pool of interview subjects, questionnaires and news diaries were completed by other members of the community organizations targeted through quota and snowball sampling. Hence, in addition to transcripts of the 100 household interviews, data were derived from several hundred questionnaires and news diaries submitted by individuals who represent a diversity of sociodemographic traits and politicoideological perspectives.[28] The unstructured interviews ranged in length from one to three hours and, in all except one-person households, enabled direct examinations of how the sociality of television usage operates within a diversity of household settings. Demographic and usage data derived from questionnaires were utilized to inform direct field observations of the interactions between household members before, during, and following news viewing. More substantive commentaries obtained from both questionnaires and news diaries were also assessed against the results of the direct observations. By means of such triangulation, the limitations peculiar to each singular method were minimized to the greatest possible extent.

The preliminary results presented here draw from the household interviews: specifically, discussions of ownership and content convergence. The sample of interviewees was diversified by age, gender, social class, household type (that is, family form or household composition), and politico-ideological perspective (identified initially by membership in particular community organizations targeted through quota sampling). It therefore encompasses a wide range of life circumstances although it is not systematically representative of the Canadian population. The age range of the interviewees extended from eighteen to eighty-nine years, with 20 percent aged between eighteen and twenty-nine years, 21 percent in their thirties, 16 percent in their forties, 18 percent in their fifties, another 18 percent in their sixties, 6 percent in their seventies, and 1 percent in their eighties. Over half of the sample (58 percent) were women. Of the 100 households in which interviews were conducted, fifty-seven were working class and the remainder were middle class.

Like most Canadian households, the majority of the households occupied by interviewees were very well-equipped with broadcast media. All of the households were equipped with at least one radio and television set, and 78 percent were cabled while 12 percent featured a satellite dish.[29] Virtually every household was equipped with at least one video cassette recorder (VCR), which was essential to the interview sessions.[30] Although print media were less directly visible during the interview sessions, interviewee questionnaires reported that newspapers were available regularly in 63 percent of the households and news magazines were available regularly in 16 percent—*Maclean's* and *Time* were cited most frequently. Only 43 percent featured a computer with Internet access, and these were reported exclusively in the middle-class households which comprised 43 percent of the sample. No more than a few of the working-class interviewees referred to the opportunity to access the Internet at their workplaces.

Television was by far the most important of these news sources, ranked as their primary news source by 61 percent of the interviewees. Radio was identified as the primary news source by 22 percent, newspapers by 18 percent, and virtually no one identified the Internet as their primary source of news.[31] The relative importance of television as a news source may have been understated by some interviewees in their questionnaire responses. Weekly hours of television viewing in the area, according to BBM data, averaged 26.7 in the spring of 2003, which exceeds the national average by 5.5 hours. Moreover, newscasts ranked third and sixth among the ten most widely viewed television programs in the area during the same period.[32] While it is difficult to obtain comparable current data regarding primary news sources for the Canadian population at large, Moscovitch cites 1998 survey data which indicate that 81 percent of Canadians called upon television as a news source, more so than any other medium.[33]

Based upon his 1990 research with focus groups in Britain, France, Germany, and the United States, Kavoori pointed to the emergence at that time of "a global culture of critical media consumption."[34] Audience groups in all four nations displayed "sweeping similarities" in their critical assessments of television news.[35] Kavoori suggests that the critical posture of audiences arises out of their familiarity with the narrative conventions of the genre and their awareness of the institutional imperatives of the media industries as well as the broader politicoideological contexts of media coverage.[36] The same critical commonalities or "sweeping similarities" were found amongst the Canadians interviewed in the current project, where it was evident that in many cases the familiarity has evolved into a weariness and accelerated frustration with the endurance of established textual strategies as well as the repetitive nature of discursive content. In addition, the Canadian interviewees directed their criticisms at both general and specific journalistic practices, beyond that toward the economic "shortcuts" pursued by national television networks and other news providers, and still beyond that to those who own and control the major news production enterprises. The critical commonalities cut across all demographic groups within the sample, although the criticisms were expressed with variant inflections of anger, frustration, and mystification as well as ridicule and satirical humor.

At the risk of anecdotalism, a brief outline of representative criticisms regarding convergence-related themes should suffice to illustrate a range of production-reception linkages. As suggested earlier, participants were much more likely to be actively and directly critical of content convergence than of ownership convergence per se. Concerns about the former were expressed far more frequently and, in almost every case, issues of cross-media content duplication were raised at the initiation of interviewees and often raised repeatedly during newscast viewing. On the other hand, throughout the unstructured interviews, it was frequently necessary to purposely introduce ownership questions or at least to clarify regular use of the vaguely ominous "they":

When you use the word 'they,' are you thinking of the producers of news programmes, or the owners, or the journalists who report the stories?
(*Female Subject*): I wouldn't blame the journalists. I think it's the producers and the owners.
(*Male Subject*): Yeah, I think the owners are saying "this is what we want" and "this is what we want you to produce" and obviously, if they want a job, and they want to get paid, then they have to go out there and do that. I'm sure many of them, they enjoy what they do but they have to do what they have to do.

Once the topic arose, many participants proceeded to attribute a great deal of power to owners, while a significant minority displayed disinterest in and/or exasperation with the issue:

I think if the owner's political views aren't followed, then things don't happen the way the producers want them to. It's the way of business. After all, the news is run as a business. It's the same thing with the CBC, because if they don't go

along with where their cheques come from, they're not gonna get their cheques
. . . I really feel that the owners of large companies and politicians are all intertwined.

I did know that he [Conrad Black] was involved with [the local newspaper] for
a little bit, but it doesn't mean anything to me, you know. I suppose I don't really care who owns anything, really. See, I'm just not, I'm not very, well, I don't
know whether the word is "worldly" or, you know. Those things just don't concern me because they don't—they probably do somewhere, but I don't know—
they don't affect the way that I go to work every day, do what I do every day. I
don't think they do, but maybe in actual fact they really do.

Whereas their actions and powers were envisioned in concrete, specific
(and often blunt) terms, Canadian media owners quite persistently occupied
the rather obscure "they" category. Only infrequently were owners or their
enterprises readily identified by name, and rarely was the true extent of their
media properties realized. Two former New Brunswick residents were among
the exceptions.[37] After detailing many of the Irving family's media and non-
media assets, the couple stated—in unison—"It was terrible!" and continued
at length (space will only permit highlights of their comments here):

(*Female Subject*): The Irvings own New Brunswick . . .
(*Male Subject*): They dominate everything . . . The news stories that come out
about them, they are edited,
(*Female Subject*): They are in control of what is written about them.
(*Male Subject*): There are very few negative things . . .
(*Female Subject*): Their family is so secretive, they don't let you know who
they are even, that they own certain companies, things like that. So they are so
in control of their own privacy that what gets printed in the newspapers is nothing. It's scary to think what they're in control of in the province . . .

Significantly, both had been employed in Irving-controlled industries,
both were keen environmentalists with special interests in the activities of
their Irving family employers, and (no doubt quite accurately) both believed
themselves to be better-informed about the Irvings than many in New
Brunswick. The couple also observed, with apparent accuracy, that there is
much less awareness of the extent of media ownership convergence on the
part of Ontario residents.

Ownership convergence is inextricably tied to the convergence of news
sources and news content. Interview subjects were frequently frustrated by
the latter, yet less often likely to connect the two. The frustration has led
some to reduce their consumption of television news and to seek alternative
news sources, such as the following middle-class woman:

I don't always turn on the news anymore because, especially the television
news, they have to fill the half hour, whether something important has happened or not. And they don't have, what was it, I guess it was Associated Press

and some of the press bureaus have been collapsed and there's only one now so there's no competing story??? So there's no two points of view.

Are you concerned about that?

No.

No?

Well, I think with the Internet, people who want to find out can. And the fact that there were two competing stories or two points of view, was it ever really discussed or pointed out ten years ago or fifteen years ago? I really can't say. I mean, I watched the news and I listened and I read *Time* magazine and stuff like that, so whether I was getting opposing views, I don't know. I used to read the *Star* in the morning, it comes here first thing in the morning, it's my morning paper. And I'd listen to CBC, and their taglines or headlines were word-for-word almost what the *Star* headlines were. And I'd think, well, who's feeding whom here? Obviously, they were getting it from the same news agency. And I wasn't aware of that ten years ago.

This response is indicative of the lack of clarity regarding news providers (evident here in the confusion about AP) as well as the tendency to assume: (a) that Internet access is widespread and (b) that such presumably widespread Internet access has rendered the issue of ownership convergence defunct. In this case, the subject enthusiastically pointed out a bookmarked on-line news source on her computer that she had started to consult regularly. Tellingly, however, when asked to identify the operator of the site, she was unable to do so. In sum, it was apparent that most participants were more immediately concerned about the manifestations of convergence, such as content duplication, and less directly concerned about ownership convergence itself.

In his typology of convergence, Taras includes the convergence of news and entertainment—evident, for example, in a tendency to frame news stories in a dramatic, sensational way that seems to value imagery even more than substance.[38] The Canadian interviewees were more inclined to associate such tabloid journalism with American news outlets. In fact, it was often seen to be a major source of distinction between Canadian and American television journalism, and one reason why the former was preferred.[39]

I won't watch American news because at an early age, about fifteen probably, that early, I noticed that their newscasts were a lot different than ours, especially in worldwide things. They like things to favor them. Everything has to favor them, and it's always someone else's fault. Or if it was their fault—well, you know! And their news is made for people with maybe a Grade 8 education. There's not a lot of big words.

Do you find Canadian news that substantially different?

Yes, and BBC news also . . . I only watch CBC and I used to watch Global news, and, a couple of weeks ago I noticed that they were having CNN clips on Global. Now, CNN is *tabloid news!* Don't try to come across like you know what you're talking about if you've got CNN news on there! I thought, I don't know what's happening to Global but there must be other news stations other than CNN that they can get information from. But maybe it comes cheap, I don't know.

When the war [in Afghanistan] was on, and you turned to CNN, that was more entertainment than it was seriousness. It was like an ongoing movie, you know, how they made it. You could sit here and watch the war going on in another country just like you would a movie, a drama. I don't know if it was a good thing or not. We need to be informed, but I don't think you need play-by-play. . . . You don't turn it on necessarily to find out what's going on in *the* world. It's entertainment, it's more like turning on that daily soap opera.

Overall, subjects principally called upon Canadian rather than American news providers in their everyday news consumption routines. CNN and other American news outlets were consulted more extensively than usual during major developments in which the United States figured prominently, such as 9/11 and the wars in Afghanistan and Iraq. At the outbreak of these "stories," it was commonly anticipated that the American networks would provide more current and somewhat more detailed reports. Many participants demonstrated a tired and irksome familiarity with Canadian dependence upon American network news feeds, which underscored their decisions to watch American news sources directly rather than await rebroadcasts of the same American reports by Canadian networks. Nevertheless, in the vast majority of cases, the American networks continued to be regarded as "supplementary" sources.

In view of their access to Canadian as well as American and other network news, participants were highly critical of the production constraints associated with television news generally, many of which were readily perceived in the newscasts that were viewed during the interview sessions. Time constraints in the form of limited story and program lengths, for example, were seen by many to necessarily preclude a comprehensive understanding of the "events" reported. These and other constraints were also seen to extend to other news media, including newspapers.

There are certain ones [stories] that may peak your interest. You'd like to know a little more and then—boom!—you're on to something else. You know, I would think that a lot of the stories that went in here, all the different news that they showed, you know, there's a lot in that short span of time, and you didn't have enough time to focus on certain things. They had a lot of different things going on in that short period of time.

I find that a lot of things I want to know information about, that I don't get the details of it that I want to hear. I just get a briefing on it, and then you are left to, you think you'll turn on the news and hear what you want to hear, but then, no, you are left to, you have to go to the newspapers. So you've got to go and find out from all different places bits and pieces of what you want to know, because you're not getting it all. . . . If there is something that I really want to know about, I'll sit here and I'll flicker through all the different news stations, and just keep going over them. And I'll have to watch the same ones a few times just to make sure that's all they're all telling us right now, you know. And it is frustrating because there are certain things you want to know about, but you can't find out as much detail as you want.

Perhaps the most definitive confirmation of television's fundamental inability to inform was experienced by interviewees who attempted to make sense of news reports that were *not* subject to conventional time constraints. The events of September 11, 2001, led broadcasters throughout the United States and Canada to abandon regular program schedules in their entirety in order to provide unprecedented amounts of continuous news coverage. Rather than render the events intelligible, however, many interviewees remained confounded and perplexed months later. For example, in November and December of that year, these participants continued to struggle with their understanding of the events:

Since September 11th they have been going on and on and on about what happened on September 11th and what's following it, the war and everything else, and yet they are beating around the bush. They are not telling very much. They are holding a lot of information back, maybe for our own protection and everything, but by the same token I would like to know if they've got a bomb over there that's gonna explode. . . . Personally, I'm not ever quite sure that I know why the attacks happened in the first place.

It gets to the point that it gets to be too much, what is seen on TV, and they're making it more difficult to sit down and watch because we watched at the beginning, when it started, when the towers came down. We watched it for a couple of days, but then it was like that's all we were hearing constantly on all the different stations, and it was getting to the point where that's all you heard. Therefore, we shut it off and said we're not going to watch the news for a while because it's getting *too* overwhelming because you're hearing it *constantly*. You know, this was on and it was repeating, you know, you'd see the buildings coming down all the time. Once was hard enough, I mean it was shocking, it was so overwhelmingly sad to see what was going on and to have to keep seeing that over and over again. So after about two days or so I had to turn it off. I couldn't keep watching the towers coming down. . . . We saw on TV, I guess, what they want us to see, and anything else is left to the imagination. And we're still left to ask what's going on with the whole situation. I think there is still the question of why it happened.

The experience of the 9/11 coverage was in itself sufficient to lead a significant number of subjects to conclude that television "hides by showing." As in the case illustrated above, some simply shut off their television sets out of sheer exasperation with the absence of comprehensible information. In a disturbing number of cases, however, the "shutdown" was of a longer-term nature—subjects, often younger subjects in working-class households, who proclaimed either a newly acquired or ongoing contentment with political apathy, derived at least in part from their frustrations with the informational limitations of television and other news media. Older and well-educated middle-class viewers were rarely driven to such extremes, equipped as most were with the means to fill in at least some of the gaps left by television news. Their frustrations with the specific content of everyday news stories were therefore somewhat abated, which enabled more reflective criticisms of the state of journalism generally in Canadian society and elsewhere. One such critique, by a subject who had participated in a strike, effectively articulated the views of many interviewees:

All the way through life now I see the essential questions never being asked. That's the problem. We saw it up close and intimate with our own issues in the strike. But the same thing applies to the focus on the corruption, let's say, in the federal government around who went to stay at whose lodge for a vacation, when in fact there is a serious *malaise* happening there, that *no one* is questioning. . . . [Journalists will ask] why is the Prime Minister behaving the way he's behaving? And there's a little conjecture, and a little of this and a little of that. But the focus is always on *the wrong thing!*
  Why do you think that is? How do you understand that yourself?
  It's frightening to me to think that there could be two reasons for it, and each one is equally frightening. One, that the journalists themselves can't see the forest for the trees. That's pretty scary. They don't know to ask the bigger questions because they don't know what the bigger question is, they're so wrapped up in chasing the minutiae. That's one theory.
  The other theory is that they have a very clear idea of what the big question is, but their editorial boards prevent them from publishing it, so therefore there's no point in asking it! That's also scary. So either one is indicating that there is a creeping rot in the actual media system. And I don't think it's a huge conspiracy, I think it's going back again to who owns it, what is the purpose? The purpose, don't forget, for the owner of the publication or the media, the purpose is not about informing the public. That is *not* their purpose. Their purpose is the bottom line, is to make money, is to consolidate their power base. Those are their purposes. Informing the public is of no particular interest whatsoever. So there you go!
  And you have a whole bunch of people who are desperate to be working, because we're churning out all of these journalists and reporters and what have you, and they're shrinking the numbers of media outlets to work in, so they'll do anything, in order to work. They're not going to risk their careers or their positions or whatever by asking the questions over and over again that their editorial board says not to. So there you go. That scares me.

The interview material that has been cited makes it apparent that, while there are indeed commonalities in the criticisms directed generally at television and other forms of journalism, there are important underlying distinctions as

well. Just like the distinctions that were observed in the more specifically eval-
uative responses evoked during the viewing of news stories, many of these
distinctions can be traced to the social locations of interviewees, which indicates the need to pursue what may or may not be rigorous classifications of
Canadian news audiences based upon class, gender, age, and so forth. Such
efforts at classification can draw usefully from the work of Press and Cole,[40]
Riggs,[41] and others who have examined age- and gender-based reception experiences at length. Political economy can certainly utilize some of the analytic
techniques of constructionism, just as Deacon and his Loughborough colleagues utilized a natural history model, derived from constructionism, to track
a particular British news story from its production through to its reception. In
their words, "the time is ripe . . . for re-tying once more the strands of production and reception."[42]

Above all, it is plainly in the interests of political economy to explore questions such as how and why contemporary journalism fails to enlighten the
impoverished and the oppressed. The research discussed in a preliminary
fashion here seeks ultimately to contribute a response to these and other related questions, and it is anticipated that further analysis of the interview
transcripts in conjunction with the questionnaires and news diaries will em-
bellish the response with insights into the ways in which the social characteristics of subjects, their social conditions, the sociality of television usage in
alternative household settings, and other considerations figure within the reception process. At this juncture, it is quite apparent that, rather than enlighten audiences, the highly converged Canadian mediascape is more inclined to generate anger and frustration; it activates audiences not in the
direction of a collective will to participate in progressive social movements,
but more commonly within the socially isolated experience of mystification
and rage that plays itself out on a daily basis in the private domain of individual households. The current extent of corporate convergence has accelerated the rage through a reduction in the already limited range of "information" sources, through extensive cross-media content duplication,
through the increased political homogeneity of news, through the aggressive
commercialization of news, and so forth. Those who point to the Internet as
a revolutionary or even "democratic" alternative need to examine the access
data and, much more importantly, need to consult Internet users about their
experiences. While many of the subjects here expressed interest in on-line
news sources, only middle-class subjects were equipped to access them
readily, reflecting the continuing class-based "digital divide" in the population at large. Furthermore, it cannot, of course, be assumed that those who
are so equipped necessarily find that their informational needs are adequately met.

It is also important to ask how and to what extent Canadian audiences have
accommodated the accelerated convergence in their everyday news usage

routines and in their general efforts to comprehend the implications of ongoing developments. In other words, how and to what extent do these highly critical postures result in a search for and use of alternative information sources? There are indications here that the contemporary scope of convergence may have led some audience groups to retreat from long-established Canadian patterns of extensive television news consumption and to seek out media, such as radio and the Internet, that are less constrained by time, the visual imperative, and other production-based limitations. Of greater concern are those audience groups who display little or no interest in on-line news or, for that matter, in any other news medium, including those whose disenchantment has led to a complete disengagement from political communication. These are the sorts of patterns easily overlooked by those who examine reception in isolation or who implicitly celebrate any and all actively critical interpretations of televisual texts.

As Hackett suggests, there is a danger that any celebration of "active" audiences, such as that found in some cultural studies works, can contribute to political quiescence and the subversion of movements to restore journalistic freedom and "media democracy."[43] Likewise, there is a pivotal need to tread carefully with presumptions about the nature and extent of the critical responses observed among audiences. At a minimum, it is necessary to distinguish between those who actively articulate a developed critique of the social world within which convergent media operate and those who merely feel obliged to conform to what Kavoori described as "the global culture of critical media consumption." At a maximum, it is necessary to determine the forms and types of resistance as well as their correlates. As the literature on social movements attests, there is little justification for the conclusion that actively critical audiences are necessarily prepared to actively engage in movements toward communicative reform.

TOWARD COMMUNICATIVE REFORM?

With those precautions in mind, it can at least be safely stated that the majority of participants in the current project would likely welcome initiatives intended to improve the communicative process in Canadian society. Despite the stability of institutional and structural imperatives, the work of Philo and others in the Glasgow University Media Group[44] suggests that the reform of journalistic practices could potentially lead to greater levels of both audience interest and audience comprehension, at least with respect to news regarding the developing world and the conflicts within it. Philo has reported about a pilot study undertaken pursuant to the Glasgow University Media Group's extensive research with 165 subjects in twenty-six focus groups.[45] The latter study found audiences both confused by and disinterested in news reports of the developing world. Group members freely acknowledged that "they simply did not understand the news and thought that the external world was not being properly explained to them,"[46] which the researchers traced directly to production practices that leave stories decontextualized and devoid of explanatory power.

In a preliminary follow-up to a rare three-dimensional analysis of production, content, and audiences, senior British journalists participated directly with BBC news viewers in a focus group discussion of how audience interest and comprehension might be affected by changes in the structure and content of such news stories. The results indicate that a greater degree of contextualization and explanatory power—especially explanations of how viewers *themselves* are impacted directly by the core system of relationships between the developed and developing worlds—can produce a distinctly pronounced change in levels of audience interest as well as audience understanding.[47] The journalists were therefore encouraged to routinely incorporate such explanations into their reports.

There can be little doubt that Canadian news audiences would respond in a similar manner. As expected (based upon audience research conducted elsewhere), participants were almost invariably inclined to be highly self-referential; those stories clearly seen to affect them directly were the stories that consistently attracted the greatest levels of interest. Unfortunately, among these were participants who felt that only local news stories could satisfy this criterion, and who therefore excluded all but local newscasts from their daily news diet. If television journalism could consistently reveal these "hidden" linkages and relationships, it might well serve to reduce the level of "symbolic violence" about which Bourdieu was led to protest.

NOTES

The research support of the Symons Trust Fund for Canadian Studies as well as the Frost Centre for Canadian Studies and Native Studies Research Committee, Trent University, is gratefully acknowledged.

1. Rodney Benson, "Making the Media See Red: Pierre Bourdieu's Campaign against Television Journalism." *French Politics and Society* 16, no. 2 (Spring 1998), 59–66. See also Pierre Bourdieu, *On Television and Journalism* (London: Pluto Press, 1998).

2. Pierre Bourdieu, "Television." *European Review* 9, no. 3 (2001): 246.

3. Bourdieu, "Television," 247.

4. Bourdieu, "Television," 248.

5. See Steve Chibnall, *Law-and-Order News: An Analysis of Crime Reporting in the British Press* (London: Tavistock, 1977), 208.

6. Chibnall, *Law-and-Order News*, 207.

7. Peter Golding and Philip Elliott, *Making the News* (London: Longman, 1979).

8. See the Kent Report (Canada, Royal Commission on Newspapers. Ottawa: Minister of Supply and Services Canada, 1981), 119–133.

9. See Graham Knight, "News and Ideology." *Canadian Journal of Communication* 8, no. 4 (September 1982), 15–41.

10. See M.E. Nichols, *(CP): The Story of the Canadian Press* (Toronto: The Ryerson Press, 1948).

11. See also Philip Elliott, "Professional Ideology and Organizational Change: The Journalist since 1800," in *Newspaper History: From the Seventeenth Century to the Present Day*, ed. George Boyce, James Curran, and Pauline Wingate (London: Constable, 1978), 183–84.

12. Knight, "News and Ideology," 24.

13. See also Elliott, "Professional Ideology and Organizational Change," 186.

14. See also Golding and Elliott, *Making the News*, 104–105.

15. See, for example, the case discussed in Debra Clarke, "Second-Hand News: Production and Reproduction at a Major Ontario Television Station," in *Communication Studies in Canada*, ed. Liora Salter (Toronto: Butterworths, 1981), 20–51.

16. Golding and Elliott, *Making the News*.

17. See, for example, Philip Schlesinger, *Putting "Reality" Together: BBC News* (London: Constable, 1978).

18. See, for example, Edward Jay Epstein, *News From Nowhere: Television and the News* (New York: Random House, 1973).

19. Michael Tracey, The Production of Political Television (London: Routledge and Kegan Paul, 1978).

20. Interview, June 1983, original emphasis.

21. See Debra Clarke, "Constraints of Television News Production: The Example of Story Geography," in *Critical Studies of Canadian Mass Media*, ed. Marc Grenier (Toronto: Butterworths, 1992), esp. Table 6.3, 119.

22. Not only was such "libel chill" evident throughout earlier observations of production at both networks, it is also readily evident to audiences. In addition to the frequent comments during interview sessions, questionnaires received to date from the total sample (including non-interviewees) indicate overwhelming agreement with the statement that "Television news is more critical of government power-holders than of other powerful people."

23. See also Clarke, "Constraints of Television News Production," esp. Figure 1, 129–30.

24. Statistics Canada, *Television Viewing Data Bank*, Catalogue # 87F0006XPE. <http://www.statcan.ca/english/pgdb/arts.23.htm> (16 January 2003).

25. Clearly, there is not the space here to engage in a necessarily lengthy discussion of the epistemological issues raised by Ang, Morley, and many others situated within and outside of the field of cultural studies. See, for example, Ien Ang, *Living Room Wars: Rethinking Media Audiences for a Postmodern World* (London: Routledge, 1996); David Morley, *Television, Audiences, and Cultural Studies* (London: Routledge, 1992); and David Morley, "'To Boldly Go . . .': The 'Third Generation' of Reception Studies," in *Rethinking the Media Audience: The New Agenda*, ed. Pertti Alasuutari (London: Sage, 1999), 195–204. The continuing disputes are addressed to a greater extent in Debra Clarke, "Class, Gender, and Much More: The Complexities of Ethnographic Audience Research," forthcoming in *Studying Social Life: Substance and Method*, ed. Dorothy Pawluch, William Shaffir, and Charlene Miall (Toronto: CSPI/Women's Press, 2004).

26. A review of this research appears in Debra Clarke, "The Active Pursuit of Active Viewers: Directions in Audience Research," *Canadian Journal of Communication* 25, no. 1 (special millennium issue, Winter 2000), 39–59.

27. Pertti Alasuutari, "Introduction: Three Phases of Reception Studies," in *Rethinking the Media Audience: The New Agenda*, ed. Pertti Alasuutari (London: Sage, 1999), 1–21. Similarly, Webster has called for "a kind of enlightened empiricism—one that makes room for a number of methods, each compensating for the limitations of the other—one that compels analysts to go into the real world, recognizing that audiences are never completely knowable." See James Webster, "The Audience." *Journal of Broadcasting and Electronic Media* 42, no. 2 (Spring 1998), 198.

28. At the time of writing, questionnaires and news diaries circulated to the larger sample, encompassing subjects who were not interviewed, are still being received. The precise total therefore remains to be determined.

29. While the questionnaires did not ask interviewees to specify the number of television sets in their households, it was evident that, in accordance with the Canadian norm, the majority were multiset households.

30. According to Bureau of Broadcast Measurement (BBM) data, 79 percent of all households in the area were equipped with VCRs in the spring of 2003 (BBM, "*BBM Spring 2003 TV Market Data Tidbits*," www.bbm.ca/Get_Data/TV_Data_Tidbits.html (15 November 2003).

31. Percentages do not total precisely 100 percent due to rounding.

32. BBM, "BBM Spring 2003 TV Market Data Tidbits."

33. Arlene Moscovitch, *Electronic Media and the Family* (Ottawa: Vanier Institute of the Family, 1998).

34. Anandam Kavoori, "Discursive Texts, Reflexive Audiences: Global Trends in Television News Texts and Audience Reception," *Journal of Broadcasting and Electronic Media* 43, no. 3 (Summer 1999): 386–99. Kavoori's research was undertaken in association with Michael Gurevitch, Mark Levy, Akiba Cohen, and Itzakh Roeh. The focus group study results are discussed in Akiba Cohen, Mark Levy, Itzakh Roeh, and Michael Gurevitch, *Global Newsrooms, Local Audiences* (London: John Libbey, 1996).

35. Kavoori, "Discursive Texts, Reflexive Audiences," 391.

36. Kavoori, "Discursive Texts, Reflexive Audiences," 396.

37. In the province of New Brunswick, it is difficult if not impossible to remain *un*aware of the power of the Irving family which, in addition to its many non-media enterprises, has exercised a nearly virtual monopoly control of all New Brunswick media since Kenneth Colin (more commonly known as "K.C.") Irving first started to purchase the daily newspapers in 1944. The early history of the family empire is discussed in Russell Hunt and Robert Campbell, *K.C. Irving: The Art of the Industrialist* (Toronto: McClelland & Stewart, 1973).

38. David Taras, *Power and Betrayal in the Canadian Media* (Peterborough: Broadview Press, updated edition, 2001), 83–86.

39. All emphases in these and other interview excerpts are original.

40. Andrea Press and Elizabeth Cole, *Speaking of Abortion: Television and Authority in the Lives of Women* (Chicago: University of Chicago Press, 1999).

41. Karen Riggs, *Mature Audiences: Television in the Lives of Elders* (New Brunswick, N.J.: Rutgers University Press, 1998).

42. David Deacon, Natalie Fenton, and Alan Bryman, "From Inception to Reception: The Natural History of a News Item." *Media, Culture & Society* 21, no. 1 (January 1999): 5–31.

43. Robert Hackett, "Taking Back the Media: Notes on the Potential for a Communicative Democracy Movement," *Studies in Political Economy* 63 (Autumn 2000): 61–86.

44. Glasgow University Media Group, "Viewing the World: A Study of British Television Coverage of Developing Countries," (London: Department for International Development, 2000) <http://www.dfid.gov.uk> (10 October 2003).

45. Greg Philo, "Television News and Audience Understanding of War, Conflict, and Disaster," *Journalism Studies* 3, no. 2 (2002), 173–86.

46. Philo, "Television News," 177.

47. Philo, "Television News," 185–86.

9

Reforming Media: Parries and Pirouettes in the U.S. Policy Process

Ben Scott

The last half of 2003 marks one of the most important moments in the history of media policy in the United States. In that span, Congress considered media ownership regulations as a top political issue on the national agenda for the first time in generations. Millions of citizens contacted Washington to advocate for a more diverse, local, and representative media system. Arguably, a national media reform movement is on the rise.

The flash point was June 2, 2003. On that date, the Federal Communications Commission (FCC) passed a controversial order concerning the structural regulation of the media system.[1] The decision dramatically loosened the rules governing media ownership to permit further consolidation. Three major rules changes were enacted. First, the 1975 ban on the cross-ownership of a broadcast station (radio or TV) and a newspaper in the same community was lifted for most markets. Second, the bar permitting local broadcast concentration was lowered, and one company was given the green light to buy two and three TV stations in a market. Finally, the networks would now be able to own stations reaching a total of 45 percent of American TV households, an increase from the 1996 cap of 35 percent. Taking the rules together, one company would now be permitted to own three TV stations, eight radio stations, the monopoly newspaper, the cable system, and an unlimited number of other nonbroadcast media properties—all in the same city. This set of numbers alarmed the American public and its representatives in Congress.

Although the Commission and Congress had been moving gradually toward business-friendly regulations for decades, the June 2 decision represented an abrupt lurch toward removing public accountability from the media system. Commissioner Jonathan S. Adelstein warned in his dissenting statement: "The majority has sealed into federal regulations the most sweeping and destructive rollback of consumer protection rules in the history of American broadcasting."[2] Members of Congress responded with extraordinarily harsh comments. Senator Byron Dorgan (D-ND) called it "the fastest, most complete cave-in to corporate interest I've ever seen by what is supposed to be a federal regulatory agency."[3] Senator Ernest "Fritz" Hollings (D-SC) blasted the move, charging that "there's no ground for it, there's no reason for it other than greed."[4] These comments echoed the sentiments of three-quarters of a million citizens and over 150 members of Congress who contacted the FCC in the run-up to June 2nd to caution the commissioners against the decision.[5] Despite this remarkable political backlash, it seemed unlikely to have the staying power to challenge the FCC. The public has not been effectively involved in media policy debates since the clash over the control of radio in the early 1930s.[6]

Yet the public did stay with the debate—in fact increasing its involvement and driving members of Congress to act. It began in the first few weeks of June when a coalition of civic organizations banded together to strike back. Spearheaded by numerous, local grassroots activist groups, this coalition represented a wide variety of political positions, including the National Rifle Association, the National Organization for Women, Parents Television Council, Children NOW, the National Council of Churches, the AFL-CIO, and online activist groups like MoveOn. Though differing in motive, they shared the goal of rolling back the rule changes and protecting the public interest. The conservatives claimed that a monopolizing media system gave more power to the liberal elites who controlled America's newsrooms. They complained that concentrated ownership would bring more indecency, sex, and violence into their living rooms. Further they feared that local control over broadcast programming would vanish. Liberals decried the reduction in the number of independent voices in the media system and a consequent threat to democracy. Despite these differences, the coalition held together—convinced that they held the high ground.

Over the course of the year, more than 3 million Americans petitioned the FCC and members of Congress to reverse the move toward media monopoly.[7] Phone calls flooded congressional offices. Town meetings were held nationwide. Local independent media groups talked up the issue. Labor unions in the media industry began educating their members about the new political drive for reform and the implications of consolidation for the livelihoods of workers. Religious and community leaders spoke to parishes and constituencies. University professors lectured on the topic. Advocacy groups specifically devoted to this issue gained members, attention, and influence. Editorials appeared in papers from the *Seattle Times* to the *Quad City Times* to the *New York Times*. Remarkably, media policy began to compete for front-page column inches with the war in Iraq.

The importance and impact of this grassroots upsurge remains to be quantified, but its implications—if it remains vibrant—point to new possibilities for systemic change. Commissioner Michael Copps concluded: "The Commission's drive to loosen the rules and its reluctance to share its proposals with the people before we voted awoke a sleeping giant. . . . The obscurity of this issue that many have relied upon in the past, where only a few dozen inside-the-Beltway lobbyists understood this issue, is gone forever."[8] His prediction, if it holds true, will mean a sea change in the way the politics of media are conducted in Washington.

Media policy has not captured national attention like this before. For decades, it has been the domain of industry lobbies, technical experts, federal bureaucrats, and a handful of powerful legislators. All this has been blown open. People are coming to understand that what they hear on the radio, see on TV, and read in their local newspaper is dependent in no small part on who owns those outlets—and larger yet—on who decides who *may* own those outlets. The FCC's greatest gift to media reformers was lifting the relationship between media content and systemic ownership structure into the light of day. As a result, huge numbers of citizens followed one of the most confusing legislative battles of the 108th Congress, participating at every twist and turn with phone calls, faxes, e-mails, and letters. The new public politics of the media is not only about learning about FCC rules, but about how the government oversees them. People are now far more aware of the problems, but they are also involved in the search for solutions and the means to activate new ideas. This is a major milestone.

Yet we should not overstate the power of the new movement. This campaign attempted to reverse policy, not to make it. By Washington standards, the nascent drive for media reform, despite its bipartisan coalition, is weak. Reformers did not win a legislative victory in 2003 in conventional terms. The political infrastructure of public advocates, civic organizations, and congressional coalitions has not yet solidified. However, the speed and potency of its development thus far suggests that this is a moment of enormous importance—but it bears considerable analysis to judge exactly how and why. The questions that will take up the remainder of this chapter are these: what exactly was won in Congress by advocates of media reform, how did they do it, and what does it mean?

There are three important points to keep in mind in the analysis that follows. First, the new public involvement in media policy is a remarkable political force. The grassroots energy that sustained the upsurge in activism across the political spectrum suggests it has staying power. It stands to reason that people angry about the current media system will not stop being angry as conditions are worsened by deregulation. For the first time there are national constituent groups dedicated solely to the democratization of media policy debates. Beside them are issue-oriented organizations that realize they are dependent on quality media. As a whole, from Main Street to Pennsylvania Avenue, the reform movement has shaken up the old political context for media policy by educating and activating citizens as stakeholders. As evidenced by the surge in traffic on media reform Web sites[9] and involvement in the political struggle, the sophistication of public knowledge about media issues has greatly improved. The combination of informed local activists groups, public-spirited Washington insiders, and a high-profile ownership fight makes for a very potent brew.

Second, the congressional response to the issue was a victory for reformers, even if the FCC's decision was not overturned. Why? Both the House and the Senate passed at least a partial reversal of the rules in the teeth of top-level Republican opposition. That is the litmus test for an issue to be taken seriously in Congress. The majority leadership was forced to exert considerable effort to beat back reform. Although for the moment the FCC's defenders will hold the line, the threat of a majority opposed to the majority cannot be held back forever. Leadership will eventually have to compromise or risk taking political damage at the polls.

Third, the conservative bloc in American politics, stretching from rural value conservatives to Wall Street business conservatives has been divided. A wedge has been driven between the family values regulation of local media ownership and the neoliberal agenda that favors the interests of corporate boardrooms. In the 108th Congress, characterized by the disciplined unity of the GOP, this kind of division was the only method of passing legislation that ran counter to the wishes of the White House. The Republican contingent in the media reform coalition was the reason progressive policy had a chance of legislative victory in 2004. It was the reason why the issue developed into such a controversy. Most Americans now recognize that we have a problem with media in this country—even if they don't agree exactly what it is. This conservative support for control of media ownership appears to have strengthened in the aftermath of George W. Bush's reelection. The moral values trumpeted by the Red states are unlikely to be satisfied by policies that enrich and embolden the media companies they blast for indecency, violence, and ethical corruption.

The defense of public-interest regulations began well before the June 2 ruling. For many years, public-interest groups in Washington like Consumers Union, the Center for Digital Democracy, Media Access Project, and the Consumer Federation of America have been monitoring and lobbying Congress on media issues. The FCC has been reviewing the broadcast ownership rules every two years since 1996. It was by no means clear that 2003 was going to be such a moment of public outcry. If anything the 2002 review (which ended in June of 2003) seemed even more of a foregone conclusion than any of the previous reviews—given Chairman Michael Powell's inclination to deregulate. Perhaps it was the brashness of this commission in neglecting public interest obligations that brought about the crisis. Perhaps it was because local grassroots organizers had built a critical mass of constituent organizations across the country. Perhaps it was commissioners Copps's and Adelstein's nationwide tour of unofficial public hearings. Perhaps it was because right-wing groups like the NRA decided to get involved for the first time. Perhaps it was the dissatisfaction many Americans felt with the press coverage of the war in Iraq in the spring of 2003. Probably it was some combination of all of these factors that led to the rising tide of opposition.

Close observers knew that these rules changes had been in the works for a long time, and that Powell was under strong pressure from the White House and media industry allies of the administration. In the face of this prevailing wind, little could stop the commission from moving forward. Ironically, it may have been corporate lobbyists who started the effort to reverse the rules. The National Association of Broadcasters (NAB), one of Washington's most powerful trade groups, was generally pleased with the idea of loosening ownership caps. However, the national broadcast ownership cap—which would allow the networks to buy more stations—would tip the balance of power in the industry toward the networks and away from the NAB's primary constituents, local and regional broadcasters. If the networks owned more stations outright, it would be easier for them to exert influence over advertising rates and programming decisions for nonowned affiliates. NAB leaned on lawmakers to keep the national cap at 35 percent to avoid that outcome, even as they pressed Congress to endorse the other rule changes.

Nudged by mounting public pressure and NAB lobbying, bipartisan companion bills were introduced in the House and the Senate which would legislate to keep the national broadcast cap at 35 percent, *even before the FCC had raised it*. In the House, it was H.R. 2052, the Burr-Dingell bill, introduced May 9 and named for its sponsors, Rep. Richard Burr (R-NC) and Rep. John Dingell (D-MI). In the Senate, it was S. 1046, the Stevens-Hollings bill, introduced May 13 and named for its sponsors Senator Ted Stevens (R-AK) and Senator Fritz Hollings (D-SC). Both bills rapidly picked up co-sponsors. By the time the Powell Commission actually raised the broadcast cap to 45 percent, a tenth of the House and Senate was on record in support of bills to roll it back. After June 2, the list of co-sponsors spiked upward and momentum gathered.

On June 12, Rep. Bernie Sanders (I-VT) introduced a more aggressive bill, H.R. 2462, a legislative reversal of the entire FCC decision—not just the 45 percent broadcast cap. Sanders's primary concern was the lifting of the ban on cross-media ownership, a move that would permit a newspaper/broadcast media giant in every city in the country. Rolling back the broadcast cap was insufficient. By the end of June, he had more than sixty co-sponsors on his legislation—about half the number held by Burr-Dingell. Such are the realities of Capitol Hill that the broadcast cap rollback—which was big on political capital and small on substance—took center stage in front of the cross-ownership ban, a rule change that would fundamentally change the American mediascape.

But Sanders's efforts were not ignored. When the Stevens-Hollings bill was marked up for consideration in the Senate Commerce Committee on June 19, a key amendment was attached to the bill that would have reinstated the ban on newspaper/broadcast cross-ownership. With that committee vote, Stevens-Hollings was transformed. It now resembled the Sanders bill more than Burr-Dingell. This proved a critical turn of events.

In response, the NAB reversed itself and turned its lobbying power to blocking the very bill that it had helped to create. This was just fine with the business conservatives allied with the Republican leadership. They were happy to have all their usual allies back on the same page. If the media ownership issue could be framed as a partisan attack, they were confident that few if any GOP votes would remain with the reform effort.

But the departure of the NAB did not break the coalition. The public interest groups had won a victory in the Senate Commerce Committee, and they redoubled organizing efforts. Senators Byron Dorgan (D-ND) and Trent Lott (R-MS) (a most unlikely pairing) announced that they would introduce a very unusual measure—a congressional veto. Under the provisions of the Congressional Review Act (CRA) of 1996, Congress could pass a "resolution of disapproval," effectively nullifying any ruling by a federal agency. The CRA had only been used once before, and its chances of passing the Senate seemed slim. Yet with a simple message of total reversal, it was easy to organize around. The public pressure and media attention generated by the CRA threat would be used to drum up more support and momentum for the new, revamped Stevens-Hollings bill.

In haste, the pro-business conservatives mobilized. Members heard complaints from those constituents they fear most—newspaper publishers and broadcast station owners. The steady flow of co-sponsors to the reform bills began to dry up. Furthermore, the powerful House Energy & Commerce Committee chairman W. J. "Billy" Tauzin (R-LA) declared his total opposition to any legislation carrying any reversal of the FCC rules. The implication was clear. Tauzin was the Republican roadblock. Senate Commerce could pass reform legislation if it liked, but if Tauzin refused to consider it in his committee, the whole effort would die on the vine. The Republicans appeared to have media ownership boxed out of play in the House. They settled in to wait out the furor.

But once again, the political pressure did not dissipate. It spilled over into another avenue—the appropriations process. Democrats had cultivated a relatively committed group of GOP value conservatives. Together they stood a real chance to win if they could execute an end-run around Tauzin by tacking a rule reversal onto an appropriations bill. An appropriations amendment might peel off enough Republican votes to make a majority to defeat the bloc of votes standing behind the majority leadership.

The difficulty of passing this measure belies the ways of Congress. The reversal of media concentration is an issue that the vast majority of Americans agree on. It is not partisan. It is hardly even contentious. It is the subject of debate in the Congress only because powerful interests have a great deal of money at stake. The Republican leadership certainly had the power to stop it cold. But could they do it without a media stink that would bring the wrath of their value-conservative constituents? The only chance for reform lay in cloaking every step in the legislative process with so much public support that any effort to stifle its chances would carry the taint of special interests.

Enter the public interest groups. Right, left, and center, advocates of media diversity and localism staged repeated campaigns throughout the summer to call, write, e-mail, and fax members of Congress and the FCC to register opposition to the rule changes. Left-wing groups—among them MoveOn, Free Press, and Common Cause—led the charge in early July. Frustrated that members of Congress had learned to ignore e-mail drives and on-line petitions, these groups asked their activists to call members of Congress directly. They provided phone numbers. Given that most congressional offices (especially in the House) receive fewer than a dozen calls from constituents per day on *any* issue, getting 50 to 100 in an afternoon comes as a shock.[10] Furthermore, every congressional staffer is trained to recognize the area codes in the caller-ID that represent a constituent. These callers are taken very seriously. When they come in such volumes that the office shuts down, it provokes quite a stir.

In a period of three days, co-sponsorship shot up on the active bills. Although these bills were blocked by Tauzin, a spike in support gave the appropriations strategy considerable momentum. Whether the phone-in campaigns were the prime mover of action on Capitol Hill or whether they greased wheels that were already turning, it is hard to say. But the people were doubtless playing a role in a way they had not before. Citizens were aware that a contest over media policy was playing out in Washington, and they made an effort to get involved. That alone is a thunderbolt.

On July 16, the House Appropriations Committee met to consider the Commerce, Justice, State appropriations bill, which allocates funding to many agencies, including the FCC. It is standard practice in Congress to attach amendments (or riders) to these bills which block the use of funds to implement particular policies. In this case, the goal was to prohibit the FCC from using any of its funds to implement the new rules. There would be one amendment blocking the broadcast cap and one blocking cross-ownership and the consolidation of local television. The first would be offered in committee and the second on the floor of the House.

In the room for the vote that morning were dozens of broadcast executives who had spent the previous two days closeted with Republicans on the appropriations committee. They thought they had it beaten. Yet, when Ranking Democrat David Obey (D-WI) introduced the amendment to block the broadcast cap, a number of Republicans spoke up in support. The rider passed 40-25, stunning everyone and leaving the broadcasters with egg on their faces. Led by Rep. Frank Wolf (R-VA), GOP committee members had voted their conscience. Wolf commented later on his defection: "I did not get elected to be a potted plant, and I don't care what the White House thinks."[11] Tauzin's fiery spokesman, Ken Johnson, acknowledged the defeat but predicted what was to come: "We may have one hand tied behind our back, but as long as we have one free hand, we can still swing a bat."[12]

The bill was set for a floor vote on July 22. The debate that afternoon was heated and the tactics complex.[13] At first, the question was whether the Republicans would attempt to strip out the Obey rider, or simply fight to block a cross-ownership amendment. Once on the floor, the Republicans said nothing about the broadcast cap and were content to debate the cross-ownership amendment, offered by Rep. Maurice Hinchey (D-NY), Rep. David Price (D-NC), and Rep. Jay Inslee (D-WA). It was thought a foregone conclusion that the Hinchey amendment would fail. The question was by how much. If it got 150 votes or more, then the House would have demonstrated respectable support for a full rollback and opened the door politically for further Senate action where support was stronger. Less than 150 would all but end the hopes of reversing the cross-ownership rule.

Activist groups responded by launching the largest call-in campaign of the year. Within two hours of the vote, practically every phone in every House office was ringing. Citizens from across the country called on their representatives to vote for the Hinchey amendment. It was a bizarre and inspiring scene, as Americans who had never heard of an appropriations rider called to demand that their representatives support one. Rep. David Price, moved by the action, said this in his speech on the House floor: "Mr. Chairman, in the history of media policy, there has never been a moment when the public was more engaged than they are right now."[14]

The Democrats responded to this public embrace awkwardly. Reps. Obey and Dingell, key Democratic leaders, spoke against the Hinchey amendment. They argued that adding a cross-ownership amendment would surely bring a Bush veto and doom any chance of a victory on the broadcast cap. Despite supporting the principle behind the Hinchey amendment, Obey warned: "The Hinchey amendment is not intended to be so, but it is a killer amendment. It will load up the camel, and it will break the camel's back."[15]

In the end, the Hinchey amendment was defeated 254-174. Sixty Democrats voted against it, thirty-four Republicans voted for it. Had the Democrats held their ground, the measure would have passed easily. Despite the tactical betrayal, the Hinchey amendment and the tens of thousands of Americans who called that day to support it, achieved a respectable vote tally, well above expectations. Further, if thirty-four Republicans were willing to vote against the entire June 2 FCC decision, all that remained to be done was to organize the Democrats into a unified block. A few days later, when the Obey-amended appropriations bill passed the House by a vote of 400-21, it made the front page of the *New York Times* and the *Washington Post*.[16] The Democrats had apparently stolen a victory from the Republican leadership in the House. But the real story that did not get mentioned, the real story that shielded the Obey amendment from harm's way, the real story of nearly unprecedented public participation in a labyrinthine legislative process—the story of the Hinchey amendment—went largely untold.

An unlikely coalition was now on the record. *Congressional Quarterly* headlined, "Unconventional Wisdom Prevails," explaining that the Tauzin roadblock in the House had been bested by the public.[17] The people had fired a shot across the GOP bow. And it was not just liberals. In the midst of the appropriations fight executive vice president of the NRA, Wayne LaPierre, issued a call to arms in the *New York Daily News*: "Tell everyone the airwaves belong to the American people, and the FCC's job is to protect the public interest—not big media barons who want a monopoly on public discourse."[18] The White House responded with a veto threat. But congressional Republican leaders were less bullish, commenting only that there was a long road to the president's desk.[19]

A few days later, Congress went into its August recess. The industry lobby went to work on district offices. The *New York Times* published an OpEd by Chairman Powell attacking his critics as misguided.[20] In late August, Americans for Tax Reform tried its hand at online activism, launching a pro-deregulation Web site.[21] The FCC went into damage control mode. On August 20, Chairman Powell announced that the commission would be launching a "Localism in Broadcasting" initiative, a taskforce aimed at collecting public testimony on the local public service of broadcasters. He declined to hold back his rule changes. Commissioner Copps called it a policy of "ready, fire, aim."[22] Finally, Republican pollster Frank Luntz released survey numbers in full-page ads in the Capitol Hill newspapers on the day members and staff returned to work in September. His data purported to show that the American public rejected government regulation of media. His message: "America Says: Don't Get Between Me and My TV."[23]

However the Republican backlash was dealt a shocking and neutralizing blow on that same day, September 3, by an event that almost no one anticipated. The 3rd Circuit Federal Court of Appeals ruled in the case of *Prometheus Radio Project vs. FCC*. Filed by a group of community radio activists and argued by public interest attorneys of the Media Access Project, the suit asked for a stay on the implementation of the FCC's June 2 media-ownership rules. Rejecting the arguments of agency and industry lawyers, the Court ruled for Prometheus. "Given the magnitude of this matter and the public's interest in reaching the proper resolution," the Court wrote, "a stay is warranted pending thorough and efficient judicial review."[24] It was a stunning victory. The *Wall Street Journal* reported that the tiny nonprofit law firm had "bested legal teams from the FCC and three of the nation's broadcast networks."[25] The lawyers at Media Access Project had opened a window for congressional action. The case would not be decided until the spring of 2004.

Senators Dorgan and Lott then announced at a press conference that they would force a vote on the CRA "resolution of disapproval." MoveOn stacked 300,000 petitions of support beside the senators' podium to drive home the point. On September 16, the Senate voted on the resolution after several hours of debate. Senator John McCain (R-AZ), who would vote against it in the end, nonetheless had this to say: "In my time as chairman of the Senate Commerce Committee, no issue has erupted so rapidly and evoked such passion from the public as media consolidation."[26] He concluded that the CRA resolution would likely pass the Senate that day, but that it would die in the House. Indeed, he chided, that may be why so many senators felt that they could vote safely in favor of it.

It passed 55-40. Once again, the vote was pushed hard by another round of public phone calls. The *New York Times* described the vote as a "stinging political rebuke of Michael K. Powell." Chairman Powell called it "bordering on the absurd."[27] He complained that "there was a concerted grass-roots effort to attack the commission from the outside in."[28] Though he said this with no irony intended, the public reform movement would likely have agreed and labeled that effort "participatory democracy." This was the high-water mark for the reformers.

In October, optimism began to fade. Burr-Dingell, Sanders, and Stevens-Hollings idled with little hope for a vote, despite a peak in support (184, 100, and 47 co-sponsors respectively). They had done their job. They had carried the baton to the appropriators. The Senate appropriations bill had also quietly taken on the broadcast cap rider in committee thanks to the insistence of Appropriations chairman Ted Stevens (R-AK).[29] But as the fall wore on, the bill looked increasingly unlikely to have a floor vote. It was fated to be wrapped up together with several other controversial spending bills in an omnibus package. The omnibus carries the weight of a must-pass bill. But it allows little opportunity for further amendment—meaning Dorgan and Lott would not have opportunity to offer an amendment blocking cross-ownership. Further, the omnibus negotiations allow much stronger influence from the White House—meaning even the broadcast cap was in danger of being stripped out. In the back channels of Senate power, the tides were turning against real legislative action.

As appropriations negotiations languished, attention returned to the CRA resolution in the House. Ignoring the will of the Senate and the public, House leadership called the resolution "dead on arrival."[30] As McCain had predicted, it was turning into a showpiece vote, not a substantive action. But the House was not finished. Led once again by Sanders and Hinchey, a new coalition was cobbled together. The goal was to get signatures on a letter to the Speaker of the House calling for an immediate vote on the Senate resolution. Once more a public call-in campaign shook up the stack and encouraged members to stand up and be counted. By late October, more than 200 members of the House (including eleven Republicans) had signed the letter. Though 200 is short of a majority, it was a clear statement to the leadership that the resolution would pass *if it were to come for a vote.* Moreover, by cross-referencing those who voted for the Hinchey amendment with those who signed the letter, a clear majority appears on the record in support of a full rollback. Speaker Dennis Hastert (R-IL) declined to bring the resolution to a vote, a privilege the Speaker enjoys under House rules.

Meanwhile, with the issue back in the limelight, the pressure was on the Senate appropriators to hold the line on the 35 percent broadcast cap in the omnibus bill. Bipartisan conferees agreed to keep the language in the bill. But at the eleventh hour in late November, Stevens met with White House counsel. He emerged with a new deal. Senator Hollings (D-SC) blasted the action: "The Republicans went into a closet, met with themselves, and announced a 'compromise,'" he said in statement. "It was a total violation of the conference agreement."[31] The new deal was as suspicious in function as it was in process. The broadcast cap would be set at 39 percent, but as a permanent statute, not a one-year appropriations rider. However, there was a catch. Any company could violate the 39 percent limit for two years without penalty before being forced to sell stations. Moreover, the commission's authority to grant a waiver to the 39 percent limit was not removed. Indeed, the new legislative language was written in such a way as to make the legal authority to change the rule intentionally murky. The clear implication was to provide the pretense of a public interest regulation while signaling to the industry that consolidation could proceed. And why 39 percent? Viacom and News Corp. stood in violation of the 35 percent limit—at 39 percent and 38 percent, respectively.[32] The "compromise" simply legalized the status quo and set up a mechanism for future violation and gradual expansion of the cap. Despite considerable opposition, the omnibus bill containing the 39 percent deal passed both the House and the Senate and became law in early 2004.

With Hastert's refusal to consider the CRA resolution and Stevens's cave-in to the White House, the policy battle for media reform was lost for 2003. However, the political battle for control of the issue was far more successful.

In six months, media ownership went from total obscurity to the top of the list of important controversies on the national political agenda. Driving the train was an odd coalition which held together through one of the most partisan sessions of Congress in recent memory. Despite Republican legislative victory, the GOP remains divided between business and value conservatives, a breach opened by serious ideological contradictions in the conservative base. Divisions like this have been few. Media ownership joins prescription drugs, civil liberties, and overtime wages on a shortlist of issues that the leadership was forced to block in conference committees to halt the will of the majority. It speaks to the power of the current administration that nothing unfavorable to the majority of the majority party passes into law. But it also shows the enormous importance of those issues that manage to get numerical majorities and require backroom "compromises" to undercut reform.

What are the prospects for keeping public interest limits on broadcast ownership in the future? By all accounts, they are good. Throughout 2004, the Congress did not significantly address media ownership again. However, the litigation in the 3rd Circuit on the June 2 rules proceeded. On June 24, 2004, the court overturned the FCC, handing the agency and its industry backers a decisive defeat. The triumph represents a tremendous victory for media diversity, localism, and the will of the general public, including the millions of citizens who have been writing, e-mailing, and calling the FCC and Congress to protest the FCC's caving in to Big Media. The court found that the FCC's decision defied logic and reason, instructing the commission to begin again on the study of media ownership rules. This ruling may yet be taken to the Supreme Court by the agency, the broadcasters, or the publishers. Regardless, it seems likely that a new Bush administration will push the commission to proceed down a similar path of deregulation once again. It raises the specter of a renewed battle on the same ground for activists and reformers.

In the public movement, the accumulated strength is considerable. A wide variety of influential civic organizations are now committed to media issues. This is particularly true in the aftermath of a highly contentious election season that featured numerous media controversies and journalistic scandals. The bedrock desire of people from all walks of life to retain control over the media system has intensified. The coalition still marshals some of the most active and effective political shock troops ever heard from on Capitol Hill. Though moderate Republican politicians may well be strong-armed into staying quiet on media reform, there is no credible evidence that conservative voters across America will do so. In short, the coalition may bend and crack on Capitol Hill, but as long as the public is unified, the issue is likely to endure.

It would be unwise to predict where the media reform movement is headed in the future. But it is certainly possible to highlight its accomplishments. The obscurity which once shrouded media policy has undeniably been cleared away. The big-picture stakes of democracy and culture have been firmly tied to the FCC and the complex legislative process in the Congress. Millions of citizens are now more aware of the problems in the media system and many hundreds of thousands have participated in potential solutions. In November of 2003, the first-ever National Conference on Media Reform was held in Madison, Wisconsin, drawing together leaders of the reform movement, members of Congress, FCC commissioners, musicians, academics, and over a thousand activists from across the country. The subject of the conference was to bring out the most important media policy issues facing the public today. Among them are low-power community radio, media and international trade deals, cable regulations, public-service obligations in digital TV, open-access spectrum rights, reforming copyright law, and many more. The ripples of educated organizing are starting to be felt in the political culture, as questions like these begin to crop up in the mainstream media and over dinner tables.

At a more concrete level, the push to reverse the June 2 FCC ruling has witnessed the majority of legislators endorse progressive, public-interest policy objectives. Perhaps most importantly, new questions are being asked by diverse groups across the country about how their members of Congress can build a better media system. And, despite being boxed out of a true legislative victory, the media reform forces inside and outside of Washington stand a real chance of winning the ownership debate in the next Congress. They have a significant chance of bringing the people—and a new agenda of public-interest media policy making—into a position as legitimate stakeholders in American media politics for years to come.

NOTES

1. The full text of the Order can be found on the FCC's Web site at: <http://hraunfoss.fcc.gov/edocs_public/attachmatch/FCC-03-127A1.pdf>

2. Adelstein, "Statement of Commissioner Jonathan S. Adelstein, Dissenting", 2 July 2003, <http://hraunfoss.fcc.gov/edocs_public/attachmatch/FCC-03-127A7.pdf, 1.>

3. Dorgan Press Release, 2 June 2003, <http://www.dorgan.senate.gov.>

4. Hollings, Press Release, 2 June 2003, <http://www.hollings.senate.gov.>

5. Copps, "Statement of Commissioner Michael J. Copps Dissenting, 2002 Biennial Regulatory Review," 2July 2003, <http://hraunfoss.fcc.gov/edocs_public/attachmatch/FCC-03-127A5.doc, 7>.

6. See Robert W. McChesney, *Telecommunications, Mass Media, and Democracy* (New York: Oxford University Press, 1993).

7. Robert W. McChesney and John Nichols, "Up In Flames," in *The Nation*, 17 November 2003, 11. The figure of 3 million should be read as an estimate. Congressional offices do not keep publicly available records.

8. Copps, 22.

9. For example: <http://www.mediareform.net>; <http://www.commoncause.org>; <http://www.futureofmusic.org>/; <http://www.childrennow.org/>; <http://www.consumersunion.org>.

10. These numbers are based on the experience of the author in Congress during this time.

11. "Congress Implements Tools to Block FCC's June Ruling," Capitol Broadcasting Company, 21 July 2003, <http://www.cbc-raleigh.com/capcom/news/2003/corporate_03/fcc_congress/fcc_congress.htm>

12. Brody Mullins, "FCC Decision Dealt Big Blow," *Roll Call*, 17 July 2003, 24.

13. This story has been told in detail at <http://www.mediareform.net/congress/updates.php?id=14>.

14. Congressional Record, House, 108th Congress, 1st Session, H7280.

15. Congressional Record, House, 108th Congress, 1st Session, H7279.

16. Stephen Labaton, "F.C.C. Media Rule Blocked in House in a 400-to-21 Vote," *New York Times*. 24 July 2003 <http://www.nytimes.com>; Christopher Stern and Jonathan Krim, "House Votes to Prevent Change in Media Rule," *Washington Post*, 24 July 2003, <http://www.washingtonpost.com>.

17. Joseph C. Anselmo, "Lawmakers Underestimate Public Concern about FCC Media Ownership Rule," *Congressional Quarterly*, 26 July 2003, 1903.

18. Wayne LaPierre, "Speak Out vs. FCC While You Can," *New York Daily News*, 18 July 2003, <http://nydailynews.com>.

19. Richard Simon and Janet Hook, "FCC Rule May Bring a Veto Standoff," *Los Angeles Times*, 25 July 2003, <http://www.latimes.com>.

20. Powell, "New Rules, Old Rhetoric," *New York Times*, 28 July 2003, <http://www.nytimes.com>.

21. <http://www.stopmediaregulation.org/>

22. "FCC Chairman Powell Launches 'Localism in Broadcasting' Initiative,'" FCC Press Release, 20 August 2003, http://www.fcc.gov; "Copps Criticizes Willingness To Let Media Consolidation Continue," FCC Press Release 20 August 2003, <http://www.fcc.gov>.

23. Memorandum: "Why Americans Support the FCC Decision," 3 September 2003, Luntz Research Companies. This memo was distributed to every congressional office.

24. Order of the United States Court of Appeals for the Third Circuit, No. 03-3388, *Prometheus Radio Project v. FCC*, 3 September 2003.

25. Yochi J. Dreazen, "No-Frills Fighter Stuns the FCC, Media Goliaths," *Wall Street Journal*, 5 September 2003, <http://www.wsjonline.com>.

26. Congressional Record, Senate, 108th Congress, 1st Session, S11507.

27. Stephen Labaton, "F.C.C. Plan to Ease Curbs on Big Media Hits Senate Snag," *New York Times*, 17 September 2003, <http://www.nytimes.com>.

28. Quoted from Michael Powell in Stephen Labaton, "F.C.C. Chief Talks of Frustration and Surprise," *New York Times*, 22 September 2003, <http://www.nytimes.com>.

29. Stephen Labaton, "Senate Panel Acts to Block TV Ownership Rule," *New York Times*, 5 September 2003, <http://www.nytimes.com>.

30. Quote from Tom DeLay in Greg Gatlin, "Reps Balk as Senate Rolls Back FCC Rules," *Boston Herald*, 17 September 2003, <http://www.bostonherald.com>.

31. Hollings Press Release, November 25, 2003, <http://hollings.senate.gov>.

32. Frank Ahrens, "Democrats Decry 'Compromise' on FCC Rule," 26 November 2003, <http://www.washingtonpost.com>

10

Angels of the Public Interest: U.S. Media Reform

Dorothy Kidd

> I think the sun came out for us today. I think that means we're on the side of the angels. And maybe they're the angels of the public interest. It's a real breath of fresh air to be here and out of Washington, to hear your views about media consolidation. This gives your voices the opportunity to join the emerging national dialogue that impacts everyone.
>
> (Federal Communications commissioner Jonathan Adelstein,
> San Francisco City Hall, April 26, 2003)

On Saturday, April 26, 2003, an overflow crowd of more than six hundred people gathered in the San Francisco City Hall chambers to discuss the Federal Communication Commission's (FCC) comprehensive review of broadcast ownership with Commissioner Adelstein.[1] The forum was extraordinary for a number of reasons. Although the hearing addressed the highly specialized concerns of a distant Washington regulator, it was jointly organized by a local media advocacy group, Media Alliance, several academic departments, a nascent national media reform network, and the two Democratic Party FCC commissioners.[2] The large turnout and informed level of debate surprised everyone, given the virtual blockade of the issue in the dominant corporate media.[3] Amidst a wide diversity of individual backgrounds and social issue constituencies, there was a marked unity of perspective. Everyone rejected the proposed new rules. Many also criticized the previous round of deregulation in the Telecommunications Act of 1996, challenging its "market" rationale. Finally, while public testimonies were limited to two minutes, several speakers went beyond just saying "no" to media consolidation and introduced alternative strategies for operating the public airwaves and media system.

The San Francisco hearing was one of twelve citizen-organized forums across the United States in the spring of 2003. The original idea was modest: to bring the problems of corporate media domination into the public sphere and begin to influence the policies governing media ownership. The national campaign grew beyond everyone's expectations, encompassing the support of more than two million people in a wide variety of organizations and constituencies, from the left to the right of the political spectrum. In addition to the hearings, the tactics ranged from letter and e-mail campaigns to the FCC and Congress, Washington lobbying, prompting mainstream journalists to cover the story, launching legal appeals in the courts, producing and circulating countermessages via the networks of old and new alternative media, and targeting both the FCC and the major corporate players in street protests.

Although the Republican majority held sway in the vote in favor of further deregulation of television and cross-media media ownership rules on June 2, 2003, the campaign achieved some considerable successes. Both Democratic commissioners voted "no" on every issue, and the majority voted for any further deregulation of radio. Then, both the House and Senate voted to reconsider some of the rules.[4] A year later, on June 24, 2004, the U.S. Court of Appeals for the Third Circuit decided in *Prometheus Radio v. FCC* to halt the rule changes. The court stipulated, among other points, that the FCC not proceed with a bias in favor of deregulation, and take more account of public concern and the local impact of media consolidation.[5]

THE ANGELS ARE NOT PHANTOMS[6]

The reemergence of the "public" interest in media consolidation and media reform was another important victory. Just days before the FCC vote, the major media outlets implicated in the decision began to cover the story.[7] Many of their reports, and those of the independent press, discussed the impact of the extensive public mobilization.[8] As well, many of the media advocacy and activist groups, and a handful of academics, have circulated analyses of the contemporary initiatives and their historical precedents.[9] However, while most commentators give credence to the "public" response, and value the "public interest," there has been little systematic analysis of the organizing experiences and concerns of the different publics outside the Washington beltway, which helped build the campaign and the broader movement for democratic media accountability.

A small, but growing number of embedded activist researchers have begun this task.[10] They trace the roots, and the prospects for further movement building, among two different sectors: the organized (counter) publics, which have historically been critical forces in social, cultural, and political change in the United States; and independent or alternative media.[11] In a departure from most of the national advocacy organizations and academic critics, their strategies for challenging the dominance of corporate commercial media are not centered on the political, economic, and media power centers of Washington, New York, and Hollywood.[12] While those arenas remain important targets, they take a more decentered and pluralistic approach, focusing instead on groups mobilizing from multiple bases in local, national, and international social and cultural networks.

My approach builds with this latter research agenda. I draw from two other radical research agendas, autonomist Marxism, and radical or alternative media. With one eye on following the money (in the growing dominating power of global capitalist communications), autonomist accounts pay more attention to the movement (the ways that people create time, space, and collective projects for communication) autonomous of that domination.[13] I also build on the growing historical record of alternative and citizens' media campaigns in the United States and elsewhere. While recognizing the sporadic, underresourced nature of many of these struggles, alternative media theorists reveal their multiple dimensions, encompassing campaigns for political, economic, cultural, and social change, affecting every aspect of the communications ecology, from infrastructure, governance, content, and aesthetics to the rights of the creator and end user.[14]

This case study of one metropolitan center provides a moment to illuminate some of the local contending actors in media and communications change in the biggest media reform campaign in U.S. history. This local lens is especially important in the United States, which leaves many central functions of government, including broadcast licensing and cable franchising, to each locality. Through analyses of the public comments, interviews, participatory observation, policy documents, and news media articles, I review the content, direction, development, and circulation of some of the counterpublics at the San Francisco hearing.[15] Situating these transcripts of struggle within the wider political, economic, and cultural context of changes in media organizations and state policy, I demonstrate that the FCC campaign was not an isolated phenomenon but a watershed moment for media change in the United States.

THE LEGACY OF THE ANGELS

If we wanted to date the birth of the campaign against the FCC, there is no better moment than the March 22, 2002, demonstration outside the FCC offices in Washington, D.C.[16] The protest was sparked by Michael Powell, the Bush-appointed chair of the commission, and an unabashed neoliberal supporter of corporate media and the rule of capital and investment in public communications policy. Powell had taken no pains to hide his contempt for the public interest, quipping: "the night after I was sworn in, I waited for a visit from the angels of the public interest. I waited all night, but she did not come." The angel-winged protesters cut short his wait, demanding that "media and communications technology should serve people over profits."[17]

Who were these angels? The list of endorsers[18] included many of the sectors Bob Hackett identified in the emerging "media democracy movement."[19] The protest itself included Washington communication advocates, independent media producers (particularly micro-radio advocates, freshly enlivened by their success with the FCC at relegalizing low-power FM), media monitoring groups, educators, and old and new social movement organizers (including those from the antiglobalization movement, and from the Indymedia Network).

The Angels' manifesto combined the "public interest" frame with the more recent global frame that "information is a world-wide good."[20] No single-issue protest, their demands spanned many of the categories of contemporary communications and media policy, including content, legal rights and entitlements, political economy, and infrastructure.[21] It also reflected the Angels' cross-generational and cross-sectoral composition, as their concerns bridged the old and new media and communication industries, intellectual property regimes, and new technologies in development. Their demands also ranged across political dimensions, from the "monopolistic concentration of media and communications systems;" to protection of public airwaves and public knowledge from privatization; pluralism and diversity of expression balancing gender, race, culture, language, and geographic region; protection of civil liberties and privacy from surveillance technology; and banning of advertisements on children's programs and taxing those targeted at adults.[22]

The Angels identified the 1996 Telecommunications Act as the low-water mark in a drastic turn toward media and communications consolidation. The paradigm of the omnibus bill, signed by President Clinton, was no longer "public service" but "market rule," and was credited for unleashing a bonanza of media and communication conglomeration. However, the first signs of major capitalist market interest in communications, and of the changing social contract between citizens, the state, and corporations, went back much further.

Some of the Angels had been involved in the last intense period of media activism, coinciding with the more general social ferment of the late 1960s and 1970s.[23] Although there had been little coordination between sectors, there had been many significant advances in the democratization of communications. African-American and other civil rights movements had successfully challenged the systemic discrimination in programming content, ownership and employment; the alternative media sector had expanded, in community radio, cable access, independent publishing, and music; and citizen advocates in Washington had pushed through policy initiatives aimed at limiting media monopolies.[24]

This period of democratization began to close during the late 1970s, with the major shift to global neoliberal policies (of market liberalization, deregulation, commercialization, and privatization).[25] Begun during the Democratic presidency of Jimmy Carter, the Reagan Republicans accelerated the process; the FCC removed many of the rules governing the structure (competition and ownership limits), programming content, and behavior (accountability to the public interest) of broadcasters.[26] The commission also deregulated the cable industry, and opened up the telephone market, enabling the first major wave of mergers and acquisitions. By the end of the 1980s, there were few remaining limits to consolidation, few content requirements (with the notable exceptions of obscenity, children's programming, and elections), and almost no accountability mechanisms.

Deregulation accelerated the growing investment in global communications enterprises. Although the number of media and communications operations stayed fairly constant, the largest global conglomerates allied to consolidate their holdings across several different industries, allowing them to expand into new markets and deter new entrants.[27] With fewer rivals, or regulatory limits, the environment shifted from a mix of commercially oriented, but variously sized companies, structured around the production and circulation of media content, to a smaller number of powerful linked conglomerates, much more oriented to marketing branded franchises to a globalized market. Their increased economic power also gave the large networks more political leverage.

Although the possibilities within the corporate media system were shrinking, radical possibilities were growing outside.[28] As global corporations extended their reach, they provided a surfeit of lower-cost, easy-to-use media production equipment and training, which were appropriated by a wide variety of small producers around the world. If the core businesses were attending more to marketing and distribution, leaving the risks to independents, this constellation allowed some degree of autonomy for the creative music, film and video, and Internet communities.[29] As well, many younger independents had moved quickly to the converged production and distribution streams of the Internet, seizing the openings to bypass the media cartel's hold over music, news, and entertainment distribution. And, while the increasing exploitation and branding of "life worlds" enraged many, the resulting sameness of global content provided common cultural references, and targets, for the latest generation of activists organizing against global capital.

Earlier generations had attempted to form coalitions that crossed lines of media industry, issue and political perspectives.[30] The Angels represented a new level of convergence of media activism. Unlike the media movements of earlier generations, their alliance represented a wider composition of social actors, dimensions of issues, and dynamics of organization. Their little demonstration that day at the FCC targeted the media ownership rules. However, among them, their visions of changes in the system as a whole were enriched by years of critique and action around corporate media representations, and of building alternative media projects and networks. Although there was very little mainstream media coverage of the protest, their call for a renewed targeting of the FCC circulated widely through the linked channels of media advocates, activists, social movements, and academics.

THE REVIEW OF MEDIA OWNERSHIP RULES

In October 2001, FCC chair Michael Powell formed a media ownership working group committed to removing all the remaining rules. Immediately, the media policy watchdog groups in Washington, including the Media Access Project, Consumers Federation of America, Consumers Union, and the Center for Digital Democracy, started a congressional lobby and press campaign to urge Congress to take action against further media concentration. The Consumer Federation of America also held town hall meetings across the country.[31] Then in September 2002, the FCC announced a biennial review of media ownership rules, a requirement from the 1996 Telecommunications Act.

The same month, the founding conference of Reclaim the Media took place in Seattle. Seattle had become a critical hub in the media activism network in late 1999, partly as a result of the organizing against the World Trade Organization (WTO) and the formation of the Indymedia Center (IMC) Network. Reclaim also drew inspiration from the counterevents to the National Association of Broadcasters (NAB) Convention, coordinated by Media Alliance in San Francisco in September 2000.[32] The NAB protest week had, in turn, boomeranged from "Seattle," combining the direct-action repertoires of street protests, agit-prop theater, and music, with more conventional social movement press campaigning and public education. As in Seattle, the aims were to expose the political and economic power nexus: in this case to highlight the political influence of the national media industry lobby group, the NAB, on national politics, and on media consolidation in the Bay area. One of the local targets was Clear Channel Radio, which had just purchased eight San Francisco stations, and fired Davy D, the popular host of a talk-show aimed at the hip-hop generation.

Another "Seattle" echo was the continuing race-and-class divide among social justice movements. The NAB events in San Francisco and the Reclaim the Media Conference in Seattle attempted to bridge these chasms, and included some key organizers from what would become the Media Justice Network, an alliance of people working in "media advocacy, media accountability and policy, cultural work and training in media production, alternative journalism, and virtual/real world technology organizing.[33]

In the final strategy session of Reclaim the Media, someone raised the upcoming FCC rule-making, and the assembled groups jumped on the opportunity to work together in a public campaign of outreach, education, and activism.[34] No one, according to Jeff Perlstein, of Media Alliance, thought there was much likelihood of overriding the Republican majority on the FCC and defeating the rule changes. Their hope was that the FCC Ownership Review, with its requirement for public comment, could provide an opportunity to raise the profile of the larger issues of corporate media consolidation and put strategies for structural change on the public agenda.

The "media diversity" frame adopted after the conference went beyond a critique of the FCC rule-making, or even media ownership. The first joint flyer's banner read: "Democracy Needs Diverse Media! Tell the FCC to defend the public interest. Join the people's campaign to stop media monopolies," and included calls for "Diversity of Views," "Diversity of Creativity, Art, Culture, Vision," "Labor Rights and Minority Ownership," "Freedom of the Net," "Localism and Community," and for additional international news sources, investigative journalism and resources for journalists, and attention to the Internet. As part of a plan to link existing efforts and groups, and encourage the involvement of new publics, Philadelphia-based Prometheus Radio and Media Tank set up an improved on-line system for filing comments to the FCC, with Web links to groups in the coalition.[35]

By January, a larger network linked the Washington watchdog groups, media workers' unions, film and video producers' associations, community and micro-radio producers, hip-hop producers, small media companies, children's advocates and civil rights organizations, and a handful of academics. When Michael Powell refused to authorize more than one official hearing, Michael Copps, the Democratic commissioner, worked with the emerging network to hold citizen-organized hearings. The first one was in New York at Columbia Law School, co-sponsored by the Writers Guild and the American Federation of Television and Radio Artists (AFTRA), with assistance from Copps's office, the Association of Independent Video and Film, the Consumers Union, and Media Access Project. While several corporate media executives from Fox, CBS and Viacom, and most of the FCC commissioners, including Michael Powell, showed up, none of the commercial TV networks covered it. Pacifica Radio covered it live throughout its national network.

THE 2003 SAN FRANCISCO HEARINGS

The successful New York event gave a new sense of urgency to groups in other regions. Commissioner Adelstein, Jeff Perlstein, executive director of Media Alliance, and the Media Studies Department of the University of San

Francisco, agreed to hold hearings in cooperation with the Berkeley Graduate School of Journalism, Stanford University's Department of Communication, and the Hastings Law School Review. A small ad hoc committee took on
coordinating site logistics, organizing panels and public comment periods,
developing outreach, creating educational instruments, and working with
the commercial and independent press.

No one imagined stopping the rule-making. As Jeff Perlstein of Media Alliance put it, the hearing would build on the existing base of key local groups,
such as independent media, media workers, youth of color, and other social
justice groups working in media transformation efforts, and spotlight these
concerns in a civic space.[36] We also discussed focusing on local case studies
of the impact of media consolidation in the Bay area, including the Hearst
purchase of the *San Francisco Chronicle* (which had left San Francisco with
one daily newspaper), the purchase of seven stations by Clear Channel, and
NBC's purchase of Telemundo TV.

The hearing itself was designed for maximum public education and participation. In contrast to those in other locales, the San Francisco group decided not to convene at one of the sponsoring universities, but in the town
hall, a space that is symbolic of the importance of civic participation in
American democracy.[37] We chose a Saturday, to encourage maximum public participation. The panels and extensive public comment periods were
designed to represent the plurality of contending perspectives, from the
corporate media, the FCC and political representatives to mainstream and
independent media workers, policy researchers, and local groups already
activated around these issues. The event was also timed to provide national
legislators an opportunity to attend during congressional recess. Finally, a
critical objective was the pitching and priming of the commercial and independent media.

In the end, the plan was modified. The president of the Board of Supervisors, Matt Gonzalez, a member of the Green Party, opened the hearing, then
left his seat to me, as the moderator from the ad hoc group. The only national
political representation was Congresswoman Woolsey's aide (Woolsey sponsored a hearing two weeks later). The greater obstacle was the reluctance of
the corporate media to accept the invitation to speak. The only corporate
media manager to do so was Dino Dinovitz, the general manager of KRON
TV, a newly independent station which had recently severed its long-time affiliation with NBC.[38]

The U.S. public has shown a growing concern with media concentration
and its impact on programming since the first wave of corporate mergers and
their regulatory approval via the Telecommunications Act of 1996.[39] Although the independent media in the Bay area had regularly featured programming on these issues, the corporate media had been almost silent.[40]
Two months prior to the hearing, the Pew Research Center for the People

and the Press reported that 72 percent of Americans had heard "nothing at all" about the FCC proceedings. The embargo of the story held fast until two days before the hearing, when Karen Stephenson, the press coordinator, successfully brokered an article in the *San Francisco Chronicle* from Commissioner Adelstein. As a result, many more members of the public heard about it and attended the hearings; and two more media workers decided to join the panels.

After only five weeks of organizing, the risky decision to call a town hall meeting to discuss national media policy paid off. The hearing opened to a packed hall, with more than two hundred more waiting outside to get in. The reluctance of media managers and media workers to testify meant that the membership of the panels changed up to the last minute. The public comment periods started off in disarray, overwhelmed by people wanting to speak. Nevertheless, the content of the day was startling. The testimonies provided more than anybody had expected; almost all the speakers thoughtfully and knowledgeably addressed existing problems of media consolidation, as well as the real consequences of two decades of privatization and deregulation, and more than a century of problems under the commercial media regime.

What had brought all these people and their concerns to City Hall? Certainly the San Francisco landscape is marked by media consolidation. Two companies, Clear Channel, and Viacom's Infinity, operate sixteen radio stations on the local dial, sharing about 50 percent of the advertising market, plus most of the city's billboards. Clear Channel alone controls most of the large concert venues. None of the major TV stations are locally owned; Viacom and Cox Enterprises, with two stations each, reach 43 percent of the city's TV audience. In the newspaper industry, the *San Francisco Chronicle* is the only significant daily.[41] However, as the panelists and public witnesses note below, the changes in ownership told only one small part of the story.

THE INDEPENDENT MEDIA

The Bay area is famous for its long history of experimentation and innovation in new communications technologies, and independent media oriented to social justice. Although the corporate media dominate the commercial market, the alternative media sector is relatively vibrant. The Press Sign-in List reflected this strength with print, radio, television and cyber-media groups, using a combination of old and cutting-edge technologies, and distribution circuits from the very local to the global.[42] During the corporate media blockade about the ownership rules, the alternative media had stepped up as the primary source of record. Their circulation of counterinformation, and their active modeling of an alternative media system, motivated many participants to attend the hearing, and cheers rang out every time their call letters or names were mentioned.

The most important national precedent for the battle against the new FCC rules had been the attempt to relegalize and extend micro-powered radio licenses. In the 1990s, Bay area micro-radio activists and their legal team from the National Lawyers Guild had successfully challenged the FCC's criminalization of low-power FM (LPFM) producers. Winning over Clinton-appointed FCC chair William Kennard, the LPFM campaign moved to the national arena; hundreds of people filed support comments at the FCC, the largest number on record until the current ownership rule-making. Prometheus Radio, the principal plaintiff in the court hearing against the FCC media ownership rules, came of age at that time.

At the San Francisco hearing, Seattle micro-radio and IMC activist Jonathan Jay called for the regulatory field to be leveled for everyone, not just the "ultra-wealthy few." "If the FCC wants to fulfill its mandate and act in the public interest, then they will stop interfering with the public's access to the public airwaves and they will allow the myriad micro-voices the chance to use the mass media. If they want to deregulate, then deregulate micro-FM of less than 10 watts on open, unused second-adjacent frequencies that LPFM licenses do not address."

The second struggle that helped educate and mobilize people in the Bay area was the crisis at veteran listener-supported and "left-oriented" KPFA-FM, and its national network Pacifica Radio. The increased economic value of their licenses, due to the overheating of the radio industry, and the cuts in funding to public broadcasting, had aggravated longstanding crises of governance. When a self-selected national board shut down KPFA, and ejected several producers in the summer of 1999, a coalition of listeners' groups, local social-justice organizations, media activists from Media Alliance, low-powered FM advocates, and other independent journalists, used a variety of tactics to regain control of the station and the network. They fought to keep the resource and to push Pacifica's commitment to internal democracy and social justice, and in particular to youth of color and recent immigrants.

As one response to the crisis, KPFA had been much more circumspect about its role, amidst the changes in the overall media landscape. The station again began broadcasting important local and national public meetings, including the first FCC hearing in New York. At the San Francisco hearing, KPFA collaborated with Poor People's Radio, KPOO-FM, an African-American community station, to reach thousands of listeners throughout the Bay area and into the Central Valley.

If the campaigns to legalize low-power FM and to save Pacifica were partly about protecting the narrow band of noncommercial radio frequencies won by the alternative media sector, some alternative media producers and artists still had to fight to stay on the radio at all. Only two months before, Sarah

Jones, a New York performance artist and musician, won a battle with the FCC over its decision to fine the community radio station that played her song "Your Revolution," which parodies the sexism in mainstream hip-hop.[43] Jones voiced the dual perspective of many alternative media producers, as both audience member and artist: "I also want to speak as an audience member to the detriment that consolidation of media represents for all of us. I can't tell you how frustrating it is to travel this country and hear the same things on the radio, to know that there are only certain artists that are going to be heard, because if Clear Channel disagrees with you, you can say good-bye to your right to freedom of expression as an artist."

MEDIA INDUSTRY WORKERS

The greatest impact of consolidation for cultural workers within the corporate media has been the restructuring of workplaces and jobs. Tens of thousands have lost jobs, including many with union protection. Remaining employees are expected to produce substantially more, as corporate management has eliminated whole departments, or combined them with others in the same conglomerate, or allied companies. At the hearing, several industry staff, and union representatives, discussed how these drastic changes had affected the localism and diversity of news production.

The Communication Workers of America (CWA) and AFTRA got involved in the national campaign early. The CWA sponsored two public meetings about the issue, as well as the first public hearing in New York City in January 2003. In San Francisco, the CWA had only recently settled a dispute over the Hearst's purchase of the *Chronicle*, which effectively ended the two-paper operating agreement. Michael Cabanatuan, president of the Northern California Media Workers Guild, Communications Workers of America, and a *Chronicle* worker, described the impact on news coverage.

> The increase in chain ownership of newspapers, the near disappearance of independent or family-owned or locally-owned newspapers, and the practice of clustering by newspaper chains has already brought a noticeable decrease in the diversity, variety and volume of news coverage. More consolidation will only make things worse.
>
> Already the consolidation of newspaper ownership has diminished the type of news coverage. Most newspapers, almost all but the major metropolitan newspapers, no longer do any investigative reporting of any substance. And very few newspapers still assign a reporter to cover what I consider a very important beat: labor. It wasn't that way 20 years ago.
>
> Attention to government affairs has also slipped at many newspapers, and certainly at broadcast outlets, which have trimmed political reporting staffs, particularly state capital bureaus. California is an excellent example. While many

California newspapers, including mine, maintain healthy bureaus in Sacramento, some do not. But that's still good news compared to the broadcast industry. It's my understanding that currently no California television stations have state capital news bureaus, and very few if any radio stations staff the state capital on a regular basis. That doesn't bode very well for the fate of newspaper bureaus if they become owned and controlled by the people who now call the shots at broadcast outlets. . . . What will also happen is that the variety of perspectives will diminish. . . . Local news coverage will probably shrink to satisfy a larger regional market, instead of having a local broad-based focus.

Roxanna Bombalier, broadcast business representative for the San Francisco Local of the American Federation of Television and Radio Artists (AFTRA), spoke about the situation in the television industry.

Fewer and fewer companies own more and more stations. The remaining independent stations are left to struggle for smaller advertising buy. In broadcast and news, due to the astronomical prices now paid for media properties, newsrooms and broadcast stations have been increasingly subjected to cost-cutting on a scale not previously seen. Consolidation means reduced staff, increased workload and hours, less labor-intensive investigative reporting, a reluctance to engage in controversial stories, and a preference of infotainment over hard news. Newspersons have complained of job losses, fewer opportunities, and increased pressures on their professional integrity.

Just as in the radio industry, the restructuring of television had affected Spanish-speaking media workers more harshly. Bombardier discussed her union's campaign against the discriminatory treatment of Spanish-speaking reporters when NBC bought Telemundo.

There are two issues that AFTRA has been campaigning at on a national level. The first issue is the disparate treatment of anchors and reporters of Spanish-speaking employees versus NBC and English-speaking employees. The second issue is the abuses of rights of Telemundo employees to organize while the NBC employees are already enjoying the benefits of a collective bargaining agreement, working in the same shop. . . . The issue is that Spanish-speaking employees at Telemundo do not receive the basic, standard compensation benefits, and workplace rights, as their English-speaking counterparts at NBC. GE has created second-class citizens out of their new Hispanic employees. This is an unacceptable double-standard that must be changed.

The mobilization of media workers was not restricted to the trade union movement. Brad Johnson is a radio engineer who worked for more than a decade for two different companies in Modesto, California, until they were both bought by Clear Channel.

I kept very busy for a few years after the Telecommunications Act of '96, breaking down long-time local stations and moving them into the corporate building.

Maybe everyone else was busy too—too busy to ask why we built five stations in one building without a newsroom.

Johnson had sought redress from Clear Channel using existing labor laws to redress violations regarding overtime, employment equity, safety violations, and recurring sexual harassment. More effectively, he had also reached out to the alternative media network and circulated his story on the Web.

URBAN RADIO: THE ELECTRONIC BACK FENCE

The veterans of African-American and Hispanic-operated radio stations were another important set of social actors at the hearing. These stations and small networks had grown during the 1970s and 1980s, partly in response to the political opportunities created by the civil rights campaign of the United Church of Christ in Jackson, Mississippi. The follow-up advocacy pushed the FCC to open up licenses for black, Hispanic and Native-American owners and women.[44] A parallel program of Employment Equity provisions opened the corporate doors for women and staff of color. Many of these new stations had built strong loyal followings, enriching the social imaginary with local music, talk and information programming, and countering the trend of the big chains toward targeting consumers with nationally syndicated talk and musical play lists.[45]

The impact of consolidation and deregulation was felt immediately. With the cuts in tax concessions and employment programs, the continuing high finance costs, and the squeeze in the advertising market, many of these stations were forced to sell out.[46] The larger conglomerates such as Clear Channel were able to reap the benefits of their rich cultural capital, and especially the tremendously popular hip-hop and Latino music styles developed at the urban stations.

Nationally, several African-American station owners fought back through lawsuits and political lobbying, led by the National Association of Black-owned Broadcasters Incorporated, (NABOB) in cooperation with the NAACP. At the San Francisco hearing, three production staff talked about their roots in the smaller community or "urban" black radio stations. Denise Maunder started at KPOO, then worked for a number of African-American-owned stations, and watched them all being sold.

I'm essentially a victim of the consolidation crunch. . . . What we're talking about is selling radio stations and losing your collective cultural memory, each and every time; losing all of your resources. It's a ripple effect. What happens is you sell stations and the communities lose their outlets for information. Grassroots information: how to get free health care, how to get some child care going, who is doing what in the community. It's the equivalent of the electronic back fence. . . .

This is incredibly crucial to our community. And then you find out that these stations are going to be sold, what's going to happen? [B]igger and bigger and bigger companies that have absolutely no connection, they just don't care.

Lesley Stoval, an announcer at the urban independent KBLX, said: "Under consolidation, everything is Velveeta . . . that is not my truth, my reality."

Marcel Ballvé is staff editor of the Pacific News Service. He commented on the changes in local Spanish-language stations.

In the Mission [District of San Francisco], one [radio] station provided three hours of local news per day. Within the last five years, it's part of a network, and now it plays three two-minute segments of news per hour at most . . . [A] two-hour public-affairs show that appeared every day and was hosted by a well-known Latino journalist was terminated and replaced by a variety-show centered around infomercials. Local Hispanic radio stations have relegated public-affairs shows to 7 A.M. slots on weekends.

MEDIA ACCOUNTABILITY

The loss of the 'electronic back fence' not only affected radio owners and staff but the communities of listeners whose social imaginary the programmers had helped shape. In 1999, Clear Channel bought two popular urban hip-hop stations in San Francisco. Known as the "people's station," KMEL had a strong following among African Americans and other youth of color. When Clear Channel fired two popular DJs, and cut their shows dealing with youth issues and local music, a coalition formed to fight the changes to what they considered their cultural resource: the Community Coalition for Media Accountability, whose member groups included Let's Get Free, Mindzeye, Media Alliance, and the Youth Media Council. Drawing on the earlier civil rights campaign, the coalition used a variety of tactics, such as media monitoring, a press campaign, and community mobilizing, as instruments in their successful campaign. They wrested some concessions from Clear Channel, including the reintroduction of a local music program and a community forum, as part of a commitment to make the station more accountable to its target audience of young listeners of color.[47]

Aimee Suzara spoke on the panel on "News and Civil Discourse" on behalf of Coalition member group, the Youth Media Council. A politically and media-savvy counterpublic, the YMC is a project of We Interrupt This Message, which is a national media training and strategy center. The council pushes the public debate about issues and perspectives of youth of color by conducting its own action research; and circulating it to their own constituencies and allies, through their own media and community meetings, as well as to the holders of media power.

At the hearing, Suzara reported on another initiative with KTVU–TV, owned by Cox and affiliated with Fox. "Speaking for Ourselves" used a content analysis and found a disproportionate focus on youth crime, almost no coverage of other youth issues, or of the larger context, and little representation from youth themselves, and especially youth leaders.[48] For example, "stories about pets and animals appeared more than four times as often as stories about youth poverty." The council approached the station to discuss ways to improve coverage of youth issues, and followed up with a meeting between station staff and youth.

Patti Miller, from Children Now, addressed the ways that younger "children's needs are not currently being served by commercial broadcasters," and are being adversely effected by media consolidation. Although there are no FCC checks for broadcasters on their programming content directed to, or about, youth, the FCC stipulates that each TV station should air a minimum of three hours per week of educational and informational programming for children.[49] These rules were also won during the upsurge of civil rights–inspired citizen interventions at the FCC.[50] Miller spoke about the cuts in original programming, local programming and innovation, and the increasing commercialism. In the fall of 2004, the FCC unanimously decided to extend the public-interest requirement for children's content rules to the new digital stations.[51]

THE NEWEST WAVE

Perhaps the largest single social justice contingent was from the peace movement, whose support in the hearing room crossed all the new and older movements. Hundreds of thousands had participated in the series of marches in San Francisco in the buildup to the war against Iraq, and the paucity of coverage of the peace perspective had enraged them. Helen Callbeck represented the Marin Media Democracy Task Force.

> This hearing reminds us that democracy can work. Walter Cronkite once said that perhaps we couldn't hold all the German citizens responsible for the Holocaust; but we could fault them for losing control of their information. Media concentration limits our access to a wide variety of sources of information and opinions. . . . Wasn't it Dan Rather, an NBC anchor, who referred to the President as his Commander in Chief? Are we to react as soldiers and think of George W as our commander? CNBC recommended to Phil Donahue that his guests should not be skeptical of the Bush administration, whereas other networks are taking every opportunity to wave the flag. Surely, skepticism is essential to our democracy.

Erin Poh is the labor representative for the Northern California Media Workers Guild.

Many of us here in this room are activists. I see people here who struggle for workers, who are calling for books not bombs, schools not jails, housing for the homeless, health care for all. I see many of you who are working to protect the environment, for the rights of women and minorities. I see many of you who have participated in non-violent direct action to avert a war that we believe is unjust.

And what are we doing here on a beautiful Saturday in late April? We're struggling for those very causes, because the cause of media diversity, even though it may not be the first and foremost cause, needs to be the second because we know the rule changes proposed by the FCC will impact us directly. We know that if the FCC drops the ban on cross-ownership, it'll be harder for us to find differing viewpoints that'll give us vital insight into those issues about which we are passionate. And it'll be harder for us to get our message out in a merged monopolistic or duopolistic media landscape.

THE "THREAT OF A GOOD EXAMPLE"[52]

The San Francisco public hearing was a remarkable moment in the history of U.S. media advocacy and activism. Nationally, the hearing played a role in the changes in policy, procedure, and framing in the state arenas of the FCC and Congress, with some ripples within media corporations such as Clear Channel Communications.[53] As importantly, the hearing and national campaign brought the debate back into the public sphere, and the "public" back into the debate, challenging both the state and corporate frames, and introducing alternative models of content, ownership, and governing structures.

The organizational strategy of bypassing the FCC and organizing autonomously combined familiar modes and purposes with more inclusive, challenging ones.[54] Recycling the well-known "town hall" format allowed for easy adaptation by groups in very different contexts across the country. In San Francisco, the symbolism of a distant and Republican-controlled commission was offset by setting the forum in a more "progressive" jurisdiction, opened by the president of the Board of Supervisors, a member of the Green Party. The formal panel structure was stretched to authorize a wider representation of people and systems of expertise, combining academics, policy consultants, and station managers with community-based advocacy organizations, hip-hop DJs, journalists, independent media-makers, trade unionists, and social movement activists.

Organizing the hearings "as if" a diversity of citizen expertise and perspectives was being officially witnessed by the FCC dramatized the contradictions of the process, reoriented "people's thinking and created the opportunity of altering patterns of participation."[55] No one spoke up for more media consolidation or deregulation. Instead, several speakers underscored a strong antimonopoly media sentiment, if not anticorporate sentiment. Iain Boal, a Berkeley professor and media critic, spoke to wide applause:

The flourishing of life . . . now depends on the re-appropriation of the commons, and that includes . . . the seizing back of the electromagnetic spectrum. As Ben Bagdikian says, an oligopoly of 20 or 4 or 2 barely makes a difference. The whole thing stinks, it is rotten. It's like trying to regulate the slaves' quarters. Let us take it out for burial. . . .

One name for our struggle is the anti-globalization movement. Another is the anti-war movement. In our sights are not only the regulations of the FCC, but the whole system. In the words of a poet at an earlier moment of reaction, at the high-tide of parliamentary privatization in England, in the wake of another devastating war, and after a police riot on a defenseless citizenry, Shelley said: "We are many, they are few."

The groups assembled at the hearing, or in the broader Angels' networks, do not yet constitute a unified movement. The differences of social power, cultural capital and resources, and of strategy are far from being resolved.[56] However, as Clemencia Rodriguez has remarked, about the parallel movement for the democratization of global communications, the hearing provided a "glimpse" of what is possible.[57] What we saw that day were a diversity of counterpublics, with a long history of working for a more just communications system. What we heard were the outlines of a three-part strategy: to extend communications access and rights within the existing corporate and state systems; create new media projects and institutions autonomous of the dominant systems; and engage existing counterpublics in widening the franchise and discourse of the public sphere.[58]

Thanks to Jeff Perlstein, Martha Wallner, Sydney Levy, Karen Stephenson, Francisco McGee, Bernadette Barker-Plummer, Seeta Peña Gangadharan, Ben Clarke, and Danielle Fairbairn for making the hearing possible, and for their contribution to the documentation.

NOTES

1. The six rules and the dates they were originally adopted: 1. Newspaper/Broadcast Cross-Ownership Prohibition (1975) 2. Local Radio Ownership (1941): Caps are set at 8 stations in a large market and five stations in a smaller market. 3. National TV Ownership (1941): Limits the number of local broadcast stations that any one broadcaster can own to 35 percent of the TV households in the United States. 4. Local TV Multiple Ownership, or "Duopoly rule" (1964): Allows for the combination of two television stations in the same market, provided: at least one of the stations is not among the four highest-ranked stations in the market. 5. Radio/TV Cross-Ownership Restriction (1970): Prevents one entity from owning both a radio station and a television station in the same market. 6. Dual Television Network Rule (1946): Prevents one broadcast network from owning another broadcast network.

2. The current commission is made up of two Democratic Party appointees and three Republican appointees,

3. Charles Layton, "News Blackout," *American Journalism Review* (December/January Issue, 2004).

4. On July 23, 2003, the House of Representatives voted 400 to 21 to roll back the television network ownership cap to 35 percent. On September 16, the Senate passed 55 to 40 a bill repealing all the new regulations. Gail Beckerman. "Tripping up Big Media,"*Columbia Journalism Review* (13 November 2003): 3.

5. Media Access Project. "Statement of Media Access Project Reacting to US Court of Appeals Media Ownership Decision," *Media Access Project* <http://www.mediaaccess.org/prometheus_decision/#summary> (14 July, 2004).

6. Drawn from the title of the edited collection: Bruce Robbins, ed. *The Phantom Public Sphere* (Minneapolis: University of Minnesota Press, 1993).

7. Charles Layton and Melissa Cirillo, "Tracking the Coverage," *American Journalism Review*. December/January, 2004. <http:www.ajr.org/article_printable.asp?id=3499.>

8. William Safire, "Regulate the FCC," *New York Times*, 16 June 2003. James Surowiecki, "All in the Family," *The New Yorker*, 16 June, 2003. Stephen Labaton, "Deregulating the Media: The Overview; Regulators Ease Rules Governing Media Ownership," *New York Times*, 3 June, 2003. Eric Boehlert. "Congress to Big Media: Not so Fast," *Salon*, 23 July, 2003. Gail Beckerman, "Tripping Up Big Media," *Columbia Journalism Review*, 13 November, 2003. John Nichols, & Robert W. McChesney, "FCC: Public Be Damned," *The Nation,* 2 June, 2003. Susan Douglas. "Seize the Moment," *In These Times*, 17 November, 2003. Norman Solomon, "Cracking the Media Walls," *In These Times*, 17 November, 2003.

9. Robert McChesney, *The Problem of the Media: U.S. Communication Politics in the 21st Century* (New York: Monthly Review Press, 2004). Mark Cooper, *Media Ownership and Democracy in the Digital Information Age* (Stanford: Center for Internet & Society, Stanford Law School, 2003). Milton Mueller, Brendan Kuerbis, and Christiane Pagé, "Reinventing Media Activism: Public Interest Advocacy in the Making of US Communication-Information Policy, 1960–2002," The Convergence Center, School of Information Studies, Syracuse University <http://www.dcc.syr.edu/ford/rma/reinventing.pdf.>(16 July, 2004).Michele Hilmes, ed., *Connections: A Broadcast History Reader* (Belmont, Calif.: Thomson Wadsworth, 2003). Kathryn C. Montgomery, *Target: Prime Time Advocacy Groups and the Struggle over Entertainment Television* (New York: Oxford University Press, 1989). Robert Horwitz,"Broadcast Reform Revisited: Reverend Everett C. Parker and the "Standing" Case (*Office of Communication of the United Church of Christ v. Federal Communications Commission*). <http://communication.ucsd.edu/people/f_horwitz_brr.html> (1997), Future of Music. "Citizens Urge FCC to Retain Current Media Ownership Rules. FCC Public Record Shows Overwhelming Opposition to Relaxing Ownership Caps." May 14, 2003.

10. Dee Dee Halleck, *Hand-Held Visions: The Impossible Possibilities of Community Media* (New York: Fordham University Press, 2002). Mark Lloyd, "Communications Policy is a Civil Rights Issue," Civil Rights Forum on Communications Policy <http://www.civilrightsforum.org/foundations.html.> (August 4, 1997). Aliza Dichter, "US Media Activism and the Search for Constituency," *Media Development* (2004): 8–13. Makani Themba-Nixon and Nan Rubin, "Speaking for Ourselves," *The Nation* 277, no. 16 (17 November 2003). Martha Wallner, "What the F.C.C. Is Going on?" *Media Alliance* (Fall 2003).

11. In the United States, "independent" media denotes noncorporate media, but not necessarily non-commercial media.

12. Thanks to James Compton for this insight. Bruce Robbins, "Introduction: The Public as Phantom," in *The Phantom Public Sphere,* ed. Bruce Robbins (Minneapolis: University of Minnesota Press, 1993), xii–xiii.

13. Nick Dyer-Witheford, *Cyber-Marx: Cycles and Circuits of Struggle in High-technology Capitalism* (Urbana and Chicago: University of Illinois Press, 1999). Scott Uzelman, "Catalyzing Participatory Communication: Independent Media Centre and the Politics of Direct Action." Unpublished M.A. Thesis, Simon Fraser University, 2002. Dorothy Kidd, "Talking the Walk: The Communications Commons amidst the Media Enclosures." Unpublished Ph.D. Dissertation. Simon Fraser University, 1998.

14. Dee Dee Halleck, *Hand-Held Visions: The Impossible Possibilities of Community Media* (New York: Fordham University Press, 2002). John Downing, *Radical Media: The Political Experience of Alternative Communication* (Boston, Mass.: South End Press, 1984). Clemencia Rodriguez, *Fissures in the Mediascape: An International Study of Citizens' Media*. 2001. William Barlow, *Voice Over: The Making of Black Radio* (Philadephia: Temple University Press, 1999). Clemencia Rodriguez, "The Renaissance of Citizens' Media," *Media Development* (April 29, 2004).

15. "Introduction," *Zerowork: Political Materials* (Brooklyn: Zero Work, 1975).

16. For a different origin story, see Beckerman, "Tripping Up Big Media."

17. Center for International Media Action (2003), The Media Policy Action Directory: Organizations Urging FCC Limits on Media Ownership. Brooklyn, NY: CIMA (3).

18. While I was not present in Washington, I endorsed the action.

19. Robert A. Hackett, "Taking Back the Media: Notes on the Potential for a Communicative Democracy Movement." *Studies in Political Economy*, 63 (Autumn 2000).

20. "The Angels of Public Interest will Descend upon the FCC." *Media Tank*. <www .mediatank.org/faceoff.html> (Last retrieved December 1, 2004.)

21. From the characterization of policy by Milton Mueller, Brendan Kuerbis, and Christiane Pagé, "Reinventing Media Activism."

22. "The Angels of Public Interest."

23. Dee Dee Halleck, *Hand-Held Visions: The Impossible Possibilities of Community Media* (New York: Fordham University Press, 2002).

24. Milton Mueller, Brendan Kuerbis, and Christiane Pagé. "The Rise of Activism," 35–44.

25. Robert Horwitz, "Broadcast Reform Revisited," Milton Mueller, Brendan Kuerbis and Christiane Pagé, "Reinventing Media Activism." Michele Hilmes, *Connections*. Susan Douglas, *Listening in*, 96.

26. The commission raised the maximum number of stations any one company could own and removed some restrictions on cross-industry ownership. They excised several programming content rules, the most important of which was the Fairness Doctrine, leaving only the indecency rules. They also eliminated many of the "behavior" rules, which required stations to demonstrate their commitment to the public interest, and to account for programming for local concerns and interests. Robert Horwitz, "On Media Concentration and the Diversity Question, p. 8.

27. James Curran, "Global Media Concentration: Shifting the Argument," Open Democracy, May 22, 2002, 3. <http://www.openDemocracy.net.>

28. Uzelman, *Catalyzing Participatory Communication*, 75.

29. David Hesmondhalgh, *The Cultural Industries* (London: Sage Publications, 2002), 22. Jeremy Rifkin, *The Age of Access: The New Culture of Hypercapitalism Where All of Life Is a Paid-For Experience* (New York: J.P. Tarcher/Putnam, 2000), 16–29.

30. Robert McChesney, *Telecommunications, Mass Media and Democracy: The Battle for the Control of U.S. Broadcasting, 1928–1935* (Oxford: Oxford University Press. 1993). Robert Horwitz. "Broadcast Reform Revisited."

31. Center for International Media Action, "The Media Policy Action Directory: Organizations Urging FCC Limits on Media Ownership." (Brooklyn, N.Y.: CIMA 2003), 3.

32. Seeta Gangadharan, "Interview with Hearings Organizers," Unpublished (2003).

33. Art McGee, Thenmozhi Soundararajan, Makani Themba-Nixon, Malkia Cyril, and Jeff Perlstein, "A Declaration of Media Independence," <http://www.mediajustice.org> (2003).

34. The list included activists from FAIR and IMC New York, Media Tank and Prometheus Radio from Philadephia, People for Better TV, Chicago Media Watch, micro-radio and IMC activists from Seattle, Third World Majority and Media Alliance from the Bay area, and key members of what would become the Media Justice Network (Gangadharan, 2003).

35. Center for International Media Action, "The Media Policy Action Directory, 3.

36. Seeta Gangadharan, "Interview with Hearings Organizers."

37. Stanley Aronowitz, "Is a Democracy Possible?" *The Phantom Public Sphere*, ed. Bruce Robbins (Minneapolis: University of Minnesota Press, 1993), 81.

38. When the Deyong Family sold the *Chronicle* to the Hearsts, they also sold KRON. In a sign of the increasing bargaining power of the networks over affiliates, NBC demanded payment for programming for the first time from the new KRON management. When they refused, NBC shifted their affiliate agreement.

39. Cooper, Mark, *Media Ownership and Democracy in the Digital Information Age* (Stanford: Center for Internet & Society, Stanford Law School, 2003), 31.

40. Layton, Charles, "Tracking the Coverage." And "News Blackout." *American Journalism Review*, December/January Issue (2003).

41. Camille Taiara, "Invasion of the Media Snatchers," *Bay Guardian*, 14 July, 2004, 26.

42. This list included KPFA, KPOO, KALX, the Bay Guardian, the BayView News, San Francisco Liberation Radio, World Link satellite TV, and several independent journalists, including two on contract with the German Deutsche Welle.

43. The FCC fined long-time community broadcaster KBOO-FM, in Portland, Oregon, $7,000 for "indecency." KBOO had fought the ruling, countering that its mission was to provide a forum for "unpopular, controversial neglected perspectives." On February 20, 2003, the Federal Communications Commission reversed its decision and rescinded the fine. Air Bubble, "Your Revolution will not be televised," <http://www.airbubble.com/your_revolution.html> (18 July 2004).

44. Mark Lloyd, "Communications Policy is a Civil Rights Issue," Civil Rights Forum on Communications Policy, <http://www.civilrightsforum.org/foundations.html.> (August 4, 1997). Robert Horwitz, "Broadcast Reform Revisited: Reverend Everett C. Parker and the "Standing" Case (*Office of Communication of the United Church of Christ v. Federal Communications Commission*). <http://communication.ucsd.edu/people/f_horwitz_brr.html> William Barlow, 25. (1997). Milton Mueller, Brendan Kuerbis and Christiane Pagé. "Reinventing Media Activism: Public Interest Advocacy in the Making of US Communication-Information Policy, 1960–2002," The Convergence Center, School of Information Studies, Syracuse University http://www. http://dcc.syr.edu/ford/rma/reinventing.pdf.> (16 July, 2004). Aliza Dichter. "Where Are the People in the "Public Interest"? US Media Activism and the Search for Constituency," *Media Development,* 2004.

45. William Barlow, *Voice*, 296. Gilbert Garcia, "Real-Deal Minority Broadcasters Face the Threat of Big Media," *San Antonio Current.* 22 January 2004.

46. The cost of purchasing a radio station can run to $80 million in a top-10 market, and between $1 million and $5 million in mid-sized markets. The price for television stations are from $650 million to $820 million in California. Carrie Solages. "If the FCC Rule Changes Survive, Minority Broadcasting May Not." *The Crisis* 10, no. 5 (Sept./Oct. 2003): 20.

47. Aliza Dichter, "US Media Reform" Presented to the Framing Communications Rights Meeting. Communications Rights in the Information Society. Geneva, Switzerland, 8 December 2003.

48. Youth Media Council, "Speaking for Ourselves: A Youth Assessment of Local TV Coverage." <http://www.youthmediacouncil.org/pdfs/speaking.pdf.>

49. Federal Communications Commission, "Children's Educational Television," http://gullfoss2.fcc.gov/prod/kidvid/prod/kidvid.htm. Last viewed December 6, 2004.

50. Several children's advocacy organizations formed in the late 1960s and 1970s, Mueller et al, 54.

51. Children Now, " Children Now Praises FCC for New Educational Television Rules." <http://www.childrennow.org/newsroom/news-04/pr-09-09-04.cfm>

52. Noam Chomsky uses the phrase to describe the threat to U.S. interests posed by countries seeking to develop independently of capitalist relations. Cited in Uzelman, 14.

53. See Kidd, McGee and Fairbairn in this same volume for the kinds of changes that Clear Channel enacted.

54. Mueller et al. "Reinventing Media Activism," 2004, chaps. 2, 7.

55. Mueller et al., "Reinventing Media Activism," 2004, chaps. 2, 7.

56. Aliza Dichter, "Where Are the People in the "Public Interest"? US Media Activism and the Search for Constituency, *Media Development*, 2004 and Makani Themba-Nixon and Nan Rubin, "Speaking for Ourselves," *The Nation* 277, no. 16 (November 17, 2003). The Listening Project, *The Makings of a Social Movement? Strategic Issues and Themes in Communications Policy Work*, April 2004

57. Clemencia Rodriguez, "The renaissance of citizen's media," *Media Development*, 29 April, 2004, <http://www.wacc.org.uk/modules.php?name=New&file+print%sid=1551>

58. Thanks to Ben Clarke, of Media Alliance and to MJ Kim, of MediAct in Korea, for suggesting similar formulations.

11

Journalism Education in the Posthistorical University

Jeanette McVicker

The University will have to become one place, among others, where the attempt is made to think the social bond without recourse to a unifying idea, whether of culture or of the state.

—Bill Readings, *The University in Ruins* (1996)

Taking Gramsci seriously would involve recasting critical studies so that they would engage constantly in dialectical self-revision and develop strategies to study the ways in which the interrelated and cultural strata of a society produce hegemonic and counterhegemonic representations in texts and other discursive systems.

—Paul A. Bove, *In the Wake of Theory* (1992)

Examining undergraduate journalism education in the United States in the period framed by two defining American historical and media events, Watergate and 9/11, reveals a tension between two competing pedagogical models that symptomatically reflects deep structural changes taking place in the function and role of the university as well as the news media in relation to the nation-state.

The first pedagogical model, typically located in English departments or writing programs, affirms the traditional values of liberal humanism in assuming the "idea" of the university generally as an institutional space imparting culture and knowledge to students who will take their place in society as democratic citizens. This model emphasizes a foundational liberal arts curriculum, adding a specialized focus on acquisition of basic news reporting and writing skills. The link between the formation of students in general to become well-rounded individual subjects of the nation-state, and training journalism students in particular to become, especially after Watergate, reluctant but necessary heroes defending an idea of "America" increasingly under erosion, is readily apparent. Students learn the craft of journalism in order to narrate "objectively" the stories of political, cultural, and social events and relations that reveal the unfolding of the democratic contract (and to point out the obstacles to this evolutionary progression of democratic freedom); students recognize their education as providing them with a traditional core of humanistic knowledge and a set of discursive skills that can take them "anywhere" to cover "anything." Students leave the university with a heightened sense of their ability to participate in the rituals of public life based on a set of presumably shared cultural and political values.

The second model, usually based in departments of communication, has its foundation in a more technologically oriented pedagogy that understands the role of journalism education as training students to master production techniques for delivery of variable content to multiple audiences, together with a foundation in rhetoric, courses in public relations, media law, analysis of mass media in society, etc. This model emphasizes its ability to give students the specific training necessary to find careers in the expanding broadcast journalism and public-affairs sectors. Because it has been able to measure the acquisition of skills more effectively, this model has adapted itself more easily, perhaps, to the economic and other changes taking place within the university than its more traditional humanities-based counterpart. In this model, students increasingly understand their education in terms of value; the goal is to gain the skills necessary to find technical and creative jobs related to media production and consumption (public relations, information technologies, broadcast news and entertainment production, and so forth) in order to enter the world of corporate media as well-trained professionals. Students leave the university with a heightened sense of their economic power to engage in the public sphere as both producers and consumers of culture.

Neither model completely excludes aspects of the other, of course; the lines I'm drawing between them are not intended to serve as rigid boundaries but rather as broad emphases in pedagogical focus leading to increasingly specific, while interrelated, ends. Neither model tends to construct itself along multi- and transdisciplinary lines;[1] neither tends to consider discourse analysis or critical/cultural theory as a cornerstone for the program.[2] Perhaps it is not surprising, then, that neither model has tended to foreground, as part of its pedagogical practice, its relation to the horizontal changes taking place within the university itself in relation to mainstream media and American (and global) society, and thus neither typically asks students to contemplate the implications of their education in a self-reflexive way that might question the political and economic foundations of these models or the ends which they serve.

"Outside" the university, this horizontal shift includes consolidation of (transnational) corporate ownership of the major news media, the explosion of information technologies that has redefined all aspects of knowledge production and consumption generally and redefined journalism specifically, the reach of global capital, the changing nature of citizenship, and so forth. At the same time, that horizonal shift "outside" the university parallels the shift taking place "inside" the university; the traditional "idea" of the university and its relation to the nation have been undergoing a controversial transformation and redefinition that includes the status of what constitutes "useful" knowledge, how it should be transmitted, and what its uses should be.

All of these changing relations carry profound ethical, social, political, economic, and cultural implications. For journalism educators and professional journalists, the debates sparked by Columbia University president Lee Bollinger's 2002 interventions regarding the future leadership and curriculum of its prestigious Graduate School of Journalism visibly constellated a number of these tensions, though they have been articulated in varying degrees of specificity by cultural theorists and media critics, particularly in the wake of 9/11. This chapter, broadly utilizing a cultural studies approach, explores some of these tensions surrounding journalism education in the United States in light of the changing relation of the university citizenship, as well as to the increasingly corporatized media and concepts of professionalism. Invoking the Columbia controversy symptomatically, it then offers some thoughts for what journalism education in a "posthistorical university," a term I borrow from the late Bill Readings's book *The University in Ruins* (1996), might strive toward.

The two models of undergraduate journalism education sketched above converge in an important way for my analysis; both assume as a point of pedagogical departure that journalists and media producers participate in the creation and maintenance of an "imagined community," the term coined by Benedict Anderson (1991), that understands the nation as "an imagined political community—and imagined as both inherently limited and inherently sovereign . . . [R]egardless of the actual inequality and exploitation that may prevail in each, the nation is always conceived as a deep, horizontal comradeship."[3] This fiction or fantasy of the nation as an imagined community fuels both pedagogical models, however differently, providing a crucial lens for understanding the shared assumptions between them as well as their divergences, and their relation to the institutions to which they are most closely linked: the university and the media. By reminding us of the tenacity of this cultural imaginary within and outside the university, and how journalism education and professional practice contribute to its hegemonic force, particularly visible following 9/11, such a concept can also assist us as we reconceptualize the stakes of journalism education, and media practice, in the United States in the post-9/11 era.

THE IDEA OF THE UNIVERSITY AND JOURNALISM EDUCATION

The idea of the public university in the United States began undergoing a profound transformation in the late 1970s and '80s in response to a number of factors too numerous and complex for me to do justice to here. We know the results of that transformation now, however: the large state university systems have experienced severe cutbacks by the state and increasingly have adopted corporate values and bureaucratic structures in order to compete in the market economy. Simultaneous with this transformation, academics primarily located in the humanities and social sciences began to critique, with the help of poststructuralist theories, the function of the university, the disciplining of knowledge, the formation of individuals as autonomous subjects, the idea of a unifying culture, and the shifting dynamic of capitalism and its erosion of the nation-state which the modern university was created to serve. One of the most provocative of these discussions came from the late Bill Readings, whose controversial book, *The University in Ruins* (1996), provided a disturbing vision of what he called "the university of excellence." I follow Readings in using the term "posthistorical university" as a way to signal a potential for rethinking how the university might provide a critical site for what he called "dissensual" thinking among "particularities" rather than an elite space for the production of subjects for the nation-state. While Readings's pre-9/11 announcement that the university had already become a transnational corporation and that the nation-state had already more or less ceased to exist may have been premature in 1994, his work continues to provide a compelling horizon for rethinking the university as a public space in the development of critical studies and citizenship, and how, in this specific context, journalism education, even within an increasingly corporatized university, might meaningfully intervene in the production and consumption of the discourses of transnational corporate media.

Readings argues that concomitant to the decline of the nation state within the context of a globalized world economy, national "'culture'—as the symbolic and political counterpart to the project of integration pursued by the nation-state—has lost its "purchase." The implications of this change are enormous for the university, he suggests, because the academy "has historically been the primary institution of national culture in the modern nation-state." Readings traces what he calls "the emergence of a discourse of 'excellence' in place of prior appeals to the idea of culture as the language in which the University seeks to explain itself to itself and to the world at large."[4]

For Readings, the corporatization of the university and the loss of its social mission must be seen in relation to the delegitimization of the nation-state. He reads the "culture wars"—this includes the tensions generated by the rise of multiethnic/multigender and cultural studies movements, for example, that still simmer in various pockets of academia—as a marker of "the incommensurability between reason and history as modes of legitimation for the modern state, once the notion of cultural identity can no longer serve to bridge the abyss."[5] Within such an erosion of the social mission of the university, he imagines three potential responses: the "conservative" position seeks to "defend and restore the social mission of the University by simply reaffirming a national cultural identity that has manifestly lost its purchase;" the "multicultural" position seeks a reinvention of cultural identity that is more broadly inclusive of "difference;" whereas the "third option is to abandon the notion that the social mission of the University is ineluctably linked to the project of realizing a national cultural identity." In practical terms, this stance also means that researchers and teachers must discard "the claim of service to the state."[6]

The implications of Readings's "difficult proposition" are, in my mind, paramount not only for a renewed understanding of the function of the university; taken seriously, they imply a radically altered way of understanding social and political interactions and reimagining concepts such as citizenship, intellectual work, community, and culture just for starters. To take up Readings's challenge furthers the project initiated by Antonio Gramsci, invoked in my second epigraph, to engage in a continual process of "dialectical self-revision." Above all, such considerations demand a radically different *thinking* and way of considering knowledge (its construction, transmission, uses, etc.) which implies a very different conception of what it means to be a critical (or specific [Foucault] or organic [Gramsci]) intellectual in relation to any reconceptualized notion of an "imagined community," a concept that would finally be exposed as a hegemonic representation. Developing critical transdisciplinary studies programs in journalism (to take only one example) might provide an experimental space for such thinking and praxis, and I will attempt to think through some possibilities for this in my conclusion. Before offering such a view, however, I want to elaborate a bit more on the way journalism programs since the Watergate era have responded to the tensions and transformations I've been outlining.

Bob Woodward and Carl Bernstein's celebrated leap into history as the reporters who broke a scandal that broke a president seemed to shore up an image of the American hero that had been fragmenting under the pressures of the Vietnam War and the aftermath of the civil rights movement in the United States. My invocation of the "heroic" here should be understood in Anderson's sense of a defense of the "imagined community." In those post-assassination, post–My Lai massacre, post–Kent State antiheroic days of the early-mid 1970s, journalists who went above and beyond the call of duty to protect "the public's right to know" seemed to offer a viable alternative for the nation's consumption. This image of the hero was smart and cynical on the surface, while at its core was a patriotic love of country and respect for the democratic process that had been subverted by the Nixon administration, had gone awry in Vietnam, and had become radicalized in the more militant versions of the civil rights movement. This heroic image especially fed the desires of liberals who saw journalism's public commitment as a way to restore belief in American values while pointing out corruption and excess in government and other areas. Leonard Downie, Jr. and Robert G. Kaiser (2002) note that as Woodward and Bernstein and the editors at the *Washington Post* "entered American mythology . . . journalism became one of the most popular majors on American campuses. Many universities created or enlarged journalism schools and departments. Newsrooms infected by Watergate fever launched into investigate journalism with fervor unmatched in the history of American newspapers."[7] In the aftermath of the press's victories in the Pentagon Papers and Watergate cases, journalism education legitimated its place within the university by participating fully in the liberal humanist story, one that linked formation of citizens through the university to the production of journalists whose democratic credentials would be above question. Ensuring the public good, always entrusted to the university as one of its primary functions, was also a hallmark of journalism now everywhere visible and celebrated.

The enduring legacy of this journalistic ideal continues to inform, however unconsciously, media critics, professional journalists, and educators. Two examples that, not accidentally, appeared just after 9/11, illustrate its tenacity.

Writing for the twenty-fifth anniversary issue of *American Journalism Review, Washington Post* columnist Marc Fisher (2002) laments the loss of that mythic time: "In the 1970s, news people could still be heroes—in our own minds and in the public imagination." Fisher's nostalgia for the journalist-as-hero comes through even more strongly as he describes the dehumanized ("postmodern") image of the journalist in the mid to late 1980s cultural imaginary: "The press, now more routinely lumped into an unkempt mass called the 'media,' took on a collective identity; instead of hero reporters, we often saw ourselves depicted as a faceless throng, a clot of shouting, hectoring goons—The Pack."[8] The metaphorical shift is striking: by the Reagan era, the journalist has lost his heroic status and the ability to see through the obfuscation of the logic impeding America's "progress;" as the neoliberal impulse has accelerated the corporate character of the media, the individual journalist has morphed into "the media," whose importance derives from the ability to (re)produce the images that represent a triumphalist America about to bring the Cold War to its predestined end. There's a concurrent shift taking place in the relation of the university to the needs and demands of the "imagined community" that is the nation-state, which is also undergoing a profound transformation in terms of its political and economic mission; the redefinition of "the press" into "the media pack" is yet another reflection of the changing horizon of capital and its embodiment in an increasingly corporatized, global media establishment. The shift in the cultural imaginary noted by Fisher signals an important change in student curricular expectations as well, particularly the concept of career training and the economic—as opposed to political and cultural—value of a journalism degree in the public consciousness.

While media theorist James W. Carey also celebrates the public disclosures accomplished by the press during the Watergate–Pentagon Papers era, calling it "the apogee of independent journalism," he understands more fully the paradox that the era ushers in:

> Showered with honors, invited to the right parties, and consulted by the political and economic elites, journalists were no longer allowed to swing free of the centers of power but were incorporated into the Establishment. At that moment, the vaunted progressivism of journalism was abandoned; or better, journalists accepted the role of progressive intellectuals with a mission to participate in the management of society and simultaneously abandoned the populist wing of progressivism with its dictate to "afflict the powerful and comfort the afflicted."[9]

Carey's criticism derives less from nostalgia for a lost age of heroic individualism than a kind of righteous indignation that the press had embraced a position abandoning the democratic role of public servant, valued since the days of Joseph Pulitzer, in order to occupy a position *within* the horizons of power. In both celebrated cases of the 1970s, he claims, the press

> engaged in and sanctioned anti-democratic practices and, in the long run, the new arrogance of the press, its self-declared dispensation from the norms of democracy, did not go unnoticed. The willingness to accept stolen documents and to tamper with grand juries in cases where the fate of the republic was not clearly at stake was a declaration that a free press was not only necessary to a democracy but that the press could disregard the welfare of other democratic institutions and go it alone.[10]

What Fisher praises as "heroic action," Carey laments as loss of journalism's special status "outside" the institutions of power while still maintaining the overall value of democratic institutions (among them, the press). Once journalists begin to act, in other words, according to the logic that getting the story by any means necessary is justifiable, the sanctity of journalism's unique role in narrating—from "outside" the halls of power—the continual unfolding of the story of American freedom is profaned. This is the liberal humanist equivalent to the mythic fall of the hero. Though their critical focuses are different, both Fisher and Carey assume that journalists' primary role is to preserve a democratic social contract between the nation-state and its citizen-subjects (including themselves). While Fisher characterizes the erosion of this role as one legacy of a "postmodernism" that emasculates the heroic individual for the faceless "pack," Carey characterizes the demise of journalism's "progressivism" as a succumbing to the hegemonic functions of the "Establishment." In other words, both understand the role of the journalist to be the primary "objective" narrator, whether hero or humble servant—and one should be able to see that they are flip sides of the same humanistic subject—of the story of an imagined "America" in which the institutions of the nation-state engage with reasonably educated citizen-subjects who, if presented with information in a coherent, objective manner, will participate freely (and wisely, one assumes) in traditional democratic rituals. While Carey's more sophisticated critique chastises the press for seeing itself as somehow above and no longer accountable to the other institutions constitutive of democracy, it is seemingly blind to the idea that journalism as an institution had always been complicitous in establishing and maintaining relations of power through its formidable ability to represent "reality" to the public, a "reality" predicated on a for-profit model, no matter how much it might legitimize itself as a performer of democratic public service. Fisher seems simply to long for the "heady days" when the public adored the journalist-hero as the last defender of liberal democracy and truly cared about what the press did and how it did it.

Both views derive from and legitimate a journalism education that is predicated on liberal humanism, the first model sketched in my introduction, one furthermore invested in what critics such as William V. Spanos have termed the "hegemonic discourse of deliverance:"

> It is the school [university] . . . that employs [this 'hegemonic discourse of deliverance'] most effectively in disciplining the young and reproducing the dominant sociopolitical order. While other ideological cultural apparatuses are situated in the material world . . . the school is represented fundamentally as a separate and value-free space in which the pursuit of knowledge is undertaken for the benefit of all 'mankind,' if not for knowledge's own sake.[11]

The formation of student-subjects within a university whose primary function is to establish and maintain a sense of national culture and civic value for the nation (the traditional humanistic "idea" of the university) undergirds the more specialized training of future journalists who will then heroically uphold democracy and faithfully defend those left out of the social contract, through journalism careers that situate them first and foremost as American citizens. Both views provide a way to understand the news media's devolution into a celebrity-driven entertainment vehicle for corporate profitability in the 1980s and after, and they both also mark the shift that journalism education took in this period. In an era of corporate mergers, as news organizations consolidated or closed, journalism's hallmark for investigative piecework—especially in coverage of international news and providing complex context for domestic issues—lost ground to the selling of "infotainment" by "star anchors" and a few telegenic reporters. It's not difficult to see how the earlier image of the journalist-as-hero feeds into this phenomenon: the press's heroic individualism turns into the media horde with the single-minded focus of image and market share in one version; in the alternative version, journalists had already allowed themselves to become celebrities of "Establishment" culture and had abandoned their more traditional "outsider" status. As the narrative story of "America" became less concerned with expanding the contractual obligations of a democratic nation-state, and more embedded in the multiple discourses of consumption and globalization, journalists' perceived role within the public consciousness shifted to that of producers of dehistoricized images and easily digested texts, conveyors of empty entertainment and bits of random "information" (which is not at all to suggest that there weren't—aren't—plenty of journalists in the print and broadcast media still trying to do their best work under increasingly adverse conditions). Within the parameters of this shift, however, the "imagined community" remains as a foundational concept. Under the pressures of globalization and market consolidation, the cultural imaginary shifts to construct an economically consumable product in an increasingly homogenized cultural idea of "America."

As this shift took hold, students entering university programs, increasingly attuned to the rising costs of education as well as their marketability upon graduation, embraced in greater numbers the second model I described in my introduction. It's no accident that this model became dominant in the 1980s and '90s, paralleling the structural shifts taking place within the university as well as the media. This model more easily marketed itself thanks to its "job training" credentials, certainly, but also, I think, because the liberal humanistic subject, both within and outside the institution of the university, generally lost its raison d'être, even in the public imagination. Poststructuralist critics' deconstruction of the fiction of the autonomous subject notwithstanding, the phenomenon of global capital and the rapid transformation of the economy to one dominated by transnational corporations had visibly eroded the force of the Enlightenment narrative whereby citizen-subjects recognize their destiny within an ever-expanding notion of political freedom realized through the imaginary community of the nation-state. The humanistic model of journalism through the 1980s and '90s increasingly became anachronistic to students more focused on their economic, rather than merely democratic, futures. Fisher and Carey rightly critique the relentless consolidation of media ownership by transnational corporate entities, the growing purveyance of "infotainment," and the increasing reliance on technology and erosion of traditional reporting that have profoundly altered the production and function of news media, all of which are essential for understanding its contemporary practices. However, their critiques fail to link the "loss" of journalism's more overtly humanistic/heroic role with the institutional transformations taking place *within the university* as well as within the media, together with the concurrent shift in emphasis from the production of national subjects as citizens to the production of subjects as primarily consumers. To contemplate the debates concerning journalism education in the United States today requires that one engage these multiple threads *together*.

Anderson's concept of an imagined community is useful for understanding both Carey and Fisher's distress at the erosion of a journalist-subject whose primary function is to maintain the liberal democratic social contract. In fact, their nostalgia for the heroic conception of the journalist masks a deeper sense of loss for a liberal version of the nation, a distinctly "progressive" version of the American imagined community that derives from the Enlightenment model of the nation-state in relation to humanist subject-citizens whose identity is constructed by means of traditional democratic rights and responsibilities. Carey imagines an idea of liberal democracy that somehow transcends capitalism, for example, a puzzling position. He suggests that "democracy" is now equated with economics,

> the existence of free and open markets. This has been true not only among the public, whom it is rather too easy to blame, but even among privileged classes, including journalists. But political democracy does not follow from the presence of effective market economy and a politically free press does not follow from an economically free one. . . . In the absence of global political institutions only nations are strong enough to contain economic forces.[12]

While Carey is right to criticize the triumphalist rhetoric that announced the victory of "democracy" over communism since 1989 as the ascendance of global capital and free markets,[13] he nevertheless seems to have forgotten that capitalism and modern liberal democracy emerged together, an inevitable process, according to Foucault: "the economic system that promotes the accumulation of capital and the system of power that ordains the accumulation of men are, from the seventeenth century on, correlated and inseparable phenomena."[14] Ironically perhaps, viable "global political institutions" in Carey's sense have little chance of emergence in an interregnum witnessing both the ascendancy of global capitalism as the dominant force on the world stage *and*, particularly post-9/11, increasingly virulent forms of "imagined communities." While I greatly admire Carey's contributions to this discussion, to suggest that the liberal nation-state needs to continue to exist in order to contain the movement of global capital seems to me unrealistic at best, and nostalgic at worst.

A similar longing for the traditional liberal model of democracy infuses the work of many scholars who wish to bridge the gap between the first and second pedagogical models of journalism education to which I have been referring in this chapter. It's interesting to note that such calls have come particularly since the turn of the century, as the imagined community of "America" has undergone rapid and profound economic, political, and ideological shifts, culminating in the post-9/11 "reality." The discussion inevitably defines itself in the renewed call for "craft" that will restore to journalism education a mission to uphold liberal democracy. Clearly committed to producing graduates who can theoretically at least intervene in the ongoing transformation turning discreet journalist-subjects into what Fisher labeled corporatized media "packs," such calls for reform continue to miss what I would suggest is the crucial horizon—the radically altered terrain of the university's function in relation to the nation-state. While I don't disagree with their goals of producing students who are more sophisticated critical thinkers inside and outside the institution, I find models such as the one offered by G. Stuart Adam, which traces its origins to such modernist heavyweights as Joseph Pulitzer and T.S. Eliot—defenders not only of an idealized view of the nation and "civilization" but of concepts of national culture that bordered, at least in Eliot's case in *Notes Toward a Definition of Culture*, the book to which Adam alludes, on proto-fascism—quite limited. For example, Adam's underlying assumption maintains that future journalists will undertake "an inquiry into the sources and methods of political obligation connecting journalism to the architecture of democratic society . . . the commitment to democracy is less a product of attitude than a product of craft. By this I mean an attachment to the principles of craft and the ambition to express them professionally constitutes the source of journalism's contribution to democracy."[15] Calls for a return to a more formalist focus on "craft" mask an assumption, however, that education can provide training in the uses of language and rhetoric that somehow maintains the fiction of an autonomous subject whose primary role upon entering the field will be to narrate the expanding story of liberal democracy—and I would argue that this nostalgic, uncritical sense of a correspondence theory of language plays right into the current Bush administration scenario for "expanding democracy" American-style around the world—through war if necessary. Those who propose a restructuring of journalism education thus need to do so within a horizon recognizing the reality that the university as a site for the production of autonomous national subjects and a unified idea of national culture, together with the nation-state it once served, are in the process of tectonic shift, if not gone already. Yet, the idea of an "imagined community" is quite alive and well, as events post-9/11 dramatically and continually reveal.

9/11 AND ITS IMPACT ON JOURNALISM EDUCATION

In the wake of 9/11 and what some critics have called the "renationalization" of the mainstream U.S. news media, the stakes of journalism education increased significantly. Carey suggests, in the same essay I've been quoting above, that, "The first and most general effect of September 11 was to draw journalists back within the body politic. . . . The press was re-nationalized, global corporations found they needed the protection of democractic practice, and journalists experienced the vulnerability that is at the root of patriotism and nationalism."[16] I would argue, however, that the press was never truly "de-nationalized;" that what Carey on the surface offers as a critique in the quotation above actually articulates the reassertion of a liberal version of an imagined community that had been increasingly challenged by conditions and practices of global capital, particularly in relation to issues of citizenship, the public sphere, and the role of the press in maintaining them. This resurgence of a more virulently ideological version of the "imagined community" post-9/11 took the form of renewed demands for the news media to function as Americans first and journalists second; it established that the narrative of the "idea" of America urgently needed articulate, involved narrators again; and it renewed calls for the heroic journalist risking his (and now her) life for the sake of the story, whether on the streets of New York City or "embedded" with the hometown troops somewhere in Afghanistan or Iraq. The nostalgia for the journalist-hero to which I've devoted much space in the opening pages of this chapter *is a particularly post-9/11 manifestation* that masks, in my view, a misplaced effort to revive the liberal idea of the nation-state and its humanist model of citizenship as a way of warding off the corporate technocrat and the domination of life by the global market and its accompanying ideologies.

All of this has direct repercussions for the debates that had been taking place for years over the direction of journalism education, which crystallized, or perhaps exploded, in July 2002, when Columbia University president Lee Bollinger dramatically called off the search for a new dean of the Graduate School of Journalism, instead initiating a task force to rethink the school's mission. For ten months, the controversy flamed among Columbia alumni and faculty as well as educators and journalists across the country. In April 2003, Bollinger issued a public statement disbanding the task force, naming a new dean, and advocating his vision, based on judgments "informed by a remarkable group of people" (including Carey) on the task force. His statement, read to J-school alumni, acknowledged the global reach of media, highlighted public concerns such as a "growing fear about how concentration of ownership narrows the scope of public debate and how commercial and technological forces increasingly drive the structure and behavior of the press;" it admitted the "understandable anxiety that monetary pressures are threatening the quality and standards of journalism."[17]

Bollinger acknowledged that "in the current deregulatory climate . . . as the government has relaxed its 'public interest' standards," the media no longer have "mandated responsibilities to operate in the 'public interest.'" Part of his answer to that is to encourage journalism's embrace of "a stronger sense of being a profession, with stronger standards and values that will provide its members with some innate resistance to other competing values that have the potential of undermining the public responsibilities of the press."[18] His obvious belief that the university (particularly Columbia) is the site for the development of such standards calls for greater resources, increased research, and awareness of but critical distance from the profession of journalism itself. He also called for instilling "certain basic capacities in its students." The teaching of craft skills would remain a prominent feature of journalism education; added to this would be a renewed commitment to fostering an intellectual ability to handle rapidly changing work conditions. The history of the profession, its "great figures," how it "developed and evolved" would be crucial if students were to gain "a sense of an identity as a professional, which includes the moral and ethical standards that should guide professional behavior."[19]

Bollinger also advocated greater general knowledge as well as more specific content for future journalists, suggesting a two-year rather than 10-month degree as the norm to encourage students to take advantage of the knowledge of other fields. Specifically, he advocated that students have "a functional knowledge of statistics, the basic concepts of economics, and an appreciation for the importance of history and for the fundamental debates in modern political theory and philosophy." In addition, "the faculty might decide upon a few of the most important subject areas of our time (e.g., religion, politics, life sciences, and the forces of globalization) and develop specific materials and course work in these as well."[20]

On the surface, the Columbia plan seems to forge a useful compromise among the many competing curricular concerns that have been percolating for years; it acknowledges the place of "craft" and skills while also providing a unified object of study and offers a foundation for professional standards and a historically relevant content based on traditional humanistic, Western values. Utilizing Foucault's genealogical approach, however, one should also remark several potentially disturbing trends in Bollinger's vision: the establishment of the history of journalism as a unified field of knowledge, i.e., the construction of a discipline with an origin, "great figures," and a stable idea of the past informing the present and future in a linear development; the construction of a "professional identity" that would increasingly establish journalistic practice in homogeneous terms and resurrect the idea of a mission by the introduction of "standards" or, adopting Foucault's terms, "normalizing techniques" that inscribe journalists' ties to institutional practices. I'll come back to these points shortly.

The marker of success for such a journalism education, Bollinger concluded, is "whether the most promising and talented people entering the profession choose to attend journalism school. . . . Our aim should be to create educational programs that are so compelling that the most promising future leaders in journalism decide that a professional education is critical to a successful career and life."[21]

Bollinger's intervention into the journalism debates was timely and strategic, coming only a few months after the 9/11 attacks, which had radically altered the terrain for the already in-progress conflicts and tensions regarding journalism education and professional journalism/media. His emphasis clearly attempts to bridge the two increasingly divergent pedagogical models by affirming *at the graduate level* the value of "craft" and necessity for a strong content foundation, based on traditional humanistic values and critical inquiry, on the one hand, while acknowledging the need for students to develop a strong sense of professionalism, on the other. Yet his statement clearly addresses at its deepest levels the broader question of how to reposition what he continually calls "the great university" between the political, civic life of a changing conception of "nation" and professional media no longer directly tied to national networks and narratives. It's no accident, of course, that this is Columbia, an Ivy League school, not a public university, that already maintains impressive economic, political, and cultural influence on U.S. journalism education, media criticism and the media generally through its alumni and faculty, its publications such as *Columbia Journalism Review*, and, not least, its fundamental connection to a journalistic tradition founded by Joseph Pulitzer. The lack of specific reference to theoretical studies of semiotics, discourse analysis, and cultural theory, for example, is troubling, and I'll come back to this absence in my conclusion.

The Columbia initiative functions symptomatically within the multiple layers I've attempted to sketch out by tacitly acknowledging the transformation of the public university's relation to the nation-state, particularly in the wake of 9/11, and the need for journalism education to be rethought within that larger cultural, political, economic, and social shift. Bollinger's statement begins by invoking Pulitzer's legacy as the founder of Columbia's journalism school and the prizes he established to recognize journalistic excellence. "These gifts came at a time of tremendous, destabilizing social change in America, a time in which the role of journalism was also changing rapidly. And they were motivated in part by Pulitzer's belief that journalism needed institutions that would help it adjust to a new role in a new era." He continues by invoking the new century, "a time of similarly profound and destabilizing changes [in which] the role of the media in America is even more critically important to society" than before. By emphasizing the exposure to content and values that "our great universities" can offer on the subjects of "religion, politics, life sciences, and the forces of globalization,"[22] he suggests that universities are still uniquely situated, not only to provide the necessary cultural glue for an increasingly heterogeneous, multiracial, and multicultural public but to foster the strategic values through which an eroded conception of the nation-state might continue to navigate the conditions of global experience, from terrorism to religious fundamentalism to the advances in biotechnology and transnational capitalism—all without naming these directly but clearly with 9/11 and its aftermath in everyone's mind. The president assumes that the university's mission and commitment to a regeneration of values are necessary and indeed, *that the university is the only institution capable of delivering such content and values* in an era in which the nation is undergoing significant redirection and transnational corporations wield ever greater power to determine the scope and speed of globalization. It's a masterful stroke that at once restores the university (or at least the private graduate school) to its unique position for the education of a class of professional intellectuals, producing future journalists steeped in multiple narratives of national and global culture—from a privileged Western position—who will perform a necessary public service for "democracy, civil society and free markets" while tacitly acknowledging that "the inexorable processes of globalization" have already made the state's ability to guarantee the balance among those three ideas shaky at best. What it maneuvers for the university is a privileged place for the production of a new kind of professional in the service of increasingly global interests rather than a strictly national one, based on a "professional identity that insists that some things simply will not be done for money."[23] Reading from one critical perspective, then, the plan seeks to replace the loss of the liberal humanist subject who was the primary embodiment of a national story produced by the "university of culture" for the nation-state with a mature professional subject who can navigate the transition from the dominance of nation-states to the dominance of transnational corporations. That such pedagogical practice happens at the graduate level and not the undergraduate level is striking in its assumptions that this new professionalism is best embodied by mature adults, not those typical college graduates still too unreliable—that is, too "youthful"—for such a mission.[24]

JOURNALISM EDUCATION IN THE POSTHISTORICAL UNIVERSITY

While no one can predict the depth or range of the impact the Columbia model will have on the future of journalism education, it has significant potential at least to move the debate from the stalled confrontation between advocates of "craft" and those who advocate more technological models. Yet as I indicated earlier, the lack of attention in the president's statement to a theoretical analysis of the function of systems of signification and representation seems troubling. Similar worries arise over the question of how future journalists, equipped with increasingly powerful technology, will play an even greater role in the construction of multiple realities, both "real" and "virtual," for multiple national and global publics. Reinscribing an overtly Western, discipline-based heritage as the primary content, together with an increasingly organized history of the field—a "usable past"—for the purposes of establishing "standards" of professionalization seems even more so. Professional journalists who might enroll in the program will not be likely to come with cultural theoretical analysis as part of their daily practice; and as I've been suggesting, most undergraduate programs are weak in teaching theory as an integrated and necessary component of journalism pedagogy. In its tacit acknowledgment of the changed world of the university in which journalism programs locate themselves, however, the Columbia plan still has the *potential* to spur those involved in the debates to contemplate more fully the significance of thinking about different pedagogical models within such a framework. By rethinking the function and relation of the university to radically revised conceptions of "imagined communities," journalism education can become a critical site of renewal within the institution while also regenerating its connections outside. Yet the Columbia model as I read it attempts to shift the role of the university from producing traditional intellectuals in service to the state to one producing a cadre of professional journalists more akin to doctors and lawyers and other professionals who leave elite graduate schools with both advanced training as well as cultural capital. Such journalists, more than doctors or even lawyers, would have more highly visible roles than current journalists in producing, interpreting, and regulating public discourse. By shifting the journalism education debates from the undergraduate to the graduate and professional levels, and, perhaps more significantly, from the public to the private, already corporatized university, Columbia's model could have significant (negative) implications for renewal of the "public sphere" and critical citizenship. After all, the challenge for democratic communication is to encourage grassroots participation, not to further professionalize elite stewardship of the public sphere.

It's not as if media educators and critics haven't attempted such shifts in teaching journalism or begun to rethink the horizon of media education in the wake of poststructuralist critiques of the production of students as "docile bodies."[25] The many volumes of work by educator-theorists written or edited by Henry Giroux, Noam Chomsky, Stanley Aronowitz, Robert W. McChesney, Paolo Freire, Armand Mattelart, and Michele Mattelart, to name only a handful, have promoted an attempt to rethink journalism/media/communication studies in critical dialogue with other disciplines such as anthropology, political science, economics, history, cultural studies, etc. David Sholle and Stan Denski's *Media Education and the (Re)Production of Culture* (1994), for example, envisioned a critical pedagogy that would reconnect teaching critical media studies to a radical idea of democracy and a reimagined public sphere, diagnosing what they perceived as a "crisis of media education," one based on its "loss of relevance to the actual life situations of the majority in the United States, to any notion of public philosophy and critical citizenship."[26]

Their book continues to offer strategies for rethinking what journalism education can accomplish, despite its rather dated historical occasion of the so-called "culture wars," because, in my view, it begins to articulate that media education is linked not only to the culture "outside" the university but to the transformations taking place within the university itself. Yet their book doesn't fully theorize what is at stake in attempting to reframe that pedagogical scene. Without linking the production of "useful subjects" within the university to the construction and maintenance of an imagined community, mediated by the university itself as well as the media, their important intervention remains incomplete.

In a complementary analysis of journalism education, David Skinner, Mike J. Gasher, and James Compton articulate a pedagogical framework in which a semiotic approach, among other critical methodologies, would reconstruct the teaching of news writing and reporting, interviewing, and photography, helping to bridge the gap between the technological, vocation model and the liberal humanist approach. Their model would help deconstruct common pedagogical models in which "students are taught a way of seeing and presenting the world without fully understanding the reasons why they are employing a particular method or the impact that the tools they utilize have on the depictions they render."[27] Their emphasis on teaching the social constructedness of news and of language in relation to historical practice is crucial for helping students to understand the ways in which power works through knowledge to establish truth-claims. Challenging journalism students to work with the assumption that news can provide only a partial version of the truth is essential in altering both the production and the reception of news, a point their work rightly emphasizes.

But I want to situate such a pedagogical emphasis within a larger critique of the formation of subjects within the university and encourage students to understand their everyday lived reality as part of this process, one undergoing profound and rapid transformation. I would also want to connect such a critique to consideration of how journalism continues to participate in constructions of the imagined community, particularly as nationalist rhetoric post-9/11 seemingly reconstitutes an idea of the homogeneously unified nation while masking the dominance of increasingly transnational economic forces. Journalism education can begin to accomplish these multisited critiques by rethinking its epistemological "home" as a more fluid transdisciplinary location.

My concept of what journalism education might strive toward in the "posthistorical university" begins with a recognition that the university, the scene of teaching itself, needs to become the initial point of a renewed critical pedagogical practice; the Gramscian reference in my second epigraph speaks to this. Engaging our students in a process of rethinking their educational location and enabling them to continually reflect and challenge the ways in which knowledge and their own desire for professional credentials are constructed, the uses to which both knowledge and professional standards and credentials are tied within and outside the university, the function of the university in a global economy, the "production" of "intellectual" and "mass" cultures both within and outside the United States, etc., will potentially transform the content of any journalism program. While content and vocation certainly must both be addressed in journalism education today, the *attitude toward thinking* that we help our students develop seems to me to be crucial, one that begins with critical exploration of the exchange between students and teachers as differently constructed "subjects." This last idea especially returns me to Readings's call for creation of a "dissensual community" of "particularities," and a rethinking of what happens if we give up the language of "production" in terms of knowledge, intellectuals, culture, and so forth. If the posthistorical university is understood as "one site among others where the question of being-together is raised,"[28] how might journalism education participate?

Roger I. Simon and Samuel Weber, among many others, have both taken up Readings's call to attempt to formulate a vision of such a site. Weber's articulation of how the economic transformation of the university necessitates a rethinking of the humanist subject in relation to it is an important point of departure and elaborates on what it means to move from the production of subjected, docile bodies to the bringing-together of "particularities." He traces this movement in the following way:

> It is the center that enables an I to doubt everything except the fact that it is I who am doing the doubting: the point in which saying and doing do not simply converge but are always and already one and the same. It is precisely this dimension of temporality, however, that returns to haunt the fantasy of pure self-identity and with it, the conception of a university that would be its institutional expression. And the manner in which it haunts that fantasy is by posing the question of the future: of a future that would not necessarily be comprehensible in terms of the past.[29]

This statement carries implications for the way students are constructed within the university as subject-citizens and especially today as consumers; it can enable them to theorize their relation to the increasingly corporate university itself and it can particularly assist them to understand the way in which media participate in maintaining such constructions of the subject at all points in the communication process. Adopting this approach could enable students together with their teachers to interrogate the subject in relation to a linear construction of history, as well as the very idea of a "stable" identity or subject-position (whether citizen, consumer, etc.). To have journalism students undertake such critical questioning would alter their understanding of sourcing, gatekeeping, context, and focus, in addition to helping them see their own role in the process of providing knowledge that is always partial in relation to the "truth" of a particular situation.

Simon attempts to locate a slightly different ground, in the wake of Readings's critique, for the scene of teaching generally; I would want to adopt his framework for a potentially transdisciplinary journalism studies program:

> If we take . . . this question of what forms of "being-together" pedagogic actions initiate, the university as a "place to think" can be characterized not so much in terms of what it redeems (the self, the social, or the checkbook), but rather, in terms of the specific obligations it engenders, precisely the obligations of thought-in-relation. This requires the reimagining of the university as an emergent "dissensual community" relinquishing the regulatory idea of communicational transparency in which the unity of thought can be realized. On these grounds, "what is called thinking is never simply a theoretical question, one that a fully grounded epistemology might answer."[30]

Simon articulates further the profoundly changed relation that faculty and students could have with each other in creating "dissensual communities" as well as how the formation of such a fluid space and relationality might impact the way that students would envision the function of their education as they exit the university and go into the field. "Teaching-learning relationships embody the ethical challenge of acknowledging and responding to the emergent specificity of others, something only available as the substance of thought-in-relation is enacted."[31] As others have attempted to point out, it means a deconstruction of the Enlightenment subject who formerly took his place at the center of the university, trained to carry forward the liberal humanist project of freedom. I've gone on at length in the early pages of this essay to demonstrate how that humanistic model has functioned in journalism education and professional media. Teaching journalism in a "posthistorical university," then, means finally letting go of this model of a subject, the university that produces him, the nation for which he is being produced, and the narrative of liberal democratic capitalism that has legitimated the horizon for the entire project. In their place, a different kind of pedagogical scene could be enacted. Simon envisions the following:

> Teaching is not exhausted in the achievement of intersubjective communication. The goal of education is not fulfilled in the achievement of a mimetic identity by the student, either as a replication of the professor as model of rigorous thoughtfulness, or as a replication of a cluster of specific knowledge and skills assumed required to take up one's place in socioeconomic systems of production and exchange, but in precisely our ability to hold open the question of education itself while substantively and productively engaging students in new concepts, ideas, perspectives, and modes of thought.[32]

Such goals stand in marked contrast, in my view, to the models proposed by well-intentioned educators and theorists such as Adam, Carey, Brent Cunningham, and others.[33] These conceptions of a journalism program would continue to produce journalists who see themselves primarily as national subjects taking their place in a long heroic tradition of narrating and maintaining the story of the ever-expanding social democratic contract. For example, in calling for the continuation of Reporting and Writing I, "the soul of the Columbia program," Cunningham rather nostalgically recounts his own first semester in the program, writing about "things like the [East Harlem] neighborhood's asthma rates . . . the grass-roots effort to block the influx of box stores like Costco and Wal-Mart; and the complicated relationship between the Anglo missionaries, who ran social programs that were instrumental in the development of East Harlem in the decades after World War II, and the rising Latino leadership class."[34] He would integrate courses with converged media platforms to acknowledge the rapidly shifting and increasingly sophisticated technological environments that journalism students will have to handle. Cunningham's well-intentioned argument unfortunately participates in the maintenance of several of the discursive practices I've been attempting to challenge in this chapter, from the myth of the journalist-hero defending the expansion of the liberal democratic contract to the "discourse of deliverance" that attempts to speak for those who have been left out of the process to a formalist focus on "craft" as the primary tool in the arsenal of the journalist who can know anything at any time. Such untheorized celebrations of journalism's heroic protection of the public interest fail to make the link between the production of uncritical subjects within the university and the production of docile consumers in the world "outside" the university, while leaving the fiction of a unified "imagined community" sharing a belief in liberal humanist values intact. It shares commonalities with Adam, Fisher, Carey, and others who don't fully interrogate, in my view, the connection between the transformations taking place inside the university as the parallel to the transformations taking place in the horizon of the social, political, economic, cultural, and global.

Unless journalism programs take what is happening within U.S. universities as their point of departure, they will continue to produce journalists and media professionals who understand themselves, particularly in the post-9/11 world, as committed to a rapidly evaporating imagined community called "America" professionally and politically, which means a commitment to the status quo (including the stranglehold of corporate interests on news media). In my mind, that means a continuing evacuation of actual critical consciousness. It's not enough, I think, to critique the increasingly corporate nature of news, or decry the lack of professional standards in the profession (or to assert that adoption of such standards would negate the former situation). A focus solely on content within journalism education won't suffice if the goal is to encourage journalists to critically interrogate and report on how various truth-claims are constructed, legitimated, and circulated. That is to say, the ritual of objectivity, fairness, and balance is insufficient, particularly if those work routines reproduce "the dominant views that are most readily available to the press."[35]

Journalism education will have to bring these locations into critical dialogue in order to confront its own investment in the myth of a free press that once served all the interests of a fully democratic society. It will also have to critique the parallel discourse of the myth of the modern university that contributed to the education of an elite professional class of national citizen-subjects and whose primary mission was the production and maintenance of a particular kind of national culture, one that reflected a liberal democracy called "America." Continuing adherence to these myths erodes the potential for a rethinking of journalism education, and thus the potential for a journalism practice that might invigorate a different kind of citizenship, a different relation to "the dominant views" that buy their way into the media.

Readings's understanding of the role of the "posthistorical university" is crucial for this task:

> How are we to reimagine the University, once its guiding idea of culture has ceased to have an essential function? . . . Once transnational capitalism has eroded the meaning of culture, and once the institutional system begins to show itself capable of functioning without reference to that term, then the role of education cannot primarily be conceived in terms of cultural acquisition or cultural resistance. This does not mean that those in the University should abandon critical judgment, become passive observers or even eager servants of capital. . . . [T]he question of value becomes more significant than ever, and it is by raising value as a question of *judgment* that the discourse of excellence can be resisted.[36]

What would it mean for journalism education in particular to heed Readings's call to relinquish "our claim to be intellectuals and giving up the claim of service to the state"? How do we "dwell in the ruins" of the university, assuming one subscribes with me to Readings's analysis? If the university no longer perceives its function as the production of national culture and national subject-citizens, but rather becomes a "ruined" site for "the thought of community that abandons either expressive identity or transactional consensus as means to unity," how can we generate "real responsibility [and] ethical probity . . . not commensurate with the grand narrative of nationalism that has up to now underpinned accounts of the social action of University research and teaching?"[37] This initiates a different kind of thinking, one that "is at once fully aware of the coerciveness of the comprehensive (narrative) structure repeatedly reconstituted and imposed on historically specific knowledge by the Western suprahistorical consciousness."[38] Taking these questions seriously, within the horizon of Readings's radical critique of the university in relation to the eroding nation-state, seems even more imperative after the events of September 11 and the current Bush administration's endless "war on terrorism" which appeals to a jingoistic nationalism, a virulent form of the "imagined community" that divides the world into "us" and "terrorists," while at the same time further consolidating the power of transnational corporate capital.

As I have suggested throughout this chapter, the present historical moment— an interregnum, if you will—bears witness to a multileveled shift implicating the production of an autonomous subject, the Enlightenment's *cogito*, that assumes a stable ground for producing knowledge and mastering the unknown. American journalism has, throughout its history, participated in the construction, maintenance, and narration of that fiction. If journalism education in the United States has any hope of emerging as a different kind of pedagogy, it must first take stock of its own site of production, questioning its role in the perpetuation of that construction and the goals to which it has thus far assumed a natural relation. It would engage "not . . . [in] a dialectical but . . . [in] a dialogic approach to the teaching of a curriculum. It would neither replace one authority with another nor produce a pedagogic context in which anything goes. It seeks to create a space that is *always already* interested yet free, contestatory yet open-ended."[39] Readings, Simon, Weber, Spanos, and many others can provide useful strategies for those of us involved in that process. This will have a jarring impact on our self-reflexive understanding of our role as scholars, teachers, intellectuals, and citizens in relation to the institution as well as the state.

CONCLUSION

To rethink what being an "intellectual" means is vital for this process of revision to occur; to put our work in the service not of an imagined community such as the nation-state but "dissensual communities" both within the institutional space of the university as well as outside it is a task we must begin to address through our critical engagements. As this process continues, the way in which we encourage students to become professional journalists dramatically shifts away from technologically trained culture producers and humanistically trained narrators. As Spanos points out, "the posthumanist specific or organic intellectual is acutely aware that *all* cultural production is finally without transcendental justification."[40]

Journalism education must, I think, radically reconceive itself in terms of its own curricular project by understanding its obligation to *challenge* forms of representation that depend on a presumed "objectivity," and to interrogate foundational claims of "Truth" at all levels. This begins by rethinking the way in which the university itself is always implicated in such a process. A reconceptualized concept of journalism education encourages students to rethink the horizon that links the production of knowledges for the imagined community with the production of knowledge and autonomous subjects for particular relations of power. In the posthistorical university, such multisituated critique can be enacted by requiring courses in which identity-formation is theorized and prioritized; students could be encouraged to take transdisciplinary courses such as introductions to women's studies, race and ethnicity studies, and/or cultural studies, which expose students directly to the linkages between epistemology, subjectivity, and representation, and the way in which the media participates in such linkages. Such a curriculum would, in my view, require courses in semiotics and discourse analysis, in order to critique the concept of representation and the instrumentalized uses of language; this would also give students exposure to what Bakhtin termed the heteroglossia of language. In addition, it would foreground epistemological processes and the uses to which knowledge—particularly knowledge delivered through media—is continually being put. A reconceptualized journalism curriculum would, at all levels of coursework, encourage students to ask who is being served by particular discourses and how particular truth-claims are being utilized in such situations? The goal of such a curriculum would be to construct a set of courses that enabled students to interrogate the connections between language, subjectivity, and citizenship and the power of the media to renew and invigorate democratic freedom; it would situate contemporary U.S. news media in relation to the increasingly privatized university and the pervasiveness of global capital. Not least, such a curriculum would encourage students to rethink the sacred five Ws: to discover not just the "who" that is doing the action but to focus as well on who is receiving the action, directly and perhaps more importantly, indirectly; to rethink the "what" by interrogating fully the implications of an action or situation that are perhaps the least obvious; to think the "where" not simply on its surface but also in relation to the economic, political, racial, gendered, classed aspects of the nation as well as the global community; to understand the "when" through a more complex engagement with history as complex genealogy rather than simple causality; and to consider the "why" and "how" from multiple epistemological sites. Once we reimagine our own roles, not as narrators of unified fictions, but instigators of thinking for continually emergent dissensual communities, journalism education can participate in the dismantling of the "imagined community" and help to revitalize the way people understand themselves and the world around them.

NOTES

1. I use these terms as a way of attempting to move beyond the standard conception of "interdisciplinary," having directed the women's studies program/minor for four years prior to coordination of the journalism minor at my home institution, both of which are considered to be "interdisciplinary" programs. In my view, the traditional conception of "interdisciplinary" assumes a bringing together of two or more disciplinary epistemologies and/or methodologies into a program (or course) that generally leaves the disciplines intact; in other words, there is

little disruption, little dialogic tension that might disturb the disciplinary boundaries through a new space generated by and within that tension. Transdisciplinarity would ideally mark a fluid space (course, program, etc.) interrogating how knowledges are constructed, for what ends and for whose benefit, through what kinds of methodologies, etc., without seeking a permanent home within the institution along traditional models of departments and disciplines. My use of this term thus signals a way of thinking as opposed to naming a methodology or creating a new structure within the university. Because there are obvious institutional risks involved in abandoning the "interdisciplinary" model, however, I acknowledge the potential usefulness of a "multidisciplinary" framework, one that attempts to generate a new space for thinking while also recognizing the need to work, at least temporarily, within those more traditional institutional locations and paradigms.

2. The relation between "communication theory," "media theory," and undergraduate journalism education is a fraught one within U.S. programs in my limited experience and research. Large research universities such as Syracuse, Berkeley, NYU, Indiana, etc. incorporate to a much greater extent a focus on "critical media studies" and communication theory rather than what I've oversimplified as the "technological training" model. Yet by and large, U.S. undergraduate programs in arts and humanities generally have not embraced critical and literary theory, cultural theory or communication/media theory. Partly this is a reflection of the tenacity of what I've equally oversimplified as the liberal humanist model, partly it's the general American "resistance to theory" at the undergraduate level in the arts and humanities. My use of the Columbia University debates as a symptomatic example of where journalism education in the United States. may be heading will attempt to reflect on this absence a bit more, as will my concluding section.

3. Benedict Anderson, *Imagined Communities: Reflections on the Origin and Spread of Nationalism*, rev. ed. (London and New York: Verso, 1991), 6–7.

4. Bill Readings, *The University in Ruins* (Cambridge, Mass.: Harvard University Press, 1996), 12–13.

5. Readings, *University*, 89.

6. Readings, *University*, 90.

7. Leonard Downie, Jr. and Robert G. Kaiser, *The News about the News: American Journalism in Peril* (New York: Vintage Books, 2002), 21.

8. Marc Fisher, "The Metamorphosis: A Quarter Century of Dramatic Change," *American Journalism Review* 24, no. 9 (November 2002): 20–25.

9. James W. Carey, "American Journalism On, Before, and After September 11," in *Journalism After September 11*, ed. Barbie Zelizer and Stuart Allan (London and New York: Routledge, 2002), 71–89.

10. Carey, "American Journalism," 84.

11. William V. Spanos, *The End of Education: Toward Posthumanism* (Minneapolis: University of Minnesota Press, 1993), 197.

12. Carey, "American Journalism," 88–89.

13. For a succinct summary of this triumphalist "end of history" discourse, and a powerful critique of it, see William V. Spanos, *America's Shadow: An Anatomy of Empire* (Minneapolis: University of Minnesota Press, 2000), especially the introduction, xv–xxiii.

14. Michel Foucault, "Truth and Power," *The Foucault Reader*, ed. Paul Rabinow (New York: Pantheon, 1984), 51–75.

15. G. Stuart Adam, "The Education of Journalists," *Journalism: Theory, Practice and Criticism* 2, no. 3 (December 2001): 315–39.

16. Carey, "American Journalism," 87.

17. Lee C. Bollinger, *Journalism Task Force Statement*. Columbia University Graduate School of Journalism, April 2003. <http://www.jrn.columbia.edu/news/2003-04/taskforce.asp> (22 Dec. 2003).

18. Bollinger, "Task Force."

19. Bollinger, "Task Force."
20. Bollinger, "Task Force."
21. Bollinger, "Task Force."
22. Bollinger, "Task Force."
23. Bollinger, "Task Force."
24. See Spanos, *End of Education*, especially the last chapter, for a discussion of this. "It is essentially by means of the curriculum thus understood as the core of a commonly shared body of knowledge that the certified professor, and the institution such a figure represents, is empowered to *cultivate* the fallow ground of youth in general in terms of the principle of *maturity*, and to inscribe the particular (though overlapping) blocs of young people—women, blacks, gays, working class, ethnic—with the affiliated sexual, racial, working class, ethnic—with the affiliated sexual, racial, cultural, sociopolitical, and international that, combined, reproduce the dominant late capitalist sociopolitical order and extend its hegemony," 207–208.
25. Michel Foucault, *Discipline and Punish: The Birth of the Prison*, trans. Alan Sheridan (New York: Vintage Books, 1979).
26. David Sholle and Stan Denski, *Media Education and the (Re)Production of Culture* (Westport, Conn.: Bergin & Garvey, 1994), 103.
27. David Skinner, Mike J. Gasher, and James Compton, "Putting Theory to Practice: A Critical Approach to Journalism Studies," *Journalism: Theory, Practice and Criticism* 2, no. 3 (December 2001): 341–60.
28. Readings, *University*, 20, 161.
29. Samuel Weber, "The Future Campus: Destiny in a Virtual World," 1999, archived at <http://www.hydra.umn.edu/weber/text1/html> (10 Jan. 2004).
30. Roger I. Simon, "The University: A Place to Think?" *Beyond the Corporate University: Culture and Pedagogy in the New Millenium*, ed. Henry A. Giroux and Kostas Myrsiades (Lanham, Md.: Rowman & Littlefield, 2001), 45–56.
31. Simon, "A Place to Think?" 53.
32. Simon, "A Place to Think?" 53.
33. Brent Cunningham, "The Mission: Searching for the Perfect J-school," *Columbia Journalism Review* (Nov./Dec. 2002) <http://www.cjr.org/issues/2002/6/school-cunningham.asp> (21 Dec. 2003). This widely cited piece responded to the controversy that was still raging at Columbia at the time. In his "fantasy school," the "core of the school—and its faculty—would be about the best reporting and writing." Such an emphasis on craft would insure coverage of "the lives of poor people in the South Bronx," Cunningham said; "most educators I talked to told me that increasingly the students coming to their graduate programs had little or no background in journalism. We cannot give students specialized knowledge in everything that they are likely to cover in their careers, but we can give them the values and the judgment and tools to guide them as they educate themselves."
34. Cunningham, "The Mission."
35. Lance W. Bennett, "Media Power in the United States," *De-Westernizing Media Studies*, ed. James Curran and Myung-Jin Park (London and New York: Routledge, 2002), 202–20.
36. Readings, *University*, 119.
37. Readings, *University*, 192.
38. Spanos, *End of Education*, 205.
39. Spanos, *End of Education*, 217.
40. Spanos, *End of Education*, 219.

12

The Alternative Communication Movement in Quebec's Mediascape

Michel Sénécal and Frédéric Dubois

The debates and forums of the World Summit on the Information Society provide an opportunity for putting the question of the democratization of the mediascape and, in particular, the right to communicate,[1] back on the political agenda. The major social stakeholders—corporations, governments, and the groups and movements that make up civil society—are, in their own ways, making the most of this international discussion to update their values, interests, and strategies through their respective logics of social communication, and from there, promoting their distinct visions of society.

The contemporary study of the appropriation of media technology demonstrates how different logics—that is, organized sets of interests and values associated with the major social stakeholders, most particularly states, corporations, civil society groups—are at work in the ways in which communication is perceived and technical systems are implemented.[2] These logics mingle, come into conflict, and interpenetrate, as a semantic fog enshrouds the very notion of the democratization of the mediascape, particularly at a time when the neoliberal project of a "global information society" reemerges.[3] These three major lines of thinking have been historically decisive in defining and applying media technologies: from the written press to audiovisual production to digital networks. These distinctions are visible to varying degrees in the definition and organization of the mediascape, locally, nationally, and globally, providing an explicit demonstration that communication is important as a terrain for social and political mobilization. The clash of these perspectives results in a paradigmatic confrontation between the social stakeholders with respect to defining distinct models of communication and their "freedom" in the mediascape.

Presently, the commercial sector is not only imposing its logic and dominating the field, it also tends to reduce the flexibility available to developing other public, community, or cooperative models. Thus, in recent years, the increased privatization and deregulation of the Canadian and Quebec mediascapes have not been isolated from market liberalization, network globalization, and the increasing supremacy of the techno-industrial and financial logic in the development of policies and practices concerning access to the media.

These tendencies are closely related to the process of transforming public policy, whereby state intervention is increasingly driven by the belief that market discipline can, on its own, ensure equitable and diversified access to media. But the reality is something altogether different when the principle of public access to the mediascape is translated into a simple formula governing the consumption of goods and services; legislators are reduced to calling on the private sector to self-regulate in order to "democratize" the mediascape. Nor is this trend confined to the national scale. Market regulation, as professed by the World Trade Organization (WTO), is intolerant of media practices supported by public policies and subsidies, considering them unfair competition.

By way of example, it is important to underline the constant pressure, applied in particular by the United States and supported by a number of other countries like Japan, to subject cultural goods and services to broader commercial negotiations. That is, every effort to resist, or intervene against, market logic in the cultural field becomes vulnerable to commercial concessions in other sectors. In Canada, the public policies most susceptible to such action are those which apply quantitative restrictions (such as Canadian-content quotas in television and radio), those which limit foreign ownership in the broadcast and telecommunications industries, and those which receive state subsidies, the most common form of policy support in the culture and communications sector.[4] Not surprisingly, then, a number of jurisdictions like Canada and Quebec defend their policies under a banner of "cultural diversity"—rather than "cultural exception"—in order to promote the idea that cultural products should not be regarded as commodities. This is a principle that some countries would like to see adopted by UNESCO as an international convention on cultural diversity by the end of 2005.

It is a significant struggle. On the one hand, the rhetoric of market globalization has an insidious impact on collective social heritage historically constructed at the local and national levels. On the other hand, regulatory adjustments that support expansionist strategies promote the commercial and financial version of the appropriation of the media at the expense of the public-interest version, supported by the groups and movements that constitute civil society. Regulation that relies solely and uniquely on market discipline, and has been designed solely in favor of the stakeholders in private industry, poses a crucial question with respect to any media system that is intended to be open and plural. That is, what can be the future of public communication spaces when the notion of market eclipses that of society, and politics is absorbed by economics?[5]

Drawing on the experience of Quebec, this chapter considers some of the ways in which the shifting logic of media regulation is foreclosing on the operations of community and alternative media outlets in that jurisdiction, and how the alternative communication movement is working to give new voice to the practice of the "right to communicate."

BARRIERS TO THE MEDIASCAPE

In May 2001, Canada's regulatory agency, the Canadian Radio-television and Telecommunications Commission (CRTC), gave the Quebecor Media group permission to acquire Videotron, the largest cable network in Quebec, with 1.5 million subscribers. Videotron also owns TVA, the largest French-language private television network, accounting for more than 30 percent of the Quebec market share.[6] This $5 billion (Cdn) acquisition occurred at a time of unprecedented levels of concentration of media ownership in Quebec. This decision also authorized cross-media ownership, making it possible for a single owner to control both a television station and a daily newspaper in the same market. Until that time, Canadian regulatory authorities had discouraged this.[7] The print media in Quebec were already heavily concentrated. Together, Quebecor and its close competitor, Gesca, a subsidiary of the Power Corporation, control 97 percent of circulation among French-language dailies in the province. That is, all the French-language dailies with the exception of the independent, small-circulation *Le Devoir*. Yet this degree of media concentration does not seem to concern the regulatory authorities. When Bell Globemedia, a subsidiary of BCE (Bell Canada Enterprises), a telecommunications leader in Canada and owner of the national daily newspaper the *Globe and Mail*, was authorized to purchase CTV, the country's largest private, English-language television network, the CRTC perceived media concentration as simply part of the governing logic behind the reorganization of the communications industry throughout the world. During the public hearings that preceded the CRTC's decision to approve Quebecor's acquisition of Videotron, numerous professional (journalists), labor (communications workers), and community (organizations and media) groups stated that the situation was particularly alarming with respect to maintaining the diversity of information sources and, more globally, with respect to preserving a public democratic space.[8] But in recent decades, the cultural protectionism and nationalism that has historically informed Canadian (and Quebec) policy seems relegated to play a minor role when facing borderless financial stakes. And a quasimonopoly is tolerated to prepare Canadian corporations to compete with powerful media groups such as AOL-Time Warner and Vivendi-Universal. But with the new hand dealt to global competition and the unprecedented grip of private enterprise on the mediascape, there is a risk that ownership concentration will become irreversible.

Similar concerns were expressed in January 1998, when the CRTC announced that cable television networks would no longer be required to host and finance community-access television channels, provided that they made a financial contribution to a Canadian audiovisual production fund that aids private, independent producers. With this ruling, the CRTC ended a thirty-year social obligation that had given community members an opportunity, if not a right, to communicate on local cable networks.[9]

Following this decision, the Quebec cable company Videotron transformed the nature of the community-access channel under its supervision, Canal VOX. It became, to some extent, an additional specialty channel, producing television programming that was similar to increasingly widespread commercial fare. With these changes, a dozen or so independent community producers operating in Videotron's exclusive territory lost their access to the community channel, with the Canal VOX programs produced in Montreal replacing time slots they once occupied.

In a very short period of time, the survival of community-based media has been seriously endangered without consideration for their contribution to the constitution of a third sector in the field of communications in Quebec and Canada, whose uniqueness has been officially recognized since the adoption of the Broadcasting Act in 1991. In Quebec, a number of independent and nonprofit broadcast production companies suddenly found themselves at the mercy of the cable distributors. As a result, community television was no longer defined as a product of citizens but a consumer product serving the brand and the editorial values of cable companies that addressed citizens as audiences with no effective programming input. The "community" was no longer the driving force behind "community television" programming, as it had been under the preceding regulatory regime. Production monies were to be invested in "house productions," leaving little or no space for the involvement and training of community members who wanted to initiate their own projects.

This situation highlights the Quebec government's change in strategy with respect to intervention in media markets. Since the Quebec government has repeatedly lost jurisdictional battles with the federal government in the communications sector—first in radio, then television and cable—it has shifted its policy aims from political motives—asserting its political independence—to financial incentives. Traditionally the political motives of the Quebec government were always accompanied by financial support to encourage the establishment of both private-sector and public-sector media structures, but by the 1980s economic incentives took precedence over the Quebec government's desire to score political points against the central government in Ottawa.

A good example of this shift to a kind of economic nationalism was the Quebec government's material support of Quebecor's acquisition of Videotron. Together, the government of Quebec and the Caisse de dépôt et placement du Québec—the government institution which manages the Quebec Pension Plan—invested $2.2 billion (Cdn) in Quebecor Media (the equivalent of 45.3 percent of its shares) to tip the scales in its bidding war against the Rogers group of Toronto, Canada's largest cable operator and a privileged partner of AT&T Canada. The president of Quebecor, Pierre Karl Péladeau, did not miss the opportunity to exploit the nationalist element of the transaction, describing the Videotron acquisition as a "social project" that would create a large, integrated communication company capable of disseminating Quebec francophone culture.[10] While attempting to defend community television before the CRTC, the Quebec minister of culture and communications was careful not to speak out with respect to the transaction in which the powerful Caisse de dépôt et placement du Québec was highly committed.

These examples confirm that in the face of increasing barriers to the mediascape brought on by escalating concentration of ownership, the various social stakeholders wield uneven amounts of influence with respect to the formulation of national communication policies.[11]

A MOVEMENT IN CONTINUAL SURVIVAL MODE

As early as 1970, critics from various labor, professional, and popular groups— the Fédération nationale des communications (FNC), the Institut canadien d'éducation des adultes (ICEA), the Fédération professionnelle des journalistes du Québec (FPJQ)—were voicing concerns over media concentration. And, over the decades, a movement committed to the democratization of the media began to emerge. This movement is composed of community television and radio stations, as well as a variety of independent magazines and newspapers and, more recently, alternative practices pertaining to the use of the Internet and open-source technologies, and today the alternative media scene in Quebec is comprised of people of different generations, using a range of technologies and approaches, and all committed to the idea of democratizing communication.

This movement is far from homogeneous. Over all those years, it was born and developed in confluence with, and under the influence of, various political conjunctures and ideologies, the ideals of the struggle for Quebec's national liberation, the counterculture utopia, the movement for progressive social change, the foundations of popular education, and the principles of cultural and community intervention. It is, therefore, hardly surprising that it is now through the antiglobalization movement that activism *in* and *through* independent and affinity-based media is once again coming to the forefront. Questions concerning women, education, health, housing, the environment, immigration, and so forth, continue to find favorable echoes on community networks, not only because they are mandated to represent the values and interests of their communities but also because those who are active within such media support these social movements.

All of this activity contributes to the defense and the realization of the right to communicate by constituting both a resistance to, and an alternative to, a mediascape that is increasingly commercialized and privatized. The fight for the recognition of a right to communicate goes hand-in-hand with the social rights being advocated in other segments of society. They all demand greater equilibrium between collective rights and private rights. This democratization movement is based on an activism for which the media serve as a means (to demystify, democratize, make the media accessible), an end (to educate, counterinform, democratize society), and even a cause when considered in the context of profound social change. Each of these concerns constitutes what Cardon and Granjon[12] refer to as informational and communicational activism.[13] As means, communication defined by proximity and reciprocity and structured as community, independent, noncommercial, and affinity-based or citizens' media, form privileged sites for a "two-fold democratization."[14] That is, they not only serve as means for democratizing the mediascape itself, but also as vehicles for democratizing society through their interventions. Since community media give democratic principles a primary place in their own activities, they may act as a catalyst for helping find such values a place within the broader public sphere.

The participatory approach of the alternative media practices translates into an emphasis on the role of the community in ownership, community members' active participation in the development of programming through broadcast projects, and the management of the organization. This is the reason for the importance given to the training of volunteers and the role played by community members in orientation, management, and production. Such democratic practice can be attributed to the collective nature of ownership and the focus placed on local and regional information, the desire for social change, and the access to nonprofessional bandwidth. These media serve as a springboard for making the missions and activities of the popular and community organizations known, for reflecting local and regional life, and for developing a place for reflection, debate, and criticism.

To ensure a lasting status for this third, community communications sector, associations were founded based on media technologies.[15] And in 1973, Quebec's Ministry of Communications (MCQ) instituted the Community Media Assistance Program (PAMEC), a financing structure within which each media sector had its own institutional representation. But over the years the Community Media Assistance Program has suffered several rounds of cutbacks and the cumulative result is that this Quebec government department has promoted the market-driven cultural industries at the expense of the community-oriented communications sector. But despite dramatic underfunding, the umbrella organizations that represent the community press, community radio, and community television are all still active.[16]

Founded in 1980, the Association des médias écrits communautaires du Québec (AMECQ) brings together about 100 community print media groups throughout Quebec. It organizes training sessions, negotiates agreements with advertisers who are likely to support community media, and lobbies governments. Although it is recognized by the Quebec government as the official representative of the community print media, AMECQ has been deserted by several members who feel it is disinclined to criticize the status quo and too closely focused on its vocation to provide institutional services and representation.

In order to play a role in defining public communication policies and regulating the sector, a large number of community radio stations joined the Association des radiodiffuseurs communautaires du Québec (ARCQ), a nonprofit organization founded in 1979. It represents the stations for purposes of consultation with the various government departments, especially the provincial communications ministry and the CRTC. In 2003, the association represented twenty-five stations broadcasting in sixteen regions in Quebec, which accounts for almost all (96 percent) of the French-language community radio stations in the province.[17] For several years now, ARCQ members have highlighted the training role played by their association. The association is also interested in technological matters, particularly new, digital methods of distribution.

Founded in November 1998, the Fédération des télévisions communautaires du Québec[18] represents more than forty nonprofit, independent community television stations. Behind an apparent single entity, the expression "community television" hides two very distinct types of structures. On the one hand there are the nonprofit organizations that we refer to as "autonomous" community television stations, of which there are still about sixty in Quebec, according to FEDETVC figures. On the other hand, there are the community programming services which are supervised and administered by the cable companies, and operated by cable company employees.

In maintaining the focus adopted in 1998, and in an effort to give priority to the private companies that provide leadership in the mediascape (including, in principle, the community sector), the CRTC, in the appendix to a public notice dated October 10, 2002, presented a *Strategic framework for communication media* in which it created a new class of broadcasting license for community television programming companies. This measure allows the CRTC to examine license applications submitted by both for-profit and non-profit applicants to operate community programming companies. The 1998 regulations gave lobbyists for profit-oriented companies an opportunity to argue that since the public had access to a wide variety of channels there was no longer any need for community television. This argument avoided any mention of the distinct character of community television, namely, the active participation of citizens in its development. ARCQ and the FEDETVC, the two community organizations primarily concerned, insisted that a portion of the broadcast industry must enjoy the regulatory requirement that those who obtain community radio or television licenses be nonprofit organizations. They feel this constitutes an essential barrier to media concentration.[19]

AN INTEGRATED LOCAL AND INTERNATIONAL PERSPECTIVE

In Quebec and in Canada, the movement to democratize communication is historically rooted in the development of local and community media practices, and it is these practices which most closely manifest what is today called the right to communicate. Since the late 1960s, however, the right to communicate has gradually become a political issue in international debates as governments in the nonindustrial nations launched an offensive invoking the domination of the West in the exchange of cultural and information productions. Central to these debates are the 1980 recommendations of the MacBride Commission.[20] The commission report insisted that the right to communicate is an extension of social progress and democracy. The report also denounced the North-South imbalance in the production of news and information, the concentration of Western media and their control of the flow of information worldwide, particularly through international press agencies, and asserted the importance of establishing a "new world information and communication order" (NWICO).[21]

More generally speaking, MacBride focused on the value of information as a privileged tool for economic development but also as a necessity and the result of the development of democratic societies. Such an approach invites citizens to become active partners in order to contribute to promoting greater variety in the messages exchanged as well as to increase the degree and quality of social representation in communication. It became clear at the time that the dominant principle should be that of reciprocity and symmetry among those who take part in the democratic process, and that information should be considered a democratic right essential to the exercise of citizenship.

The Western industrialized nations accepted the report's general orientation, but remained faithful to the sacrosanct free-flow doctrine, which had, until then, dominated international exchanges and produced a continual shift of television and radio networks to the private sector. The most vocal advocates of neoliberal thought at the time, Ronald Reagan and Margaret Thatcher went so far as to withdraw their countries from UNESCO in the mid-1980s. This political gesture sent a strong a message of disapproval for the MacBride Commission's endorsement of a right to communicate.

The 1980s saw the entrance on the international scene of "grassroots" organizations that made it their goal to promote the right to communicate.[22] These included the World Association of Community Radio Broadcasters (AMARC), the World Association for Christian Communication (WACC), the Association for Progressive Communication (APC) and Videazimut (a coalition promoting audiovisual communication). Often, these alternative networks started on a local level, then concentrated on the regional, national, and even continental levels. AMARC and Videazimut[23] were founded in Quebec in 1983 and 1990, respectively, as assemblies initiated by alternative media activists from Quebec eventually developed into full-fledged international networks. AMARC still has its global head office in Montreal.

Beginning with the Rio Summit in 1992, these associations became official stakeholders in global debates. Their emergence coincided with fundamental changes in the international communication policies of multilateral organizations. In 1989, UNESCO developed a new communication strategy which officially rejected the central tenets of the MacBride Commission and, in effect, pushed aside visions for participatory communication and the democratization of the mediascape.

A number of media organizations also met under various international banners, including Voices 21, which was founded in March 1999 to build a new social movement around media and communication problems. They included such groups as the Platform for Democratic Communication, the Peoples' Communication Charter, the Cultural Environment Movement, the MacBride Roundtable on Communication, the WACC, the APC, AMARC, the Center for Development Communication, Videazimut, Deep Dish TV, and EcoNews Africa. These informal groups opposed the increasing concentration and control of capital in a smaller number of hands, and led to the emergence of an economic censorship more subtle than the traditional censorship practiced by governments. They are interested in communication from the citizen's perspective, play a role in a social context that is marked by the dynamics created through struggles against the Multilateral Agreement on Investment (MIA), discussed by the Organization for Economic Cooperation and Development (OECD) between 1995 and 1998, and against the summit held by the World Trade Organization (WTO) in Seattle in 1999. The first World Social Forum (WSF), held in 2001 in Porte Alegre, Brazil, as an alternative to the World Economic Forum (WEF) in Davos, Switzerland, gave social groups from around the world (unions, NGOs, movements and organizations, intellectuals and artists) an opportunity to discuss the bases of "another possible world," much different from the world that only values the markets and money.

TOWARD NEW TERRITORY IN A DETERRITORIALIZED MEDIASCAPE: CMAQ AND RMA

The development of the Internet and the multiplication of communication spaces organized into networks that are not directly linked to a specific territory call into question the notion of a public sphere grounded in a specific national space under the jurisdiction of a nation-state.[24] But despite this apparent freedom, the Internet should not become a hiding place for community media practitioners, who no longer want to confront the economic and political barriers to entering the national mediascape. Losing sight of local and national realities, and ceasing to intervene, even accepting the commercialization of the conventional media structure, is a major political risk. Even if this new, on-line media space can serve to create an unprecedented communication network for social stakeholders with converging interests who are prepared to mobilize on a global level, other levels such as the national and the local remain pertinent.

In the face of this technology with seemingly limitless potential for public access, some of the historical benefits that were hard won by community media activists are seriously endangered. The deregulation of community television in Canada is one example, and the lack of mobilization in response to this policy shift demonstrates just how fragile the intervention culture of the social groups and movements in this field is. For this reason, the development of these new digital devices and networks has resuscitated the questions raised with respect to conventional media—specifically, the matter of the exclusion of certain stakeholders.

Although the Internet remains, in fact, a means of communication that imposes few barriers to entry as a result of the relatively modest capital needs— at least compared to print media, radio, and television—this does not necessarily mean that access to this emerging public sphere is more equitable for most citizens. Communicating over the Internet requires a minimum amount of computer knowledge and Web sites still require considerable resources (material, capital, human) for content production. Moreover, access to the Internet is still very limited in most countries of the world, a shortcoming which groups dedicated to popular education in Quebec, such as Communautique,[25] are attempting to overcome.

This does not mean that the independent media on the Internet are secondary as such. On the contrary, the Internet is the battlefield that provides coverage for various theaters for social mobilization, both locally and internationally. The development of the Independent Media Centers (IMC) network, better known as Indymedia, created in Seattle in 1999 in the rush of antiglobalization activities, is a good example.[26] However, working to maintain traditional forms of community media, and keeping local, regional, and national communities involved in the effort, is key if community voices are to be heard and the right to communicate maintained and enlarged. The Centre for Media Alternatives—Québec (CMAQ) and the Réseau des médias alternatifs du Québec (RMA)—are two Quebec-based initiatives to do just that.

Created within the international cooperative NGO Alternatives, the Centre for Media Alternatives—Québec (cmaq.net) project joined the Indymedia network in 2000, becoming Quebec Indymedia. A complex mixture of radical counter-information and political activism specific to grassroots movements, the phenomenon of Indymedia combines the skillful deployment of digital network technologies with a horizontal and multilateral mode of organization. Here, media activism is characterized by a multilocal, multilinguistic, multimedia, decentralized, and nonhierarchical approach. It entails the establishment of a global, open-publishing press agency, which is intended to disseminate information and opinions that can be transmitted more easily by means of a decentralized digital network such as the Internet than by means of the traditional media, which are confined to specific territories and whose use is subject to strict regulation. Moreover, considering organizational form as a political gesture, Indymedia defends consensus decision making.[27]

In this context, CMAQ was designed to provide alternative coverage of the Summit of the Americas, held in Quebec City in April 2001. The core idea was to allow citizens to film, record, write, and publish their contributions through a decentralized, open platform so that they could testify to public resistance to the Free Trade Area of the Americas (FTAA).

CMAQ, then, was developed at the crossroads of two identifiable trends in the Internet activist movement, which were consolidated at the end of the 1990s. First, there is the tradition of community activism, a tradition close to the hearts of the alternative Quebec community media and which positions the Internet in a historical sequence of media technologies (print, radio, TV, video, etc.). This tradition is critical of the dramatic influence of the economic concentration of the media and the control of corporate power over the Internet and thus promotes alternative practices with digital technologies and open-source software. The second trend is part of a series of sporadic, anticapitalistic activities and mobilizations that continue to grow in number around the world, using network technologies. This trend is one of radical rupture. It is strongly guided by the principles of freedom of speech as evoked in the First Amendment of the American Constitution. These activists serve specifically as watchdogs over government institutions, a practice that has strong roots in the United States where Indymedia initially developed.[28]

With more than 1,000 contributors and a self-managed collective of about twenty active members, CMAQ provides an alternative to the mass media. Employing a democratic and horizontal structure, activists engaged in the communications process can transmit their own ideas instantaneously and debate them collectively. The success of this project does not depend solely on its open-publishing Web site. In fact, those who created the center have conducted educational workshops criticizing the media and organized a community life around the project, particularly by holding discussion sessions and cultural or social activities.

Unlike most of the approximately one hundred sites that belong to the Indymedia network, CMAQ always intended to maintain a singular identity, with strong roots in its community. As a result, the collective decided to become independent of the NGO alternatives and, to some extent, from the Indymedia network itself, incorporating as a nonprofit organization, managing its own server and funding its activities by offering e-mail and Web site hosting services. In this way, CMAQ has worked to position itself as an alternative to the alternative. Its webmasters have acquired experience by developing open-source code (weaving their own code) and particular software solutions.

Characterized by openness to all progressive political trends, opposed either directly or indirectly to the neoliberal agenda, CMAQ has managed to attract content from extremely diverse sources, in terms of both subject matter and the perspectives from which they are engaged. The center has a deliberate international focus, maintaining a site in three languages (French, English, and Spanish) and closely monitoring social and political developments in Northern and Southern countries, particularly events in Latin America.

For the past three years, in addition to mobilizing around the meetings held by multilateral organizations such as the WTO, the IMF, the World Bank, and the G8, CMAQ has sent a delegation of media activists to the World Social Forum (WSF), held in Porto Alegre in Brazil and Mumbai in India. At each WSF, an independent media room is set up. CMAQ volunteers have contributed to this as well as to efforts to set up local media production facilities. Each of these actions incorporates an international as well as a local dimension. The Global CN (globalcn.org) event, organized in October 2002 by the World Forum on Community Networking in Montreal, and the organization of a mini-WTO meeting in Montreal in July 2003, gave CMAQ militants two prime opportunities to make a content production space available to the community.

According to CMAQ, the combination of idealistic technical thinking, anarchistic political and social thinking, and community activism makes it possible to create a sustainable mediascape that cannot be dissociated from social mobilization and the intensive use of digital communication tools. This is particularly notable since the media activists at CMAQ and similar collectives have appropriated and learned to handle communication tools that correspond to their values of self-organization and self-management.

In recent years, several conferences and meetings have been organized for alternative media, based essentially on the idea of launching a national alternative newspaper[29] or evoking a possible coalition of alternative media. With this in mind, CMAQ called for a "Convergence of independent media" in May of 2002, in order to share the idea of developing a network for independent radio, newspapers, and video workers and, in January 2003, the Réseau des médias alternatifs du Québec (RMA) was created. The network's first accomplishment, the Web portal for alternative media (reseaumedia.info), was launched during an information and activity week devoted to alternative media.[30] The primary characteristics of this network are that it is informal, open to the four media sectors (print, radio, TV/video, Internet) and promotes participatory communication for the people, by the people.

The RMA boasts thirty members after one year of operation. These alternative media are nonprofit grassroots ventures advocating cooperation over competition. In print, for instance, it counts on the input of the satirical newspaper *Le Couac* and the street newspaper *l'Itinéraire*; in radio, the multilingual Radio Centre-Ville and the student-run CHOQ FM; in video and TV, the Montreal video activist collective Les Lucioles and the regional community TV station TVCBF. On the Internet, the network reaches out to groups such as the Indymedia Quebec collective CMAQ and feminist Web portal Cybersolidaires.

Also known as Réseaumedia, the RMA is organized in a decentralized manner and uses Internet-based technologies. For example, the network uses groupware that is accessible to all members everywhere. It contains information concerning the constitution of the network, minutes, its charter, as well as a list of members and their contact information. An e-mail distribution list is used to coordinate the working committees and communicate at little cost.

The Web portal includes the major headlines for each medium registered. The mosaic presented is a double demonstration of the group's desire to practice the right to communicate through the creation of an alternative mediascape, and the desire to ensure a plurality in the information that is being provided. The convergence of several types of media on a single Internet site demonstrates the versatility of the platform. This type of network must be viewed as a cooperative space; each stakeholder contributes in his own manner, in a collective effort to exchange content, experiences, skills, and expertise.

The Internet portal uses streaming to disseminate radio programs and videos produced by collectives of committed videographers. The cybermedia are able to "syndicate" their content, which means that the submissions are simultaneously updated on the specific media site in question as well as on the portal. The written media use the portal to complement their hardcopy publication, enhancing visibility and their contribution to the network.

This new form of network is not, however, solely linked on-line. Monthly meetings are necessary to develop a true community. A virtual community is not enough for organizing and implementing a veritable alternative media strategy. Community members feel a need to see one another, to debate and discuss in face-to-face communication. This has been observed and expressed by many media activists who seek to create and sustain a true sense of complicity and solidarity between individuals who are not always likeminded and come from different walks of life.

The charter of the RMA stipulates, moreover, that one of the organization's two principal objectives remains the exchange of services among RMA members for the benefit of developing a true community of alternative media. The other major objective is to reach out to a large community audience, who may know little or nothing about the alternative, autonomous, and independent media. This joining of forces based on shared affinities and technological synergies might well result in an alternative mediascape, with a goal to influence the larger public sphere.

As a result, the media that were initially closed off in their own medium-specific sectors are coming out of their isolation and learning to find inspiration in the experiences of other, similar media practitioners. Moreover, a large number of these media groups have already undertaken reciprocal joint efforts and projects which, without a network of solidarity, would possibly have taken longer to emerge. By gathering a plurality of dispersed media and media sectors, CMAQ is playing the role of catalyst, in forming a coalition of media resistance fronts.

CONCLUSION: THE NECESSARY COALITION OF MEDIA RESISTANCE FRONTS

Paradoxically, while technological advances make the multiplication and variety of channels of communication possible, from an economic or regulatory point of view, we are witnessing a reduction in the actual capacities of citizens to develop their own media, in keeping with their need for expression and collective organization.[31] The current wave of neoliberalism embedded in communication policies is threatening the survival and development of community, independent, and noncommercial media. Survival and development rely increasingly on the political support of civil society for the principle of community and democratic appropriation of communication technologies. In fact, only strong community mobilization will engender a regulatory framework that supports autonomous community media. This should be combined with a joint initiative on the part of all community media. This is essential for breaking out of their isolation and ensuring a solid framework for setting aside the marginality in which authorities prefer to relegate them. It is necessary to make the case that the quality of democratic life requires the democratization of the media, in order to prevent public communication spaces from falling completely under the control of market logic and the power of private corporations.

Moreover, action to protect and develop community media must be combined with other fronts of resistance to neoliberal market forces and rally other sectors that are committed to the democratization of communication.[32] These fronts, or fields, of resistance provide a basis for a broad social coalition with the democratization of communication as its political underpinning.[33] Some of the fronts that might be combined here are listed below.

The first is the *institutional front*. Groups or organizations working at this level are characterized by lobbying and political intervention at the state level. It aims at reforming the legal and political framework of institutions. Then there is the *organizational front*, which consists of progressive and creative initiatives developed by labor and professional groups within commercial or public mass media. The *alternative front* represents the struggle to develop autonomous, participative, and democratic media. The *educational front* includes media literacy and actions of media consumer groups. And, finally, the *academic front* encourages critical research on information, culture, and communication. We can add to this list the *cultural front*, which has been organized more recently around the defense and maintenance of cultural diversity.

The convergence of these diverse forms of action is all the more necessary since it permits each party, in its own manner and in keeping with its particular experience, to work toward developing alternative public spheres that favor the exercise of the right to communicate. Thus, it is all the more essential to develop a global and critical approach with respect to democratization projects, taking into consideration the various economic, legal, political, technological, and cultural dimensions that their deployment implies in the current context of globalization.

The decline of public debate in the field of broadcasting and telecommunications throughout the world reflects the growth in the power of capital and the shrinking of political culture. Since the balance of power is on the side of the global market, there is a concern that a balance between the representative logics will not be possible. If it is still possible to balance the notions of market and common good, it will require a return to the politicization of communication, in the sense that the definition and focus of communication will require public political choices that should not be reduced to private interests such as those that motivate the current neoliberal trend and endanger the attainment of social justice.

NOTES

This text has been translated by Sheryl Curtis.

1. Specifically, the Communication Rights in the Information Society (CRIS) campaign, launched in November 2001, is intended to mobilize civil organizations for the World Summit on the Information Society (WSIS) (http://www.crisinfo.org). See also the World Forum on Communication Rights (www.communicationrights.org), held in parallel with the WSIS and organized by the World Association of Community Radio Broadcasters (AMARC), the Association for Progressive Communication (APC), the CRIS secretariat, the World Association for Christian Communication (WACC), Peoples' Charter of Communication, etc.

2. Michel Sénécal, *L'espace médiatique. Les communications à l'épreuve de la démocratie* (Montréal: Liber, 1995).

3. Armand Mattelart, *Histoire de la société de l'information* (Paris: La Découverte coll. "Repères", 2003).

4. Ted Magder, "Franchising the Candy Store: Split-Run Magazines and a New International Regime for Trade in Culture," in *Canadian-American Public Policy* 34 (Apr 1998). <http://www .alanalexandroff.com/Magder.htm> (10 Dec. 2004).

5. Serge Latouche, "La mondialisation et la fin du politique: Diagnostic et perspectives," *La Revue du MAUSS* 1, no. 9 (1997): 137–50.

6. For a broader understanding, see the report of the *Centre d'Étude sur les Médias* (Laval University) on media concentration (in French only): "Portrait de la propriété dans le secteur de la télévision" <http://www.cem.ulaval.ca/ConcentrationCadre.html>

7. A stance also taken in June 2003 by the Federal Communications Commission (FCC) in the United States, which has since had to step back after more than two million citizens expressed opposition to this new focus and a federal appeal court suspended the implementation of this project. The FCC, chaired by Republican Michael K. Powell, is apparently inclined essentially to give preference to the industrial stakeholders with respect to reconsidering and possibly abolishing the rule that has prohibited cross-media ownership since 1975.

8. La Fédération Nationale des Communications (FNC-CSN), "Mémoire présenté au CRTC sur la Demande (2000-2309-4) présentée par Quebecor Média Inc. (QMI)," (March 2001). <http://www.fncom.org/accueil/memoire/m_mars_2001.htm> (22 July 2004).

9. Fédération des télévisions communautaires autonomes du Québec (FEDETVC), "La Télévision Communautaire, en Extinction de Voix!" (16 Dec. 1999) <www.fedetvc.qc.ca/Communiques/ Communique_1999_Decembre_VoixDextinction.doc> (22 July 2004).

10. Canoe.com, "Le CRTC se penche sur la transaction Quebecor-Videotron," 26 March 2001, <http://lcn.canoe.com/economie/nouvelles/archives/2001/03/20010326-001306.html> (23 June 2004).

11. Marc Raboy, *Accès inégal. Les canaux d'influence en radiodiffusion* (Sainte-Foy: Les Presses de l'Université du Québec, 1995).

12. Fabien Granjon and Dominique Cardon, "Mouvement altermondialiste et militantisme informationnel," (paper presented at the Association of Internet Researchers Conference, Toronto, On., October 2003).

13. Translation from French of "militantisme informationnel et communicationnel."

14. David Held, "Democracy and the International Order," in *Cosmopolitan Democracy: An Agenda for the New World Order*, eds. David Held and Daniele Archibugi (Cambridge: Polity Press, 1995), 96–120; John Keane, *The Media and Democracy* (Cambridge: Polity Press, 1991).

15. In this respect, it must be said that if, during the '70s–'80s, the community television stations came into being partially as a result of the development of cable technology and technical advances in portable videotape recording, radio stations had recourse to recording,

processing and broadcasting technologies that were more accessible in terms of both costs and use. The same applies to the digital technologies for data acquisition, processing and networking that can be used today to explore new ways in which to handle communication.

16. Nevertheless, they have shown little inclination to date to form alliances with other, less institutionalized groups.

17. Although the number of community radio stations in Quebec has changed little since the 1980s, the CRTC did however grant licenses to student radio stations CKUT (1987) and CISM (1991), one associated with McGill University and the other with the Université de Montréal. Since these radio stations are associated with universities, they are generally located in urban settings. They enjoy a certain independence with respect to government and commercial structures as a result of their status as university radio stations, and are partly funded by student contributions. This arrangement is not without obligations, of course. These two campus radio stations are members of the NCRA (National Campus Radio Association), which has its head office in Montreal.

18. This federation is the result of a series of groups formed in the community TV sector: the RTCL (Regroupement des télévisions communautaires et locales), which grew out of the 1988 merger of the ROCCQ (Regroupement des organismes de communication communautaire du Québec), created in 1978, and the ATVQ, founded at the start of the 1980s by community television stations in the Montreal region.

19. Association des Radiodiffuseurs Communautaires du Québec (ARCQ), "Proposition de cadre stratégique pour les médias communautaires," *Réponse à avis public CRTC 2001-129* (February 2002).; Fédération des Télévisions Communautaires Autonomes du Québec (FEDETVC), *Allocution sur l'étude de l'état du système canadien de radiodiffusion,* presented to the Canadian Heritage standing committee, (March 19, 2002). Although it was possible for private networks to set up operations in certain regions as a result of a local media network that was already in place and well established in the area, they could still develop further through acquisition strategies.

20. UNESCO, *Voix multiples un seul monde* (Paris: UNESCO, 1980).

21. Herbert I. Schiller, *Communications and Cultural Domination* (New York: International Arts and Science Press, 1976).

22. Alain Ambrosi, "Difficile émergence des réseaux de communication démocratique dans l'espace politique global," in *Vers une citoyenneté simulée. Médias, réseaux et mondialisation,* dir. Serge Proulx et André Viatlis (Rennes: Apogée, 1999), 99–122.

23. Videazimut has since ceased its operations.

24. See John Keane, "Structural Transformations of the Public Sphere," *The Communication Review,* 1, no. 1 (1995). For instance, in Canada, the CRTC decided in 1999 not to regulate the Internet, since most of the material contained on the Internet is not considered relevant to broadcasting in the meaning provided in the Broadcasting Act and because Canadians were already major content producers on the World Wide Web.

25. In 2002, Communautique has launched the Quebec's Citizen Internet Platform to promote the use of Internet tools by and for social groups and the general public (www .communautique.qc.ca).

26. Dorothy Kidd, "Indymedia.org: The Development of Communication Commons," *Democratic Communiqué* 18. (Summer 2002).

27. Scott Uzelman, "Catalyzing Participatory Communication: Independent Media Centre and the Politics of Direct Action," unpublished Masters' Thesis (Burnaby: Simon Fraser University, 2002).; John Downing, "Independent Media Centres: A Multi-local, Multi-media Challenge to Global Neo-liberalism," in *Global Media Policy in the New Millennium,* ed. Marc Raboy, (Luton: University of Luton Press, 2002), 215–32.

28. Bram Dov Abramson, "The Politics of Broadband: Virtual Networking and the Right to Communicate," in *Global Media Policy in the New Millennium,* ed. Marc Raboy (Luton: University of Luton Press, 2002), 233–50.

29. See the resolutions adopted at the conference *La presse alternative à la Une*, organized by the magazine Recto Verso, in partnership with the Service aux collectivités at the Université du Québec à Montréal (UQÀM). Fall 2001.

30. The RMA managed to mobilize about thirty alternative media during the week of September 2 to October 2, 2003, at UQÀM. This gave hundreds of university students an opportunity to ask questions about these practices and discuss them with media workers.

31. Michel Sénécal, "La part réduite de l'appropriation collective : vers un déficit démocratique de l'espace médiatique," in *Vers une citoyenneté simulée. Médias, réseaux et mondialisation*, dir. Serge Proulx and André Vitalis, (Rennes: Apogée, 1999),183–203.

32. Michael Warner, *Publics and Counterpublics* (New York: Zone Books, 2001), 334.

33. Rafael Roncagliolo, "Las nuevas technologies pueden contrarrestar la homogeneizacion," *Corto Circuito* no. 7 (April 1989); Jean-Pierre Boyer, "Marchandisation ou démocratisation? - Pour une 'poléthique' de la communication sociale," in *Petits écrans et démocratie*, ed. N. Thede and A. Ambrosi (Paris: Syros-Alternatives, 1992), 249–58; Marc Raboy and Peter Bruck, eds., *Communication For and Against Democracy* (Montreal: Black Rose Press, 1989), 3–16; Robert Hackett, "Taking Back the Media: Notes on the Potential for a Communicative Democracy Movement," *Studies in Political Economy* (Fall 2000): 61–86.

13

Canadian Cyberactivism in the Cycle of Counterglobalization Struggles

Nick Dyer-Witheford

While the growth of corporate media empires is a salient feature of North American mediascapes, so too is the search for ways to elude or explode this dominant information regime. One direction of this search is the emergence of "cyberactivism"—the use of the Internet by movements contesting the established relations of social power. Cyberactivism, so defined, is a contradictory phenomenon, embracing Net-use by left and right, fascists and ecologists, feminists and fundamentalists.[1] But perhaps its most significant manifestations arise from a sequence of global struggles against the institutions of the world market waged by a transnational opposition that I will term the "counterglobalization" movement. This chapter examines counterglobalizing cyberactivism in a context that richly reveals its possibilities and problems—Canada.

GLOBALIZATION, COUNTERGLOBALIZATION, AND THE ELECTRONIC FABRIC OF STRUGGLE

At the end of twentieth century, the collapse of state socialism, growth of multinational corporations, expansion of financial markets, innovation in communication and transportation, and widespread hegemony of neoliberal economic policies seemed to throw the operations of the world market to a new level of extension and intensification. "Globalization" was the code word by which this was announced and applauded, a euphemism for the supposedly inevitable worldwide triumph of capitalism.

Quite unanticipated by proponents of "globalization" was the scope and depth of opposition its processes would elicit. Trades unions feared capital's mobility threatened wages and working conditions; ecologists that it allowed business to escape environmental regulation; citizen's groups that it destabilized welfare states and undermined the very concept of national sovereignty; the poor that, for all these reasons, it would make them poorer.

From these sources sprung a sequence of uprisings, beginning in the global South with the anti-IMF riots of the late 1980s, passing to anti–free trade movements in the global North, and spiraling around the planet with increasing velocity from the jungles of Chiapas to the streets of Paris, and from Seattle to Prague to La Paz. This upwelling of opposition combined many points of resistance, some taking aim at the practices of specific companies such as Nike, Monsanto, or McDonalds, others challenging the overarching policies of neoliberalism, and yet others taking aim at institutions such as the IMF (international Monetary Fund), World Bank, and World Trade Organization.[2]

Characterizing this newest social movement has proved difficult for friends, foes, and sociologists alike. It is "anticorporate," in that it takes aim at the massive multinational conglomerates; its more radical elements are "anticapitalist," challenging the overall logic of a social system based on general commodification. Opponents, and some participants, call it an "antiglobalization" movement. But while certain sectors are nationalist, fundamentalist, ethnocentric, and/or economically protectionist, others are committed to global intercourse, albeit on a basis radically different from neoliberalism. They are in favor of "fair trade" rather than "free trade," or of a globalism that "levels up" rather than "a race to the bottom."[3] Some activists speak of an "other," or "higher" globalization, a "new internationalism," a "global justice" movement; a "globalization from below"; many refer to an emergent "global civil society"; yet others of an uprising of "the multitude" against the "empire" of the world market.[4] I call this new activism the "counterglobalization movement," encompassing a tension between the "antiglobalization" elements (*counter*globalization) and "alternative globalization" (counter*globalization*) components.

The counterglobalization movement renews a "cycle of struggles" that has characterized the history of capitalism. That is to say, it represents a new phase in a perennial conflict between capitalism and its creative, exploited subjects that is constantly shifting in its forms, manifestation, and the strategies of the antagonists. "Primitive capitalism" saw fights over enclosure and commons, slavery, and the Luddite challenges to machine domination; "industrial capitalism" generated the classic conflict with the mass worker's socialist, social democratic, and trades union movements; and the revolts of the 1990s mark the ignition of a new wave of contestation against "global capital." The concept of a cycle of struggles permits recognition that, rather than being made once over, the forces pushing for an exodus from capitalism perpetually transform themselves.[5]

One aspect of this transformation is the emergence of digital communication networks as a major factor in the collision between world capital and the counterglobalization movement. Global marketization would be unthinkable without telecommunications and computer networks that now circulate money, commodities, and power. On the other hand, counterglobalization movements also use digital networks- to raise awareness of their concerns, to organize protests, and for forms of action, ranging from e-mail lobbying to "hacktivism."[6] As Harry Cleaver observes of the single most famous example of cyberactivism—the use of the Internet to call world attention to the Zapatista revolt in Mexico—counterglobalization movements have woven an "electronic fabric of struggle."[7] While many activists are enthusiastic about these digital prospects, others are more skeptical—controversies to which we return in our conclusion. But first, we examine the Canadian patches in the electronic fabric of struggle.

CANADIAN CONTENT

In Canada, social-democratic, labor, feminist, environmental, and nationalist movements have contested globalization in a society with one of the highest rates of digital connection in the world. As part of the North American telecommunications hub, Canada is more "wired" than most of the rest of the world, while its domestic politics place it further "left" than the United States. This equation renders it the site of a very intense convergence between counterglobalization and cyberactivism.

From 1987, the date of the Canada-U.S. Free Trade Agreement, Canada's governing political parties of the right and center have always embraced neoliberal policies in office, even if oscillating in opposition. But these policies have been repeatedly challenged. Counterglobalization sentiment has flourished because neoliberal "free trade," with its associated logic of privatization and deregulation, threatens an array of Canadian welfare state institutions (public health care, broadcasting, and education systems), while the risk of job flight to the southern United States, Mexico, or farther afield also menaces a residual Fordist "social contract" between capital and labor. These issues are entwined to Canadian nationalist sentiment and a historical suspicion of the United States that makes "Washington consensus" globalization a hot-button issue—although in Quebec it has often been seen as an opportunity for Francophone leverage against Anglophone domination, and there are other important regional variations.

Though social democratic traditions and trades unions have been critical in generating opposition to neoliberalism, the Canadian counterglobalization movement (like those everywhere else on the planet) involves other, often far more radical, dissenting forces: feminist and environmental movements, the activism of indigenous peoples and of immigrant communities involved in a contested multiculturalism and linked to social struggles across the globe, urban youth and student movements grappling with McJobs and endless debt. Many of these groups have little reason to be nostalgic about the Canadian national welfare state to which they had never been fully dealt in, but plenty of cause to suspect even worse from a borderless pan-capitalism. The interplay of these forces added up to a rich, if inchoate, brew of counter-globalization tendencies

A central concern of nearly all these elements has been the filtering of social communication by corporate media empires. Four issues, already well discussed by other contributors to this volume, can be briefly mentioned: (a) *The influence of U.S. media*, whose transborder flows of news and entertainment both ignore Canadian issues and have a pronouncedly corporate skew. (b) A series *of mergers and acquisitions in Canadian domestic media*, typified by the activities of Canada's home-grown media moguls, Conrad Black and the Asper family, a process again narrowing the spectrum of public discourse in a pro-business direction. (c) *The crisis of Canadian public service media*, embodied in the Canadian Broadcasting Corporation, which, having established an expectation that the mediascape should include non-U.S. and noncorporate sources, was itself threatened by budget cuts and right-wing attacks. (d) Countering the previous three points, a tradition of Canadian experimentation with *alternative media*—in the press, in community radio ventures, in video-activism, and in independent film.

Cyberactivism was both an extension of these earlier lines of media activism and a breach if them since it involved a new set of digital skills whose acquisition tended to be generational. What made the exploration of computer networking attractive and possible for social activists was the rapid diffusion of computer and Internet use in Canada. In 1987 (the first year for which Statistics Canada reports figures), 20 percent of Canadian households had a computer, in 2001 60 percent did; 7.4 percent had in-home Internet connection in 1996, but 50 percent in 2001, with higher numbers connecting from work, school, university, and public libraries.[8] These figures are broadly comparable with those for the United States, although Canadian rates of broadband connection are higher. By comparison, in 2001, the UK had Internet in 33 percent of households, Germany in about 25 percent and France in 20 percent of homes. Only a handful of countries in Asia, Africa, and Latin America have connection rates of over 10 percent of households, and in very many the percentage is miniscule.[9]

There are, of course, huge disparities in access between different sectors of Canadian society.[10] As elsewhere across the world, income remains the single most reliable predictor of connection, in combination with a rapidly shifting mix of gender, age and ethnicity, and urbanism. Cyberspace has historically been gender-biased, with use of the Internet by women and girls only matching (or perhaps even exceeding) that of men and boys in the later 1990s in North America. There are important regional differences, with rates of connection lowest in Quebec—a reflection of the hegemony of English in cyberspace—and higher in urban rather rural areas. The continued existence of multiple digital divides continues, as we will see, to pose serious dilemmas for Canadian cyberactivists in "global justice" movements. Nonetheless, over the very period when such movements were coalescing in Canada, Internet access and digital know-hows were becoming widespread.

NORTHERN NETWORKS

Although this quantitative diffusion of computers and connectivity was dramatic, numbers alone conceal qualitative shifts in cyber-culture, whose history can itself be seen as a hyperaccelerated cycle of appropriations and counterappropriations by different social agencies at the blinding speed of Net time. We can schematize five stages in this process, though these overlap: (i) *Military* development of computer communications during the 1960s and '70s by the U.S. Defense Department, seeking command and control systems for nuclear war. (ii) Civilian takeover and extension of the network by an *academic-hacker* culture in the 1980s, spilling over into virtual community experiments that pushed the Net onto a trajectory of exponential growth. (iii) Mounting *government* interest—marked by the U.S. 1992 "information highway" initiative—in digital networks as a means of accelerating economic growth and cutting social costs. (iv) Belated *corporate* recognition of the commercial possibilities of the Net, intensifying from 1995 on, and launching an increasingly frenzied e-business drive that would culminate in the dot.com boom and its dramatic bust in 2000. (v) *Resistant and alternative* net use, from cyberactivism to open source software to peer to peer networks, exploding simultaneously with phases (iii) and (iv), involving a molecular proliferation of technohobbyists, artists, pirates, activists, media guerrillas, and cypherpunks, creating a "hydra-headed" world of anticommercial net practices.[11]

The very first, military-industrial stage of Internet history touched Canada only indirectly, through its involvement in NORAD, an air defense system crucial to the U.S. nuclear war-fighting systems. But from then on Canadians were involved in all phases of Net history. Researchers at the Universities of Toronto, British Columbia, Alberta and McGill contributed to the early culture of shared protocols and open access; Canadians were enthusiastic users of bulletin boards such as FidoNet and also participated extensively in the brief North American flowering of "Freenets" or nonprofit community networks. As Susan Bryant and Richard Smith observe, "virtually all of this effort was produced on a nonprofit, voluntary basis or as part of research projects at universities."[12] This widening arena of voluntary cyber-*activity* was by no means explicitly cyber-*activist*; most of the new netizens were on-line for academic, social, or leisure interests. But some saw virtual communication as a new dimension of social mobilization.

Amongst these were members of the Canadian labor movement. Eric Lee, the historian of labor on the net, credits the British Columbia Teachers Federation as the first trades union to, in 1981, use computer communication to link officers and shop stewards of locals, a step inspired by the typically Canadian problem of organizing over vast distances. Other Canadian unions followed suit.[13] The Canadian Union of Public Employee's Solinet was an early experiment of the possibilities of trade union networking.[14] Other initiatives were more informal: for many years the email news service operated by Sid Shniad, the research officer British Columbia Telecommunications Workers Union, was an important resource for Canadian activists in numerous different movements. The primary thrust of electronic labor organizing was usually the facilitation of trades unions' internal organization. But it also opened onto wider horizons; Canadian e-activists were involved in the projects for internationalist labor e-communication, and at attempts at coordinating actions of international solidarity with imprisoned trades unionist and embattled strikers, from Liverpool to Seoul to Moscow.

In other types of e-activism the current of influence flowed from the United States, with a mingled stream of counter-cultural politics and digital knowledge running from San Francisco to Vancouver being particularly important. In 1984 Silicon Valley activists founded Peace Net, linking social-justice, antiwar, and human-rights movements. Its coalition with related initiatives—Eco-Net, Conflict Net, Green Net, LaborNet and Women's Net—eventually created the Association for Progressive Communications (APC). Supported by charitable foundations and by the United Nations Development Program, APC provided discussion forums, new services, and technical support for social movements in numerous countries.

Canadians' link to the APC was Web Networks, an ISP founded in 1987 that for nine years operated on a nonprofit basis, providing service to some 3,500 organizations and individuals. APC networks were used by environmental and indigenous groups opposing Hydro-Quebec's Great Whale Hydroelectric Project, by protestors against right-wing provincial governments in Ontario, and by the green activists halting logging in British Columbia's Clayquot Sound.[15] But, as Rory O'Brian, a Canadian APC activist and "techie" notes, the high-water mark of APC activism was its coordination of networking services for NGOs at the series of global summits convened by the United Nations from the 1992 "Earth Summit" on Environment and Development in Rio, to the 1995 United Nations World Conference on Women. At these events, the APC's role in providing a "communications venues for disseminating official government policy documents, background reports, and negotiating stances of the NGOs, "made it apparent that "the use of computer communications . . . gave an identity and power to the international coalitions of organizations . . . that they had never experienced before."[16]

The forums of APC, and other early cyberactivist exchanges such as ACTIVE-L, a North American activist listserv, carried the messages and manifestoes of environmentalists, feminists, indigenous peoples, and trades unionists—groups with different agendas and often in conflict with one another. Yet this untidy electronic cohabitation encouraged shared initiatives and informational cross-overs. Common cyberspaces implicitly asserted interconnections, even though participants might still be searching for the explicit formulation of such links. This convergence would soon be deepened by the struggle against "free trade."

SOUTHERN EXPOSURES: NAFTA AND APEC

The late 1980s and early '90s saw two related policy developments in Canada, one "cyberspatial," the other "terrestrial." The "cyberspatial" development entailed state promotion and management of the unforeseen growth of the Internet. In the United States, the Clinton-Gore "information highway" initiative was facilitating commercial development of digital networks through subsidization and deregulation; Canada followed suit through the programs and consultations of the Information Highway Advisory Council. The "terrestrial" policy initiative was Canada's participation in a series of trade liberalization agreements—the 1987 Canadian-American Free Trade Agreement, the 1992 NAFTA (the North American Free Trade Agreement), and, simultaneously, regional and global negotiations such as those for APEC (Asia Pacific Economic Cooperation), GATT (General Agreement on Tariffs and Trade) and the (WTO) World Trade Organization. Seemingly distinct, these two developments actually associated. Policy elites' interest in managing digital networks arose in part from their desire to assure a communications infrastructure adequate to the financial and commodity flows anticipated from trade liberalization. Free trade and information highways were both facets of what Vincent Mosco and Dan Schiller term "integrating North America for cybercapitalism."[17]

This process also, however, partially integrated struggles within and against cybercapitalism. The "borderless" logic of free trade had implications for labor standards, environmental regulation, social programs, and a wide range of other issues. Opposition therefore encouraged the formation of broad, diverse coalitions, involving trade unions, greens, welfare state defenders, and citizens rights groups, and gave a powerful impetus to the regional and multinational connection of these coalitions. This process rested on exchanges and connections of all kinds—among which computer-communications was one important part.

When the negotiation of the U.S.-Canada Free Trade Agreement detonated a controversy in the midst of a Canadian election campaign in 1987, opposition to the deal not only generated the Pro-Canada Network, later renamed Action Canada Network, but also saw the establishment of the first free trade conference on the APC, "webfreetrade." for which the major suppliers of information and analysis were Canadian environmental and public interest research groups.[18] The scope of such discussion was radically enlarged five years later, when the North American Free Trade Agreement (NAFTA) saw the inclusion of Mexico in a continental trade deal.

NAFTA rapidly encountered resistance in all three countries. But co-ordination of a trilateral opposition faced serious obstacles. In the United States and Canada the anti–free trade movement often tended toward a nationalist protectionism focused on walling out competition from "cheap" Mexican labor. Development of a more internationalist perspective, based on supporting Southern struggles for improved labor and social conditions and linking trade policy to issues such as debt relief, depended on contact with and understanding of Mexican social movements.

In the event, the anti-NAFTA struggles generated many cross-border activist exchanges, including both on the ground contacts, particularly visits to *maquiladoras* by U.S. and Canadian workers, and a circulation of newsletters and journals, videos, and alternative radio and television broadcasts. Despite relatively low levels of Mexican Internet connection, computer networking, sometimes accompanied by technical assistance from Northern NGOs, was an important part of this process. John Brenner and Fredrick Howard have both made inventories of the anti-NAFTA organizations using online communication.[19] These include the North American Worker-to-Worker Network, supporting the connections, within and without official union frameworks, between U.S., Canadian and Mexican workers in the automobile, telecommunications, and electronics sectors, feminist organizations, such as Mujer a Mujer, which organized a Tri-National Working Women's Conference on NAFTA whose reports were posted on-line, and environmental such as the Pesticide Action network and Greenpeace.

Although the anti-NAFTA coalitions mobilized a depth of opposition entirely unexpected by neoliberals, they failed to stop the deal. But their cross-sectoral and transcontinental organizing seriously checked the chauvinist element in North American opposition to free trade, and it opened pathways for future cross-border connections, including electronic ones, such as the Canadian-based Maquiladora Solidarity Network, which to this day tracks labor, environmental, and human rights abuses along the US-Mexico border using e-mail alerts. Perhaps the most significant legacy of NAFTA cyberactivism was, however, its unwitting preparation of the electronic terrain for the uprising of the Zapatistas.

The Mayan peasant revolt of the EZLN (Ejército Zapatista de Liberacion Nacional) against the Mexican government in 1994—a revolt that specifically denounced capitalist globalization as the culmination of a centuries-long dispossession of the people of Chiapas—is one whose virtual dimension is now well known.[20] The (apocryphal) story of Subcommandante Marcos inputting dispatches on a laptop plugged to the lighter socket of an old pickup truck has entered the realm of digital folklore, and the (real) success of Zapatista supporters in using the Net to attract international attention to their insurrection, and prevent its immediate military repression, is a counterglobalization landmark. There are, however, two aspects of this story of direct relevance to Canadian cyberactivism, one to do with the preconditions for Zapatista cyberactivism, the other with its consequences.

In his analysis of the EZLN's "electronic fabric of struggle," Cleaver suggests its success was largely due to the tissue of Internet activism established during the NAFTA campaigns.[21] These created a set of forums and discussions on the APC and Usenet news already alert to news about social struggles in Mexico, in which the significance of Marcos's bulletins was immediately understood, and through which they were rediffused, accompanied by additional information, analysis, and discussion, into other parts of the Internet, and from thence into left-wing newspapers, magazines, and radio stations, and, eventually, into the mainstream press.[22] The phenomenon of "Zapatistas in cyberspace" did not fall from the sky, but emerged on the basis of a lacework of cyber connections already established by U.S., Mexican, and Canadian activists.

Conversely, however, the Zapatista example had a galvanizing effect on counterglobalization activism in general, and especially cyberactivism. In the 1996 First International Encounter for Humanity and against Neoliberalism—one of a series of *encuentros* organized by the EZLN to stimulate global opposition to neoliberalism—Zapatista representatives called for the creation of an "intercontinental network of alternative communication against neoliberalism, an intercontinental network of alternative communication for humanity."[23] Zapatismo and its "Ya Basta" World Wide Web site inspired a wealth of Web sites and of discussion about the possibilities of Internet mobilization. The bulletin boards and Web sites associated with Chiapas became the points for a convergence of communication about other struggles, particularly those of indigenous peoples threatened by global capital, such as the Ogoni, battling Shell Oil in Nigeria, and the East Timorese, resisting occupation by an Indonesian government well-supported by multinational corporations interested in one of Asia's most populous and resource-rich markets.[24]

The dynamics of free trade very shortly threw the East Timorese case into high Canadian profile. In 1997, the Organization for Asia-Pacific Economic

Cooperation, a regional free trade forum, convened in Vancouver, and was met by demonstrators. The protestors had a range of concerns, but a special focus was the presence of Indonesian president Suharto. This created an occasion to highlight the human rights abuses of a regime with which Canada had strong economic ties, including the imprisonment of labor and social activists, and the occupation of East Timor, where military repression on a genocidal scale had proceeded under a veil of quiet obscurity.

This veil was, however, beginning to shred, largely due to various types of media activism. British television journalists had filmed a massacre of student demonstrators in Dilli; Noam Chomsky and Edward Hermann's *Manufacturing Consent*, in text and film versions, exposed press silences about Timor.[25] At the same time, international solidarity groups, such as the East Timor Action Network (which had a particularly active chapter in Vancouver) had created numerous e-mail lists and Web sites that in turn drew on a range of net communications from Indonesian dissidents, including Timorese students using the Internet connections of Indonesian universities.[26]

The Vancouver APEC demonstration reflected this growing awareness of the underside of Indonesia's international economic connections. But when the RCMP pepper sprayed participants and preemptively arrested organizers, it also revealed the hazards of both street protest and cyberactivism. A CBC reporter, Terry Milewski, raised questions as to whether the Prime Minister's Office had ordered extreme security measures to protect the Indonesian delegation. In the course of his reporting, Milewski had an e-mail correspondence with an anti-APEC protester in which he referred to the police as "the forces of evil." This e-mail was unearthed by the Prime Minister's Office and used as evidence for a complaint to the CBC that Milewski was engaged in partisan reportage and "milking" the APEC issue. Although Milewski was eventually exonerated by a CBC ombudsperson, the immediate result of the complaint was to have him removed from covering the story.

The NAFTA protests, the Zapatistas in cyberspace, and the APEC incident all showed that anti–free trade organizing had acquired a virtual aspect. Although the Milewski incident demonstrated that this dimension carried hazards of surveillance, cyberactivism was enabling a circulation of news previously marginalized by mainstream media, and new transnational connections, both with allies in the well-wired United States, and also, on occasion, with activists in the global South. Counterglobalizers and globalizers alike were constructing cyberspatial infrastructures.

MULTITUDES ON LINE AND THE MAI-NOT

By the late 1990s the conditions of Internet activism, in Canada and throughout advanced capitalist society, were changing. In 1999 nearly a quarter of

Canadian households had in-home internet access, more than three times as many as three years previously. The World Wide Web protocols had converted a "geeky," unwieldy, text-based technology into a convenient, hyperlinked, and graphic medium. The Net was being transformed from a marginal experiment to a cultural power.

The forces driving this expansion did not, at first sight, seem propitious for cyberactivism. By the mid 1990s, business had belatedly woken up to the Internet, and the rush to commercially exploit the electronic frontier was on. Across North America massive corporate ISP's, such as America On-Line, and, in Canada, lesser entities such as Bell and Rogers, were selling Internet connection as a necessity of contemporary life; the banners, pop-ups, and mass spamming of e-advertisers were sweeping across the networks, and the mounting frenzy of the dot.com boom, exemplified for Canadians by the surging value of Nortel stocks, made the virtual a topic of delicious speculation.

Many left observers looked on this development with deep foreboding, anticipating the closing of any window of digital dissent by a familiar model of corporate domination. But these predictions proved incomplete. Commercialization of digital space did undercut initiatives such as the Freenets and specialized "activist" ISPs. At the same time, however, cybercapital increased the potential scope of activism—by enlarging the numbers it could reach, normalizing digital skills, and spreading to low-cost authoring tools. New groups, such as the Toronto-based Media Collective experimenting with a synthesis of hip hop culture, computer hacking, and anticorporate organization showed that e-activism was not fading, but changing.[27] Exposure to a capitalist e-culture was not merely producing branded consciousness and ideological conformity; in training an entire generation to surf, search, and design cyberspace it also disseminated a capacity to reappropriate and refunction elements of the digital milieu.

By the closing years of the decade a "multitude"—to use Hardt and Negri's phrase—of Canadian counterglobalization groups were using the Internet. Many were components of transnational mobilizations: anti-sweatshop struggles against Nike and the Gap; the Jubilee Third World debt abolition project, the Attac campaign against speculative financial capital were all multinationally networked organizations with strong Canadian involvement. Some of these initiatives started in Canada. In Winnipeg, the Rural Advancement Foundation International (RAFI), a clearing-house for transnational movements fighting biotechnological enclosures, used data-base searches to identify pending corporate patent claims, and disseminated its analysis via World Wide Web. In Vancouver, Adbusters, whose internationally famous campaigns against corporate advertising originated in West Coast environmentalism, took "culture jamming" on line. The most dramatic instance of Canadian cyberactivism in this period was, however, the battle against the Multilateral Agreement of Investment (MAI).

The MAI was intended as an agreement on the conditions of foreign investment amongst the powerful capitalist economies of the Organization for Economic Cooperation and Development (OECD). This projected treaty included major limitations on the powers of governments to support domestic industries, fund public services, or protect the environment if these measures contradicted the interests of foreign investors. Negotiations began in 1995, and, though not strictly secret, received almost no press attention, largely because they were depicted as technical and noncontroversial, and involved no consultation with public interest groups.

It was only after some two years that this cone of silence broke. NGO's, such as the Third World Network in Malaysia, began to ask questions. Disputes within the negotiating group started to appear. In spring of 1997 a draft text of the agreement was leaked—according to some reports, by the Canadian delegation. This found its way to the hands, and Web sites, of the Council of Canadians, which had emerged as the major Canadian public interest group contesting corporate globalization, and Ralph Nader's Global Trade Watch for Public Citizens, who denounced the negotiations as a stealth attack on state sovereignty and citizen rights. In response, the OECD released an official draft text on a special Web site, and attempted a conciliation of its critics, a step which, however, only clarified the degree of conflict, and precipitated a full-scale counterglobalization campaign to scuttle the MAI.

This was the first international campaign in which the do-it-yourself authoring capacity of the World Wide Web was fully deployed by activists, and Canadian groups were prominent. A study by Peter Jay Smith and Elizabeth Smythe enumerates 352 Web sites devoted to the MAI—the majority critical of it—and originating in more than 25 countries. Of these, seventy-one—17.6 percent— were originating in more than 25 countries. Of those originating more was the United States, with 129 sites, or 31.9 percent. As Smith and Smythe observe, "the significant number of U.S. sites is no surprise, but the relatively large number of Canadian sites, relative to population . . . is striking."[28]

The importance of Canadian cyberactivism is borne out by their more detailed analysis: when sites with more than 60 percent original content are ranked by national origin, the United States again emerges first, with 20, but Canada was second, with 16. The most frequently visited MAI-related site was the OECD's official page. But after this, occupying positions two to five, come four Canadian sites: MAI Not, originating from OPIRG (Ontario Public Interest Research Group), the National Centre for Sustainability, in Victoria, B.C.; Appleton, a law office in Toronto; and YUCC (the personal site of a York University law student). Also frequently visited were the Web sites of the Council of Canadians and the Canadian Centre for Policy Alternatives, making six of the ten most accessed sites Canadian.

The leak of the draft text and the anti-MAI campaign attracted sudden, wide media coverage. Net activism itself became part of the story; the Canadian *Globe and Mail* eagerly reported the assertion by Maude Barlow, chairwoman of the Council of Canadians, that, "If a negotiator says something to someone over a glass of wine, we'll have it on the Internet within an hour, all over the world."[29] As attention to the MAI intensified, the pressures on negotiators, and hence the splits amongst them, increased. Several governments commenced legislative hearings on the treaty, starting with Canada in the fall of 1997, followed by Australia, France, the United Kingdom, and the European Parliament. In December 1998 the French government withdrew from the MAI negotiations, sounding their death knell.

Many MAI proponents ascribed the debacle to cyberactivism. "This is the first successful Internet campaign by non-governmental organizations," said one diplomat. "It's been very effective."[30] The *Globe and Mail* declared that, "the OECD's efforts to harness the Internet have not caught up in color, content and consumer friendliness to those of the advocacy groups" and reported an official's rueful comment that it had failed on a "strategy on information, communication and explication."[31] Such an interpretation neglects the underlying causes of conflict between the OECD and the counterglobalization movements, the splits between negotiators, and the amount of very traditional, on-the-ground in-person organizing—meetings, marches, demonstrations, in the anti-MAI mobilization. Nonetheless, the circulation of information and analysis made possible by the Web had clearly been very important to campaigns that, as Smith and Smith observe "despite having virtually no access initially to mainstream media" was able to "articulate an alternative vision and critique of globalization which challenged the prevailing discourse in a number of OECD countries."[32] This challenge was very shortly to reerupt with unanticipated force.

INDYMEDIA: FROM SEATTLE TO QUEBEC CITY

The protests against the meetings of the WTO in Seattle in December of 1999 were a watershed in the emergence of the counterglobalization movement. Although there had been many massive, and violent, protests in the global South against the institutions of neoliberal globalism, the Seattle demonstrations marked a leap in the movement's "on the ground" presence in North America—a leap that threw authorities into disarray, and abruptly seized the attention of the mainstream media. Integral to this shift was a new phase of cyberactive practices, marked by the appearance of the Interdependent Media Centres (IMC).

The IMC network was created by a convergence of U.S. alternative media activists from groups such as Free Speech TV, Protest.net, Paper Tiger TV, and Deep Dish TV. Assisted by the WTO's choice of a host city that, as a center of information capital was also crawling with digital expertise, IMC organizers raised donations, registered the indymedia.org Web site, mustered volunteers and established a multimedia newsroom with computers, Internet lines, and digital editing systems using the innovative "Open Publishing" software that allowed anyone with a modem to upload real-time audio, video, texts, and photos.[33]

"Indymedia," as the IMC became known, built on earlier net activism, but bought to it a new sensibility. It was the creation of a generation of activists rendered intimately familiar with digital media by a capitalist youth culture built around Internet use, video games, and viral advertising, at home not only with the keyboard and modem but also with streaming video, digital photography, and MP3 audio. These activists had an exceptional "im-mmediacy" in their relation to media technologies and practices, a "media savvy" that knew every depiction of the world was a edit, but insisted on making the cut for itself, a perspective that saw every subject as a potential media producer—a view expressed in the slogan of the Italian IMC: "become the media."

This marked a shift—and sometimes a rift—in the media practices of the counterglobalization movement, a contrast analyzed by Dorothy Kidd as "press conferences versus web-cam witnesses."[34] The well-established NGOs, public interest groups, and trades unions who saw themselves as the mandated, responsible representatives of "civil society" had also made media preparations for Seattle. However, they followed what Kidd terms a "vertical" model of alternative reportage, using Web sites, teach-ins, and press conferences primarily as channels through which counterexperts in trade, labor, and environmental issues could challenge the WTO. Indymedia had a different, "flatter" model. The Seattle IMC "did not prep professional communicators":

> Instead a motley crew of several hundred volunteers took their cameras, microphones and writing implements to the streets to bring witness from the demonstrators, which other crews then rapidly edited and circulated to a global audience on the web.

Rather than focusing on "alternative content," IMC's "do-it-yourself approach" acted "to change relations of production and reception too," making what Kidd terms a shift from "alternative" to "autonomous" media.[35]

From its inception, Indymedia's new style of reportage was associated with another new experience for counterglobalization movements in North America—massive confrontation with the armed power of the state. Seattle saw the exercise of police force against demonstrators on an unprecedented scale. As the city streets of Seattle filled with tear gas, the protests grabbed the attention of corporate media in a way unlike any other counterglobalization event. But their coverage—particularly that on U.S. television network news—depicted the violence as the responsibility of demonstrators, focusing on a few incidents of vandalism, obscuring the role of the police in precipitating mayhem, and ignoring the issues inspiring the protests.[36]

IMC reporters, in contrast, covered the events from the point of view of the protestors, articulated their concerns seriously, presented their justifications for civil disobedience actions, and offered a different interpretation of the violence on Seattle streets—as a panicky police riot, unleashing disproportionate force and rampant abuse of civil liberties. On the spot footage of demonstrators being systematically beaten, of point-blank tear gas volleys fired into crowds of passive demonstrators, and of short-range use of rubber bullets were uploaded to IMC Web sites. This not only influenced the perception of events by the thousands of sympathizers and curious who logged on but also appears to have had some success in altering corporate network's reporting, particularly in immediately and irrefutably contradicting official denials that rubber bullets had been fired.[37] Later, the widely circulated film, "This Is What Democracy Looks Like," made from IMC footage, provided an account of the protests in which police action appeared as the unraveling of liberal democracy facing a challenge to corporate power.

While there was a very large contingent of Canadians at Seattle—a city conveniently close to the border—they were not centrally involved in the creation of the IMC. But the "five days that shook the world" in Seattle set in motion a very rapid circulation of struggles, inspiring a sequence of summit protests, in New York, Washington, Prague, Barcelona, and Québec City.[38] Accompanying this was a transnational diffusion of the IMC's linked by a common philosophy, a focus on grassroots reporting and online publication, and a well-maintained technical infrastructure. By the end of 2000 over thirty Indymedia were scattered across the globe, and two years after the first Indymedia hit the Web, this number had grown to over sixty—eleven of them in Canada.

The vortex of widening street protests and intensifying cyberactivism truly touched down in Canada, however, at the Summit of the Americas in Quebec City in April 2001. It was widely anticipated that this inauguration of Free Trade Area of the Americas would see confrontation between globalizing and counterglobalizing forces. The mounting intensity of protests was bringing problems for both sides. Summit organizers made extensive security preparations, including the fencing in of the entire meeting site, preparations that in turn became a focus of wide public criticism. Meanwhile, the possibility of a violent collision with security forces split the counterglobalization forces.

On the days of the demonstrations, the civil society organizations lead a march of some 30–50,000 people away from the fence to a jamboree of speeches in a vacant industrial parking lot. However, about 10,000 activists, most of them young, marched to the barrier and stormed sections of it before being repelled. Clashes between activists and police went on throughout the day. Streets once again filled with tear gas, police fired some 350 plastic bullets, deployed water cannons, and arrested 460 people.

Again, the IMC, organized by the Centre des Média Alternatifs-Québec 2001 (CMAQ), was in the thick of the action. A series of preparatory workshops—*ateliers de formation*—on the manufacturing and dissemination of dissenting news had been organized by the Comité d'acceuil du Sommet des Amériques (CASA) (Quebec City) and Convergence des Luttes Ant-Capitalistes (CLAC), the two main Franco-Canadian groups involved in the demonstration, and also two of the most youthful and most militant.[39] Even in the run-up to the demonstrations, IMC centers in Quebec and elsewhere had been raided by police. Over the days of the protest, the CMAQ was headquartered in the Méduse art complex, a short walk away from the security perimeter. The same building housed medics, who helped those harmed by tear gas and rubber bullets, and became a point of rendezvous and recuperation for exhausted or lost activists. On the afternoon of the main protests, as security forces pushed demonstrators down the streets of the Old City, tear gas billowed into the building, and doors were barricaded in expectations of a police assault. Although there was now no shortage of corporate and public media coverage of the widely anticipated clash, with reporters and cameras stategically situated at every vantage point, it was IMC who were the first to report events such as the police take-downs of targeted activists, and it was IMC networks who would continue to track the unfolding legal cases long after they faded from mainstream news.

Indymedia's hallmark continued to be the Web dissemination of original, firsthand coverage of counterglobalization events through print, photos, audio, and video. This emphasis on raw reporting was its strength, as an experiment in participatory media democracy, but it could also be a weakness, creating problems of focus and reliability, and intense debates about creation of an "editorial" policy. But in this respect, Indymedia were complemented, in Canada as elsewhere, by an explosion of radical on-line journalism.

The attempt to find a virtual equivalent for the daily newspaper or weekly newsmagazine was now an integral part of the dot.com boom, explored both by corporate news empires and by a spate of "alternative" cultural and political projects hoping to end run such media giants. Part of this latter strain was the appearance in the late 1990s of numerous electronic newsletters and on-line journals, from a left of center position. In Canada, these included *Straight Goods,* started by Ish Theilheimer and friends in 1998–1999, *rabble.ca* founded by the veteran socialist and feminist activist Judy Rebbick in 2000, and, a little later, *Dominion,* set up by journalists of the Canadian University Press. It is also of note that a Canadian, Stephen

Marshall, previously active in alternative television production, was a co-founder of one of the most successful of U.S. radical on-line journalism ventures, *Guerrilla News Network*.

These projects were, like the IMC, part of the ambience of the counter-globalization movements. But whereas IMC was outrightly "agitational" the on-line radical journals were more "analytic"; both were forms of activist-journalism, but the accent fell on different sides of the hyphen. In *Straight Goods* or *rabble.ca* one would find detailed reports of news items systematically unreported by the mainstream press, such as the series of World Social Forum meetings held in Porto Alegre from 1998 on, the success of Hugo Chavez's embattled populist regime in Venezuela, or struggles over water-privatization in Bolivia. The on-line journals had regular issues. They were founded by people who had background as journalists, and their contributors were sometimes professional writers, or, more often, had ambitions to become such. They grappled, more or less successfully, with the problem of financial support, either by subscription, donation, or sponsorship. This combined diffusion of the activist IMC and left on-line journalism gave the Canadian counterglobalization movement not just sporadic "cyberactivism" but something approaching an ongoing "cyberactive culture."

CRISIS: GENOA AND 9/11

In 2001 the protests at the Genoa meeting of the G8 bought the intensifying collision of counterglobalization forces with the neoliberal state to a crisis. The shooting of Carlo Giuliani by Italian Carabineri, an event whose photographed sequence was almost instantaneously uploaded to Web sites and subject to incessant interpretation, made counterglobalization protest a matter of life and death. The subsequent attack by Italian police on the IMC headquarters near the Diaz school in Genoa also showed how far the communicative capacity of the counterglobalization movement has become, in the eyes of police and protestors alike, the nerve center of protest. It also, ironically, demonstrated how incorrigible this capacity was, for despite the security force's orgy of beatings and humiliations, and the destruction and confiscation of computers, news of the rampage disseminated very rapidly.

In the aftermath of Genoa both globalizers and counterglobalizers seemed taken aback, wrong footed by the rapidity of escalation. In Canada, the decision to remove the next G8 summit to a remote wilderness location in Kanasakis more or less thwarted protesters, though at the price of symbolically marginalizing the negotiators. Both sides in the spiraling contestation paused, uncertain as to how it would play out. This question would, however, never be answered in the terms it was initially conceived—for on September 11, 2001, the situation was abruptly changed.

The attack on the World Trade Center cut a trail of flame across the rising arc of counterglobalization struggles. Neoliberal proponents of globalization saw all their sunny optimism go up in smoke as the ferocity of social antagonisms unfolding within the world-market exploded in their face, but the movements of Seattle and Quebec City were also rocked back on their heels by a conjunction that now included not only the WTO and the Zapatistas but also al-Qaeda. The Bush administration's announcement of "war on terror" diverted attention from issues of global equity and economics. Any form of dissent risked stigmatization amidst suspensions of civil liberties, intensification of surveillance, and enhanced danger of arbitrary arrest. Within a year or so, elements of the counterglobalization movement were part of the international protests against the U.S. invasion of Iraq, protests that unfolded across a new political terrain and with new demands—that the war on terror not be used as a veil for U.S. imperial interests, for remedy of the fundamental conditions of human insecurity that generate terrorism, and for new transnational institutions of peace.

Canadian cyberactivists were deeply involved in these events. The e-mailers of trade unions and social movements, the on-line journalism of Straight Goods, rabble.ca, Dominion, and the network of IMC's contributed in the mobilization of the Canadian antiwar movement. They were also important in ensuring that in a war situation issues of global trade and investment policy were not totally eclipsed. When the 2003 meeting of the WTO in Cancun, Mexico, saw a revolt of the poor nations against the refusal of the developed world to submit its own agricultural and intellectual property regimes to the logic of "free" trade, much of the best analysis of the resulting paradoxes was in media that were both alternative and digital. These events occurred, however, in a context transfigured by a massive remilitarization of planetary politics whose consequences remain uncertain, so it seems appropriate to halt our narrative of Canadian counterglobalizing cyberactivism, and make a tentative evaluation.

CONCLUSION

In Canada the use of the Net is now common throughout the counterglobalization movements. Cyberactivism is an important aspect of an oppositional culture that has surprised opponents both by its emergence and by its persistence. Web sites and e-mail lists are normal parts of the organizing operation of many of its component organization, and the IMCs and radical on-line journals constitute an embryonic alternative news system. At certain key junctures, such as the Zapatista revolt, the anti-MAI campaign, and the street protests in Seattle, Quebec City, Genoa, and elsewhere, the dissemination of news via the Internet has been important in attracting public attention to events that were under- or mis-reported by the mainstream media. Government officials, corporate spokespeople, and mainstream journalism often partially ascribed the "backlash" against policies of economic globalization to the skillful cyberactivism of social movements, and hasten to prepare counterstrategies.[40]

Many counterglobalization advocates believe cyberactivism's effects on the movement are both far-reaching and positive. The Canadian activist/author Naomi Klein suggests that the Internet is "shaping the movement in its own image," permitting the emergence of "an activist model that mirrors the organic, decentralized, interlinked pathways of the Internet."[41] Though she notes that this process is not without its problems, she sees it as transcending many historical problems of the left:

> Thanks to the Net, mobilizations are able to unfold with sparse bureaucracy and minimal hierarchy; forced consensus and laboured manifestoes are fading into the background . . .[42]

Indeed, some theorists suggest that the "immaterial labor" or "cognitariat" involved with computers, telecommunications, and other media networks occupy as important a position in the cycle of counterglobalization struggles as the industrial proletariat did in the cycle of struggles against industrial capital.[43]

By no means all involved in the counterglobalization movement, however, have a positive evaluation of cyberactivism. Suggestions that the speed, volume and decontextualization of Internet communication might actually be inimical to critical analysis and democratic debate are not uncommon. The Canadian scholar Judith Hellman, for example has recently argued that uncritical acceptance of the EZLN's cyber-communiqués amongst Northern supporters produced a "flattened," "reductionist" perspective on the complexities of terrestrial class struggles in Chiapas, and an illusory, misdirected sense of involvement based on the "appeal of events seen from a great distance."[44] The much-celebrated "Zapatistas in cyberspace" were, she claims, at least in part, the product of a "magical realism" arising from "technological fetishism."[45]

Even many committed net activists often express concerns about the efficacy of cyber-organizing, concerns that might be summarized by asking "Is cyberactivism preaching to the converted, and are the converted overloaded?" The Net, as is often remarked, is a "pull" medium dependent on users selection from an expanding universe of virtual data. "Push" media, such as newspapers, TV, and radio, have a greater capacity to attract attention to a previously unsuspected issue headlines and news bulletins. Cyberactivists face here the same problem of "clutter cutting" that beset e-capitalists and virtual marketers, except that political principle inhibits them from unlimited spamming, and lack of resources prevents enormous off-line promotional efforts. Digital networks can rapidly circulate information amongst supporters and sympathizers, but expanding the radius of the circuit to reach new participants is difficult, while, for many within the cyberactivist circle, merely managing the inflow of data, let alone responding to or acting on it, is a major problem.[46]

A third obstacle squarely confronting counterglobalization cyberactivism is that of unequal access. There is a very obvious paradox in advancing the cause of planetary equality and democracy through a medium characterized by a vast "digital divide." As we have seen, Canadian counterglobalization cyberactivism has flourished within a specific, and, globally speaking, highly propitious technoeconomic context. Even within this relatively favored situation, half Canadian households do not have easy Net access. When one comes to a global perspective, with at most 10 percent of the world's population connected, and exclusions running along multiple axes of gender, ethnicity, and affluence, the disparities are breathtaking.

Such inequities mean, for example, that, although cyberactivism enables Canadian, U.S., and European counterglobalizers to obtain news about, and act in support of, movements in the global South, the conditions of this communicative exchange remain heavily weighted in favor of Northern cyberactivists. The evident danger is the emergence of a so-called counterglobalization movement whose digitalized, high technology communication networks are saturated with the perspectives, analysis, and prescription of Northern anti corporate forces—a cyberactive chorus of "we are the world."

However, despite these problems, I suspect that cyberactivism will continue to play an increasingly important, and probably constructive, part in the development of counterglobalization struggles. Some of the objections made against it are more serious than others. Criticisms of the quality of analysis sent and received on the net, such as Hellman's attack on the Chiapas networks, ascribe to cyberactivism problems endemic to all international solidarity politics (perhaps just all *politics*), regardless of medium: oversimplification, romanticism, and a surplus of rhetorical over real involvement manifest in face-to-face, in print, or broadcast exchanges, not just their cyberform. Clearly cyber-circulated information should be subjected to the same critical evaluation about origins, authoritativeness, and interests that activists bring to other media, but developing this critical sensibility in the new arena of cyberspace is an issue that time and intelligence can handle.

Far more intractable are issues of reach and access, whose resolution will seriously test counterglobalizers self-organizing skills. Virtual activism is often rightly described as bypassing conventional media, but it does not negate the need for the counterglobalization movement to develop a presence within such media, which continue to be accessible on a wider basis, and in easier ways. In a series of trenchant discussions of this issue, Dorothy Kidd has suggested that Northern media activists learn from the example of their Southern counterparts, who are compelled to attend far more closely to integrating the flows of cyber-information into cascading relays of radio, print and oral communication.[47] Net-separatist tendencies, which fetishize the supposed freedom of digital networks, needs to be distinguish from integrated cyberactivism that connects itself to such hybrid alternative networks, and cultivate the crossovers and symbiosis between these networks and sympathetic journalists and media workers involved in the mainstream channels.

In the long term, capitalist globalization itself favors the widening scope of cyberactivism. The world market has a history of disseminating the communication technologies that are the vital infrastructures for all its operations, far faster than many others of its benefits—which often in fact fail to arrive at all. Television and radios are today often quite common in otherwise utterly immizerated areas of the planet. If the wired or wireless distribution of digital networks follows the same pattern, they will become increasingly, though still unevenly, available for activists in Asia, Africa, and Latin America to communicate their struggles against the unavailability of far more basic resources—food, water, shelter, medicine, unpolluted environments, and safe habitats.

The globe-girdling powers of the Internet have helped establish communications between oppositional movements in Canada and those elsewhere in the world—in the United States, Italy, Mexico, Indonesia, Malaysia, Korea, and many other places. This has been one, although only one, important element in the formation of what André Drainville terms "transnational subjects," protagonists not of an antiglobalization movement of nationalist and local resistances, but of an *altermondialiste* movement fighting to free planetary development from the constraints of commodification.[48] If activists can reflexively and self-critically recuperate the digitally expansive drive of capital, computer-networking will continue to be crucial in this effort, and Canada's pioneering cyberactivism become merely a moment in the making of the species-beings who will wage the social struggles of the twenty-first century.

NOTES

1. In the burgeoning literature on cyberactivism, see Martha McCaughey and Michael D. Ayers, eds. *Cyberactivism: Online Activism in Theory and Practice* (New York and London: Routledge, 2003); Graham Meikle, *Future Active: Media Activism and the Internet* (New York: Routledge, 2002); Geert Lovink, *Dark Fiber: Tracking Critical Internet Cultue* (Cambridge, Mass.: MIT Press, 2002); John Downing, with Tamara Villareal Ford, Geneve Gil, and Laura Stein. *Radical Media: Rebellious Communication and Social Movements* (Thousand Oaks, Calif.: Sage, 2001); Frank Webster, ed., *Culture and Politics in the Information Age: A New Politics?* (New York: Routledge, 2001).

2. Recent overviews include: Maude Barlow and Tony Clarke, *Global Showdown: How the New Activists Are Fighting Global Corporate Rule* (Toronto: Stoddart, 2001); Amory Starr, *Naming the Enemy: Anti-Corporate Movements Confront Globalization* (London: Zed Books, 2000; David McNally, *Another World Is Possibe: Globalization and Anti-Capitalism* (Winnipeg: Arbeiter Ring, 2002); William Fisher and Thomas Ponniah, *Another World Is Possible: Popular Alternatives to Globalization at the World Social Forum*, (Halifax, N.S.: Firewood, 2003).

3. On this discussion see David Held and Anthony McGrew, *Globalization/Anti-Globalization*. (Cambridge: Polity, 2002).

4. For these terms see: Nick Dyer-Witheford, *Cyber-Marx: Cycles and Circuits of Struggle in High-Technology Capitalism* (Urbana: University of Illinois Press, 1999); John McMurtry, *Value Wars: The Global Market versus the Life Economy* (London; Pluto, 2002); Peter Waterman, *Globalization, Social Movements, and the New Internationalisms* (London: Mansell, 1998); Jeremy Brecher and Tim Costello, *Global Village or Global Pillage* (Boston: South End, 1994); Tony Dowmunt, "An Alternative Globalization: Youthful Resistance to Electronic Empires, " in *Electronic Empires : Global Media and Local Resistance*, ed. Daya Kishan Thussu (London: Arnold, 1998), 243; George Monbiot, *The Age of Consent: A Manifesto for a New World Order* (London: Flamingo, 2003); Barlow and Clarke, *Global Showdown*; Michael Hardt and Antonio Negri, *Empire* (Cambridge, Mass.: Harvard University Press, 2000).

5. For more on the "cycle of struggles" see Hardt and Negri, *Empire*, and Dyer-Witheford, *Cyber-Marx*.

6. Sandor Vegh, "Classifying Forms of Online Activism: The Case of Cyberprotests against the World Bank." in *Cyberactivism*, ed. McCaughey and Ayers, 72.

7. Harry Cleaver, "The Chiapas Uprising," *Studies in Political Economy* 44 (1994), 143.

8. Statistics Canada, "Selected Dwelling Characteristics and Household Equipment," http://www.statcan.ca/english/Pgdb/famil09c.htm (7 November 2002).

9. Global household connection rates from Cyber-Atlas, "The Big Picture: Global Internet Population Moves Away from US," by Michael Pastore, <http://cyberatlas.internet.com/big_picture/geographics/article/0,,5911_558061,00.html> (15 October 2003). Although this data comes from market research sources, its picture of global demographics is broadly verified by sources, such as the United Nations Development Project, *Human Development Report 2002: Deepening Democracy in a Fragmented World* (New York: UNDP, 2002) and Mark Balnaves et al., eds. *The Penguin Atlas of Media Information: Key Issues and Global Trends* (New York: Penguin, 2001), which, however, do not report data in terms of household connection rates.

10. See William Birdsall, "The Digital Divide in the Liberal State: A Canadian Perspective," *First Monday*, 5: 12 (2000), <http://firstmonday.org/issues/issue5_12/birdsall/index.html> (17 November 2003)

11. Nick Dyer-Witheford, "E-Capital and the Many-Headed Hydra," in *Critical Perspectives on the Internet*, ed. Greg Elmer (New York: Rowman & Littlefield, 2002), 129–63.

12. Susan Bryant and Richard Smith, "Computers and the Internet," in *Mediascapes: New Patterns in Canadian Communication*, ed. Paul Attallah and Leslie Reagan Shade (Scarborough, Ont.: Nelson, 2002), 235.

13. Eric Lee, *The Labour Movement and the Internet: The New Internationalism* (London: Pluto Press, 1997), 49–54.

14. Lee, 64–66; Patricia Mazepa, "The Solidarity Network in Formation: A Search for Democratic Alternative Communication" (paper presented at the Canadian Communication Association Annual Conference, University of Ottawa, 2 June 1998).

15. Donald Gutstein,. *E.Con: How the Internet Undermines Democracy* (Toronto: Stoddart, 1999), 273–77.

16. Rory O'Brien, "Civil Society, the Public Sphere and the Internet," <http://www.web.net/~robrien/papers/civsoc.html> (Nov. 11, 2003).

17. Vincent Mosco and Dan Schiller, eds., *Continental Order: Integrating North America for Cybercapitalism* (Lanham, Md.: Rowman & Littlefield, 2001).

18. Howard Frederick, "North American NGO Networking against NAFTA: The Use of Computer Communications in Cross-Border Coalition Building" (paper presented at XVII International Congress of the Latin American Studies Association, Los Angeles, 24–27 September 1994).

19. Joseph Brenner, "Internationalist Labor Communication by Computer Network: The United States, Mexico and Nafta," School of International Service, American University, Washington, D.C., 1994; Frederick, "North American NGO Networking."

20. See Cleaver, "The Chiapas Uprising"; Donna Kowal, "Digitizing and Globalizing Indigenous Voices: The Zapatista Movement," in *Critical Perspectives on the Internet*, ed. Greg Elmer (New York: Rowman & Littlefield, 2002), 105–29; Maria Garrido and Alexander Halavais, "Mapping Networks of Support for the Zapatista Movement: Applying Social Networks Analysis to Study Contemporary Social Movements," in *Cyberactivism*, ed. McCaughey and Ayers, 145–64.

21. Cleaver, "The Chiapas Uprising," 15.

22. Cleaver, "The Chiapas Uprising," 16.

23. EZLN (Zapatista Army of National Liberation), "Second Declaration of La Realidad (Reality) for Humanity against Neoliberalism," August 3, 1996.

24. See Harry Cleaver, "The Zapatista Effect: The Internet and the Rise of an Alternative Political Fabric, *Journal of International Affairs*, 5:2 (1998): 621–40.

25. Noam Chomsky and Edward S. Herman, *Manufacturing Consent: The Political Economy of the Mass Media* (New York: Pantheon, 1988); *Manufacturing Consent*, film directed by. Mark Achbar and Peter Wintonick, coproduced by Neccessary Illusions and Natinal Film Board of Canada, 1992.

26. See Sharon Scharfe, "Human Rights and the Internet in Asia: Promoting the Case of East Timor," in *Human Rights and the Internet*, ed. Steven Hick (London: Macmillan, 2000), 129–39; Andreas Harsano, "Indonesia: From Mainstream to Alternative Media," *First Monday* 1:3 (1996), http://www.firstmonday.dk/issues/issue3/harsono/index.html (April 14, 2002); Dana Cloud, "Doing Away with Suharto—And the Twin Myth of Globalization and New Social Movements," in *Counterpublics and the State*, ed. Robert Aspen and Daniel C. Brouwer (New York: State University of New York Press, 2001) 235–63.

27. See Jesse Hirsh, "The Media Cluster: Communalizing Intellectual Property While Socially Appropriating the Media Conglomerate," in *E-Commerce vs E-Commons: Communications in the Public Interest*, ed. Marita Moll and Leslie Reagan Shade (Ottawa: Canadian Centre for Policy Alternatives, 2001), 57–69.

28. Peter Jay Smith and Elizabeth Smythe, "Globalization, Citizenship and Technology: The Multilateral Agreement on Investment (MAI) Meets the Internet," in *Culture and Politics in the Information Age: A New Politics*, ed. by Frank Webster (London: Routledge, 2001), 183–206. See p. 196.

29. "How the Net Killed the MAI," *Globe and Mail*, 29 April, 1998, 1.

30. "How the Net Killed the MAI."

31. "How the Net Killed the MAI."

32. Smith and Smythe.

33. On the IMC, see, Dorothy Kidd, "Indymedia.org: A New Communications Commons," in *Cyberactivism*, ed. McCaughey and. Ayers, 47–69; Gene Hyde, "Independent Media Centers: Cyber-Subversion and the Alternative Press," *First Monday* 7:4 (2002), <http://firstmonday.org/issues/issues_4/hyde/index.html> (15 June 2003), and DeeDee Halleck, "Gathering Storm: Cyberactivism After Seattle," in *Media, Profit and Politics: Competing Priorities in an Open Society*, ed. Joseph Harper and Thom Yantek (Kent, Ohio: Kent State University Press, 2003), 202–14.

34. Dorothy Kidd, "From Carnival to Commons: the Global IMC Network," in *Confronting Capitalism*, ed. Eddie Yuen, George Katsiaficas, and Daniel Burton Rose (New York: Softskull Press, forthcoming).

35. Dorothy Kidd, "From Carnival to Commons."

36. See John Guiffo, "Smoke Gets in Your Eyes," *Columbia Journalism Review* (September/October 2001), <http://archives.cjr.org/year/01/5/giuffo.asp> (17 November 2003).

37. Hyde, "Independent Media Centers."

38. Alexander Cockburn and Jeffrey St. Clair, *Five Days That Shook the World: Seattle and Beyond* (London and New York: Verso, 2000).

39. André Drainville, "Québec City 2001 and the Making of Transnational Subjects," in *Socialist Register 2002: A World of Contradictions*, ed. Leo Panitch and Colin Leys (London: Merlin, 2001), 32

40. See John Arquilla and David Ronfeldt, "Cyberwar Is Coming!" *Comparative Strategy*, 12.2 (1993): 141–65, and John Arquilla and David Ronfeldt, eds., *In Athena's Camp: Preparing for Conflict in the Information Age* (Santa Monica, Calif.: Rand, 1997); Eveline Lubbers, "The Brent Spar Syndeome," in Josephine Bosma et al., eds., *Readme! Filtered By Nettime: ASCII Culture and the Revenge of Knowledge* (New York: Autonomedia 2000), 281–85; Dorothy Denning, "Hacktivism: An Emerging Threat to Diplomacy," <http:www.afsa.org/fsj/sep00/Denning.html> (April 6, 2002).

41. Naomi Klein, "The Vision Thing," *Nation* 27 June 2000, 12. See also her "Farewell to 'The End of History': Organization and Vision in Anti-Corporate Movements," in *Socialist Register 2002: A World of Contradictions*, ed. Leo Panitch and Colin Leys (London: Merlin, 2001), 1–14.

42. Klein, "The Vision Thing," 12.

43. Hardt and Negri, *Empire;* Franco Berardi, "Bifo/Berardi, interview on "The Factory of Unhappiness,"2001 <http://www.nettime.org> (June 21, 2002).

44. Judith Hellman, "Real and Virtual Chiapas: Magic Realism and the Left," *Socialist Register 2000: Necessary and Unnecessary Utopias*, ed. L. Panitch and Colin Leys (London: Merlin, 1999), 180. Also on-line at <http://www.yorku.ca/socreg>.

45. Hellman "Real and Virtual Chiapas," 181. For responses, from the scorching to the temperate, see Harry Cleaver, "The Virtual and Real Chiapas Support Network," <http://www.eco.utexas.edu/Homepages/Faculty/Cleaver/chiapas95.html> (12 May 2002) and Justin Paulson, "Peasant Struggles and International Solidarity: The Case of Chiapas," in *Socialist Register 2001: Working Classes, Global Realities*, ed. Leo Panitch and Colin Leys (London: Merlin, 2000), 275–88. See also Hellman's "Virtual Chiapas: A Reply to Paulson," in *Socialist Register 2001*, 289–93.

46. For an excellent discussion of these points, see Steve Wright, "Pondering Information and Communication in Contemprary Anti-Capitalist Organizations," *The Commoner* 7 (Spring/Summer 2003), <http://www.commoner.org.uk/01-7groundzero.htm> (19 November 2003).

47. Kidd, "Indymedia.org," "From Carnival to Commons," and "Which Would You Rather: Seattle or Porto Alegre?" presentation for "Our Media, Not Theirs," Barcelona, July 2002.

48. Drainville, "Québec City 2001 and the Making of Transnational Subjects," 15.

14

Turning the Tide

David Skinner, James R. Compton, and Mike Gasher

Over the last few years, readers of the business pages will have found numerous stories and opinion columns heralding the end of media convergence—dismissing it as yet another fleeting business fad. The widely publicized troubles faced by AOL Time Warner since its watershed merger in 2000 have tested the faith of many former convergence believers. Slumping stock prices and unhappy investors forced Time Warner executives to drop AOL from the company's corporate letterhead. That reluctant move came after AOL founder Steve Case and former Time Warner chairman Gerald Levin fell on their swords and resigned their company posts. Both men left amid disgruntlement among shareholders that company financial returns were not sufficiently robust. Plummeting stock values also forced the resignation of Vivendi Universal's chief executive Jean-Marie Messier in 2002. The former French water and sewage utility had been transformed by Messier into a multi-media giant with its purchase of Seagram's Universal music and film operations. The same business publications that had uncritically cheered the rise of the so-called new digital economy, were suddenly printing stories about the hubris of merger-happy media moguls whose reach extended beyond their grasp. Stock characters adapted from mythic tales of the "fallen man" replaced rigorous political economic analysis.

As illustrated in the chapters in this volume, it is premature to dismiss the logic of corporate and media integration as a fleeting business fad. Shareholder concerns at Time Warner, Vivendi, and CanWest Global, along with other media organizations strapped with high debt loads, can be traced to a number of factors. These companies bought into the merger mania at the top of the stock-market bubble of 2000. When that bubble burst it helped usher in an overall economic downturn that hammered advertising revenues, which in turn impacted the bottom line and aroused the wrath of shareholders. Despite these difficulties, corporate interest in cross-media mergers and acquisitions continues apace. Lobbyists working on behalf of major media conglomerates exacted enormous pressure in 2003 to ensure the Federal Communications Commission would revamp its regulatory policy and raise the cap on radio and television cross-ownership. In Canada, CanWest Global and Quebecor, among others, remain fully committed to the project. And as General Electric's merger of Vivendi Universal and NBC and ComCast's 2004 courting of Disney indicate, vertical integration is not dead.

But news-media convergence is in its infancy, and many media companies are still struggling to find a stable and profitable business model for their converged multimedia businesses. Some of the largest newspaper chains in the United States and Canada, owned by Belo, Knight Ridder, Tribune, and Can-West Global, have recommitted themselves to on-line convergence strategies by investing in large-scale, fully integrated news Web sites and newsrooms.[1] Other companies are engaged in a struggle to reaggregate fragmented audiences using their integrated properties. At the heart of these efforts, three strategies of multimedia convergence—repurposing resources, cross-promotion, and the creation of new synergistic business opportunities—are still very much in play.

As we have seen, the same forces are reshaping markets on both sides of the border. As Mosco and Schiller point out, these forces are part of the larger wiring of North America for transnational cyber-capitalism.[2] Economic elites lobbied hard for broadcast and telecommunications regulatory reform because of fears "that significant blockages were preventing the global expansion of the market and eroding opportunities for business."[3] In their view, the principal hurdles to be overcome were "national control over key institutions and policy levers, and public service principles restricting advertising and emphasizing rights of access irrespective of market power."[4] In the United States, during the 1980s and 1990s, government regulations established to meet public interest and public-service goals were targeted for elimination and replaced by market standards of performance. The twin pillars of this policy revamp were: (1) the removal of general content regulations; and (2) the removal of ownership limit restrictions. These goals were eventually achieved with the FCC's elimination of the Fairness Doctrine in 1987 and the adoption of the 1996 U.S. Telecommunications Act. The Canadian Radio-Television and Telecommunications Commission's 1996 convergence policy had similar effects in Canada.

This trend toward liberalization of U.S. and Canadian media industries is part of a worldwide movement supporting neoliberal trade policies. The undermining and privatization of public enterprises, including public-service broadcasting, occurred throughout Europe, Canada, and Australia. The structural reform ushered in by the Canada-U.S. Free Trade Agreement (FTA) and the North American Free Trade Agreement (NAFTA) forwarded the hegemony of this neoliberal policy agenda. Foreign direct investment in the U.S. communications industry increased, along with investment in a communications infrastructure that served to link those transnational corporations. And in the midst of this broad economic restructuring, formerly national media networks, such as NBC, CBS, and ABC, were restructured "along global lines, both in business and consumer markets."[5]

In Canada, corporate pressure to transnationalize the media system has been slower to develop. This is due, in part, to Canadian ownership regulations and tax incentives that both restrict foreign ownership in the broadcast and telecommunication fields and dissuade Canadian advertisers from patronizing foreign-owned newspapers. But by 2003, more of the Canadian cultural exemptions that had been negotiated into the FTA and NAFTA texts were under siege from corporate lobbying. Bell Canada Enterprises (BCE), Canada's largest telecommunications company and the owner of the country's largest private television network (CTV), one of Canada's two national newspapers (*The Globe and Mail*) and one of the nation's largest Web portals (sympatico.ca) began pushing for the lifting of foreign-ownership restrictions in telecommunications. CanWest Global, the owner of Canada's dominant newspaper chain and the second-largest private English-language television network (Global), recommended the restrictions in other media industries receive similar treatment.

Given that relaxing ownership rules would likely provide a healthy boost to their share prices, their position is not without self-interest. Two separate parliamentary committees reported on the issue and took opposite sides, with a majority of federal cabinet members in the Liberal government signaling in September 2003 that they supported the elimination of foreign-ownership restrictions in the cable and telecom industries.[6] A decision is pending, but given the converged nature of these industries, it would seem that if these regulations change, newspaper and broadcast restrictions might not be far behind.

The technological convergence of media platforms, along with the promotional integration of print, broadcast, and on-line newsrooms, is part of a much larger social process involving the state, the development of new digital technologies, and the implementation of institutional logics designed to produce economic and symbolic synergies. As such, corporate concentration and media convergence present significant challenges to the viability of the public-service ideal in the communications realm, and to journalism's ability to serve democracy. Vincent Mosco draws a direct connection between the digitization of communications media and the commodification of news and information.[7] Digitization, he argues, occurs within the context of commodification, "or the transformation of use to exchange or market value," and at the same time "expands the commodification of content by extending the range of opportunities to measure and monitor, package and repackage information entertainment and information."[8] Digitization permits the precise measurement of each "information transaction" and thus helps sell audiences to advertisers,[9] it further commodifies labor by broadening the job description of reporters into photography, editing, page production,[10] and it breaks down the legal and institutional bounds between media sectors, facilitating, even stimulating, corporate mergers and acquisitions.[11]

This is the logic that drives the convergence efforts of companies such as Tribune and CanWest Global. Today's news workers find themselves in a hypercommercialized media environment in which their work is ramified and, increasingly, made to serve the promotional needs of large, vertically and horizontally integrated media conglomerates. Increasingly, reporters must adapt themselves to flexible work routines. They must file to print, broadcast and on-line services. Whereas a newspaper reporter used to work to one main deadline a day, he or she now faces multiple deadlines in order to update stories over a now dominant twenty-four-hour news cycle— time that used to be spent doing more reporting, making an extra call, providing more context. Lise Lareau, president of the Canadian Media Guild, told a Canadian Senate committee investigating media performance that media workers are being stretched thin.

> [M]any of our people are being asked to serve many media and file the same story in radio, TV, print or whatever. You have heard that. It is a concern from workload and stress view, and we are dealing with that in a traditional union way. However, there is no question that those are developments that also lead to fewer points of view out there and fewer eyeballs on a story. This is what happens in the markets that you are referring to with the cross-ownership issue.[12]

Many print and broadcast newsrooms still retain their separate cultures, but they are under pressure to integrate in order to improve organizational efficiency. Converged news organizations, such as those run by Tribune, insist on multitasking. Reporters at national broadcasters and cable news channels, tied as they are to the organizational demands of a twenty-four-hour production regime, increasingly find themselves involved in the construction of global media spectacles, such as the mourning of Princess Diana or Monicagate. During the U.S.-led invasion of Iraq, for example, the trumped-up story of the rescue of Private Jessica Lynch was compelling fodder for all the major American broadcasters. The nineteen-year-old soldier was travelling with the Army's 507th Maintenance Company when the convoy was ambushed after taking a wrong turn. Lynch was taken prisoner after she sustained serious injuries to her legs and spine. But it was the dramatic story of the photogenic soldier's rescue—complete with grainy video—that caught the world's attention. Her mythic status as an American hero made her image easily transposable. It was the perfect image commodity, and it was repurposed and repeated endlessly by news, current affairs, and all-talk programming. Before ABC's Diane Sawyer secured the first exclusive interview, all three main American broadcasters moved aggressively to win Lynch's sympathy, with CBS offering a package that would have seen the Lynch story bundled into a book deal and a possible made-for-TV movie. Corporate synergy meets militainment.[13] These spectacles are historically unique, but the rationalization of labor that produces them is not. As William Solomon reminds us, news workers have been subject to systems of rationalized production since the beginning of the commercial press in the early nineteenth century, as they shifted from treating news as a craft to producing it as a commodity.[14] Recent events like those described in this volume are just one more step down this path of corporate rationalization.

Two responses to media convergence are outlined in this volume:[15] (i) media reform, particularly in terms of restructuring media policies regarding corporate media; (ii) the development of independent media, not only to fill in the gaps in public discourse found in corporate media but perhaps, more importantly, to create new lines and modes of social communication. In these two positions we see two different, but not contradictory, responses to public life. Both start from the position that the institutions and processes of public communication are themselves an integral part of political culture. Where they differ is on the location of politics. Media reformers emphasize the need to use the regulatory power of the state, or the strengthening of professional standards of social responsibility, to curb the excesses of corporate power, and to, thereby, democratize a mainstream media system that is presumed to be part of a centralized public sphere. Independent media producers, such as the Indy Media Web sites created in 1999 in Seattle, present a more decentred challenge to media power by encouraging the production of media by average citizens. Theirs is a radical plea for a plurality of voices set against the power of the state, and overtly opposed to professional standards of objectivity.

First, we turn to the reform agenda. Of course, comprehensive reform of the corporate media would involve a multifaceted approach, too complex to detail here.[16] However, there are several policy areas in need of attention in both the United States and Canada. Key among these are ownership regulations and antitrust law.

In the United States, ownership caps in broadcasting have experienced increasing upward pressure since they were eased in 1996. And in Canada the lack of consistent public policy regarding ownership on the part of government and the CRTC has been a major contributor to escalating levels of concentration. The attendant problems of concentration are well illustrated by Clear Channel's dominant position in radio broadcasting in the United States, and Canadian broadcaster CanWest Global's ownership of both a national television network and thirteen dailies newspapers which enjoy a 28.8 percent share of total daily Canadian circulation.[17] Cross-media ownership compounds these problems and it can be a particular concern in terms of both the ways in which converged newsrooms tend to undermine the diversity of news available in local communities and the pressures it puts upon news workers. CanWest's dominance is particularly pronounced in Vancouver where the company controls the city's two dailies and its top-rated supper-hour newscast enjoys a 70.6 percent market share.[18] Similar problems led a recent Parliamentary Committee in Canada to recommend strengthening policies regarding newsroom separation in cross-media ownership situations as well as the development of "a clear and unequivocal policy statement concerning cross media ownership."[19] Indeed, based upon recent evidence, it is clear that in both the U.S. and Canadian jurisdictions, capping, perhaps even rolling back, ownership levels, particularly cross-media ownership, is key to providing the ground on which media diversity might grow.[20]

Increasing the scope of antitrust law in the United States and competition law in Canada would provide a second avenue for maintaining corporate diversity. McChesney has recently forwarded four suggestions in this regard that have application on both sides of the border.[21] First, antitrust and competition regulators must move beyond their fixation with the power of media companies to fix prices in advertising markets. Noneconomic factors, such as diversity of expression in news and ideas and "self-censorship," must be given the attention they deserve.[22] Second, concentration in media industries should not be assessed in the same manner as nonmedia industries, such as heavy manufacturing, where the high costs of production discourage thousands of competitors. Radio, in particular, can be produced relatively cheaply.[23] Third, regulators must deal head-on with vertical and horizontal integration and reduce it. And finally, any government media policy must encompass the entire industry. It must, he suggests, break from the "piecemeal logic of current antitrust thinking" in which policy is implemented on a case-by-case basis. Overall goals of reduced concentration must inform all deliberations.[24]

In both countries efforts also need to be made to keep media regulations out of trade agreements. This has particular importance in Canada, where ensuring adequate representation of Canadian perspectives in the media has been an historic problem. However, on both sides of the border, local control of the ways in which media are financed and organized is paramount to maintaining the representation of local, regional, and even national perspectives on the events shaping citizens' lives. On another front, public broadcasting also requires renewed support on both sides of the border. Although it operates on two very different models in Canada and the United States, public broadcasting, with its public-service mandate, provides for a much different disposition of resources than profit-driven media and thereby yields patterns of representation different from private, commercial media.[25]

Another reform idea that has been brought forward in Canada is to restructure existing provincial press councils so as to give them more independence from the newspapers that sponsor them. Indeed, although self-regulation of newspapers has not proved particularly successful on either side of the border, it does provide a foothold for developing a degree of regulatory oversight and perhaps it is time to finally implement the recommendations in this regard made by the Hutchins and Davey enquiries.

Finally, in Canada, there has been some discussion of legislating a code of professional practice or code of ethics that would help protect journalists and other media workers from undue influence and possible obstructions by owners. While the idea has drawbacks in that it might be used to hold journalists, rather than media managers, responsible for shortcomings in news coverage, it is one idea in a larger struggle to find ways to protect and empower labor in the face of this latest and ongoing round of rationalization. Since at least the 1930s, journalists have been key actors in resisting corporate rationalization in the newspaper business. They have been at the forefront of developing professional codes and practices to maintain the firewall between the business and editorial sides of news organizations, and working to countermand corporate tendencies to interfere with news production.[26] And despite the problems endured by labor during convergence, this tradition continues today.

For instance, *Montreal Gazette* journalists, who belong to the Montreal Newspaper Guild (a local of TNG Canada/CWA, which is, in turn, an arm of The Newspaper Guild, based in Washington, D.C.), won three important arbitration settlements in 2003 and 2004 against their employer, CanWest Global Communications.

In December 2001, a number of *Gazette* journalists withdrew their credit lines as part of a protest against CanWest's chain-wide "national editorials" policy. They also established a protest Web site and wrote an open letter of dissent, which was published by other Montreal newspapers and the nationally circulated *Globe and Mail*. Gazette management responded with a "gag order" prohibiting its employees not only from public criticism of the national editorial policy but broader criticisms of the company. The union, in turn, filed a grievance with the company, which resulted in a court-sanctioned arbitration hearing.

In October 2003, a Quebec arbitrator ruled that *Gazette* journalists had the right to withhold their by-lines "as they see fit." And in February 2004, the union declared a double victory following an arbitration settlement which affirmed their right to "contribute to and participate in open public debate" over the newspaper's editorial policies. The decision came in response to two grievances filed by the union. The first concerned the December 2001 "gag order" imposed by *Gazette* managers. The second was prompted by a formal warning issued to reporter William Marsden after he participated in a public debate on media concentration at a Canadian Association of Journalists conference. In March 2004, TNG Canada/CWA established a Web site entitled Your Media[27] as, in the words of TNG Canada/CWA director Arnold Amber, "a national gathering place, information source and rallying point for those who cherish and demand freedom of expression, full diversity of voices and unfettered independence of the media outlets that serve their communities." The victories in Montreal established an important precedent in journalists' struggle to regain some measure of control of the labor process. They illustrate the extent to which collective bargaining provides a venue in which to fight for the public-service values of journalism and the importance of local struggles in the context of continental forces of rationalization.

As important as the project of corporate reform is, however, it is not the answer to all that ails the news media. As has been well illustrated by media scholars, patterns of omission in the news are not simply the product of concentration of ownership or meddling by owners. Rather, they can also be traced to the ways in which both news values and journalistic practices tend to foreclose on the range of perspectives included in the news. As Hackett and Zhao point out:

> news values, like the practices of objectivity, typically assume and amplify a presumed consensus around basic social values of liberal capitalism. . . . (and) journalism . . . is predisposed towards maintaining certain types of social power—technological expertise, patriarchy, private capital—and the liberal state. Oppositional actors who want to publicly challenge the nature of this consensus will find themselves marginalized and denigrated.[28]

While, as Schudson argues, it would be a mistake to adhere too rigidly to a model of the news media that sees "large corporations and the media working hand in glove to stifle dissent or promote a lethargic public acceptance of the existing distribution of power," as Cooper points out there is ample evidence of blind spots and patterns of omission in the news offered by the corporate media.[29]

The sources of these problems of representation are complex. In part, they can be directly traced to the fact that, as Hackett and Zhao put it, the "commercial logic" of corporate media has "editorial consequences" in that organizational resources are oriented toward maximizing advertising revenue.[30] As a result, "news and commentary . . . are shaped by a consumerist orientation" and the drive to capture audiences with particular demographic qualities.[31] But these problems are also woven between a set of professional codes and practices, such as journalists' dependence on official sources, to help define the meaning of events and the propensity of journalists to frame events in terms of dominant ideas and stereotypes.[32] Digitization, the repurposing of news stories from one medium to another, and the "spectacularization" of news plays upon and accelerates these tendencies. And while pinpointing the cause of specific biases and omissions is an empirical problem, the net result of these practices is that the corporate press tends to provide a stilted and partial perspective on social events and circumstances.

When media reform is approached from this perspective, it raises the issue of whether the kinds of reforms discussed above would adequately address the ways in which news production practices—particularly those set within large, private, profit-oriented corporations—routinely foreclose upon the representation of a wide range of ideas and perspectives. At the least, this work casts doubt on some of the more far-reaching goals of reform in this regard.

Neither does the Web promise to solve the problems associated with concentration of ownership in news production, even though it is often touted as panacea for the problems presented by shrinking forums for public expression.[33] Not only are many Americans and Canadians still without access to the Internet in their homes,[34] but, as Paterson points out (in chapter 7 of this volume), in the face of the "cybermediation" of news agency content, there is some question as to the originality of much news on the Web. Independent operators of "news" Web sites operate largely as aggregators of information rather than producers, and the production of consistent quality content is generally beyond their means. More than two-thirds of the most popular news sites on the Web are owned by the twenty largest media companies.[35] Add to this the efforts of some of the larger portals to operate their sites as "walled gardens" and confine Web surfers to their own news and information sites, and the Web loses much of its allure as an alternative source of news and information.[26]

All of this is not to say that it is not worth keeping up the fight for the reform of corporate media and working to redefine communicative rights and responsibilities in favor of the public interest over corporate profit. Indeed, recent efforts to raise corporate media reform on the public agenda have shown success in both countries. As Robert McChesney suggests, the media ownership fight of 2003 was an "unprecedented moment in U.S. history. For the first time in generations, media policy issues were taken from behind closed doors and made the stuff of democratic discourse."[37] Similarly, ongoing pressure from a range of labor and public-interest groups in Canada has resulted in a Senate inquiry into concentration of ownership. The greatest success has been had in the United States, however, where organizations such as Freepress and Media Matters for America have begun to stitch together a broad-based coalition organized around a relatively broad set of reform goals.[38] These efforts provide a glimpse of what might be accomplished with hard work and determination. Learning from that success and building on it in both countries is crucial.

Given the obstacles facing comprehensive reform of corporate media, however, working to bolster independent and community media is also an important and pressing project, as well as perhaps the only way to guarantee that a wide range of perspectives is available through public communication.[39] The anarchistic Independent Media Center (IMC) movement has provided a powerful example of a de-centered alternative to the convergence of corporate media. As John Downing argues, from the beginning the Seattle IndyMedia Web sites eschewed top-down hierarchical forms of organization. "There was no ambition to be any kind of Leninist directing center, any more than there was an interest in allying IMC work with any mainstream political party."[40] Instead, IMCs were developed by local activists—feminists, environmentalists, labor, students—who utilized the open publishing software made available by IMC organizers. The goal was to invert the longstanding division of labor between media producers and consumers in a bid to encourage, to use Nick Couldry's phrase, "new hybrid forms of media *consumption-production.*"[41] Anyone with a modem could become a reporter by filing a text, audio, or video report. In the process, as Nick Dyer-Witheford argues, the IMCs facilitated an "intense convergence between counter-globalization and cyberactivism."[42] The IMCs are part of a broader transnational struggle against the circuits of corporate globalization, and as such, have positioned themselves as a positive example of social convergence—the sharing of resources by diverse and loosely associated groups and individuals to serve broader public, and not private commercial, interests.

On another front, in the United States, Deep Dish TV—one of the founding members of the IMC movement—provides a growing, flexible mode of distribution for a broad range of programming. First developed as the distribution arm of Paper Tiger Television, its programs are shown on more than 200 cable systems across the country and link local-access producers and programmers, independent video makers, and activists. In a similar vein, Free Speech TV offers a national satellite broadcast channel 24/7, mandated to provide a range of programming focussed on supporting independent producers, building partnerships with social justice organizations, and helping build progressive social movements. On the print front, the Independent Press Association (IPA) is a nonprofit organization that helps small, generally progressive magazine and newspaper publishers develop and build their operations.[43] With its innovative advertising pool, IPA New York provides a particularly interesting model for helping promote the growth and stability of ethnic and community newspapers. As well, there are a number of community media centers across the United States that provide shining examples of what might be done at the local level.[44] In radio, the widespread institution of low-power FM holds promise for invigorating local radio.

Independent media are also on the rise in Canada, although community media are generally better organized in Quebec than the rest of the country. And while there are some examples of particularly innovative not-for-profit broadcast organizations in Canada—such as the Aboriginal Peoples Television Network (APTN)—generally, independent media outlets in that country are not as well-organized as their American cousins. Community television is in particular trouble, having suffered a blow in Canada in the late 1990s when the federal regulator ended compulsory funding by cable companies. On a more hopeful note, a recent parliamentary committee on broadcasting made a range of recommendations to help boost not-for-profit and community broadcasting and in Quebec the Web is being used as a point of convergence for the efforts of a number of different types of community media outlets.

Still, there remains much to spur development of alternative and community media in both jurisdictions. In both countries (Canada particularly), a better understanding of what the operators of these media perceive to be their needs—in terms of both direct aid and policy development toward building economic infrastructure—is required. Similarly, strengthening relationships between social justice groups, other NGOs, and alternative media is in order. This is especially so in terms of exploiting any synergies that might be had by, on one hand, alternative media developing publics and public awareness for these groups, and, on the other hand, these groups helping develop audiences, circulation, and readership for alternative media outlets. Finally, and particularly in Canada, there needs to be more effort to build local, regional, and national associations or cooperatives to undertake efforts and activities such as those that the IPA undertakes, as well as programs to create and support local nonprofit and/or cooperative community media centers.

Liberal democracy has historically privileged an individual's right to be free from forms of state domination. This assumed negative right is at the core of journalism's heavily mythologized "gatekeeper" role. However, the same right has all too often been used successfully by corporate owners of news media to defend their so-called natural right to dispose of their private property as they deem fit—sometimes in open defiance of the public good. We agree with Jeff Noonan, who argues that the struggle for democracy must move beyond a "rights-based conception of democracy," to a "needs-based conception" that accounts for the practical requirements of democratic life. "A radical democracy is one that is rooted in democratic control over natural and social resources and posits as its end not simply the political empowerment of citizens, but their all-round development as active, self-creative beings."[45] The ultimate solution to the convergence of corporate media and the rationalization of media content it is producing lies in an invigorated public-service media—that is, media devoted to developing public consideration and discussion of the issues and concerns that animate our lives. There are signs that people are becoming more critical of the news fed to them by the networks; that their interests are diverging from those of the converging media giants. Harnessing that alienation to fuel reform and the development of alternative media is the key to turning the tide of convergence in the public interest. If there is hope in our story, this is where it lies.

NOTES

1. J.D. Lasica, "The Rise of the Digital Networks," *Online Journalism Review*, <http://www.ojr.org/ojr/lasica/p1018588363.php> (11 April, 2002).

2. Vincent Mosco and Dan Schiller, eds., *Continental Order?: Integrating North America for Cybercapitalism* (Lanham, Md.: Rowman & Littlefield, 2001).

3. Mosco and Schiller, *Continental Order?* 28.

4. Mosco and Schiller, *Continental Order?* 29.

5. Mosco and Schiller, *Continental Order?* 29.

6. Tuck, Simon. "CanWest Urges Removal of Ownership Limits," *Globe and Mail* (28 February 2003), B4.

7. Vincent Mosco, *The Digital Sublime* (Cambridge, Mass.: MIT Press, 2004).

8. Mosco, *Digital Sublime*, 156.

9. Mosco, *Digital Sublime*, 157–58.

10. Mosco, *Digital Sublime*, 158.

11. Mosco, *Digital Sublime*, 159–61.

12. Canada, Standing Senate Committee on Transport and Communications, *Interim Report on the Canadian News Media* (Ottawa, April 2004), 79.

13. James Compton, *The Integrated News Spectacle: A Political Economy of Cultural Performance* (New York: Peter Lang, 2004).

14. William S Solomon, "The Site of Newsroom Labor: The Division of Editorial Practices," in *Newsworkers: Toward a History of the Rank and File*, eds. Hanno Hardt and Bonnie Brennen (Minneapolis: University of Minnesota Press, 1995), 112.

15. A common third avenue of response, media education, is not covered here. For more information in this area see the Action Coalition for Media Education at <http://www.acme.org.>

16. For a more comprehensive discussion of the possible dimensions of media reform in the United States, see www.freepress.org. For the same in Canada, see <http://www.presscampaign.org>.

17. Rowland Lorimer and Mike Gasher, *Mass Communication in Canada*, 5th edition (Toronto: Oxford University Press, 2004), 201.

18. Standing Senate Committee, *Interim Report*, 45.

19. Canada. Standing Committee on Canadian Heritage, *Our Cultural Sovereignty: The Second Century of Canadian Broadcasting* (cited 18 June, 2003), 631.

20. However, in Canada, presumably because of the legal impediments to forcing divestiture of media properties, a recent government report concludes that such divestiture is "not conceivable." See Canada, Department of Heritage. "Media Studies: Concentration of Ownership in the Media Part II," 12.

21. Robert McChesney, *The Problem of the Media* (New York: Monthly Review Press, 2004), 238–39.

22. McChesney, *The Problem of the Media*, 238.

23. McChesney, *The Problem of the Media*, 238.

24. McChesney, *The Problem of the Media*, 239.

25. James H. Wittebols, "News from the Non-institutional World: U.S. and Canadian Television News Coverage of Social Protest," *Political Communication* 13, no. 2 (1996): 345–61.

26. See Robert W. McChesney and Ben Scott, eds. *Our Unfree Press: One Hundred Years of Radical Media Criticism* (New York: The New Press, 2004).

27. See <http:www.yourmedia.ca>

28. Robert Hackett and Yeuzhi Zhao, *Sustaining Democracy: Journalism and the Politics of Objectivity* (Toronto: Garamond Press: 1998), 149–50.

29. Michael Schudson, "The Sociology of News Production Revisited (Again)," in *Mass Media and Society*, eds. James Curran and Michael Gurevtich (New York: Oxford University Press, 2000) 180.

30. Hackett and Zhao, *Sustaining Democracy*, 65.

31. Robert Hackett, Richard Pinet, and Myles Ruggles, "From Audience Commodity to Audience Community: Mass Media in B.C.," in *Seeing Ourselves: Media Power and Policy in Canada* (Toronto: Harcourt, Brace, Jovanovich, 1992), 14.

32. See Schudson, "Sociology"; Mark Fishman, *Manufacturing the News* (Austin: University of Texas Press, 1980); Todd Gitlin, *The Whole World Is Watching* (Berkley: University of California Press, 1980); Herbert Gans, *Deciding What's News* (New York: Pantheon, 1979).

33. For instance, speaking for many, News Corporation chief executive Rupert Murdoch suggests that "with the Internet it's so easy and so cheap to start a newspaper or start a magazine that there's just millions of voices . . . the old ideas of it being too concentrated, I think that's just fading away," <www.smh.com.au/articles/2004/04/07/1081222511084.html> (5 Dec. 2004).

34. Dwayne Winseck, "Lost in Cyberspace," *Mediascapes: New Patterns in Canadian Communication*, eds. Paul Attallah and Leslie Regan Shade, eds. (Scarborough, Ont.: Thomson Nelson, 2002), p. 330.

35. Project for Journalism Excellence, "State of the News Media 2004," <http://www.state ofthenewsmedia.org. (7 Jan. 2005).

36. Jeffrey A. Chester, "Web behind Walls" *Technology Review*, June 2001, <http://www .technologyreview.com/articles/reviews0601.asp> (31 Jan. 2004).

37. McChesney, *The Problem of the Media*, 295.

38. See <http://www.freepress.net> (5 Jan. 2005).

39. Britain has experienced similar problems in this regard. Three postwar royal commissions dealing with the press failed to effectively challenge the power of publishers and their self-defensive rhetoric of press freedom. See James Curran, "Rethinking Media and Democracy," in *Mass Media and Society*, James Curran and Michael Gurevitch, eds. (London: Arnold, 2000).

40. John Downing, "The Independent Media Center Movement and the Anarchist Socialist Tradition," in *Contesting Media Power: Alternative Media in a Networked World*, eds. Nick Couldry and James Curran (Lanham, Md.: Rowman & Littlefield, 2003), 251.

41. Nick Couldry, "Beyond the Hall of Mirrors?: Some Theoretical Reflections on the Global Contestation of Media Power," in *Contesting Media Power: Alternative Media in a Networked World*, eds. Nick Couldry and James Curran (Lanham, Md.: Rowman & Littlefield, 2003), 45.

42. Nick Dyer-Witheford, "Canadian Cyberactivism in the Cycle of Counter-Globalization Struggles," chapter 12 of this volume.

43. See <www.indypress.org> (17 Feb. 2004).

44. See <www.grcmc.org> (16 March 2004).

45. Jeff Noonan, "Rights, Needs, and the Moral Grounds of Democratic Society," *Rethinking Marxism* 16, no. 3 (July 2004): 322.

Bibliography

Abramson, Bram Dov. "The Politics of Broadband: Virtual Networking and the Right to Communicate." Pp. 233–50 in *Global Media Policy in the New Millennium*, edited by Marc Raboy. Luton: University of Luton Press, 2002.

Ackerman, Seth. "The Most Biased Name in News: Fox Channel's Extraordinary Right-wing Tilt." *FAIR*, August 2002.

Adam, G. Stuart. "The Education of Journalists." *Journalism: Theory, Practice and Criticism* 2, no. 3 (December 2001): 315–39.

Adelstein, Jonathan. "Statement of Commissioner Jonathan S. Adelstein, Dissenting," July 2, 2003, <http://hraunfoss.fcc.gov/edocs_public/attachmatch/FCC-03-127A7.pdf>.

Ahrens, Frank. "Making Radio Waves: Rivals Fear Clear Channel Trying to Muscle Them Out." *Washington Post*, 22 August 2001.

——. "Democrats Decry 'Compromise' on FCC Rule," 26 November 2003. <http://www.washingtonpost.com>.

Air Bubble."Your Revolution Will Not Be Televised." 2004. <http://www.airbubble.com/your_revolution.html> (18 July 2004).

Airplay Monitor. "What Effect Will FCC's Indie Policy Have?" *Airplay Monitor*, 2 May 2003.

Alasuutari, Pertti. "Introduction: Three Phases of Reception Studies." Pp. 1–21 in *Rethinking the Media Audience: The New Agenda*, edited by Pertti Alasuutari. London: Sage, 1999.

Albarran, Alan B., and John W. Dimmick. "An Assessment of Utility and Competitive Superiority in the Video Entertainment Industries." *Journal of Media Economics* 6 (1993).

Alterman, Eric. *What Liberal Media: The Truth about Bias and the News*. New York: Basic Books, 2002.

Ambrosi, Alain. "Difficile Émergence des Réseaux de Communication démocratique dans l'espace Politique Global." Pp. 99–122 in *Vers une Citoyenneté Simulée. Médias, Réseaux et Mondialisation*, under the direction of Serge Proulx and André Vitalis. Rennes: Apogée, 1999.

Amster-Burton, L., and M. Amster-Burton. "News Media, Old Bias: Reuters On-line Provides Instant Access to Views of Establishment Men." *FAIR Extra!* (January/February): 25.

Anderson, Benedict. *Imagined Communities: Reflections on the Origin and Spread of Nationalism*. Rev. edition. London and New York: Verso, 1991.

305

Anderson Forest, Stephanie with Tom Lowry. "Is Clear Channel Hogging the Airwaves?" *Business Week*. October 1, 2001, <http://www.businessweek.com/magazine/content/01_40/b3751043.html>.

Ang, Ien. *Living Room Wars: Rethinking Audiences for a Postmodern World*. London: Routledge, 1996.

Anselmo, Joseph C. "Lawmakers Underestimate Public Concern about FCC Media Ownership Rule." *Congressional Quarterly*, 26 July 2003, 1903.

Ansolabehere, Stephen, and Shanto Iyengar. "Riding the Wave and Claiming Ownership Over Issues: The Joint Effect of Advertising and News Coverage in Campaigns." *Public Opinion Quarterly* 58 (1994).

Aronowitz, Stanley. "Is a Democracy Possible?" Pp. 75–92 in *The Phantom Public Sphere*, edited by Bruce Robbins. Minneapolis: University of Minnesota Pres, 1993.

Associated Press. "Clear Channel Growth the Result of 1996 Deregulation." *Salt Lake Tribune*, 21 September 2003, <http://www.sltrib.com/2003/Sep/09212003/business/94315.asp>.

Association des Radiodiffuseurs Communautaires du Québec, (ARCQ), *Proposition de cadre stratégique pour les médias communautaires*, Réponse à avis public CRTC 2001–129, February 2002.

Aufderheide, Patricia. "After the Fairness Doctrine: Controversial Broadcast Programming and the Public Interest." *Journal of Communication* 40, no. 3 (1990): 47–72.

———. "Niche-Market Culture, Off and On Line." Pp. 43–57 in *The Electronic Grapevine: Rumor, Reputation, and Reporting in the New On-Line Environment*, edited by D. Borden and K. Harvey. Mahwah, N.J.: Lawrence Erlbaum Associates, 1998.

———. *Communications Policy and the Public Interest: The Telecommunications Act of 1996*. New York: Guilford Press, 1999.

Auletta, Ken. "The State of the American Newspaper." *American Journalism Review*, June 1998.

Babe, Robert. "Empires in TV Land." *Search* (Spring 1979), 15.

———. *Canadian Television Broadcasting Structure, Performance and Regulation*. Hull, Quebec: Minister of Supply and Services, 1979.

———. *Telecommunications in Canada: Technology, Industry, and Government*. Toronto: University of Toronto Press, 1990.

Bachen, Christine, Allen Hammond, Laurie Mason, and Stephanie Craft. Diversity of Programming in the Broadcast Spectrum: Is there a Link Between Owner Race or Ethnicity and News and Public Affairs Programming? (Santa Clara University, December 1999).

Bagdikian, Ben. *The Media Monopoly*. Boston: Beacon Press, 1992.

———. *The Media Monopoly*. Boston: Beacon Press, 2000.

Baker, C. Edwin, *Advertising and a Democratic Press*. Princeton, N.J.: Princeton University Press, 1994.

———. "Giving the Audience What It Wants." *Ohio State Law Journal* 58 (1997).

———. "Giving Up on Democracy: The Legal Regulation of Media Ownership," Attachment C, Comments of Consumers Union, Consumer Federation of America, Civil Rights Forum, Center for Digital Democracy, Leadership Conference on Civil Rights and Media Access Project (before the Federal Communications Commission, In the Matter of Cross Ownership of Broadcast Station and Newspaper/Radio Cross-Ownership Waiver Policy, MM Docket No. 01-235, 96–197, 3 December 2001).

———. *Media, Markets and Democracy*. Cambridge: Cambridge University Press, 2001.

———. "Turner Broadcasting: Content-Based Regulation of Persons and Presses." Pp. 57–128 in *The Supreme Court Review 1994*, edited by Dennis J. Hutchinson, David A. Strauss, and Geoffrey R. Stone. Chicago: University of Chicago Press, 1995.

Baker, Nigel. "Invisible Giants, Quiet Revolution." Pp. 63–78 in *International News in the Twenty-First Century*, edited by C. Paterson and A. Sreberny. Luton: Luton University Press, 2004.

Ballvé, Marcelo. "The Battle for Latino Media." *NACLA Report on the Americas*. 37, no. 4 (2004).

Balnaves, Mark, James Donald, and Stephanie Hemelryk Donald, eds. *The Penguin Atlas of Media Information: Key Issues and Global Trends*. New York: Penguin, 2001.

Barber, B. R. *Jihad v. McWorld*. New York: Ballantine, 1996.

Baril, Hélène. "Quebecor engranger les profits de Star Académie," *La Presse*, May 9, 2003, D 1.

Barker, David C., *Rushed to Judgment*. New York: Columbia University Press, 2002.

Barlow, William. *Voice Over: The Making of Black Radio*. Philadelphia: Temple University Press, 1999.

Barlow, Maude, and Tony Clarke. *Global Showdown: How the New Activists Are Fighting Global Corporate Rule*. Toronto: Stoddart, 2001.

Bass, Jack. "Newspaper Monopoly." In *Leaving Readers Behind*, edited by Gene Roberts, Thomas Kunkel, and Charles Clayton. Fayetteville: University of Arkansas Press, 2001.

Bates, Stephen. "Realigning Journalism with Democracy: The Hutchins Commission, Its Times, and Ours," <http://www.annenberg.northwestern.edu/pubs/hutchins/default.htm> (December 8, 2004).

BBC On-line. "Web Is 'Shrinking,'" *BBC On-line*. 1999 <news2.thls.bbc.co.uk/hi/english/sci/tech/newsid%5F428000/428999.stm>.

———. "Yahoo links with New York Times," *BBC On-line*, 2001 <news.bbc.co.uk/1/low/business/1168993.stm>.

Beam, Randal A. "What It Means to Be a Market-Oriented Newspaper," *Newspaper Research Journal* 16 (1995).

———. "Size of Corporate Parent Drives Market Orientation," *Newspaper Research Journal* 23 (2002).

Beckerman, Gail. "Tripping Up Big Media." *Columbia Journalism Review*, 13 November 2003.

Benkler, Yochai. "Intellectual Property and the Organization of Information Production." *International Review of Law and Economics* 22, no. 1 (2002): 81–107.

Bennett, W. Lance, and Regina G. Lawrence. "News Icons and the Mainstreaming of Social Change." *Journal of Communication* 45 (1995): 20–39.

———. "Media Power in the United States." Pp. 202–220 in *De-Westernizing Media Studies*, edited by James Curran and Myung-Jin Park. London and New York: Routledge, 2002.

Benoit, William L., and Glenn Hansen. "Issue Adaptation of Presidential Television Spots and Debates to Primary and General Audiences." *Communications Research Reports* 19 (2002).

Benson, Rodney. "Making the Media See Red: Pierre Bourdieu's Campaign against Television Journalism." *French Politics and Society* 16, no. 2 (Spring 1998): 59–66.

Berardi, Franco. "Bifo/Berardi, Interview on "The Factory of Unhappiness." 2001. <http://www.nettime.org> (21 June 2002).

Berger, P. L., and T. Luckman. *The Social Construction of Reality: A Treatise in the Sociology of Knowledge*. Garden City, N.Y.: Anchor Books, 1996.

Berkowitz, Dan, and David Pritchard. "Political Knowledge and Communication Resources." *Journalism Quarterly* 66 (1989): 697–702.

Bernier, Yvan. "Politiques Culturelles et Commerce International." In *Variations sur l'Influence Culturelle Américaine*, edited by Florian Sauvageau, Presses de l'Université Laval, Ste-Foy, Quebec, 1999.

Bernstein, James M., and Stephen Lacy. "Contextual Coverage of Government by Local Television News." *Journalism Quarterly* 69 (1992): 329–40.

Berss, Marcia. "Greener Pastures." *Forbes* (23 October 1995): 56–60.

Bimber, Bruce. "The Internet and Political Transformation: Populism, Community and Accelerated Pluralism." *Polity* 31, no. 1 (1998): 133–60.

Birdsall, William. "The Digital Divide in the Liberal State: A Canadian Perspective."*First Monday* 5, no.12 (2000). <http://firstmonday.org/issues/issue5_12/birdsall/index.html> (Nov. 17, 2003).

Bishop, Ronald and Ernest A. Hakanen. "In the Public Interest? The State of Local Television Programming Fifteen Years After Deregulation." *Journal of Communications Inquiry* 26, no. 3 (2002): 261–76.

Bissinger, Buzz. "The End of Innocence." Pp. 75–108 in *Leaving Readers Behind*, edited by Gene Roberts, Thomas Kunkel, and Charles Clayton. Fayetteville: University of Arkansas Press, 2001.

Blackwell, Richard. "Asper Wants Martin to Back Foreign Control." *Globe and Mail*, 14 November 2003.

Blatchford, Christie. "The Curious Trust We Share with Readers." *National Post,* 20 June 2002, <http://www.montrealnewspaperguild.com/canwestlinks.htm>.

Blevins, Fred. "The Hutchins Commission Turns 50: Recurring Themes in Today's Public and Civic Journalism," <http://mtprof.msun.edu/Fall1997/Blevins.html> (8 Dec. 2004).

Boehlert, Eric. "Is Pay-for-Play Finally Finished?" *Salon* (20 February 2003). <http://www.salon.com/ent/music/feature/2003/02/20/pay_for_play/index.html>.

———. "Congress to Big Media: Not so Fast." *Salon* (23 July 2003), <http://archive.salon.com/news/feature/2003/07/23/fcc/>.

———. "Radio's Big Bully." *Salon* (22 September 2003), <http://www.salon.com/ent/clear_channel/>.

Bogart, Leo. *Preserving the Press: How Daily Newspapers Mobilized to Keep Their Readers.* New York: Columbia University Press, 1991.

Bollinger, Lee C. *Journalism Task Force Statement.* Columbia University Graduate School of Journalism online, April 2003. (22 December 2003.)

Bordon, D. and K Harvery. *The Electronic Grapevine: Rumor, Reputation, and Reporting in the New Online Environment.* Mahwah, N.J.: Lawrence Erlbaum Associates, 1998.

Borjesson, Kristina. *Into the BUZZSAW.* Amherst, N.Y.: Prometheus Books, 2002.

Bourdieu, Pierre. "Television." *European Review* 9, no. 3 (2001): 245–56.

———. *On Television and Journalism.* London: Pluto Press, 1998.

Bove, Paul A. "The Function of the Literary Critic in the Postmodern World." Pp. 25–47 in *In the Wake of Theory*, edited by Paul A. Bove. Hanover, N.H.: Wesleyan University Press, 1992.

Boyer, Jean-Pierre. "Marchandisation ou démocratisation? - Pour une 'poléthique' de la communication sociale." Pp. 249–258 in *Petits écrans et démocratie*, edited by N. Thede and A. Ambrosi. Paris: Syros-Alternatives, 1992.

Boyd-Barrett, Oliver. "Media Imperialism: Towards an International Framework for the Analysis of Media Systems." Pp. 116–35 in *Mass Communication and Society*, edited by James Curran, Michael Gurevitch, and Janet Woollacott. London: Edward Arnold, 1977.

———. *The International News Agencies.* London: Constable, 1980.

———. "Global News Agencies." In *The Globalization of News*, edited by O. Boyd-Barrett and T. Rantanen. London: Sage, 1998.

Boyd-Barrett, Oliver, and K. Thussu. *Contra-Flow in Global News.* London: John Libbey, 1992.

Boyd-Barrett, Oliver, and Terhi Rantanen. *The Globalization of News.* London: Sage, 1998.

———. "News Agencies as News Sources: A Re-evaluation." Pp. 31–46 in *International News in the Twenty-First Century* edited by Chris Paterson and Annabelle Sreberny. Eastleigh, UK: John Libbey Press, 2004.

Bradford, William D. "Discrimination in Capital Markets, Broadcast/Wireless Spectrum Service Providers and Auction Outcomes." School of Business Administration, Univ. of Washington, 5 December 2000.

Brazeal, LeAnn M., and William L. Benoit. "A Functional Analysis of Congressional Television Spots." *Communications Quarterly* 49 (2001): 436–54.

Brecher, Jeremy, and Tim Costello. *Global Village or Global Pillage?* Boston: South End, 1994.

Breaux, Julie. "Deregulation Changing the Sound, Ownership of Radio in the Basin." *Odessa American.* 1 August 2004. <http://www.oaoa.com/news/nw010804c.html>.

Brians, Craig L. and Martin P. Wattenberg. "Campaign Issue Knowledge and Salience: Comparing Reception for TV Commercials, TV News, and Newspapers. *American Journal of Political* Science 40 (1996): 172–93.

Brill, Ann. "Way New Journalism: How Pioneers Are Doing." *Electronic Journal of Communication* 7, no. 2 (1997). <http://www.cios.org/getfile\Brill_V7N297>.

Broadcaster. "Making a Difference: Giving Back to the Community Remains a Top Priority at CanWest." *Broadcaster* 62, no. 1 (January 2003): 24.

Broadcaster. "Taking It to the Next Level: Leonard Asper Reveals His Convergence Strategy." *Broadcaster* 62, no. 1 (January 2003).

Broadcaster. "CanWest Global Milestones." *Broadcaster* 62, no. 1 (January 2003): 10.

Broadcasting & Cable. "NBC to Report Record Revenue." *Broadcasting & Cable* (4 December 2000).

Broadcasting & Cable Yearbook, 2002–2003. New York: Broadcasting and Cable, 2003.

Broadcasting Yearbook. New York: Broadcasting, 1980.

Brown, DeNeen L. "Journalists Feel Shackled by New Owner." *International Herald Tribune.* (January 31, 2002). <http://www.iht.com/articles/46496.html>.

Browning, Lynnley. "Making Waves on Air: Big Radio's Bad Boy." *New York Times,* 19 June 2002.

Bryant, Susan, and Richard Smith. "Computers and the Internet." Pp. 235–31 in *Mediascapes: New Patterns in Canadian Communication,* edited by Paul Attallah and Leslie Reagan Shade. Scarborough, Ont.; Nelson, 2002.

Bureau of Broadcast Measurement (BBM). BBM Spring 2003 TV Market Data Tidbits. (15 November 2003). <http://www.bbm.ca/Get_Data/TV_Data_Tidbits.html>.

Burden, P. "Interactivity and On-line News at the BBC." *CMCR*. Unpublished Masters Dissertation: University of Leicester, 1999.

Busterna, J.C. "Television Station Ownership Effects on Programming and Idea Diversity: Baseline Data." *Journal of Media Economics* 1, no. 2 (Fall 1988): 63–74.

Campaign for Press and Broadcasting Freedom. "Media Reform," 2003 <http://www.press campaign.org/proposals.htm>.

Campaign for Press and Broadcast Freedom. "Ownership Tables," 2004<http://www.press campaign.org> (5 March, 2004).

Canada. *Building the Information Society: Moving Canada into the 21st Century.* Ottawa: Mnister of Supply and Services, 1996.

Canada. Department of Heritage. Media Studies: Concentration of Ownership in the Media Part I, 2001, <www.pch.gc.ca/culture/convergence/pch/isspap1.html.> (7 Sept. 2004).

Canada. Information Highway Advisory Council. *Preparing Canada for a Digital World.* Ottawa: Industry Canada, 1997.

Canada, Industry Canada. "Convergence Policy Statement," 1996 <http://strategis.ic.gc.ca/epic/internet/insmt-gst.nsf/en/sf05265e.html> (12 Dec. 2004).

Canada. Ministry of Heritage. *Diversity and Concentration of Ownership in the Cultural Sector.* May 23, 2000, <http://www.pch.gc.ca/progrs/ac-ca/progs/esm-ms/divers2_e.cfm> (March 10, 2004).

Canada. Restrictive Trade Practices Commission. *Report: Concerning the Production and Supply of Newspapers in the City of Vancouver and Elsewhere in the Province of British Columbia* (Ottawa: 1960), 175.

Canada. Royal Commission on Corporate Concentration. *Report*. Ottawa: Minister of Supply and Services Canada, 1978.

Canada. Royal Commission on Newspapers (Kent Report). *Report*. Ottawa: Minister of Supply and Services Canada, 1981.

Canada. Royal Commission on the Development of the Arts, Letters and Sciences, *Report*. Ottawa: King's Printer, 1951.

Canada. Special Senate Committee on Mass Media (Davey Committee). *Uncertain Mirror: Report of the Special Senate Committee on Mass Media.* Vol. 1. Ottawa: Queen's Printer, 1970.

Canada. Standing Committee on Canadian Heritage. *Our Cultural Sovereignty: The Second Century of Canadian Broadcasting. Report of the House of Commons Standing Committee on Canadian Heritage*, Ottawa: Communication Canada, 2003.

Canada. Task Force on Broadcasting Policy. *Report*. Ottawa: Minister of Supply and Services, 1986.

Canadian Broadcasting Corporation (CBC). "CBC/Radio-Canada Annual Report 2002–03." *Cbc.radio-canada.* <http://cbc.radio-canada.ca/htmen/annual_report/2002-2003/pdf/CBC_2002-2003_annual_report.pdf> (10 November 2003).

Canadian Heritage Standing Committee. *Our Cultural Sovereignty: The Second Century of Canadian Broadcasting*. Ottawa: Canadian Government Publishing, 2003. <http://www.parl.gc.ca/InfoComDoc/37/2/HERI/Studies/Reports/herirp02-e.htm>.

Canadian Journalists for Free Expression. *Not in the Newsroom! CanWest Global, Chain Editorials and Freedom of Expression in Canada*, <http:www.cjfe.org/specials/canwest/canwintro.html> (26 March 2004).

Canadian Press. "CanWest Global May Sell More Assets." *Charlottetown Guardian*, 22 January, 2003, B11.

Canadian Press. "CanWest Is Dropping the Historic Name of its Southam Newspapers Group, Founded by the Southam Family 126 Years Ago and Purchased by CanWest from Hollinger Inc. Three Years Ago." *Canadian-Press-Newswire*, 28 January 2003.

Canadian Radio-Television and Telecommunications Commission. *Canadian Ownership of Broadcasting*. Ottawa: Minister of Supply and Services, 1974.

Canoe. "Le CRTC se penche sur la transaction Quebecor-Videotron." *Canoe* 26 March 2001, <http://lcn.canoe.com/economie/nouvelles/archives/2001/03/20010326-001306.html> (23 June 2004).

Capital Broadcasting Compay. "Congress Implements Tools to Block FCC's June Ruling." Capitol Broadcasting Company, July 21, 2003, <http://www.cbc-raleigh.com/capcom/news/2003/corporate_03/fcc_congress/fcc_congress.htm>.

Carey, James W. "American Journalism On, Before, and After September 11." Pp. 71–90 in *Journalism After September 11*, edited by Barbie Zelizer and Stuart Allan. London and New York: Routledge, 2002.

Carroll, Raymond L. "Market Size and TV News Values." *Journalism Quarterly* 66 (1989): 49–56.

Carroll, Raymond L., and C. A. Tuggle. "The World Outside: Local TV News Treatment of Imported News." *Journalism and Mass Communications Quarterly* 74, no. 1 (Spring 1997): 123–33.

Carter, Sue, Frederick Fico, and Joycelyn A. McCabe. "Partisan and Structural Balance in Local Television Election Coverage." *Journalism and Mass Communications Quarterly* 79, no. 1 (2002): 41–53.

CBC News. "CanWest Selling Ontario Newspapers to Osprey Media." *CBC News* (27 January 2003). <http://www.cbc.ca/stories/2003/01/27/canwest_030127>.

Center for International Media Action. *The Media Policy Action Directory: Organizations Urging FCC Limits on Media Ownership*. Brooklyn, N.Y.: CIMA, (2003).

Center for Public Integrity. "Well Connected: The Data Bases." <http://www.openairwaves.org/telecom> (2003).

Central Intelligence Agency. *The World Fact Book: Canada*. <http://www.odci.gov/cia/publications/factbook/geos/ca.html> (22 March 2004).

Chaffee, Steven H., Xinshu Zhao, and Glenn Leshner. "Political Knowledge and the Campaign Media of 1992." *Communications Research*, 21 (1994): 305–24.

Chan-Olmsted, Sylvia, and Jung Suk Park. "From On-Air to Online World: Examining the Content and Structures of Broadcast TV Stations' Web Sites." *Journalism & Mass Communication Quarterly* 77, no. 2 (2000): 321–39.

Chang, Jeff. "Urban Radio Rage." *Bay Guardian*, 22 January 2003. <http://www.sfbg.com/37/18/cover_kmel.html>.

Chen, Christine Y. "The Bad Boys of Radio" *Fortune*; 3 March 2003.

Chibnall, Steve. *Law-and-Order News: An Analysis of Crime Reporting in the British Press*. London: Tavistock, 1977.

Children Now. "Children Now Praises FCC for New Educational Television Rules." 2004 <http://www.childrennow.org/newsroom/news-04/pr-09-09-04.cfm>.

Choi, Hyeon Cheol, and Samuel Becker. "Media Use, Issue/Image Discrimination." *Communications Research* 14, no. 3 (1987): 267–90.

Christopher, L. Carol. "Technology and Journalism in the On-Line Newsroom." Pp. 123–41 in *The Electronic Grapevine: Rumor, Reputation, and Reporting in the New On-Line Environment*, edited by D. Borden and K. Harvey. Mahwah, N.J.: Lawrence Erlbaum Associates, 1998.

Chyi, Hsiang Iris, and Dominic L. Lasora. "An Exploratory Study on the Market Relation between Online and Print Newspapers." *The Journal of Media Economics* 15 (2002).

Clarke, Debra. "Class, Gender, and Much More: The Complexities of Ethnographic Audience Research." Forthcoming in *Studying Social Life: Substance and Method*, edited by Dorothy Pawluch, William Shaffir, and Charlene Miall. Toronto: CSPI/Women's Press, 2005.

———. "The Active Pursuit of Active Viewers: Directions in Audience Research." *Canadian Journal of Communication* 25, no. 1 (Winter 2000): 39–59.

———. "Constraints of Television News Production: The Example of Story Geography." Pp. 107–31 in *Critical Studies of Canadian Mass Media*, edited by Marc Grenier. Toronto: Butterworths, 1992.

———. "Second-Hand News: Production and Reproduction at a Major Ontario Television Station." Pp. 20–51 in *Communication Studies in Canada*, edited by Liora Salter. Toronto: Butterworths, 1981.

Clarke, Steve. "London: International News Capital." *Variety*, 18 December 1995.

Clear Channel Inc. "Clear Channel Cuts Ties with Independent Promoters," Press Release. Clear Channel, 9 April 2003. <http://www.clearchannel.com/documents/press_releases/20030409_Corp_Indies.pdf>

Clear Channel, Inc. Company webpage. <http://www.clearchannel.com/company_history.php> (14 September 2003).

Cleaver, Harry. "The Chiapas Uprising," *Studies in Political Economy* 44 (1994): 141–57.

———. "The Zapatista Effect: The Internet and the Rise of an Alternative Political Fabric." *Journal of International Affairs* 5, no. 2 (1998): 621–40.

Cloud, Dana. "Doing Away with Suharto and the Twin Myth of Globalization and New Social Movements." Pp. 235–63 in *Counterpublics and the State*, edited by Robert Aspen and Daniel C. Brouwer. New York: State University of New York Press, 2001.

CNews. "Davis Leaves CanWest Global." *CNews Media News*. 2003 <http://cnews.canoe.ca/CNEWS/MediaNews/2003/05/16/89119-cp.html> (16 May 2003).

Cobden, Michael. "The Danger of CanWest's National Editorials." *Globe and Mail*, 30 January 2002, B15.

Cockburn, Alexander, and Jeffrey St. Clair, *Five Days That Shook the World: Seattle and Beyond*. London and New York: Verso, 2000.

Cockburn, Neco. "CanWest Plans Book Unit." *Toronto Star*, 1 April 2004, D3.

Cohen, A., M. Levy, I. Roeh, and M. Gurevitch. *Global Newsroom, Local Audiences: A Study of the Eurovision News Exchange*. London: John Libbey, 1996.

Cohen, Bernard. *The Press and Foreign Policy*. Princeton, N.J.: Princeton University, 1963.

Collins-Jarvis, Lori A. "Gender Representation in an Electronic City Hall: Female Adoption of Santa Monica's PEN System." *Journal of Broadcasting and Electronic Media* (1993).

Colon, Aly. "The Multimedia Newsroom." *Columbia Journalism Review* 39, no. 1 (June 2000): 24–27.

Commission on Freedom of the Press. *A Free and Responsible Press: A General Report on Mass Communications—Newspapers, Radio, Motion Pictures, Magazines, and Books*. Chicago: University of Chicago Press, 1947.

Compaine, Benjamin M., and Douglas Gomery. *Who Owns the Media? Competition and Concentration in the Mass Media Industry*. 3rd edition, Mahwah, N.J.: Erlbaum, 2000.

Compton, James R. *The Integrated News Spectacle: A Political Economy of Cultural Performance*. New York: Peter Lang, 2004.

Congressional Research Service, Statistical Analysis of FCC Survey Data: Minority *Broadcast Station Ownership and Minority Broadcasting*. Washington, D.C.: U.S. Government Printing Office, 1988.

Congressional Research Service, *Minority Broadcast Station Ownership and Broadcast Programming: Is There a Nexus?* Washington, D.C.: Library of Congress, 1988.

Conseil de la Radiodiffusion et des Télécommunications Canadiennes (CRTC), press release "Le CRTC ne réglementera pas internet, " 17 May 1999. <http://www.crtc.gc.ca/FRN/NEWS/RELEASES/1999/R990517.htm>.

Consumer Union, Consumer Federation of America, Center for Digital Democracy and Media Access Project. "Comments of the Consumer Federation of America, et al.," *In the Matter of Cross Ownership of Broadcast Stations and Newspaper; Newspaper/Radio Cross-Ownership Waiver Policy* (Federal Communications Commission, MM Docket Nos. 01-235, 96–197), December 4 2001.

Cook, Timothy E. *Governing with the News: The News Media as a Political Institution*. Chicago: University of Chicago Press, 1998.

Cooper, Mark N. *Cable Mergers and Monopolies: Market Power Digital Media and Communications Networks* Washington, D.C.: Economic Policy Institute, 2002.

——. "Inequality in Digital Society." *Cardozo Journal On Media and the Arts* 73 (2002).

——. *Media Ownership and Democracy in the Digital Information Age*. Center for Internet and Society, Stanford Law School, 2003.

Copps, Michael. "Statement of Commissioner Michael J. Copps Dissenting, 2002 Biennial Regulatory Review," July 2, 2003, <http://hraunfoss.fcc.gov/edocs_public/attachmatch/FCC-03-127A5.doc>.

Cottle, Simon. "From BBC Newsroom to BBC Centre: On Changing Technology and Journalist Practices." Unpublished Paper, 1999.

Couldry, Nick. "Beyond the Hall of Mirrors?: Some Theoretical Reflections on the Global Contestation of Media Power." Pp. 39–54 in *Contesting Media Power: Alternative Media in a Networked World*, edited by Nick Couldry and James Curran. Lanham, Md.: Rowman & Littlefield, 2003.

Coulson, David C. "Impact of Ownership on Newspaper Quality." *Journalism Quarterly* (1994).

Coulson David C., and Anne Hanson. "The Louisville Courier-Journal's News Content After Purchase By Gannett." *Journalism & Mass Communication Quarterly* 72, no. 1 (Spring 1995): 205–15.

Coulson, David C., and Stephen Lacy. "Newspapers and Joint Operating Agreements." In *Contemporary Media Issues*, edited by E. Sloan David and Emily Erickson Hoff. Northport, Ala.: Vision Press, 1998.

Council of Canadians, Campaign for Press and Broadcasting Freedom. *Policies for a Democratic Media: Confronting the Problem of Media Ownership Concentration in Canada*. Spring 1997.

Crabtree, Susan, and Justin Oppelaar. "Clear Channel Snips Indie Promo Ties." *Daily Variety*, 10 April 2003.

Craig, Gully. "Corporate censorship: CanWest muzzles staff." *Index on Censorship*. 2002. <http://www.indexonline.org/news/20020418_Canada.shtml> (April 18, 2002).

Cranberg, Gilbert, Randall Bezanson, and John Soloski. *Taking Stock: Journalism and the Publicly Traded Newspaper Company*. Ames: Iowa State University Press, 2001.

Crenson, Matthew A., and Benjamin Ginsberg. *Downsizing Democracy*. Baltimore: Johns Hopkins University Press, 2002.

Crigler, Ann N., ed. *The Psychology of Political Communications*. Ann Arbor: University of Michigan Press, 1996.

Cullen, Jim. *The Art of Democracy: A Concise History of Popular Culture in the United States.* New York: Monthly Review Press, 2002.

Cundy, Donald T. "Political Commercials and Candidate Image." Pp. 210–34 in *New Perspectives in Political Advertising,* edited by Lynda Lee Kaid. Carbondale, Ill.: Southern Illinois University Press, 1986.

Cunningham, Brent. "The Mission: Searching for the Perfect J-school." *Columbia Journalism Review* online. November/December 2002 (21 December 2003.)

Curran, James, *Media and Power.* London: Routledge, 2002.

Curran, James. "Global Media Concentration: Shifting the Argument." *OpenDemocracy.* 2002. <http://www.openDemocracy.net> (May 22, 2002).

Curtin, Michael. *Redeeming the Wasteland: Television Documentary and Cold War Politics.* New Brunswick, N.J.: Rutgers University Press, 1995.

Dahlberg, Lincoln. "The Internet and Democratic Discourse." *Information, Communications and Society* 4, no. 4 (2001): 615–33.

Damsell, Keith. "CanWest Wins License to Launch Jazz Radio." *Globe and Mail.* 2002. <http://www.friendscb.org/articles/GlobeandMail/globe020809.htm> (9 August 2002).

———. "CanWest Scales Back Policy." *Globe and Mail,* 12 February 2002, B8.

———. "CanWest Set to Launch News Hub." *Globe and Mail,* 20 January 2003, B20.

Davie, William R., and Jung-Sook Lee. "Television News Technology: Do More Sources Mean Less Diversity?" *Journal of Broadcasting and Electronic Media* 37, no. 4 (1993): 453–64.

Dawkins, Walter, and Mathew S. Scott. "Battle for the Airwaves!" *Black Enterprise* 33, no. 10 (May 2003).

Deacon, David, Natalie Fenton, and Alan Bryman. "From Inception to Reception: The Natural History of a News Item." *Media, Culture & Society* 21, no. 1 (January 1999): 5–31.

de Bonville, Jean. *La Presse Québécoise de 1884 à 1914: Genèse d'un Media de Masse.* Quebec: Presses de l'Université Laval, 1988.

Dellinger, M. "It's O.K., I'm with Clear Channel." *New York Times,* 29 June 2003.

Demers, David. "Corporate Newspaper Bashing: Is it Justified?" *Newspaper Research Journal,* 20, no. 1 (Winter 1999): 83–97.

Denning, Dorothy. "Hacktivism: An Emerging Threat to Diplomacy," <http:www.afsa.org/fsj/sep00/Denning.html> (April 6, 2002).

Dichter, Aliza. "U.S. Media Reform." Presented to the Framing Communications Rights Meeting. Communications Rights in the Information Society. Geneva, Switzerland, December 8, 2003.

———. "Where Are the People in the 'Public Interest'? U.S. Media Activism and the Search for Constituency." *Media Development,* 2004.

Dicola, Peter, and Kristin Thomson. *Radio Deregulation: Has It Served Citizens and Musicians?* Future of Music Coalition, (18 November 2002).

Digital Television. "Profile with Bob Wright: The Agony Before the Ecstasy of Digital TV." *Digital Television,* April 1999.

Dimmick, John B. "The Theory of the Niche and Spending on Mass Media: The Case of the Video Revolution." *Journal of Media Economics* 10 (1997): 33–43.

Diversity of Voices. "Is Freedom of the Press Being Lost, One Newsroom at a Time?" *Globe and Mail* 6 June 2002, A7. [advertisement for www.DiversityOfVoices.ca]

Domke, David, David Perlmutter, and Meg Spratt. "The Primes of Our Times? An Examination of the 'Power' of Visual Images." *Journalism* 3, no. 2 (2002): 131–159.

Dorner, Andreas. *Politainment.* Frankfurt/Main: Surhkamp, 2001.

Dougherty, J. "Indian Ruin: The Zuni Tribes Plans for Phoenix Billboards Were Abruptly Canceled by Clear Channel." *Phoenix New Times,* 6 February 2003.

Douglas, Susan. "Amateur Operators and American Broadcasting: Shaping the Future of Radio." In *Imagining Tomorrow: History, Technology and the American Future,* edited by Joseph J. Corn. Cambridge, Massachusetts: MIT Press, 1986.

———. "Seize the Moment," *In These Times,* 17 November, 2003, 15.

Dowmunt, Tony. "An Alternative Globalization: Youthful Resistance to Electronic Empires." Pp. 243–56 in *Electronic Empires: Global Media and Local Resistance,* edited by Daya Kishan Thussu. London: Arnold, 1998.

Downie, Jr., Leonard, and Robert G. Kaiser. *The News about the News: American Journalism in Peril.* New York: Vintage Books, 2002.

Downing, John, with Tamara Villareal Ford, Geneve Gil, and Laura Stein. *Radical Media: Rebellious Communication and Social Movements.* Thousand Oaks, Calif.: Sage, 2001.

Downing, John. "Independent Media Centres: A Multi-local, Multi-media Challenge to Global Neoliberalism." Pp. 215–32 in *Global Media Policy in the New Millennium.* edited by Marc Raboy. Luton: University of Luton Press, 2002.

——. "The Independent Media Center Movement and the Anarchist Socialist Tradition." Pp. 243–57 in *Contesting Media Power: Alternative Media in a Networked World,* edited by Nick Couldry and James Curran. Lanham, Md.: Rowman & Littlefield, 2003.

Drainville, André. "Québec City 2001 and the Making of Transnational Subjects." Pp.15–45 in *Socialist Register 2002: A World of Contradictions,* edited by Leo Panitch and Colin Leys. London: Merlin, 2001.

Dreazen, Yochi J. "No-Frills Fighter Stuns the FCC, Media Goliaths." *Wall Street Journal Online.* 2003. <http://www.wsjonline.com> (5 September 2003).

Drew, Dan, and David Weaver. "Voter Learning in the 1988 Presidential Election: Did the Media Matter?" *Journalism Quarterly* 68 (1991).

Dubin, Jeff, and Matthew L. Spitzer. "Testing Minority Preferences in Broadcasting." *Southern California Law Review* 68, no. 4 (May 1995): 841–84.

Dugger, Ronald. "The Corporate Domination of Journalism." Pp. 27–56 in *The Business of Journalism,* edited by Williams Serrin. New York: New Press, 2000.

Dumas, Hugo. "Congédiement arbitraire de TVA." *La Presse,* 1 May 2004, A1.

Dunbar, John and Aron Pilhofer. "Big Radio Rules in Small Markets." The Center for Public Integrity. *Openairwaves* 2003. <http://www.openairwaves.org/telecom/report.aspx?aid=63>.

Dutton, William H., Jay G. Blumler, and Kenneth L. Kraemer, ed. *Wired Cities: Shaping the Future of Communications.* Boston: K. G. Hall, 1987.

Dyer-Witheford, Nick. "E-Capital and the Many-Headed Hydra." Pp 129–63 in *Critical Perspectives on the Internet,* edited by Greg Elmer. Lanham, Md.: Rowman & Littlefield, 2002.

——. *Cyber-Marx: Cycles and Circuits of Struggle in High-Technology Capitalism.* Urbana: University of Illinois Press, 1999.

Editor and Publisher. "Reporter Apologizes for Iraq Coverage." *Editor and Publisher,* 29 March 2004.

Edge, Marc. *Pacific Press: The Unauthorized Story of Vancouver's Newspaper Monopoly.* Vancouver: New Star Books, 2001.

Edwards, Stephen. "CanWest on Mission to Woo U.S. Investors." *Vancouver Sun,* 10 February, 2004, D7.

Elliott, Philip. "Professional Ideology and Organizational Change: The Journalist since 1800." Pp. 172–91 in *Newspaper History: From the Seventeenth Century to the Present Day,* edited by George Boyce, James Curran, and Pauline Wingate. London: Constable, 1978.

Ellis, John. "Why the Pirates Will Win: Television May Hurt, Rather than Help, the New Media Moguls as They Work to Make Convergence a Reality." *Marketing* 106, no. 8 (26 February 2001): 25.

Epstein, Edward Jay. *News From Nowhere: Television and the News.* New York: Random House, 1973.

Esslin, Martin. *The Age of Television.* New Brunswick, N.J.: Transaction, 2002.

Ettema, James and Whitney D. Charles, eds. *Audience Making: How the Media Create the Audience,* Thousand Oaks, Calif.: Sage, 1994.

European Journalism Centre. *The Future of the Printed Press: Challenges in a Digital World.* 1998. <www.ejc.nl/hp/fpp/execsum.html>.

Evans, Akousa Barthewell. "Are Minority Preferences Necessary? Another Look at the Radio Broadcasting Industry." *Yale Law and Policy Review* 8 (1990).

Evans, W. "Content Analysis in an Era of Interactive News: Assessing 21st Century Symbolic Environments." Pp. 161–71 in *The Electronic Grapevine: Rumor, Reputation and Reporting in the New On-Line Environment,* edited by D. Borden and K. Harvey. Mahwah, N.J.: Lawrence Erlbaum Associates, 1998.

Everett, Robert, and Frederic J. Fletcher. "The Mass Media and Political Communication in Canada." Pp. 165–78 in *Communications in Canadian Society,* Fifth Edition, edited by Craig McKie and Benjamin D. Singer. Toronto: Thompson Educational Publishing Inc., 2001.

EZLN (Zapatista Army of National Liberation). "Second Declaration of La Realidad (Reality) for Humanity against Neoliberalism," 3 August 1996.

Fairchild, Charles. "Deterritorializing Radio: Deregulation and the Continuing Triumph of the Corporatist Perspective in the USA." *Media, Culture & Society* 21, no. 4 (1999): 549–61.

FCC, Public Service Responsibility of Broadcast Licensees. Washington, D.C.: FCC, 1946.

———. "National Proposed Rule Making 96–90." 1996 <http://www.fcc.gov/Bureaus/Mass_Media/ Orders/1996/fcc96090.txt>.

———. Report and Order and Notice of Proposed Rulemaking, 2002 Biennial Regulatory Review–Review of the Commission's Broadcast Ownership Rules and Other Rules Adopted Pursuant to Section 202 of the Telecommunications Act of 1996 (MB Docket 02-277). Adopted June 2, 2003; released July 2, 2003.

———. Localism Task Force. 2004 <http://www.fcc.gov/localism>.

Federal News Service. "Hearing of the Senate Commerce, Science and Transportation Committee: Hearing on Media Ownership." *Federal News Service Inc.,* 30 January 2003.

Fédération des Télévisions Communautaires Autonomes du Québec (FEDETVC). "Allocution sur l'étude de l'état du système canadien de radiodiffusion" (2002), presented to the Canadian Heritage standing committee, 19 March.

———. "La Télévision Communautaire, en Extinction de Voix!" (16 Dec, 1999) <www.fedetvc .qc.ca/Communiques/Communique_1999_Decembre_VoixDextinction.doc> (22 July 2004).

Fedlin, E. "Rethinking the News Story for the Internet: Hyperstory Prototypes and a Model of the User *Journalism Monographs* (1997): 163.

Fenby, Jonathan *The International News Services,* Twentieth Century Fund Report. New York: Schocken Books, 1986.

Ferrall, V. E. "The Impact of Television Deregulation." *Journal of Communication* 39, no. 1 (1992): 8–38.

Fife, Marilyn D., *The Impact of Minority Ownership on Broadcast Program Content: A Case Study of WGPR-TV's Local News Content.* Washington, D.C.: National Association of Broadcasters, 1979.

———. *The Impact of Minority Ownership on Broadcast Program Content: A Multi-Market Study.* Washington, D.C.: National Association of Broadcasters, 1986.

Figueroa, Maria, Damone Richardson, and Pam Whitefield. *The Clear Picture on Clear Channel Communications, Inc: A Corporate Profile.* 28 January 2004. Ithaca, N.Y.: Cornell University Press.

Firestone, Charles M., and Jorge M. Schement. *Toward an Information Bill of Rights and Responsibilities.* Washington, D.C.: Aspen Institute, 1995.

Fisher, Marc. "The Metamorphosis: A Quarter Century of Dramatic Change." *American Journalism Review* 24, no. 9 (November 2002): 20–25.

Fisher, William, and Thomas Ponniah, eds. *Another World is Possible: Popular Alternatives to Globalization at the World Social Forum.* Black Point, NS.: Fernwood, 2003.

Foot, Kirsten A., and Steven M. Schneider. "Online Action in Campaign 2000: An Exploratory Analysis of the U.S. Political Web Sphere." *Journal of Broadcasting and Electronic Media* 46, no. 2 (2002): 222–44.

Foss, Krista. "CanWest Presses Ottawa on Media Legislation." *Globe and Mail,* 2 March 2002, B4.

Foucault, Michel. *Discipline and Punish: The Birth of the Prison.* Trans. Alan Sheridan. New York: Vintage Books, 1979.

———. "Truth and Power," Pp. 51–75 in *The Foucault Reader,* edited by Paul Rabinow. New York: Pantheon, 1984.

Future of Music. Joint Statement on Current Issues in Radio; American Federation of Musicians (AFM), American Federation of Television and Radio Artists (AFTRA), Artist Empowerment Coalition (AEC), Association for Independent Music (AFIM), Future of Music Coalition (FMC), Just Plain Folks, Music Managers Forum (MMF), Nashville Songwriters Association International (NSAI), National Association of Recording Merchandisers (NARM), Recording Artists' Coalition (RAC). 2002. <http://www.futureofmusic.org/news/radioissuesstatement .cfm> (May 24, 2002).

Future of Music. "Citizens Urge FCC to Retain Current Media Ownership Rules. FCC Public Record Shows Overwhelming Opposition to Relaxing Ownership Caps." 2003. <http://www .futureofmusic.org/news/PRFCCdocket.cfm> (May 14, 2003).

Galtung, Johan, and Mari Holmboe Ruge. "The Structure of Foreign News." *Journal of Peace Research* 2 (1965): 64–91.

Gangadharan, Seeta. "Who Cares, What's Wrong, and Why It Matters: A Guide for Reporters Covering the Biggest Media-Regulation Battle of 2003." Media Alliance and the Centre for International Media Action, 2003.

———. "Why Are Civil Rights Groups Neglecting Media Policy" *Alternet.org.* 2002. <http://www .alternet.org/print.html?Story ID=12841>.

Gans, Herbert J. *Democracy and the News.* Oxford: Oxford University Press, 2003.

Garcia, Gilbert. "Real-Deal Minority Broadcasters Face the Threat of Big Media." *San Antonio Current.* 22 January 2004.

———. "When Latino Doesn't Mean Latino. Real-Deal Minority Broadcasters Face the Threat of Big Media." *San Antonio Current.* 22 January 2004.

Garner, Amy Korzick, ed. *Investing in Diversity: Advancing Opportunities for Minorities in Media.* Washington, D.C.: Aspen Institute, 1998.

Garrido, Maria, and Alexander Halavais. "Mapping Networks of Support for the Zapatista Movement: Applying Social Networks Analysis to Study Contemporary Social Movements." Pp. 145–64 in *Cyberactivism: Online Activism in Theory and Practice,* edited by Martha McCaughey and Michael D. Ayers. New York & London: Routledge, 2003.

Gasher, Mike. "From Sacred Cows to White Elephants: Cultural Policy Under Siege." Pp.13–29 in *Canadian Cultures and Globalization,* edited by Joy Cohnstaedt and Yves Frechette. Montreal: Association for Canadian Studies, 1997.

———. "Point of View: Does CanWest Know What All the Fuss Is About?" *Media Magazine.* Winter 2002 <http://www.caj.ca/mediamag/winter2002/pov.html>.

Gatlin, Greg. "Reps Balk as Senate Rolls Back FCC Rules," *Boston Herald.* 2003. <http://www .bostonherald.com> (17 September 2003).

Gauger, T. G. "The Constitutionality of the FCC's Use of Race and Sex in Granting Broadcast Licenses," *Northwestern Law Review* (1989).

George, Éric. "Le Droit à Communiquer entre Médias Traditionnels et l'Internet." Pp. 325–42 in *Philosophie et Mondialisation,* sous la direction de Yves Bonin. Quebec: Presses de l'Université Laval, 2001.

Giffard, Anthony, and Nancy Rivenburgh. "News Agencies, National Images, and Global Media Events." Paper for the IAMCR Annual Conference, Glasgow, 1998.

Gimpel, James G. *Separate Destinations: Migration, Immigration and the Politics of Places.* Ann Arbor: University of Michigan Press, 1999.

Gish, Pat, and Tom Gish. "We Still Scream: The Perils and Pleasures of Running a Small-Town Newspaper," Pp.1–26 in *The Business of Journalism,* edited by William Serrin. New York: New Press, 2000.

Gitlin, Todd. "Bits and Blips: Chunk News, Savvy Talk and the Bifurcation of American Politics." Pp. 119–36 in *Communications and Citizenship: Journalism and the Public Sphere*, edited by P. Dahlgren and C. Sparks. London: Routledge, 1991.

Glasgow University Media Group. Viewing the World: A Study of British Television Coverage of Developing Countries. London: Department for International Development, 2000, <http://www.dfid.gov.uk> (10 October 2003).

Globe and Mail. "Let's Press for Press Freedom." *Globe and Mail*, 19 April 2002, A13.

Godin, Pierre. *La lutte pour l'information: Histoire de la presse écrite au Québec*. Montréal: Le Jour, 1981.

Goldberg, Bernard, *Bias*. Washington, D.C.: Regnery, 2002.

Golding, Peter and Philip Elliott. *Making the News*. London: Longman, 1979.

Goyette, Charles. "How to Lose Your Job in Talk Radio: Clear Channel Gags an Anti-war Conservative." *American Conservative*. 2004. <http://www.amconmag.com/1_19_04/article3.html> (February 2, 2004)

Graber, Doris, *Mass Media and American Politics*. Washington, D.C.: Congressional Quarterly, 1997.

———. *Processing Politics*. Chicago: University of Chicago Press, 2001.

Granjon, Fabien and Dominique Cardon. "Mouvement altermondialiste et militantisme informationnel." Paper presented at the Association of Internet Researchers Conference, Toronto, On., October 2003.

Grant, T. "Media Spat: Profit vs. Free Speech." *The Christian Science Monitor*. 2002. <http://www.csmonitor.com/2002/0215/p06s01-woam.htm> (15 February 2002).

Gray, J. "Waiting for the Wave: BCE and CanWest Global Bet Big on Convergence, Counting on a Surge of Revenue. But It Might Turn into One Long Drought." *Canadian Business* 74, no. 9 (May 14, 2001): 30–32, 34–36.

Grove, Lloyd, 2002. "The Reliable Source." *Washington Post*, 19 November, C3.

Guiffo, John. "Smoke Gets in Your Eyes." *Columbia Journalism Review*. September/October 2001, <http://archives.cjr.org/year/01/5/giuffo.asp> (Nov. 17, 2003).

Gunther, Albert C. "The Persuasive Press Inference: Effects of Mass Media on Perceived Public Opinion." *Communications Research* 25 (October 1998): 481–99.

Gutstein, Donald. *E.Con: How the Internet Undermines Democracy*. Toronto: Stoddart, 1999.

Gwiasda, Gregory W. "Network News Coverage of Campaign Advertisements: Media's Ability to Reinforce Campaign Messages." *American Politics Research* 29 (2001).

Ha, T. T. "Sparks Fly in Quebec over Changes at Gazette." *Globe and Mail*, December 21, 2001, A7.

Habermas, Jürgen. *The Structural Transformation of the Public Sphere*. Cambridge: Polity, 1989.

———. *Between Facts and Norms*. Cambridge: Polity, 1996.

Hackett, Robert, Richard Pinet, and Myles Ruggles. "From Audience Commodity to Audience Community: Mass Media in B.C." Pp. 10–20 in *Seeing Ourselves: Media Power and Policy in Canada*, edited by David Taras and Helen Holmes.Toronto: Harcourt, Brace, Jovanovich, 1992.

Hackett, Robert and Yeuzhi Zhao. *Sustaining Democracy: Journalism and the Politics of Objectivity*. Toronto: Garamond Press, 1998.

Hackett, Robert. "Taking Back the Media: Notes on the Potential for a Communicative Democracy Movement." *Studies in Political Economy* 63 (Autumn 2000): 61–86.

Hagen, Lutz. "Foreign News in German Media in 1979 and in 1995." Paper for the IAMCR Annual Conference, Sydney, 1996.

Halleck, Dee. *Hand-Held Visions: The Impossible Possibilities of Community Media*. New York: Fordham University Press, 2002.

———. "Gathering Storm: Cyberactivism After Seattle." Pp.202–14 in *Media, Profit and Politics: Competing Priorities in an Open Society*, edited by Joseph Harper and Thom Yantek. Kent, Ohio: Kent State University Press, 2003.

Hamilton, James T. *Channeling Violence: The Economic Market for Violent Television Programming*. Princeton, N.J.: Princeton University Press, 1998.

————. *All the News That's Fit to Sell: How the Market Transforms Information Into News.* Princeton, N.J.: Princeton University Press, 2004.

Hanchette, John. "USA Today' Editors Should Not Emerge Unscathed," Says Pulitzer Winner," *Editor and Publisher*, 22 March 2003.

Hansen, Glenn J., and William Benoit. "Presidential Television Advertising and Public Policy Priorities, 1952–2002," *Communications Studies* 53 (2002).

Hanson, Christopher. "The Dark Side of On-Line Scoops." *Columbia Journalism Review* (May/June 1997).

Hanson, John Mark. "The Majoritarian Impulse and the Declining Significance of Place, in *The Future of American Democratic Politics*, edited by Gerald M. Pomper and Marc D. Weiner. New Brunswick, N.J.: Rutgers University Press, 2003.

Hardt, Michael, and Antonio Negri. *Empire.* Cambridge, Mass.: Harvard University Press, 2000.

Harper, Christopher. "The Daily Me." *American Journalism Review* (April 1997): 40–44.

Harris, Jay. "Luncheon Address to ASNE." Address presented at American Society of Newspaper Editors. ASNE Reporter. 6 April 2001. <http://www.asne.org/index.cfm?id=1525> (22 Sept. 2003).

Harris Leslie & Associates. (2001) Media Diversity: A Status Report.

Harsano, Andreas. "Indonesia: From Mainstream to Alternative Media." *First Monday* 1, no. 3 1996 <http://www.firstmonday.dk/issues/issue3/harsono/index.html> (April 14, 2002).

Hart, Jr., T. A. "The Case for Minority Broadcast Ownership." *Gannet Center Journal* (1988).

Hayuk, Ronald, and Kevin Mattson, eds., *Democracy's Moment: Reforming the American Political System for the 21st Century.* Lanham, Md.: Rowman & Littlefield, 2002.

Held, David. "Democracy and the International Order." Pp. 96–120 in *Cosmopolitan Democracy: An Agenda for the New World Order*, edited by David Held and Daniele Archibugi. Cambridge: Polity Press, 1995.

Held, David, and Anthony McGrew. *Globalization/Anti-Globalization.* Cambridge: Polity, 2002.

Helland, Knut. "Public Service and Commercial News." Doctoral Dissertation. University of Bergen, 1995.

Hellman, Judith Adler. "Virtual Chiapas: A Reply to Paulson." Pp.289–93 in *Socialist Register 2001: Working Classes, Global Realities*, edited by Leo Panitch and Colin Leys. London: Merlin, 2000.

Herman, Edward S. and Noam Chomsky. *Manufacturing Consent: The Political Economy of the Mass Media.* New York: Pantheon, 1988.

Hesmondhalgh, David. *The Cultural Industries.* London: Sage Publications, 2002.

Hickey, Neil. "Unshackling Big Media." *Columbia Journalism Review* (March/April 2002).

————. "We, the Media: With the FCC Leaning toward Relaxing Regulations on Ownership of TV and Radio Stations and Newspapers, Expect More Consolidation of Media Properties into a Few Huge Corporations and Less Diversity of Content and Viewpoint." *Metroland.* Albany, May 15, 2003. Vol. 26, Issue 20. p. 16.

Hills, Jill, and Maria Michalis. "The Internet: A Challenge to Public Service Broadcasting?" *Gazette* 62, no.6. (2000): 477–93.

Hilmes, Michelle. *Only Connect: A Cultural History of Broadcasting in the United States.* Belmont, Calif.: Wadsworth/Thomson Learning, 2002.

Hirsh, Jesse. "The Media Cluster: Communalizing Intellectual Property While Socially Appropriating the Media Conglomerate." Pp. 57–69 in *E-Commerce vs E-Commons: Communications in the Public Interest*, edited Marita Moll and Leslie Reagan Shade. Ottawa: Canadian Centre for Policy Alternatives, 2001.

Hjarvard, S. Internationale TV-nyheder. En historisk analyze af det europeiske system for *udvkesling af internationale TV-nyheder.* Copenhagen: Akademisk Forlag: 1995.

————. "TV News Flow Studies Revisited" *Electronic Journal of Communication* 5, no. 2 (1995): 24–38.

Hoge, J. "Foreign News: Who Gives a Damn." *Columbia Journalism Review.* 1997. <http://www .cjr.org/year/97/6/foreign.asp>.

Horwitz, Robert Britt. *The Irony of Regulatory Reform: The Deregulation of American Telecommunications*. New York: Oxford University Press, 1989.

——. "Broadcast Reform Revisited: Reverend Everett C. Parker and the "Standing" Case (Office of Communication of the United Church of Christ v. Federal Communications Commision). 1997 <http://communication.ucsd.edu/people/f_horwitz_brr.html>.

——. "On Media Concentration and the Diversity Question." 2003. <http://www.communication.ucsd.edu/people/ConcentrationpaperICA.htm> (6 Dec. 2004).

Huckfeldt, Robert, and John Sprague. "Political Parties and Electoral Mobilization: Political Structure, Social Structure, and the Party Canvas." *American Political Science Review* 86 (1992): 70–86.

Hunt, Russell, and Robert Campbell. *K.C. Irving: The Art of the Industrialist*. Toronto: McClelland & Stewart, 1973.

Hyde, Gene. "Independent Media Centers: Cyber-Subversion and the Alternative Press." *First Monday* 7, no.4 (2002) <http://firstmonday.org/issues/issues_4/hyde/index.html> (June 15, 2003).

International Federation of Journalists. "Corporate Control of Editorial Policy in Canada Threatens Press Freedom Says IFJ," *ifj.org.* 2001. <http://www.ifj.org/publications/press/pr/281.html> (20 December 2001).

International Press Institute "IPI Condemns Firing of Canadian Publisher." *Orbicom. 2002.* <http://www.orbicom.uqam.ca/in_focus/news/archives/2002_juin/2002_juin_18_b.html. (18 June 2002).

Iosifides, Petros. "Diversity versus Concentration in the Deregulated Mass Media." *Journalism and Mass Communications Quarterly* 76, no. 1 (Spring 1999): 152–62.

Iyengar, Shanto, and Donald R. Kinder, *News That Matters: Television and American Opinion*. Chicago: University of Chicago Press, 1987.

Jackson, Wes. *New Roots for Agriculture*. Lincoln: University of Nebraska Press, 1980.

Jansen, Sue Curry. *Censorship: The Knot That Binds Power and Knowledge.* New York: Oxford University Press, 1991.

Jenkins, Kent, Jr. "Learning to Love Those Expensive Campaigns." *U.S. News and World Report*, 122, no. 10 (1997).

Johnson, Brad. FCC Hearings, City Hall, San Francisco, April 26, 2003.

Johnson, Thomas J., and Wayne Wanta. "Newspaper Circulation and Message Diversity in an Urban Market." *Mass Communications Review*, 1993.

Johnston, Pete. "Lemann Sees Two-Year Program Going beyond ABCs to Science, Business, Law." *Columbia University Graduate School of Journalism Alumni Journal*, Fall 2003, 1–2, online. (22 December 2003.)

Jones, Nicholas. *Soundbites and Spindoctors: How Politicians Manipulate the Media—and Visa Versa*. London: Cassel, 1995.

Jordan, Tim. *Cyberpower*. London: Routledge, 1998.

Joslyn, Mark, and Steve Cecolli. "Attentiveness to Television News and Opinion Change in the Fall of 1992 Election Campaign." *Political Behavior* 18 (1996).

Joslyn, Richard. "The Impact of Campaign Spot Advertising Ads," *Journalism Quarterly* 7 (1981).

Just, Marion, R., Ann N. Crigler, Dean F. Alger, Timothy E. Cook, Montague Kern, and Darrell M. West, *Crosstalk: Citizens, Candidates and the Media in a Presidential Campaign*. Chicago: University of Chicago Press, 1996.

Just, Marion R., Ann N. Crigler, and W. Russell Neuman. "Cognitive and Affective Dimensions of Political Conceptualization," Pp. 133–48 in *The Psychology of Political Communications*, edited by Ann N. Crigler. Ann Arbor: University of Michigan Press, 1996.

Kahn, Kim Fridkin, and Patrick J. Kenny. "The Slant of News: How Editorial Endorsements Influence Campaign Coverage and Citizens' Views of Candidates." *American Political Science Review* 96 (2002).

Kahn, Kim Fridkin, and Patrick J. Kenney, *The Spectacle of U.S. Senate Campaign.* Chicago: University of Chicago Press, 1999.

Kaid, Lynda Lee, Dan D. Nimmo, and Keith R. Sanders, eds., *New Perspectives in Political Advertising.* Carbondale: Southern Illinois University Press, 1986.

Kaid, Lynda Lee, et al. "Television News and Presidential Campaigns: The Legitimation of Televised Political Advertising." *Social Science Quarterly* 74, no. 2 (1993): 274–85.

Kapica, Jack. "Edison's Noisy Children." *Digital Journal.com.* 2003. <http://www.digitaljournal.com/news/?articleID=3630&page=3> (July 2003).

Kaplan, David. "Concert Promoter Lous Messina Sees World of Opportunity as Noncompete Clause with Old Boss Expires." *Houston Chronicle,* 8 August 2003.

Karr, Albert. "Television News Tunes Out Airwaves Auction Battle," *Wall Street Journal,* 1 May 1996.

Kavoori, Anandam. "Discursive Texts, Reflexive Audiences: Global Trends in Television News Texts and Audience Reception." *Journal of Broadcasting and Electronic Media* 43, no. 3 (Summer 1999): 386–99.

Keane, John. *The Media and Democracy.* Cambridge: Polity Press, 1991.

———. "Structural Transformations of the Public Sphere." *The Communication Review* 1, no. 1 (1995): 1–22.

———. *Civil Society.* Stanford, Calif.: Stanford University Press, 1998.

Kelly, Michael. "Left Everlasting." *Washington Post,* 11 December 2002.

Kennedy, Peter. "Asper Blasts Critics of Editorial Policy." *Globe and Mail,* 31 January 2002, A6.

Kent, Tom. "Concentration with Convergence—Goodbye, Freedom of the Press." *Policy Options/Options Politiques* (October 2002): 26–28.

———. "The Times and Significance of the Kent Commission." Pp. 21–39 in *Seeing Ourselves: Media Power and Policy in Canada,* edited by H. Holmes and D. Taras. Toronto: Harcourt Brace Jovanovich Canada Inc, 1992.

Kern, Montague, *30 Second Politics: Political Advertising in the Eighties.* New York: Praeger, 1988.

Kesterton, Wilfred, and Roger Bird. "The Press in Canada: A Historical Overview." Pp. 29–49 in *Communications in Canada,* edited by Benjamin D. Singer, Scarborough, Ont.: Nelson, 1991.

Kidd, Dorothy. "From Carnival to Commons: The Global IMC Network." In *Confronting Capitalism,* edited by Eddie Yuen, George Katsiaficas, and Daniel Burton Rose. New York: Softskull Press, forthcoming.

———. "Indymedia.org: A New Communications Commons." Pp. 47–70 in *Cyberactivism: Online Activism in Theory and Practice,* edited by Martha McCaughey and Michael D. Ayers. New York & London: Routledge, 2003.

———. "Which Would You Rather: Seattle or Porto Alegre?" Paper presented at "Our Media, Not Theirs," Barcelona, July 2002.

———. "Indymedia.org: The Development of Communication Commons," *Democratic Communiqué* 18 (Summer 2002).

Kim, Sei-Hill, Dietram A. Scheufele, and James Shanahan. "Think about It This Way: Attribute Agenda Setting Function of the Press and the Public's Evaluation of a Local Issue." *Journalism and Mass Communications Quarterly* 79 (2002).

Khagram, Sanjeev, James V. Riker, and Kathryn Sikknik, eds. *Restructuring World Politics: Transnational Social Movements, Networks and Norms.* Minneapolis: University of Minnesota Press, 2002.

Klieman, Howard. "Content Diversity and the FCC's Minority and Gender Licensing Policies." *Journal of Broadcasting and Electronic Media* 35, no. 4 (1991): 411–29.

Klein, Naomi. "Farewell to 'The End of History': Organization and Vision in Anti-Corporate Movements." Pp. 1–14 in *Socialist Register 2002: A World of Contradictions,* edited by Leo Panitch and Colin Leys. London: Merlin, 2001.

Klugman, Paul. "In Media Res." *New York Times,* 29 November 2002.

———. "Channels of influence." *New York Times,* 25 March 2003.

Knight, Graham. "News and Ideology." *Canadian Journal of Communication* 8, no. 4 (September 1982): 15–41.

Kovach, Bill, and Tom Rosenstiel. *Warp Speed: America in the Age of Mixed Media.* New York: The Century Foundation Press, 1999.

Kowal, Donna. "Digitizing and Globalizing Indigenous Voices: The Zapatista Movement." Pp. 105–29 in *Critical Perspectives on the Internet,* edited by Greg Elmer. Lanham, Md.: Rowman & Littlefield, 2002.

Krosnick, Jon A., and Donald R. Kinder. "Altering the Foundation of Support for the President through Priming," *American Political Science Review* 84 (1990).

Krotoszynski, Ronald J., Jr., and A. Richard M. Blaiklock. "Enhancing the Spectrum: Media Power, Democracy, and the Marketplace of Ideas," *University of Illinois Law Review* (2002).

Kunkel, Thomas, and Gene Roberts. "Leaving Readers Behind: The Age of Corporate Newspapering." *American Journalism Review* (May 2001).

Labaton, Stephen. "A Lone Voice for Regulation at the F.C.C." New York Times, 30 September 2002, B. 1.

———. "A Media Rule by the FCC is in Jeopardy in the House." *New York Times,* 33 July 2003, <http://query.nytimes.com/gst/abstract.html?rcs=F20A16FB3F5B0C708EDDAE0894DB404482>.

———. "F.C.C. Media Rule Blocked in House in a 400-to-21 Vote." *New York Times.* 24 July 2003, <http://www.nytimes.com>.

———. "Senate Panel Acts to Block TV Ownership Rule." *New York Times,* 5 September 2003, <http://www.nytimes.com>.

———. "F.C.C. Plan to Ease Curbs on Big Media Hits Senate Snag." *New York Times,* 17 September 2003, <http://www.nytimes.com>.

———. "F.C.C. Chief Talks of Frustration and Surprise." *New York Times.* 22 September 2003, <http://www.nytimes.com>.

Lacy, Stephen. "A Model of Demand for News: Impact of Competition on Newspaper Content." *Journalism Quarterly* 66 (1989): 40–48.

Lacy, Stephen, David C. Coulson, and Charles St. Cyr. "The Impact of Beat Competition on City Hall Coverage." *Journalism & Mass Communication Quarterly* 76 (1999): 325–40.

Lacy, Stephen, Mary Alice Shaver, and Charles St. Cyr. "The Effects of Public Ownership and Newspaper Competition on the Financial Performance of Newspaper Corporation: A Replication and Extension." *Journalism and Mass Communication Quarterly* 73, no. 2 (Summer 1996): 332.

Lacy, Stephen, and Todd F. Simon, eds. *The Economics and Regulation of United States Newspapers.* Norwood, N.J.: Ablex, 1993.

La Fédération Nationale des Communications (FNC-CSN). "Mémoire présenté au CRTC sur la Demande (2000-2309-4) présentée par Quebecor Média Inc. (QMI)," (March 2001). <http://www.fncom.org/accueil/memoire/m_mars_2001.htm> (22 July 2004).

Laing, Rachel. "FCC Rules Signal Confusion for Cross-Border Broadcasting; Clear Channel's Stations in Mexico May Cross the Line." *San Diego Union-Tribune,* 15 July 2003.

Langfield, Amy. "Net News Lethargy Most Sites Fail to Make Use of the Medium's Main Strength-Speed." *Online Journalism Review* 1992, <http://www.ojr.org/ojr/reviews/1017864558.php>.

Lapham, Lewis. "American Jihad." *Harper's Magazine* 304, no. 1820 (January 2002): 7–9.

LaPierre, Wayne. "Speak Out vs. FCC While You Can." *New York Daily News,* 18 July 2003, <http://nydailynews.com>.

Lasica, J.D. "The Rise of the Digital Networks." *Online Journalism Review* 2002, <http://www.ojr.org/ojr/lasica/p1018588363.php> (11 April, 2002).

Latouche, Serge. "La mondialisation et la fin du politique: diagnostic et perspectives." *La Revue du MAUSS* 1, no. 9 (1997): 137–50.

Lauzen, Martha M., and David Dozier. "Making a Difference in Prime Time: Women on Screen and Behind the Scenes in 1995–1996 Television Season." *Journal of Broadcasting and Electronic Media* (Winter 1999).

Lavoie, Marie-Hélène, and Chris Dornan. *Concentration of Newspaper Ownership: An 'Old' and Still Unresolved Problem*, edited by Florian Sauvageau, Centre d'études sur les medias. Ottawa: Department of Canadian Heritage, 2001, <http://www.pch.gc.ca/progs/ac-ca/progs/esm-ms/prob1_e.cfm>.

Layton, Charles. "What Do Readers Really Want?" *American Journalism Review* (March 1999).

———. "What the FCC Did." *American Journalism Review*. December/January Issue (2004), <http://www.ajr.org/article.asp?id=3498>.

———. "Tracking the Coverage." *American Journalism Review*. December/January Issue (2004), <http://www.ajr.org/article.asp?id=3499>.

Layton, Charles and Jennifer Dorroh. "Sad State," *American Journalism Review* (June 2002).

Lee, Eric. *The Labour Movement and the Internet: The New Internationalism*. London: Pluto Press, 1997.

Lee, Jennifer. "On Minot, N.D., Radio, A Single Corporate Voice." *New York Times*, 31 March 2003.

Leeds, Jeff. "Firm Skirts Radio Caps in San Diego." *Los Angeles Times*, 4 October 2002.

Leiss, William, Stephen Kline, and Sut Jhally. *Social Communication in Advertising: Persons, Products, & Images of Well-Being*. Scarborough, Ont.: Nelson Canada, 1990.

Lemert, James B., William R. Elliott, and James M. Bernstein. *News Verdicts, the Debates, and Presidential Campaigns*. New York: Praeger, 1991.

Lessig, Lawrence, *The Future of Ideas: The Fate of the Commons in a Connected World*. New York: Random House, 2001.

Levin, Harvey J. "Competition, Diversity, and the Television Group Ownership Rule." *Columbia Law Review* 70, no. 4 (May 1970): 791–835.

———. "Program Duplication, Diversity, and Effective Viewer Choices: Some Empirical Findings." *American Economic Review* (1971).

Levine, Peter, *Building the Electronic Commons*. Washington, D.C.: Democracy Collaborative, 5 April 2002.

———. "Can the Internet Rescue Democracy? Toward an On-Line Commons." In *Democracy's Moment: Reforming the American Political System for the 21st Century*, edited by Ronald Hayuk and Kevin Mattson. Lanham, Md.: Rowman and Littlefield, 2002.

———. "The Internet and Civil Society." Report from the University of Maryland, Institute for Philosophy & Public Policy 20, no. 4 (Fall 2000).

Levy, Pierre. *Cyberculture*. Minneapolis: University of Minnesota Press, 2001.

Lewandowski, Rene. "Anger Management." *National Post Business Magazine* (July 2003): 56.

Lichter, S. Robert. "Depends on How You Define 'Bias.'" *Washington Post*, 18 December 2002.

Lipscomb, Georgina. "BBC Online Put Under Scrutiny." *Broadcast* (January 2001).

Listening Project, The. *The Makings of a Social Movement? Strategic Issues and Themes in Communications Policy Work*. April 2004.

Lloyd, Mark. "Communications Policy Is a Civil Rights Issue." Civil Rights Forum on Communications Policy. August 4, 1997. <http://www.civilrightsforum.org/foundations.html.>

Localism Task Force. Federal Communications Commission. <http://www.fcc.gov/localism>. 2004.

Lorek, L.A. "Clear Channel Sweetens Its Profit Despite Sour Economy." *San Antonio Express-News*, 30 July 2003.

Los Angeles Times. "Music Execs Upset with Clear Channel Pacts." *Los Angeles Times*, <http://www.cincypost.com/2002/sep/05/clear090502.html.> (September 5, 2002).

Loudon, K. C. "Promise versus Performances of Cable," in *Wired Cities: Shaping the Future of Communications* edited by William H. Dutton, et al. Boston: K. G. Hall, 1987.

Lovink, Geert. *Dark Fiber: Tracking Critical Internet Culture.* Cambridge, Mass.: MIT Press, 2002.

Lubunski, Richard. "The First Amendment at the Crossroads: Free Expression and New Media Technology." *Communications Law and Policy 2,* no. 2 (Spring 1997).

MacBride, Sean, et al. *Voix multiples un seul monde,* La Documentation française, Paris, 1980.

Magder, Ted. "Taking Culture Seriously: A Political Economy of Communications." Pp. 278–96 in *The New Canadian Political Economy.* edited by Wallace Clement and Glen Williams. Kingston and Montreal: McGill-Queen's University Press, 1989.

———. *Canada's Hollywood: The Canadian State and Feature Films.* Toronto: University of Toronto Press, 1993.

———. "Franchising the Candy Store: Split-run Magazines and a New International Regime for Trade in Culture." In *Canadian-American Public Policy* 34 (Apr. 1998), <http://www.alanalexandroff.com/Magder.htm> (10 Dec. 2004).

Magid, L. "All Roads Lead to Reuters." *Currents.net* (1997). <www.currents.net/magazine/national/1513/uout1513.html>

Malik, R. "The Global News Agenda." *Intermedia* 20, no.1 (1992).

Marotte, Bertrand. "Rogers Creates Multi-Media Giant with Maclean Hunter Takeover." *Ottawa Citizen,* 9 March, 1994, C1.

Martin, Shannon E. "How News Gets from Paper to Its Online Counterpart" *Newspaper Research Journal* 19 (Spring, 1998): 64–73.

Mason, Laurie, Christine M. Bachen, and Stephanie L. Craft. "Support for FCC Minority Ownership Policy: How Broadcast Station Owner Race or Ethnicity Affects News and Public Affairs Programming Diversity," *Comm. Law Policy* 6 (2001).

Massey, B., and M. Levy. "Interactivity, OnLine Journalism, and English-Language Web Newspapers in Asia." *Journalism and Mass Communication Quarterly* 76, no.1 (1999): 138–51.

Mattelart, Armand. "Les laissés-pour-compte du cyberspace." *Le Monde diplomatique* (August 2003)

———. *Histoire de la société de l'information.* Paris: La Découverte coll. "Repères", 2003.

Maxwell, Kim. *Residential Broadband: An Insider's Guide to the Battle for the Last Mile.* New York: John Wiley, 1999.

Mazepa, Patricia. "The Solidarity Network in Formation: A Search for Democratic Alternative Communication." Paper presented at the Canadian Communication Association Annual Conference, University of Ottawa, 2 June 1998.

McCarthy, John P. "Pitfalls of Media Mega-Mergers." *America* 182, no. 16 (6 May 2000): 12–17.

McCarthy, Shawn, and Jeff Sallot. "Publisher's Firing Sets Off Storm." *Globe and Mail.* 18 June 2002. <http://friendscb.ca/articles/GlobeandMail/globe020618-2.htm>.

McCaughey, Martha, and Michael D. Ayers, eds. *Cyberactivism: Online Activism in Theory and Practice.* New York & London: Routledge, 2003.

McChesney, Robert W. *Telecommunications, Mass Media, and Democracy.* New York: Oxford University Press, 1993.

———. *Rich Media, Poor Democracy,* New York: The New Press, 1999.

———. "The Titanic Sails On: Why the Internet Won't Sink the Media Giants." *Extra!* (March/April 2000).

———. *The Problem of the Media: U.S. Communication Politics in the 21st Century.* New York: Monthly Review Press, 2004.

McChesney, Robert W., and John Nichols. "Up in Flames: The Public Revolts against Monopoly Media." *The Nation* 277, no. 16 (November 17, 2003).

McChesney, Robert W., and Ben Scott. *Our Unfree Press: One Hundred Years of Radical Media Criticism.* New York: The New Press, 2004.

McCombs, Maxwell E., and Donald Shaw. "The Agenda-Setting Function of the Mass Media," *Public Opinion Quarterly* 36 (1972).

McConnell, Bill. "Strike Two for FCC EEO Rules." *Broadcasting & Cable* 131, no. 4 (22 January 2001.): 102.

———. "The National Acquirers: Whether Better for News or Fatter Profits, Media Companies Want in on TV/Newspaper Cross-ownership." *Broadcasting & Cable* 131, no. 51 (December 2001).

McFarland, Janet, and Keith Damsell. "CanWest Unveils Management Shuffle." *Globe and Mail,* 29 January 2003, B3.

McGee, Francisco. "Transcripts of the San Francisco Public Hearings on FCC Rule-Making on Media Ownership." University of San Francisco Media Group (2003).

McGee, Art, Thenmozhi Soundararajan, Makani Themba-Nixon, Malkia Cyril, and Jeff Perlstein. "A Declaration of Media Independence." (2003). <http://www.mediajustice.org>.

McKean, Michael L., and Vernon A. Stone. "Why Stations Don't Do News." *Communicator* (1991).

McKercher, Catherine. *Newsworkers Unite: Labor, Convergence, and North American Newspapers.* Lanham, Md.: Rowman & Littlfield, 2002.

McKie, David. "First Word: What Were They Thinking?" *Media Magazine.* Summer 2002. <http://www.caj.ca/mediamag/summer2002/firstword.html>.

McLeod, Douglas M. "Communicating Deviance: The Effects of Television News Coverage of Social Protests." *Journal of Broadcasting & Electronic Media* 39 (1995).

McManus, John. "How Objective Is Local Television News?" *Mass Communications Review* 18 (1991): 26–27.

———. *Market-Driven Journalism: Let the Citizen Beware?* Thousand Oaks, Calif.: Sage, 1994.

McMurtry, John. *Value Wars: The Global Market versus the Life Economy.* London; Pluto, 2002.

McNally, David. *Another World Is Possible: Globalization and Anti-Capitalism.* Winnipeg: Arbeiter Ring, 2002.

Media Access Project. "Statement of Media Access Project Reacting to U.S. Court of Appeals Media Ownership Decision," <http://www.mediaaccess.org/prometheus_decision/#summary> (14 July, 2004).

Meikle, Graham. *Future Active: Media Activism and the Internet.* New York and London: Routledge, 2002.

Meyer, Thomas, *Media Democracy.* Cambridge: Polity Press, 2000.

Meyerowitz, Joshua. *No Sense of Place: The Effect of Electronic Media on Social Behavior.* New York: Oxford, 1985.

Miller, John. *Yesterday's News: Why Canada's Daily Newspapers are Failing Us.* Halifax, N.S.: Fernwood Publishing, 1998.

———. "Do Editorials Matter?" *Straight Goods.* <http://www.straightgoods.ca/ViewFeature.cfm?REF=264> (February 17, 2002).

Miller, Steven E. *Civilizing Cyberspace.* New York: ACM Press, 1998.

Mills, Russell. "Under the Asper Thumb." *Globe and Mail,* 19 June 2002, A15.

Mitchell, Bill. "Media Collaborations," *Broadcasting & Cable* (10 April 2000).

Mitchell, Gregg. "Keller Defends Judith Miller in Statement." *Editor and Publisher* 28 (March 2004).

Mock, Brentin. "Station Identification; WAMO, the City's Historic Black Radio Station, Once Had the Community to Itself. Now It's Counting on That Sense of Community to Compete against Monoliths." *Pittsburgh City Paper,* 23 July 2003.

Molina, Gabriel. "The Production of Mexican Television News: The Supremacy of Corporate Rationale." Unpublished Doctoral Dissertation, University of Leicester, (1990).

Moll, Marita, and Leslie Regan Shade, eds. *Seeking Convergence in Policy and Practice: Communications in the Public Interest.* Ottawa: Canadian Centre for Policy Alternatives, 2004.

Monbiot, George. *The Age of Consent: A Manifesto for a New World Order.* London: Flamingo, 2003.

Montgomery, Kathryn C. *Target: Prime Time Advocacy Groups and the Struggle over Entertainment Television.* New York: Oxford University Press, 1989.

Morley, David. "'To Boldly Go . . .': The 'Third Generation' of Reception Studies." Pp. 195–204 in *Rethinking the Media Audience: The New Agenda*, edited by Pertti Alasuutari (London: Sage, 1999).

———. *Television, Audiences, and Cultural Studies.* London: Routledge, 1992.

Morton, John. "Everything Is Coming Up Profits for Papers." *American Journalism Review* (June 1999): 80.

Mosco, Vincent. *The Pay-Per Society: Computers & Communications in the Information Age.* Norwood, N.J.: Ablex, 1989.

———. *The Political Economy of Communication.* Thousand Oaks, Calif.: Sage, 1996.

———. *The Digital Sublime: Myth, Power, and Cyberspace*, Cambridge, Mass.: MIT Press, 2004.

Mosco, Vincent, and Janet Wasko, eds. *The Political Economy of Information.* Madison: University of Wisconsin Press, 1988.

Mosco, Vincent, and Dan Schiller, eds. *Continental Order: Integrating North America for Cybercapitalism.* Lanham, Md.: Rowman & Littlefield, 2001.

Moscovitch, Arlene. *Electronic Media and the Family.* Ottawa: Vanier Institute of the Family, 1998.

Moses, Lucia. "TV or Not TV? Few Newspapers Are Camera Shy, But Sometimes Two into One Just Doesn't Go." *Editor and Cable*, 21 August 2000.

Motto, Massimo, and Michele Polo. "Concentration and Public Policies in the Broadcasting Industry." *Economic Policy* 24 (Spring 1997): 331–33.

Mueller, Milton, Christiane Pagé, and Brenden Kuerbis. "Civil Society and the Shaping of Communication-Information Policy: Four Decades of Advocacy." (2003).

Mueller, Milton, Brendan Kuerbis, and Christiane Pagé. "Reinventing Media Activism: Public Interest Advocacy in the Making of U.S. Communication-Information Policy, 1960–2002." The Convergence Center, School of Information Studies, Syracuse University, <http://www. http:// dcc.syr.edu/ford/rma/reinventing.pdf.> (16 July, 2004).

Mulder, Ronald. "The Effects of Televised Political Ads in the 1995 Chicago Mayoral Election." *Journalism Quarterly* 56 (1979).

Mullins, Brody. "FCC Decision Dealt Big Blow." *Roll Call*, 17 July 2003, 24.

Murdock, Graham, and Peter Golding. "Digital Possibilities, Market Realities: The Contradictions of Communications Convergence." Pp.111–30 in *Socialist Register 2002: A World of Contradictions*, edited by Leo Panitch and Colin Leys. London: Merlin, 2001.

Napoli, Philip. "Deconstructing the Diversity Principle." *Journal of Communication* 49, no. 4 (Autumn 1999): 7–34.

———. "Market Conditions and Public Affairs Programming: Implications for Digital Television Policy." Prepared for Benton Foundation (1999)

———. "Audience Valuation and Minority Media: An Analysis of the Determinants of the Value of Radio Audiences." *Journal of Broadcasting and Electronic Media*, 46 (2002).

———. *Foundations of Communications Policy: Principles and Process in the Regulation of Electronic Media.* Cresskill, N.J.: Hampton Press, 2001.

National Association of Black Owned Broadcasters and the Rainbow Push Coalition. "Petition for Reconsideration." Before the Federal Communications Commission. In the matter of the 2002 Biennial review of the Commission's Broadcast Ownership Rules, 4 September 2003. 10. <http:// www.nabob.org/Press_Releases/9_4_2003-Petition.pdf>

National Council for Civil Liberties, *Liberating Cyberspace.* London: Pluto Press, 1999.

Neiman Reports. *The Business of News, the News about Business*, Neiman Reports (Summer 1999).

Netanal, Neil, *Is the Commercial Mass Media Necessary, or Even Desirable, for Liberal Democracy?* paper presented at Telecommunications Policy Research Conference on Information, Communications, and Internet Policy (October 2001).

Newhagen, J., and M. Levy. "The Future of Journalism in a Distributed Communication Architecture." Pp. 9–21 in *The Electronic Grapevine: Rumor, Reputation, and Reporting in the New On-Line Environment*, edited by D. Borden and K. Harvey. Mahwah, N.J.: Lawrence Erlbaum Associates, 1998.

Newspaper Association of America. "U.S. Daily and Sunday/Weekend Newspaper Reading Audience," 2000. <http://www.naa.org/info/facts00/02.html> (19 Sept. 2003).

———. "Total U.S. Non-Daily Newspapers" 2000. <http://www.naa.org/info/facts00/27.html> (24 Sept. 2003).

———. "Daily Newspaper Readership Trends." 2002. <http://www.naa.org/artpage.cfm?AID=1613&SID=1022> (19 Sept. 2003).

———. "Trends and Numbers." 2003. <http://www.naa.org/artpage.cfm?AID=1610&SID=1022> (2 Oct. 2003).

———. "2002 Daily and Sunday Newspaper Report." 2002. <http://www.naa.org/marketscope/DSN2002/DSNAud2002Final.pdf> (19 Sept. 2003).

———. "U.S. Daily Newspaper Circulation." 2003. <http://www.naa.org/info/facts03/14_facts2003.html> (17 Nov. 2003).

Newspaper Guild of Canada. "The Newspaper Guild Calls on CanWest Global to Change Policies in Name of Public Trust." [press release]. <http://www.montrealnewspaperguild.com/News/pr-feb202002.htm> (February 20, 2002).

———. "Citizen Asper: Publisher, Fired for Editorial, Fires Back with Libel Lawsuit." <http://www.newsguild.org/gr/gr_display.php?storyID=849> (July 12, 2002).

Nichols, M.E. *(CP): The Story of the Canadian Press*. Toronto: The Ryerson Press, 1948.

Nichols, John, and Robert W. McChesney. "FCC: Public Be Damned." *The Nation* 2 June 2003.

Noonan, Jeff. "Rights, Needs, and the Moral Grounds of Democratic Society." *Rethinking Marxism*, 16, no. 3 (July 2004): 311–325.

Nutt, Rod. "Southam Gives up North Shore's Real Estate Weekly in Swap of Assets." *Vancouver Sun*, 15 September 1998, D4.

Oberholzer-Gee, Felix, and Joel Waldfogel, *Electoral Acceleration: The Effect of Minority Population on Minority Voter Turnout*, NBER Working Paper 8252 (Cambridge, Mass.: National Bureau of Economic Research, 2001).

O'Brien, Rory. "Civil Society, the Public Sphere and the Internet." <http://www.web.net/~robrien/papers/civsoc.html> (Nov. 11, 2003).

Ofori, Kofi A., *When Being No. 1 Is Not Enough: The Impact of Advertising Practices on Minority-Owned and Minority-Targeted Broadcast Stations*. Civil Rights Forum on Communications Policy, 1999.

O'Keefe, Garrett J. "Political Malaise and Reliance on the Media." *Journalism Quarterly* (1980).

Olson, Kathryn. "Exploiting the Tension between the New Media's 'Objective' and Adversarial Roles: The Role Imbalance Attach and Its Use of the Implied Audience." *Communications Quarterly* 42, no. 1 (1994).

O'Sullivan, Patrick B. "The Nexus between Broadcast Licensing Gender Preferences and Programming Diversity: What Does the Social Scientific Evidence Say?" Santa Barbara: Department of Communication, University of California Santa Barbara, 2000.

Ottawa Citizen. "Mills Firing Dominates Parliamentary Debate." *Ottawa Citizen*, 19 June 2002, A1.

Overholser, Geneva. "Editor, Inc." Pp. 157–88 in *Leaving Readers Behind: The Age of Corporate Newspapering*, edited by Gene Roberts, Thomas Kunkel, and Charles Layton. Fayetteville: University of Arkansas Press, 2001.

Owen, Bruce, and Steven Wildman, *Video Economics*. Cambridge, Mass.: Harvard University Press, 1992.

Page, Benjamin I., *Who Deliberates*. Chicago: University of Chicago Press, 1996.

Paletz, David L., *The Media in American Politics: Contents and Consequences*. New York: Longman, 1999.

Pan, Zhongdang, and Gerald M. Kosicki. "Priming and Media Impact on the Evaluation of the President's Performance." *Communications Research* 24 (1997).

Papazian, Ed, ed. *TV Dimensions 2003.* New York: Media Dynamics, 2003.

Paraskevas, Joe. "Kent Takes Aim at Media Convergence: Senate Hearings Begin: Ex-commissioner's Views Dismissed as 'Old-Fashioned'." *National-Post,* 30 April 2003, FP4.

Pastore, Michael. "Cyber-Atlas–The Big Picture: Global Internet Population Moves Away from US." <http://cyberatlas.internet.com/big_picture/geographics/article/0,,5911_558061,00.html> (Oct 15. 2003).

Paterson, Chris. "News Production at Worldwide Television News (WTN): An Analysis of Television News Agency Coverage of Developing Countries." Doctoral Dissertation, University of Texas, 1996.

———. "Global Battlefields," Pp.79–103 in *The Globalization of News,* edited by O. Boyd-Barrett and T. Rantanen. London: Sage, 1998.

———. "Internet News: Source Concentration and Cybermediation." *EURICOM Colloquium on the Political Economy of Convergence.* London, 1999.

———. "An Exploratory Analysis of the Transference of Frames in Global Television." Pp. 337–53 in *Framing in the New Media Landscape,* edited by Stephen Reese, A. Grant, and Oscar Gandy. Mahwah, N.J.: Erlbaum, 2000.

———. "Media Imperialism Revisited: The Global Public Sphere and the News Agency Agenda." Pp. 77–92 in *News in a Globalized Society,* edited by Stig Hjarvard (Göteborg: NORDICOM, 2001).

Patterson, Thomas E., and Robert D. McClure. *The Unseeing Eye: The Myth of Television Power in National Politics.* New York: Putnam Books, 1976.

———. *The Vanishing Voter.* New York: Alfred A. Knopf, 2002.

Paulson, Justin. "Peasant Struggles and International Solidarity: The Case of Chiapas." Pp.275–88 in *Socialist Register 2001: Working Classes, Global Realities,* edited by Leo Panitch and Colin Leys. London: Merlin, 2000.

Pearson, Patricia. "See No Evil, No More." *Globe and Mail,* 19 April 2003, A19.

Peers, Frank. *The Politics of Canadian Broadcasting: 1920–1951.* Toronto: University of Toronto Press, 1969.

Pendakur, Manjunath. "United States-Canada Relations: Cultural Dependence and Conflict." Pp. 165–84 in *Critical Communications Review.* Volume II: *Changing Patterns of Communications Control,* edited by Vincent Mosco and Janet Wasko. Norwood, N.J.: Ablex Publishing, 1984.

Perlstein, Jeff. "Clear Channel Stumbles." *Media File,* 2002.

———. "Clear Channel: The Media Mammoth That Stole the Airwaves." *CorpWatch,* 14 November 2002. <http://www.corpwatch.org/issues/PID.jsp?articleid=4808> (22 Sept. 2003).

———. "Letter from the E.D." *Media Alliance.* Fall 2003.

Pfau, Michael. "A Channel Approach to Television Influence." *Journal of Broadcasting and Electronic Media* 34 (1990): 195–214.

Pfau, Michael, and Henry C. Kenski. *Attack Politics.* New York: Praeger, 1990.

Phillips, Peter, and Project Censored, *Censored 2003.* New York: Seven Stories, 2002.

Philo, Greg. "Television News and Audience Understanding of War, Conflict, and Disaster." *Journalism Studies* 3, no. 2 (2002): 173–86.

Picard, Robert G. "The Economics of the Daily Newspaper Industry." Pp. 111–30 in *Media Economics: Theory and Practice,* edited by Alison Alexander, James Owers and Rodney Carveth. Mahwah, N.J.: Erlbaum, 1998.

Policy Statement on Comparative Broadcast Hearings, 1 FCC 2d 393 (1965).

Pomper, Gerald M., and Marc D. Weiner, eds. *The Future of American Democratic Politics.* New Brunswick, N.J.: Rutgers University Press, 2003.

Postman, Neil, *Amusing Ourselves to Death: Public Discourse in the Age of Show Business.* New York: Viking, 1985.

Powell, Michael. "New Rules, Old Rhetoric," *New York Times,* 28 July 2003, <http://www.nytimes.com>.

Press, Andrea, and Elizabeth Cole. *Speaking of Abortion: Television and Authority in the Lives of Women.* Chicago: University of Chicago Press, 1999.

Project for Excellence in Journalism. "Special Report: Local TV News." Supplement to *Columbia Journalism Review* (Nov./Dec. 2001).

———. "Does Ownership Matter in Local Television News: A Five-Year Study of Ownership and Quality," 17 February (2003).

Proulx, Gilles. *L'aventure de la radio au Québec.* Montréal: La Presse, 1979.

Quebecor Media. "Mémoire Sur la Demande Présentée au CRTC en vue du Transfert du Contrôle des Entreprises de Radiodiffusion de Vidéotron et du Groupe TVA à Quebecor Média," 2001, <http://www.quebecor.com/crtc/>.

Québec. Comité Conseil sur la Qualité et la Diversité l'Information, *Les Effets de la Concentration des Medias au Quebec: Problématique, Recherches et Consultations.* January 2003, <http://www.mcc.gouv.gc.ca/publications/rapportst-jenatome_2.pdf>

Québec. Secrétariat des commissions. *Mandat d'Initiative Portent sur la Concentration de la Presse.* <http://www.assnat.qc.ca/fra/publications/rapports/rapcc3.html> (March 22, 2004)

Rabasca, Lisa. "Benefits, Costs and Convergence." *Presstime* (2001).

Raboy, Marc, and Peter Bruck. "The Challenge of Democratic Communication." Pp. 3–16 in *Communication For and Against Democracy,* edited by Marc Raboy and Peter Bruck. Montreal and New York: Black Rose Books, 1989.

Raboy, Marc. *Accès Inégal. Les Canaux d'Influence en Radiodiffusion.* Les Presses de l'Université du Québec, Sainte-Foy, 1995.

Read, Donald. *The Power of News: The History of Reuters 1849–1989.* Oxford: Oxford University Press, 1992.

Readings, Bill. *The University in Ruins.* Cambridge, Mass.: Harvard University Press, 1996.

Reguly, Eric. "Consumers Beware: Canada Is a Haven for Media Oligopolies." *Globe and Mail,* 28 February 2002, B17.

Rifkin, Jeremy. *The Age of Access: The New Culture of Hypercapitalism Where All of Life Is a Paid-For Experience.* New York: J.P. Tarcher/Putnam, 2000.

Riggs, Karen. *Mature Audiences: Television in the Lives of Elders.* New Brunswick, N.J.: Rutgers University Press, 1998.

Robbins, Bruce. "Introduction: The Public as Phantom." Pp.vii–xxvi In *The Phantom Public Sphere,* edited by Bruce Robbins. Minneapolis: University of Minnesota Press, 1993.

Roberts, Gene, and Thomas Kunkel. *Breach of Faith: A Crisis of Coverage in the Age of Corporate Newspapering.* Fayetteville, Ark: University of Arkansas Press, 2002.

Roberts, Gene. "Corporatism vs. Journalism," *The Press-Enterprise Lecture Series* 31, no. 12 (February 1996).

Roberts, Gene, and Thomas Kunkel, eds. *Breach of Faith: A Crisis of Coverage in the Age of Corporate Newspapering.* Fayetteville: University of Arkansas Press, 2002.

Roberts, Gene, Thomas Kunkel, and Charles Clayton, eds. *Leaving Readers Behind.* Fayetteville: University of Arkansas Press, 2001.

Robin, R. "Mixed-up Media: CanWest Is Hyping the Benefits of Convergence. Trouble Is, No One Knows What It Actually Means." *Canadian Business* 74, no. 19 (October 15, 2001): 65–68.

Robinson, J. P., and D. K. Davis. "Television News and the Informed Public: An Information Process Approach," *Journal of Communication* 40, no. 3 (1990): 106–19.

Robinson, John P., and Mark R. Levy. "New Media Use and the Informed Public: A 1990s Update," *Journal of Communication* 46, no. 2 (Spring 1996): 129.

Rodriguez, America. "Made in the USA: The Production of the Noticiero Univision." *Critical Studies in Mass Communication* 13, no.1 (1996): 59–82.

Rodriguez, Clemencia. *Fissures in the Mediascape: An International Study of Citizens' Media.* Cresskill, N.J.: Hampton Press, 2001.

Roncagliolo, Rafael. "Las Nuevas Technologies Pueden Contrarrestar la Homogeneizacion." *Corto Circuito,* no. 7 (April 1989).

Ross, Steven, and Don Middleberg. *1998 Media in Cyberspace Study.* 1998. <www.middleberg.com/toolsforsuccess/cyberstudy.cfm>.

Rowland, Willard D. "U.S. Broadcasting and the Public Interest in the Multichannel Era: The Policy Heritage and Its Implications." In Michele Hilmes. *Connections: A Broadcast History Reader.* Belmont, Calif.: Thomson Wadsworth, 2003.

Rowse, Arthur E. *Drive-By Journalism.* Monroe, Maine: Common Courage Press, 2000.

Rowse, Edward, *Slanted News: A Case Study of the Nixon and Stevenson Fund Stories.* Boston: Beacon, 1975.

Rutenberg, Jim. "To Interview Former P.O.W., CBS Offers Stardom." *New York Times,* 16 June 2003: A1.

Rutherford, Paul. *The Making of the Canadian Media.* Toronto: McGraw-Hill Ryerson, 1978.

Saco, Diana, *Cybering Democracy.* Minneapolis: University of Minnesota Press, 2002.

Safire, William. "Regulate the FCC." *New York Times,* 16 June 2003.

Sallot. Jeff. "Mills Flouted Principle, CanWest Says." *Globe and Mail,* 21 June 2002, A4.

Sarker, M., B. Butler, and C. Steinfield. "Intermediaries and Cybermediaries: A Continuing Role for Mediating Players in the Electronic Marketplace." *Journal of Computer-Mediated Communication,* 1995. <http://www.ascusc.org/jcmc/vol1/issue3/sarker.html>.

Scharfe, Sharon. "Human Rights and the Internet in Asia: Promoting the Case of East Timor." Pp. 129–39, in *Human Rights and the Internet,* edited by Steven Hick. London: Macmillan, 2000.

Schiff, F. "The Associated Press: Its Worldwide Bureaus and American Interests." *International Communication Bulletin* 31, no.1-2 (Spring 1996): 7–13.

Schiller, Herbert I. *Communications and Cultural Domination.* New York: International Arts and Science Press, 1976.

Schlesinger, Philip. *Putting 'Reality' Together: BBC News.* London: Constable, 1978.

———. *Putting 'Reality' Together: BBC News.* 2nd ed. London: Routledge, 1987.

Schudson, M. "The Sociology of News Production Revisited." Pp.141–59 in *Mass Media and Society,* edited by I. Curran and M. Gurevitch. New York: Routledge, 1992.

———. *The Sociology of News.* New York: Norton, 2003.

Scoffield, Heather. "Ottawa and the Goliaths." *Globe and Mail,* 26 March 2001, R1.

Scott, David K., and Robert H. Gobetz. "Hard News/Soft News Content of the National Broadcast Networks: 1972–1987." *Journalism Quarterly* 69, no. 2(2000): 407.

Sénécal, Michel. *L'espace médiatique. Les communications à l'épreuve de la démocratie.* Montreal: Liber, 1995.

———. "La part réduite de l'appropriation collective: Vers un déficit démocratique de l'espace médiatique." Pp. 183–203 in *Vers une citoyenneté simulée. Médias, réseaux et Mondialisation,* edited by Serge Proulx and André Vitalis. Rennes: Apogée, 1999.

Serrin, William, ed., *The Business of Journalism.* New York: New York Press, 2000.

Shapiro, Carl and Hal R. Varian. *Information Rules: A Strategic Guide to the Network Economy.* Boston: Harvard Business School Press, 1999.

Shaw, David. "Heard the Local News? It May Soon Be Harder to Find." *Los Angeles Times,* 1 June 2003, E12.

Shecter, Barbara. "Editorial Policy 'Mischaracterized.'" *National Post,* 31 January 2002. <http://www.nationalpost.com/home/story.html?f=/stories/20020131/1294510.html>.

———. "BCE Loses Interest in Prized Media Assets" *National Post,* 10 January 2004, FP1.

Shipp, E. R. "Excuses, Excuses: How Editors and Reporters Justify Ignoring Stories." Pp. 57–74 in *The Business of Journalism,* edited by William Serrin. New York: New Press, 2000.

Sholle, David, and Stan Denski. *Media Education and the (Re)Production of Culture.* Westport, Conn.: Bergin & Garvey, 1994.

Siegelman, Peter, and Joel Waldfogel. "Race and Radio: Preference Externalities, Minority Ownership and the Provision of Programming to Minorities." *Advances in Applied Microeconomics,* 10 (2001).

Silcoff, Sean. "Peladeau: A Year of Redemption." *National Post,* 23 December 2003, FP7.

Simon, Roger I. "The University: A Place to Think?" Pp. 45–56 in *Beyond the Corporate University: Culture and Pedagogy in the New Millenium*, edited by Henry A. Giroux and Kostas Myrsiades. Lanham, Md.: Rowman & Littlefield, 2001.

Simon, Richard, and Janet Hook. "FCC Rule May Bring a Veto Standoff." *Los Angeles Times*, 25 July 2003. <http://www.latimes.com>.

Sinclair, Jon R. "Reforming Television's Role in American Political Campaigns: Rationale for the Elimination of Paid Political Advertisements." *Communications and the Law* (March 1995).

Sine, N. M., et al. "Current Issues in Cable Television: A Re-balancing to Protect the Consumer." *Cardozo Arts & Entertainment Law Journal* (1990).

Singhania, Lisa. "Will Congress Tackle Pay-for-Play?" *AP*, 19 September 2003.

Skinner, David, Mike J. Gasher, and James Compton. "Putting Theory to Practice: a Critical Approach to Journalism Studies." *Journalism: Theory, Practice and Criticism* 2, no. 3 (December 2001): 341–60.

Slattery, Karen L., and Ernest A. Hakanen. "Sensationalism Versus Public Affairs Content of Local TV News: Pennsylvania Revisited," *Journal of Broadcasting and Electronic Media* 38, no. 2 (1994): 205–16.

Slattery, Karen L., Ernest A. Hakanen, and Mark Doremus. "The Expression of Localism: Local TV News Coverage in the New Video Marketplace." *Journal of Broadcasting and Electronic Media* 40, no. 3 (1996): 403–13.

Sleigh, Stephen R. *On Deadline: Labor Relations in Newspaper Publishing*. Bayside, N.Y.: Social Change Press, 1998.

Sloan, David, E., and Emily Erickson Hoff, eds. *Contemporary Media Issues*. Northport, Ala.: Vision Press, 1998.

Smulyan, Susan. *Selling Radio: The Commercialization of American Broadcasting 1920–1934*. Washington, D.C.: Smithsonian Institution Press, 1994.

Smythe, Dallas. *Dependency Road: Communications, Capitalism, Consciousness and Canada*. Norwood, N.J.: Ablex, 1981.

Snider, James H., and Benjamin I. Page. "Does Media Ownership Affect Media Stands? The Case of the Telecommunications Act of 1996." Paper delivered at the Annual Meeting of the Midwest Political Science Association, April 1997.

Snow, David, and Danny Trom. "The Case Study and the Study of Social Movements." Pp. 146–72 in *Methods of Social Movement Research*, edited by Bert Klandermans and Suzanne Staggenborg. Minneapolis: University of Minneapolis Press, 2002.

Solages, Carrie. "If the FCC Rule Changes Survive, Minority Broadcasting May Not." *The Crisis*. 110, no. 5 (September/October 2003): 20.

Solomon, Norman. "Cracking the Media Walls." *In These Times*, 17 November 2003.

Solomon, William S. "The Site of Newsroom Labor: The Division of Editorial Practices," Pp. 110–34 in *Newsworkers: Toward a History of the Rank and File*, edited by Hanno Hardt and Bonnie Brennen. Minneapolis: University of Minnesota Press, 1995.

Sotiron, Minko. *From Politics to Profit: The Commercialization of Canadian Daily Newspapers, 1890–1920*. Montreal: McGill-Queens University Press, 1997.

Spanos, William V. *The End of Education: Toward Posthumanism*. Minneapolis: University of Minnesota Press, 1993.

Sparks, Glenn G., Marianne Pellechia, and Chris Irvine. "Does Television News about UFOs Affect Viewers' UFO Beliefs?: An Experimental Investigation." *Communication Quarterly* 46 (1998): 284–94.

Sparrow, Bartholomew H. *Uncertain Guardians: The News Media as a Political Institution*. Baltimore: Johns Hopkins University Press, 1999.

Sreberny-Mohammadi, Annabelle, Kaarle Nordenstreng, Robert Stevenson, and Frank Ugboajah. *Foreign News in the Media: International News Reporting in 29 Countries*. Reports and Papers in Mass Communication, no. 93, Paris: UNESCO, 1985.

Standing Senate Committee on Transport and Communications. *Interim Report on the Canadian News Media* (Ottawa, April 2004).

Stanger, Howard. "Newspapers: Collective Bargaining Decline Amidst Technological Change." Pp. 179–216 in *Collective Bargaining in the Private Sector*, edited by Paul F. Clark, John T. Delaney, and Ann C. Frost. Champaign, Ill: Industrial Relations Research Association, 2002.

Stark, P. "Cumulus' Lew Dickey on Chicks, Indies, More." *Airplay Monitor*, 1 August 2003.

Starr, Amory. *Naming the Enemy: Anti-Corporate Movements Confront Globalization*. London: Zed Books, 2000.

Statistics Canada. Television Viewing Data Bank, Catalogue # 87F0006XPE. <http://www.statcan.ca/english/pgdb/arts.23.htm> (16 January 2003).

Statistics Canada. "Population by Mother Tongue, Provinces and Territories" <http://www.statcan.ca/english/Pgdb/demo_18b.htm> (22 March 2004).

Stavitsky, Alan G. "The Changing Conception of Localism in U.S. Public Radio." *Journal of Broadcasting and Electronic Media* 38 (1994): 19–38.

Stempell, Guido H., III, and Thomas Hargrove. "Mass Media Audiences in a Changing Media Environment." *Journalism and Mass Communications Quarterly* 73, no. 3 (Autumn 1996): 549–58.

Stepp, Carl Sessions. "Whatever Happened to Competition," *American Journalism Review* (June 2001).

Stern, Christopher, and Jonathan Krim. "House Votes to Prevent Change in Media Rule." *Washington Post*, 24 July 2003, <http://www.washingtonpost.com>.

Stone, Vernon A. "Deregulation Felt Mainly in Large-Market Radio and Independent TV." *Communicator* (April 1987).

——."New Staffs Change Little in Radio, Take Cuts in Major Markets TV." *RTNDA Communicator* (1998).

Street, John, *Mass Media, Politics and Democracy*. New York: Palgrave, 2001.

Streeter, Thomas. "The Cable Fable Revisited; Discourse, Policy, and the Making of Cable Television." *Critical Studies in Mass Communications* (1987).

Strupp, Joe. "Local News Wins Popularity Contest on Newspaper Web Sites." *Editor and Publisher*. (30 June 1999).

——. "Three Point Play." *Editor and Publisher*, 21 August 2000.

Sunstein, Cass. "Television and the Public Interest." *California Law Review*, 8 (1999).

——. *Republic.com*. Princeton, N.J.: Princeton University Press, 2001.

Surowiecki, James. "All in the Family." *New Yorker*, 16 June, 2003.

Taiara, Camille. "Invasion of the Media Snatchers." *Bay Guardian*, 14 July, 2004.

Taras, David. *Power and Betrayal in the Canadian Media* (updated edition). Peterborough: Broadview Press, 2001.

Themba-Nixon, Makani, and Nan Rubin. "Speaking for Ourselves." *The Nation* 277, no. 16. (17 November 2003)

Tompkins, Al, and Aly Colon. "NAB 200: The Convergence Marketplace." *Broadcasting and Cable*, 10 (April 2000).

Toomey, Jenny. "Radio Deregulation: Has It Served Citizens and Musicians?" Testimony submitted by the Future of Music Coalition for "Media Ownership: Radio" Hearings. Before the Senate Committee on Commerce, Science and Transportation, 30 January 2003.

Tracey, Michael. *The Production of Political Television*. London: Routledge & Kegan Paul, 1978.

Tremayne, Mark. "Internet: Is the Medium the Message?" Unpublished Paper. University of Texas, Department of Journalism, 1997.

Tuchman, Gaye. *Making News: A Study in the Construction of Reality* New York: Free Press, 1978.

Tuck, Simon. "CanWest Urges Removal of Ownership Limits." *Globe and Mail*, 28 February 2003, B4.

Underwood, Doug. *When MBAs Rule the Newsroom: How the Marketers and Managers Are Reshaping Today's Media*. New York: Columbia University Press, 1991.

United Nations Development Project. *Human Development Report 2002: Deepening Democracy in a Fragmented World.* New York: UNDP, 2002.

University of San Francisco Media Group. "San Francisco Hearings on Local Ownership." Unpublished Transcript, 26 April 2003.

Unknown author. "What Effect Will CC's Indie Policy Have? Clear Channels Decision to End Ties with Independent Promoters." *Airplay Monitor.* 2 May 2003. <http://find articles.com/p/articles/mi_hboo4is_200305/ai_hibm1g1101680725>

Uzelman, Scott. "Catalyzing Participatory Communication: Independent Media Centre and the Politics of Direct Action," unpublished Masters' Thesis, Simon Fraser University, 2002.

Van Der Molen, Juliette H. Walma, and Tom H. A. Van Der Voort. "The Impact of Television, Print, and Audio on Children's Recall of the News." *Human Communication Research,* 26 (2001).

Van Orden, Bob. "Top Five Interactive Digital-TV Applications." *Multichannel News,* 21 June 1999, 143, 145.

Vane, Sharyn. "Taking Care of Business." *American Journalism Review* (March 2002).

Vasil, Adria. "World Domination." *Ryerson Review of Journalism* 20, no. 2 (2003): 56–61.

Vegh, Sandor. "Classifying Forms of Online Activism: The Case of Cyberprotests against the World Bank." Pp. 71–96 in *Cyberactivism: Online Activism in Theory and Practice,* edited by Martha McCaughey and Michael D. Ayers. New York and London: Routledge, 2003.

Vigilante, Richard. *Strike: The Daily News War and the Future of American Labor.* New York: Simon & Schuster, 1994.

Vipond, Mary. *The Mass Media in Canada.* Toronto: James Lorimer & Co., 1992.

———. *The Mass Media in Canada.* Revised edition. Toronto: James Lorimer & Co., 2000.

Voakes, Paul S., Jack Kapfer, David Kurpius, and David Shano-yeon Chern. "Diversity in the News: A Conceptual and Methodological Framework." *Journalism and Mass Communications Quarterly* 73, no. 3 (Autumn 1996): 582–93.

Waklshlag, Jacob, and William Jenson Adams. "Trends in Program Variety and the Prime Time Access Rule." *Journal of Broadcasting & Electronic Media* 29, no. 1 (Winter 1985): 23–34.

Waldfogel, Joel. Comments on Consolidation and Localism, Federal Communications Commission, Roundtable on Media Ownership (29 October 2001).

———. *Preference Externalities: An Empirical Study of Who Benefits Whom in Differentiated Product Markets,* NBER Working Paper 7391. Cambridge: National Bureau of Economic Research, 1999.

———. *Who Benefits Whom in Local Television Markets?* Philadelphia: Wharton School, November 2001.

Waldfogel, Joel, and Lisa George. *Who Benefits Whom in Daily Newspaper Markets?* NBER Working Paper 7944. Cambridge: National Bureau of Economic Research, 2000.

Waldfogel, Joel, and Felix Oberholzer-Gee. *Tiebout Acceleration: Political Participation in Heterogeneous Jurisdictions.* Cambridge: National Bureau of Economic Research, 2001.

Walker, Leslie. "AOL Time Warner Sites Dominate Data." *Washington Post,* 27 February 2001.

Wallis, Roger., and Stanley Baran. *The Known World of Broadcast News.* London: Routledge, 1990.

Wallner, Martha. 2003. "What the F.C.C. Is Going On?" *Media Alliance.* Fall 2003.

Walton, Mary, and Charles Layton. "Missing the Story at the Statehouse." In *Leaving Readers Behind,* edited by Gene Roberts, Thomas Kunkel, and Charles Clayton. Fayetteville: University of Arkansas Press, 2001.

Wanta, Wayne, and Thomas J. Johnson. "Content Changes in the St. Louis Post-Dispatch during Different Market Situations." *Journal of Media Economics* 7, no. 1 (1994): 13–28.

Warner, Michael. *Publics and Counterpublics.* New York: Zone Books, 2001.

Waterman, Peter. *Globalization, Social Movements, and the New Internationalisms.* London: Mansell, 1998.

Weber, Samuel. *The Future Campus: Destiny in a Virtual World,* <http://www.hydra.umn.edu/weber/text1/html> (10 January 2004).

Webster, Frank, ed. *Culture and Politics in the Information Age: A New Politics?* New York: Routledge, 2001.

Webster, James G., and Patricia F. Phalen. *The Mass Audience: Rediscovering the Dominant Model.* Mahwah, N.J.: Erlbaum, 1997.

Webster, James. "The Audience." *Journal of Broadcasting and Electronic Media* 42, no. 2 (Spring 1998): 190–208.

Weston, Greg. "Freezing the Free Press; The Firing of Russell Mills Will Make any CanWest Journalist Covering Politics Think Twice before Printing the Truth—It's an Incredible Opportunity for the PM." *Toronto Sun,* 20 June 2002. <http://www.montrealnewspaperguild.com/canwestlinks.htm>.

Weston, Tracy. "Can Technology Save Democracy?" *National Civic Review* 87, no. 1 (1998): 47.

Westwood One, Inc. *Securities and Exchange Commission filing 8-K.* 5 Aug. 2003. <http://www.sec.gov/Archives/edgar/data/771950/000077195003000033/0000771950-03-000033.txt> (22 Sept. 2003).

White David M. "The 'Gate Keeper': A Case Study in the Selection of News." *Journalism Quarterly* 27, no. 4 (1950): 383–90.

Wicks, Robert H., and Montague Kern. "Factors Influencing Decisions by Local Television News Directors to Develop New Reporting Strategies during the 1992 Political Campaign." *Communications Research* 22, no. 2 (1995): 237–55.

Wilde Mathews, Anna. "Legal Quirks Aid Radio Empire." *Wall Street Journal,* 4 October 2002.

Wildman, Steven. "One-Way Flows and the Economics of Audience Making." Pp. 115–41 in *Audiencemaking: How the Media Create the Audience,* edited by James Ettema and Whitney D. Charles. Thousand Oaks, Calif.: Sage Publications, 1994.

Wildman, Steven, and Theomary Karamanis. "The Economics of Minority Programming." Pp. 47–65 in *Investing in Diversity: Advancing Opportunities for Minorities in Media,* edited by Amy Korzick Garner. Washington, D.C.: Aspen Institute, 1998.

Williams, Vanessa. "Black and White and Red All Over: The Ongoing Struggle to Integrate America's Newsrooms." Pp. 95–116 in *The Business of Journalism,* edited by William Serrin. New York: New York Press, 2000.

Willis, Andre. "An Income Trust Would Cure What's Ailing Asper's CanWest." *Globe and Mail,* 4 November 2004, B21.

Wilonsky, Robert. "What's Left of the Dial: How One Nonprofit Helped Save Radio. Sort of. For Now." *Dallas Observer,* 19 June 2003.

Wimmer, Kurt A. "Deregulation and the Future of Pluralism in the Mass Media: The Prospects for Positive Policy Reform." *Mass Communications Review* (1998).

Winerip, Michael. "Looking for an 11 O'Clock Fix." *New York Times Magazine* (11 January 1998): 30–63.

Winseck, Dwayne. *Reconvergence: A Political Economy of Telecommunications in Canada.* Cresskill, N.J.: Hampton Press, 1998.

Winston, B. "Rejecting the Jehovah's Witness Gambit," *Intermedia* (1990).

Wise, Richard. *Multimedia: A Critical Introduction.* London: Routledge, 2000.

Wittebols, James H. "News from the Noninstitutional World: U.S. and Canadian Television News Coverage of Social Protest." *Political Communication* 13, no. 2 (1996): 345–61.

Woodward, Bob, *Bush At War.* New York: Simon & Schuster, 2002.

Wright, Steve. "Pondering Information and Communication in Contemporary Anti-Capitalist Organizations," *The Commoner* 7 (2003), <http://www.commoner.org.uk/01-7groundzero.htm> (19 November 2003).

Yezbak, C. "Media Giant Clear Channel Sued for Policy of Working Employees Off-the-Clock without Pay." *US Newswire.* <http://www.usnewswire.com/topnews/qtr1_2003/0331-125.html.> (31 March 2003).

Youth Media Council. Is KMEL the People's Station? A Community Assessment of 106.1 KMEL. *Youth Media Council.* <http://www.youthmediacouncil.org/pdfs/BuildAPeoplesStation.pdf> (Fall 2002).

Youth Media Council. "Speaking for Ourselves: A Youth Assessment of Local TV Coverage," <http://www.youthmediacouncil.org/pdfs/speaking.pdf>.

Yuen, Eddie, Daniel Burton Rose, and George Katsiaficas. *The Battle of Seattle: The New Challenge to Capitalist Globalization*. New York: Soft Skull Press, 2002.

Zaller, John R. *The Nature and Origins of Mass Opinion*. New York: Cambridge University Press, 1992.

Zerowork. *Zerowork: Political Materials*. Brooklyn: Zero Work, 1975.

Zhao, Xinshu, and Steven H. Chaffee. "Campaign Advertisements versus Television News as Sources of Political Issue Information." *Public Opinion Quarterly* 59 (1995): 41–65.

Index

List of Contributors

Debra Clarke is associate professor in the Department of Sociology, Trent University in Peterborough, Ontario, where she is also an associate member of the Frost Centre for Canadian Studies and Native Studies. Her publications have been focussed upon the convergence of media ownership, state regulation of the media industries, the political economy of network television information production, professional journalistic practices and ideologies, and contemporary ethnographic audience research. Her current research interests are directed toward the household uses of communication technologies and variations in the process of media reception among the diverse family forms and household types found within Canadian society.

James R. Compton is an assistant professor in the department of Information and Media Studies at the University of Western Ontario. A former reporter and editor with Canadian Press/Broadcast News, he is author of *The Integrated News Spectacle: A Political Economy of Cultural Performance* (Peter Lang, 2004). His work can also be found in the journals *Journalism Studies* and *Journalism: Theory, Practice and Criticism*.

Mark Cooper is director of research at the Consumer Federation of America and a Fellow at the Stanford Law Center for Internet and Society and the Columbia Institute for Tele-Information. He holds a Ph.D. from Yale University and is a former Yale University and Fullbright Fellow. He is the author of numerous articles in trade and scholarly journals on telecommunications and digital society issues and three books—most recently, *Cable Mergers and Monopolies* (2002).

Frédéric Dubois is a Montreal-based social activist and independent journalist. As part of the Research Observatory on Alternative Communication (ORCA), he recently graduated with a Masters in Communications from the University of Quebec in Montreal (UQÀM). Along with Andrea Langlois, he is co-author of *Autonomous Media: Activating Resistance and Dissent* (Cumulus Press, 2005).

Nick Dyer-Witheford is associate professor in the Faculty of Information and Media Studies at the University of Western Ontario in London, Ontario. Author of the highly acclaimed *Cyber-Marx: Cycles and Circuits of Struggle in High-Technology Capitalism* (Illinois University Press, 1999), Dyer-Witheford's research interests include emergent forms of counterpower against high technology, globalized capital and the political economy of the computer and video-game industry. He is currently researching a book on the drive to convert libraries from "books to bytes."

Danielle Fairbairn recently graduated from the University of San Francisco. She plans to work in the nonprofit sector in areas of media advocacy and public policy.

Mike Gasher is associate professor and the graduate program director in the Department of Journalism at Concordia University in Montreal. A former newspaper reporter, he is the author of *Hollywood North: The Film Industry in British Columbia* (UBC Press, 2002) and co-author of the fourth and fifth editions of the textbook *Mass Communication in Canada* (Oxford University Press, 2001, 2004).

Robert B. Horwitz is professor of communication in the Department of Communication, University of California San Diego. He is the author of two books—*Communication and Democratic Reform in South Africa* (Cambridge University Press, 2001) and *The Irony of Regulatory Reform: The Deregulation of American Telecommunications* (Oxford University Press, 1989)—as well as numerous articles and book chapters on communication law and policy.

Robert Jensen is associate professor in the School of Journalism at the University of Texas at Austin, where he teaches courses in media law, ethics, and politics. Prior to his academic career, he worked as a professional journalist for a decade. He is the author of *Writing Dissent: Taking Radical Ideas from the Margins to the Mainstream* (Peter Lang, 2002); co-author with Gail Dines and Ann Russo of *Pornography: The Production and Consumption of Inequality* (Routledge, 1998); and co-editor with David S. Allen of *Freeing the First Amendment: Critical Perspectives on Freedom of Expression* (New York University Press, 1995).

Dorothy Kidd has been involved as a community media producer, policy advocate, and educator in the growing media democracy movement in Canada, the United States, and internationally. Her research and writing examines the development of autonomous media and the communications commons. She teaches media studies at the University of San Francisco.

Francisco McGee is a senior in the undergraduate Media Studies program at the University of San Francisco. Under the direction of Professor Dorothy Kidd, he is working on "La Piel de la Memoria," a documentary about a public art project that transpired in the Colombian city of Medellín in 2001.

Jeanette McVicker is professor of English at SUNY Fredonia and coordinator of the interdisciplinary program in journalism, in addition to serving as faculty adviser to the student newspaper, *The Leader*. From 1996 to 2000, she directed the Women's Studies program. Her most recent work can be found in Robyn Wiegman (ed.) *Women's Studies On Its Own: A Next Wave Reader in Institutional Change* (Duke University Press), and *Woolf Studies Annual* v. 9 and 10 (Pace University Press).

Chris Paterson is a lecturer at the University of Ulster, Northern Ireland. He previously taught at the University of San Francisco and the University of Leicester. His doctoral dissertation concerning international television news agencies was completed for the University of Texas at Austin, in 1996. Chris has been a visiting researcher or lecturer in the UK, Finland, and South Africa, and has worked in television production in the United States. His coedited book "International News in the Twenty-first Century" was published in 2004, and he has contributed chapters to numerous other anthologies. He has published articles in the *Review of African Political Economy* (1998), and the *Journal of International Communication* (1997).

Ben Scott is the policy director for Free Press in Washington, D.C. Before joining Free Press, he spent a year working as a legislative fellow handling telecommunications policy in the U.S. House of Representatives for Rep. Bernie Sanders (I-VT). Ben is in the final stages of his doctoral degree in communications from the University of Illinois. He holds a bachelors degree from Northwestern University and a masters from the University of Sussex (UK). He is the author of several articles on American journalism history and the politics of media regulation as well as co-editor of *Our Unfree Press* (The New Press, 2004) with Robert W. McChesney.

Michel Sénécal is professor of communication at Télé-université, Université du Québec, in Montréal (Canada). He is founder and co-director of ERADEC (Equipe de recherche sur les acteurs, dispositifs et enjeux de la communication). He is head of the ORCA project, a digital collaborative platform for the development of an International Research Observatory on Alternative Communication. Most of his research work is in the field of history and geopolitics of communication systems, democracy, and social movements.

Leslie Regan Shade is an associate professor at Concordia University's Department of Communication Studies, where her teaching and research focuses on the social, policy, and ethical aspects of information and communication technologies. She is the author of *Gender and Community in the Social Construction of the Internet* (Peter Lang, 2002); co-editor with Paul Attallah of *Mediascapes: New Patterns in Canadian Communication* (Nelson Canada, 2002); co-editor with Sherry Ferguson of *Civic Discourse and Cultural Politics in Canada: A Cacophony of Voices* (Ablex, 2002); and with Marita Moll, *Seeking Convergence in Policy and Practice: Communication in the Public Interest* (Canadian Centre for Policy Alternatives, 2004).

David Skinner is assistant professor in the Communication Studies Program at York University in Toronto. He was the founding chair of the Bachelor of Journalism program at the University College of the Cariboo in British Columbia and has written a number of articles on broadcasting and alternative media in Canada. He is also the author of *The Ethical Investor: A Guide to Socially Responsible Investment in Canada* (Stoddart, 2001).

0 1341 1412747 2

CPSIA information can be obtained at www.ICGtesting.com
Printed in the USA
LVOW07s2235290914

406390LV00001B/105/P

9 780739 113066